jrp|ringier

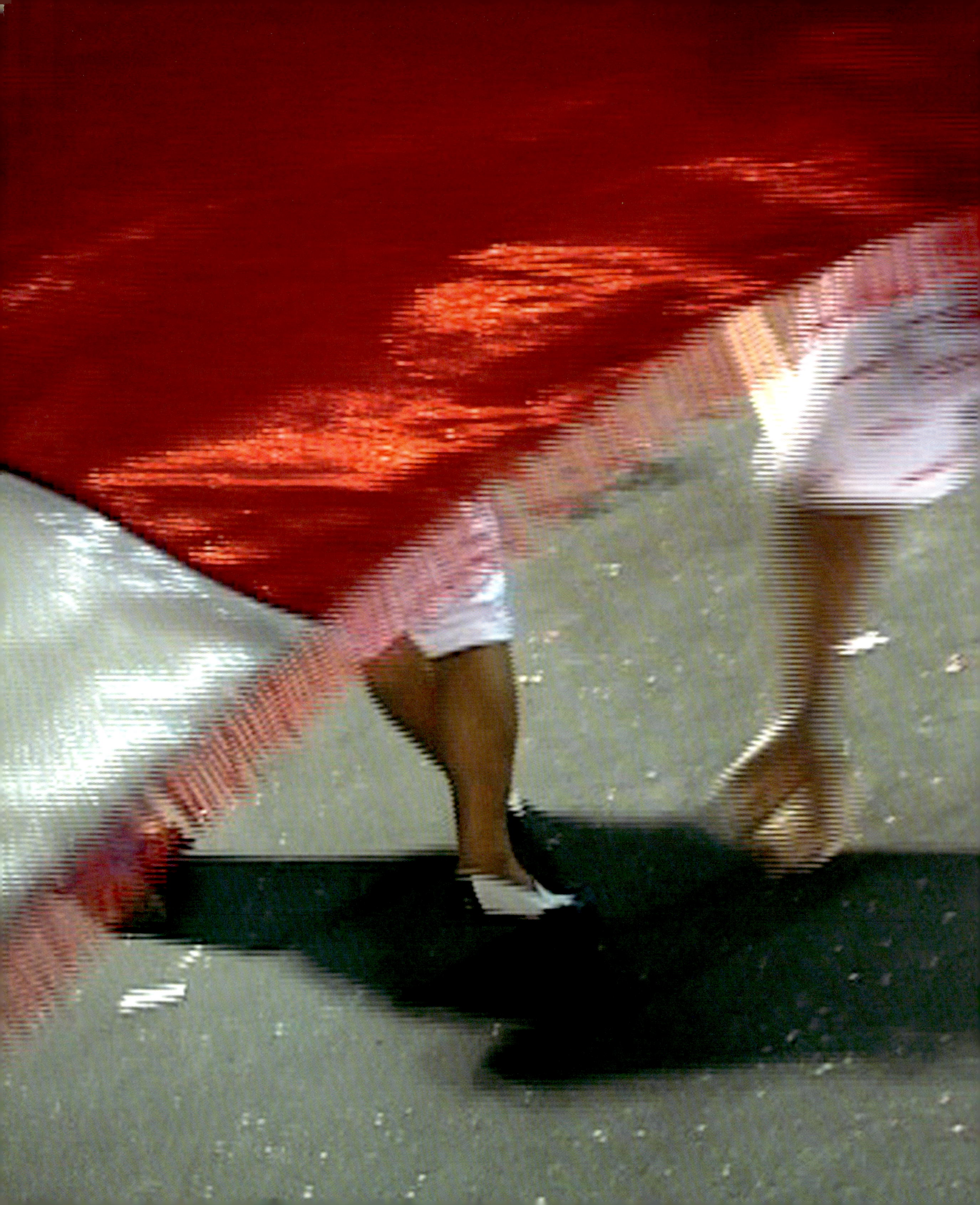

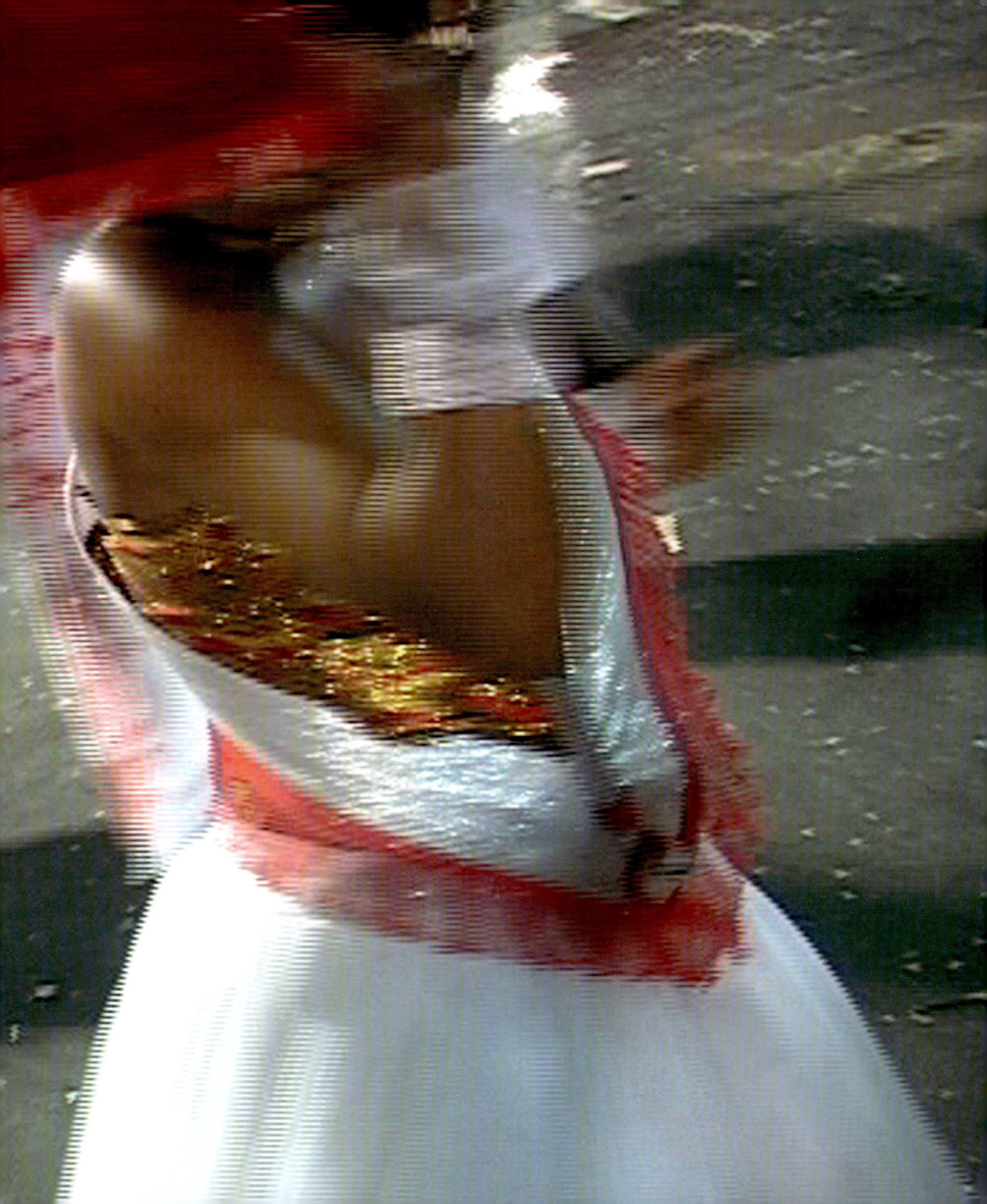

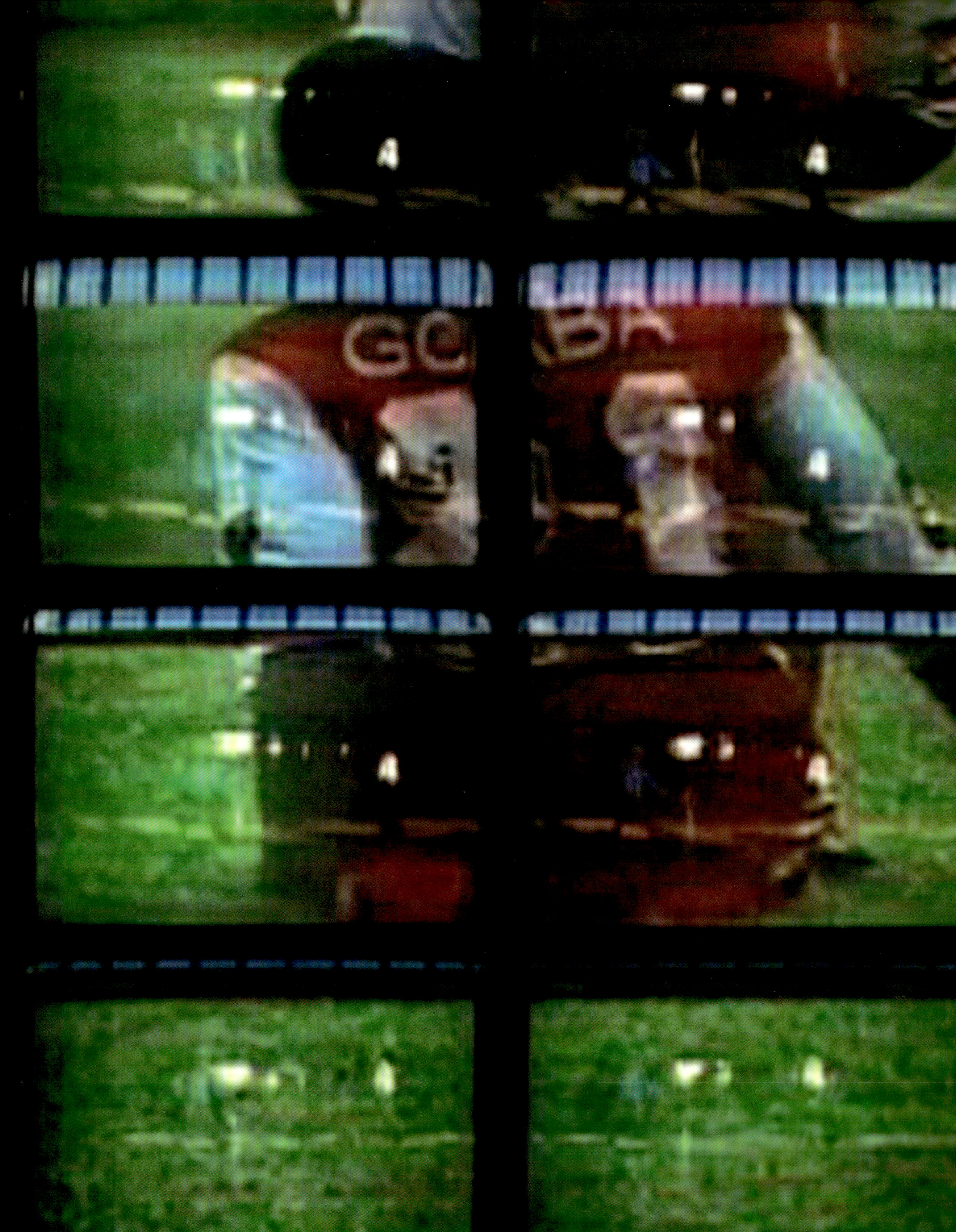

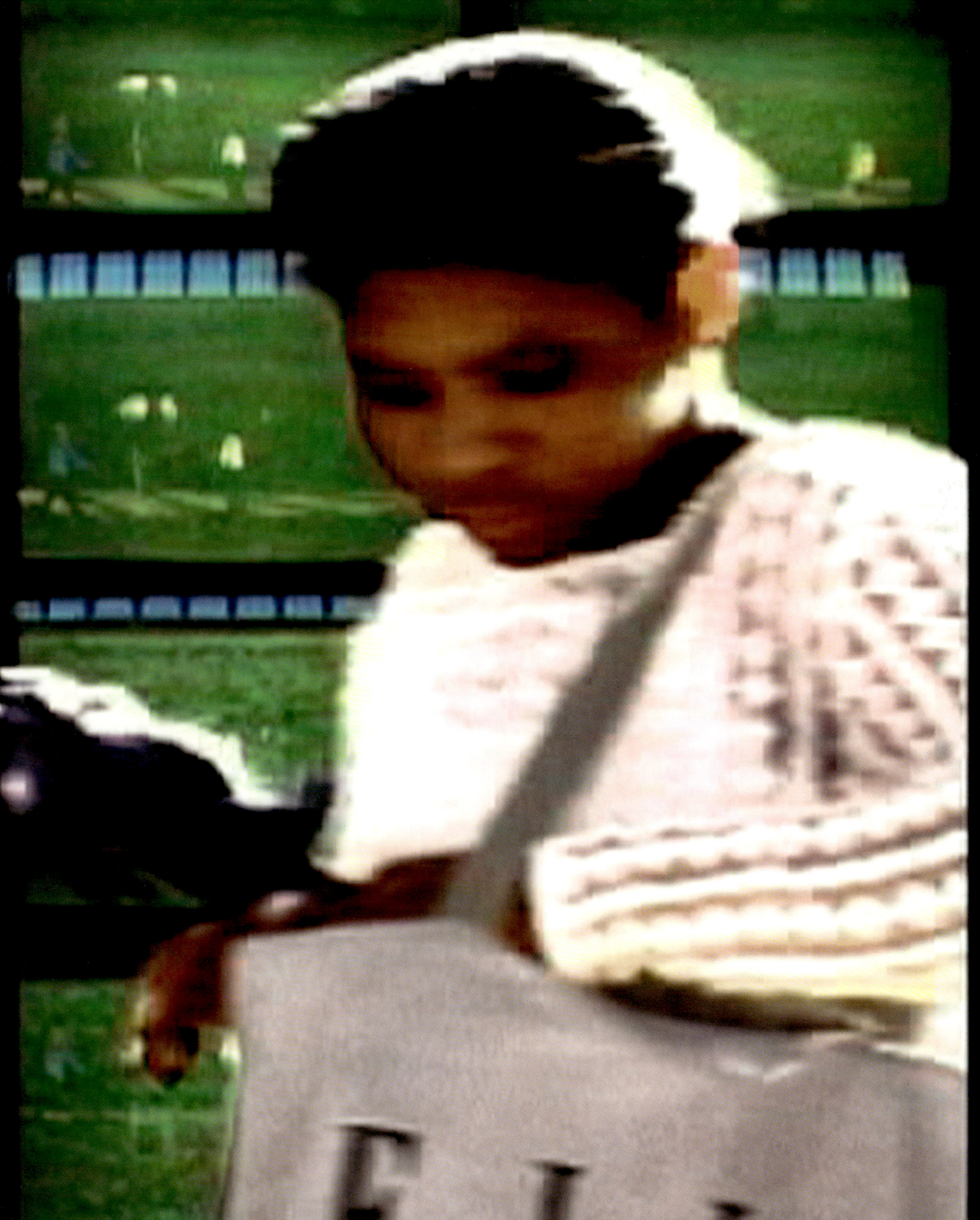
FI

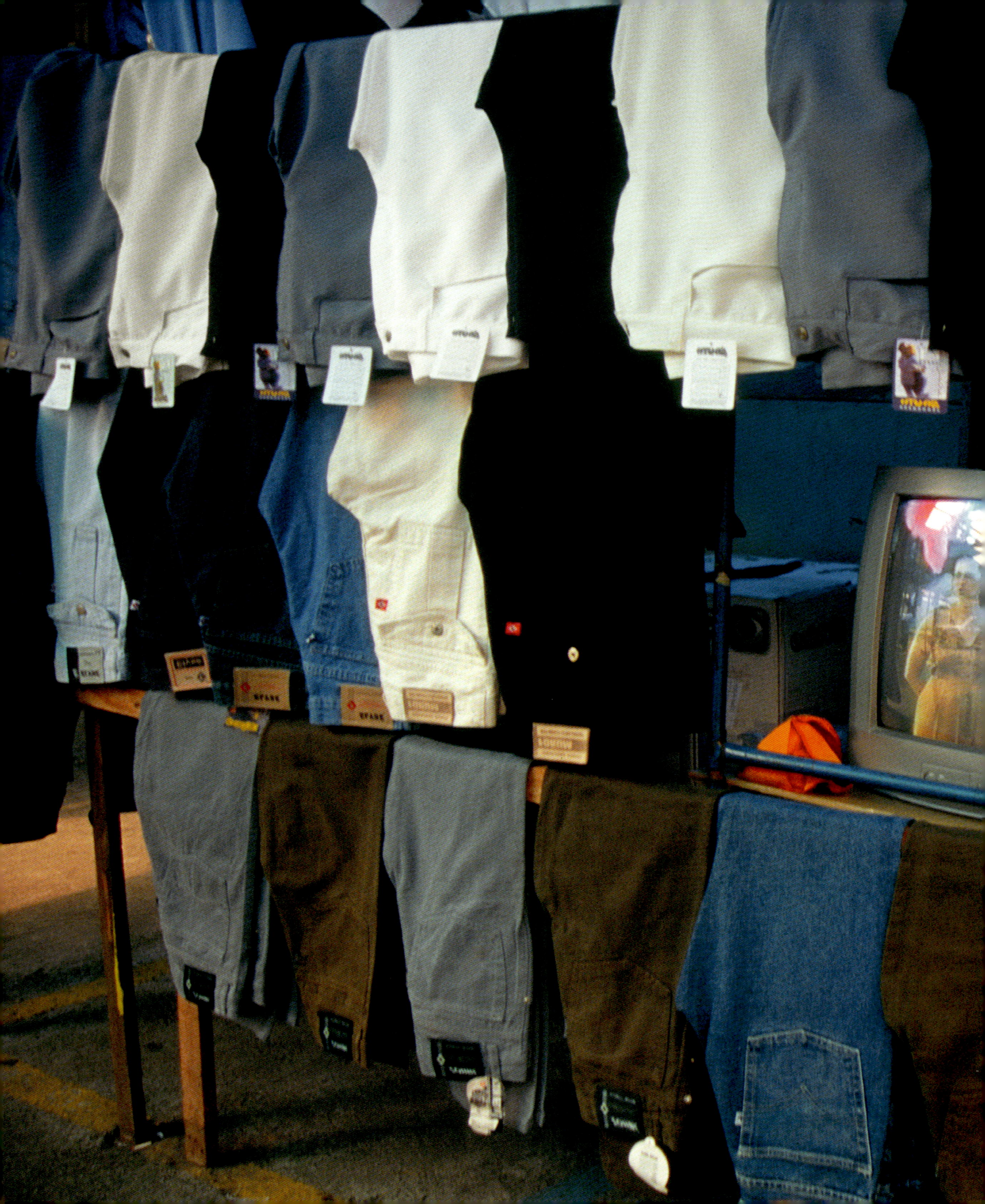

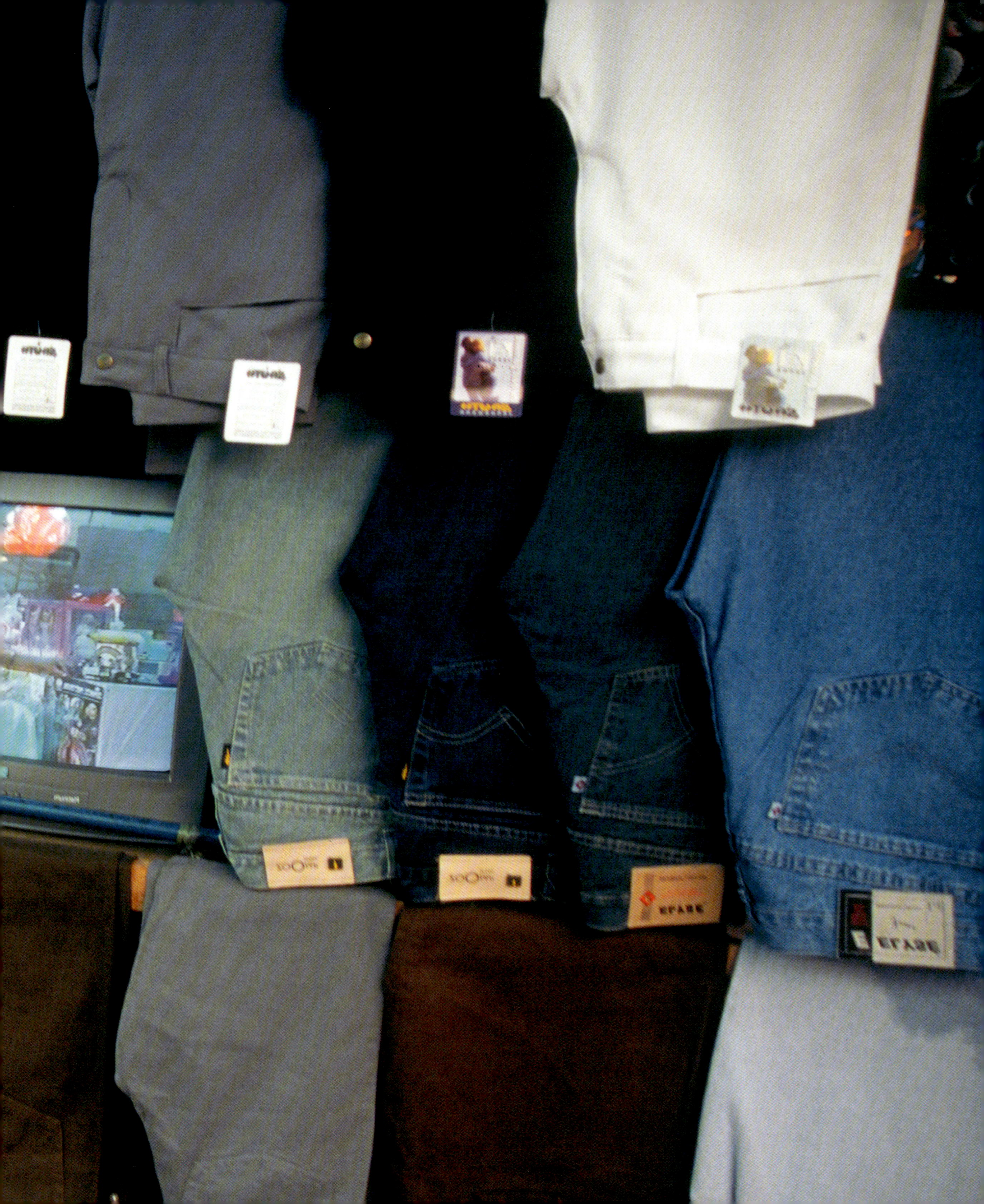

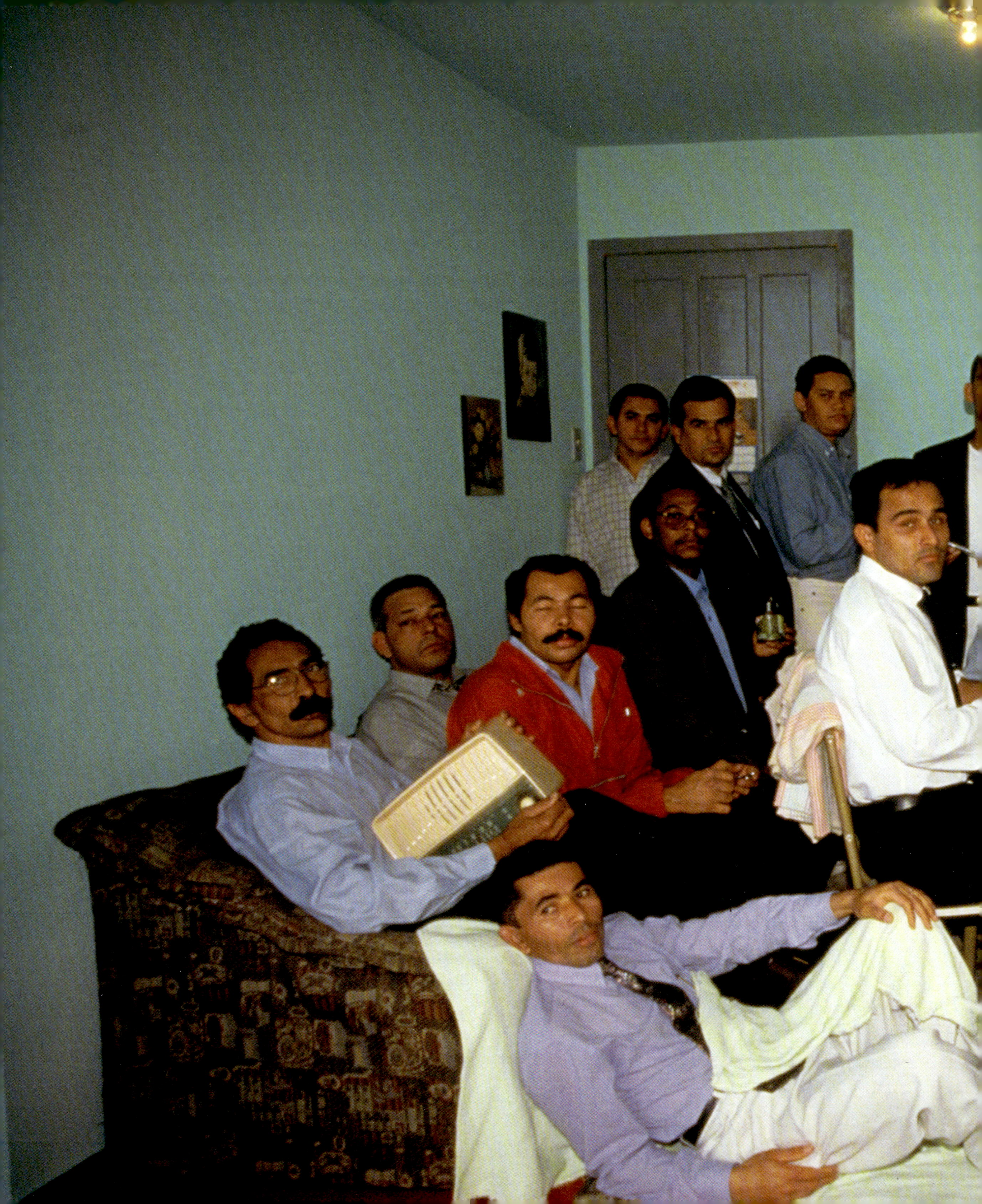

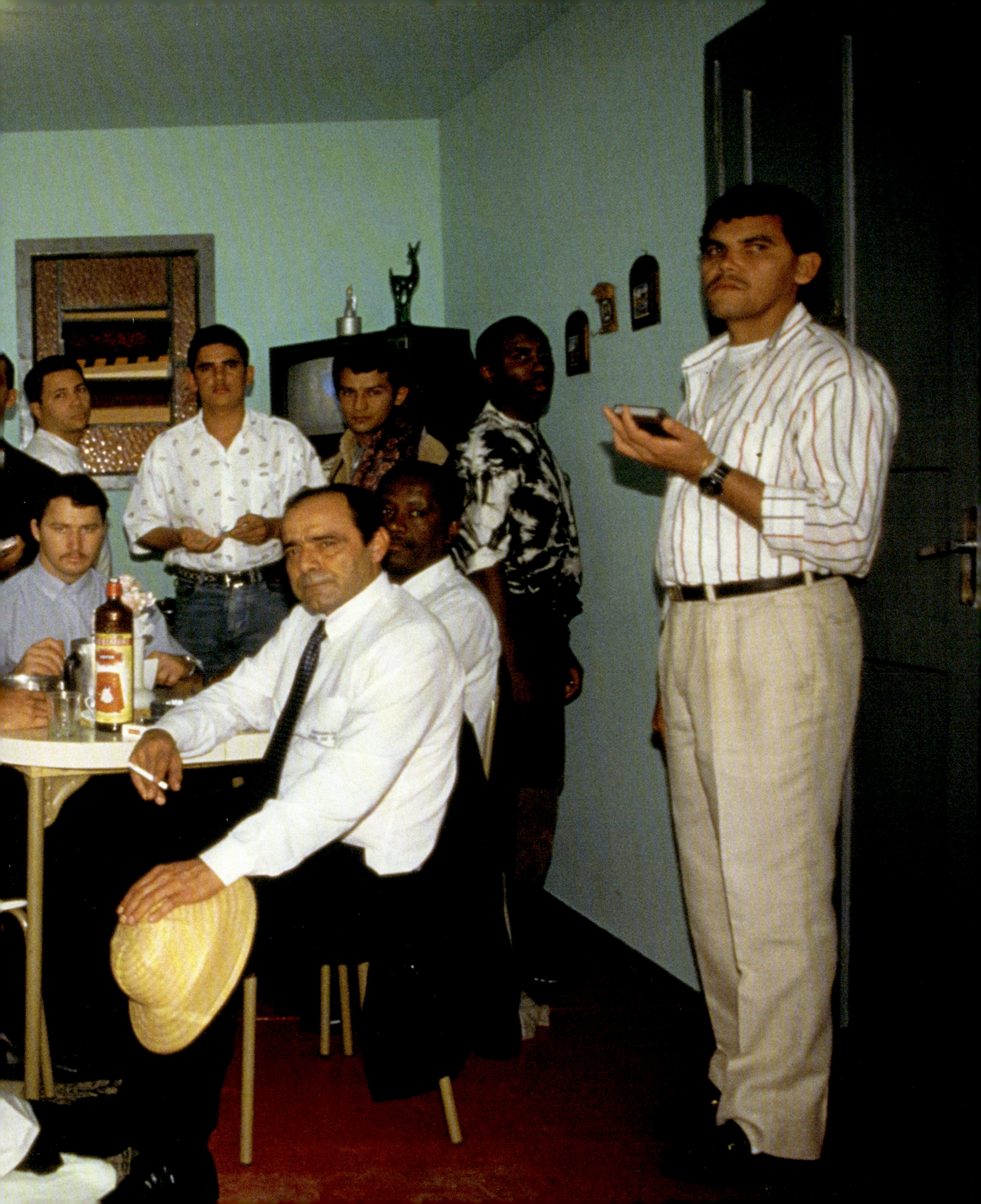

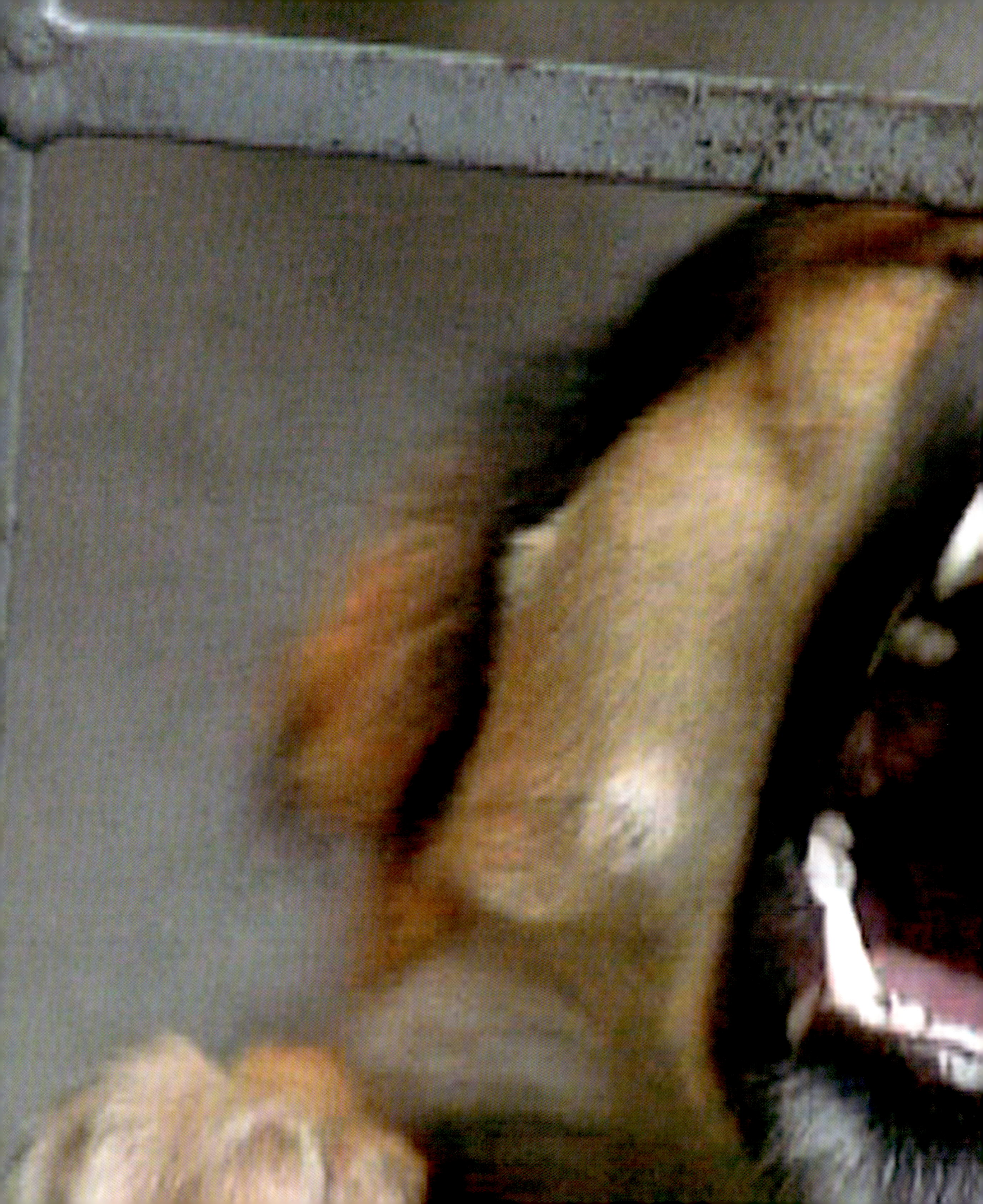

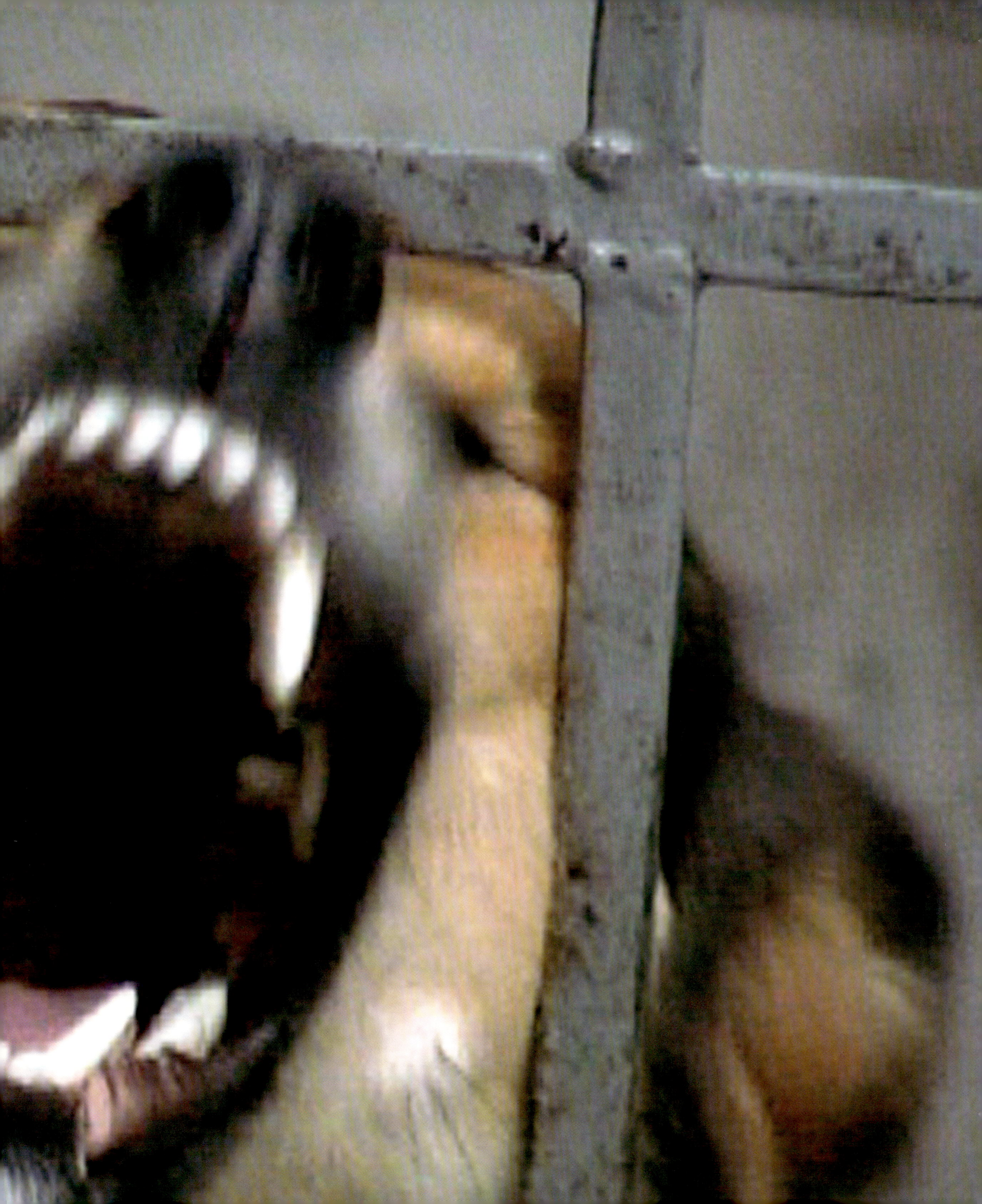

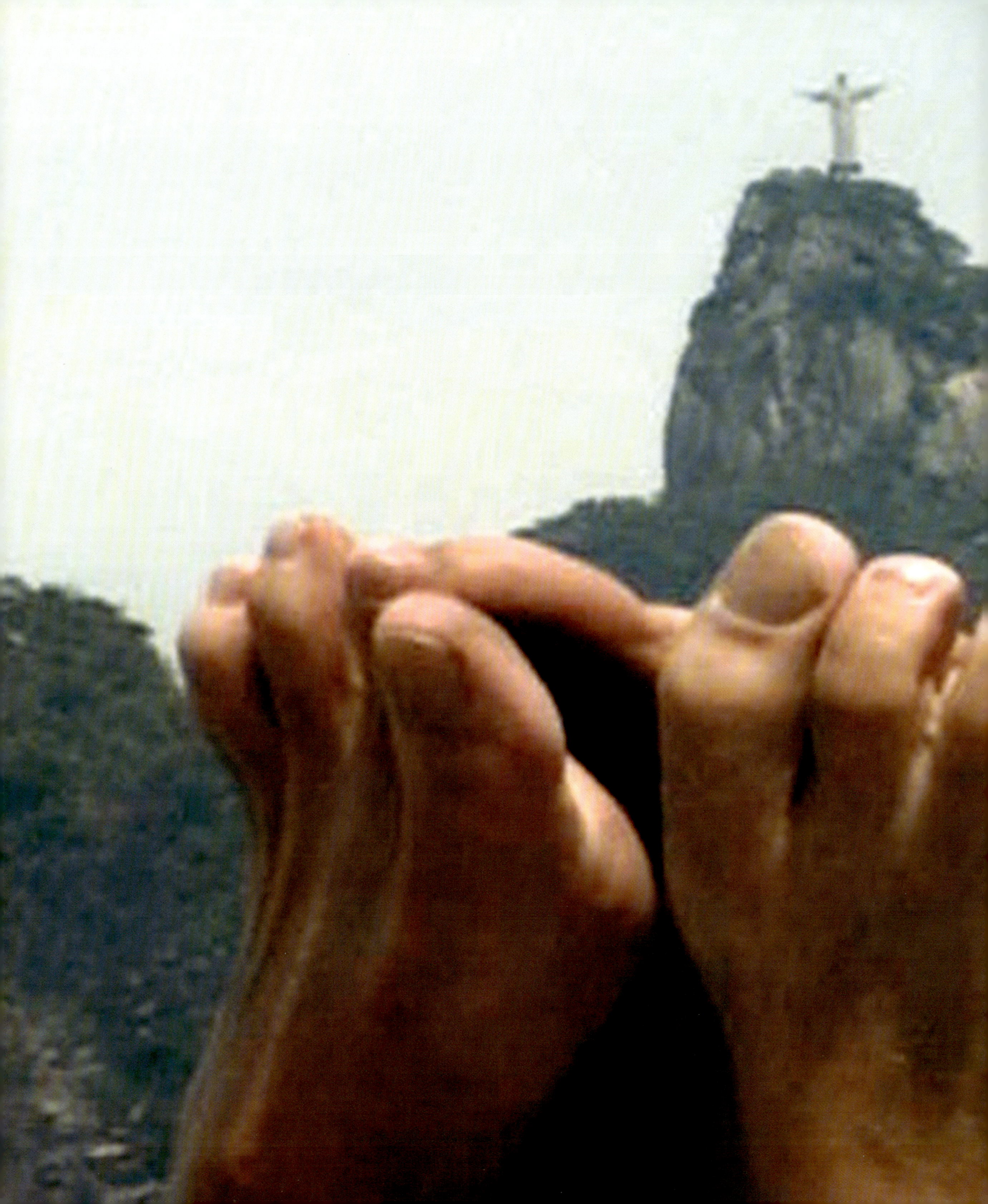

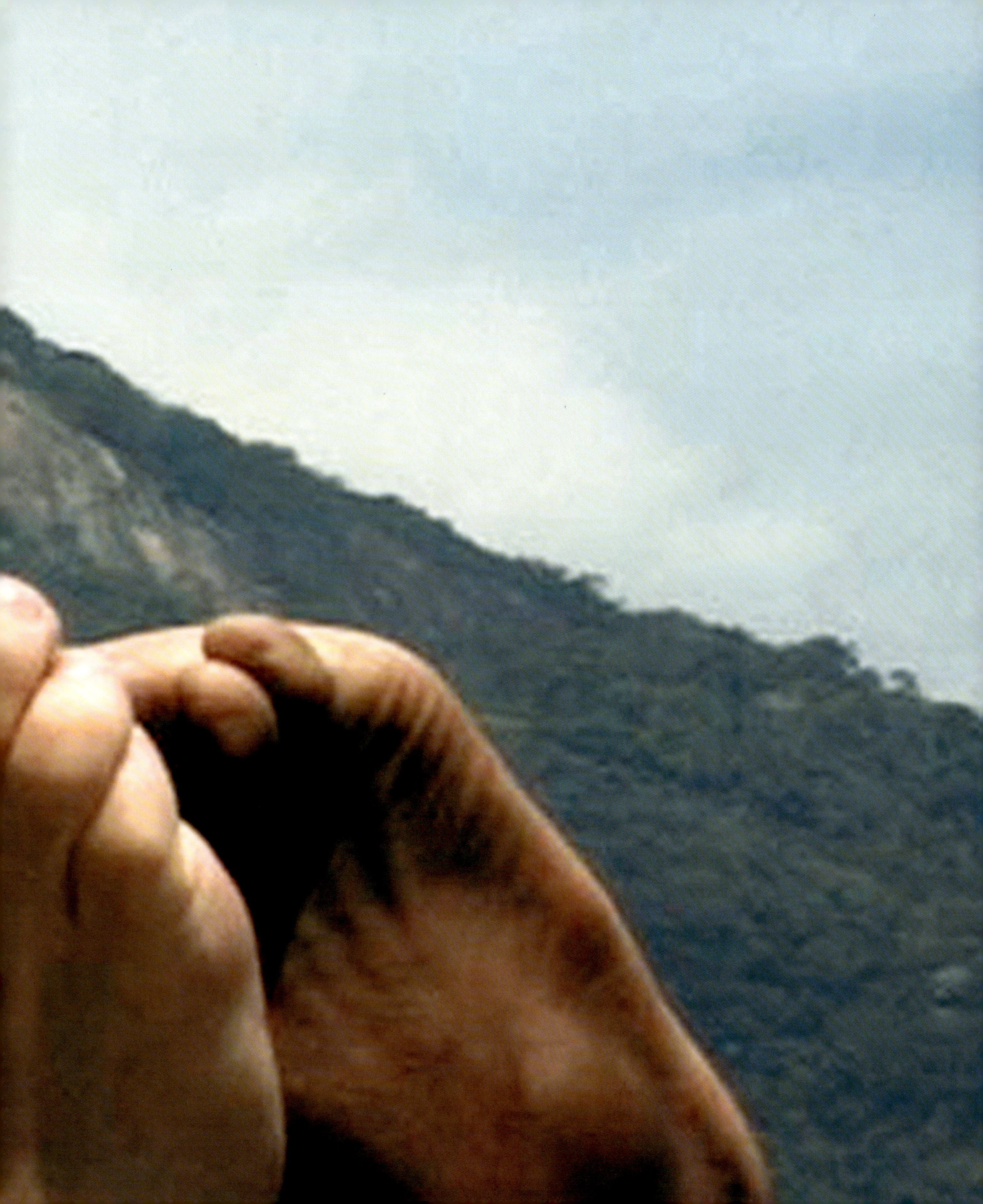

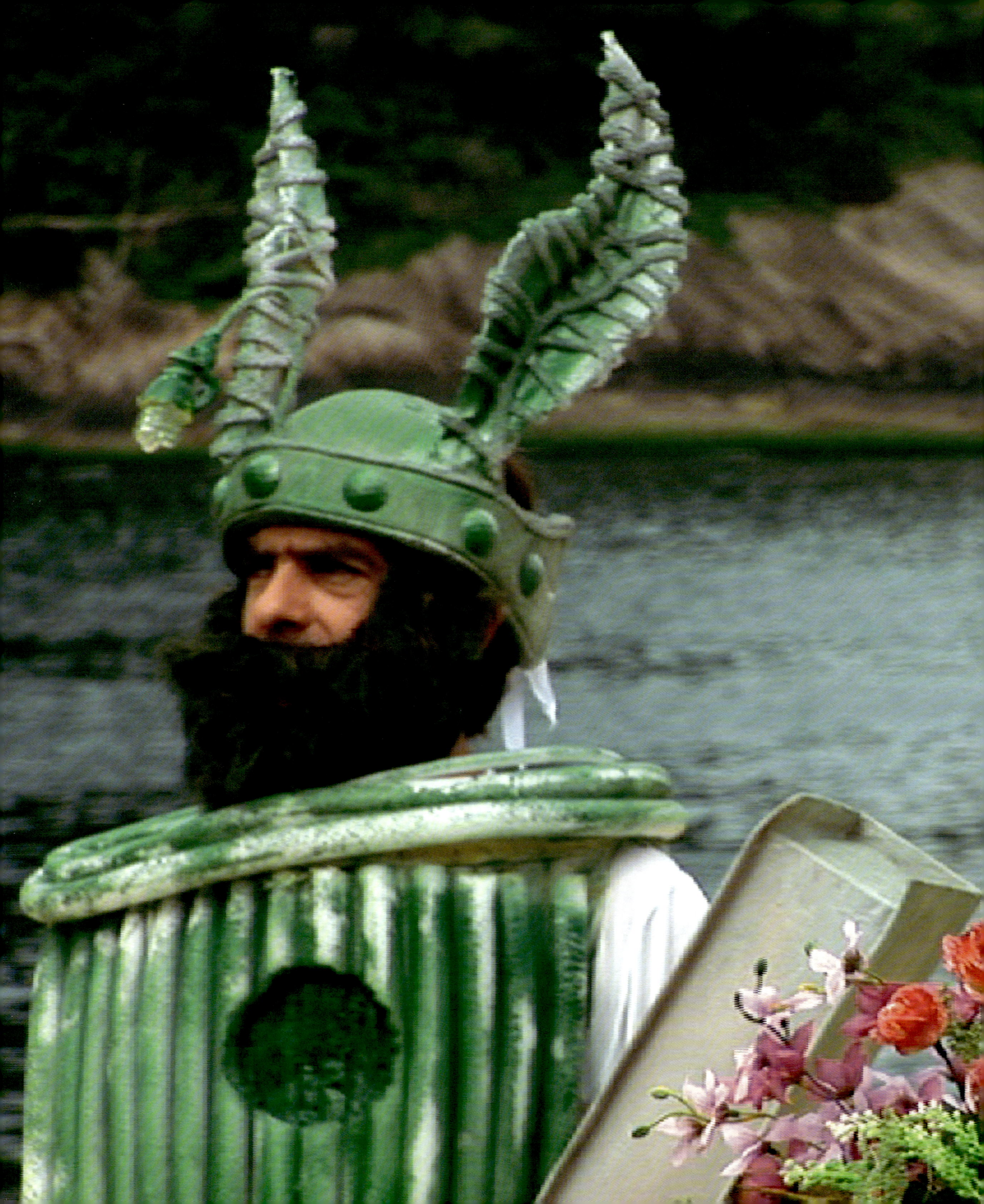

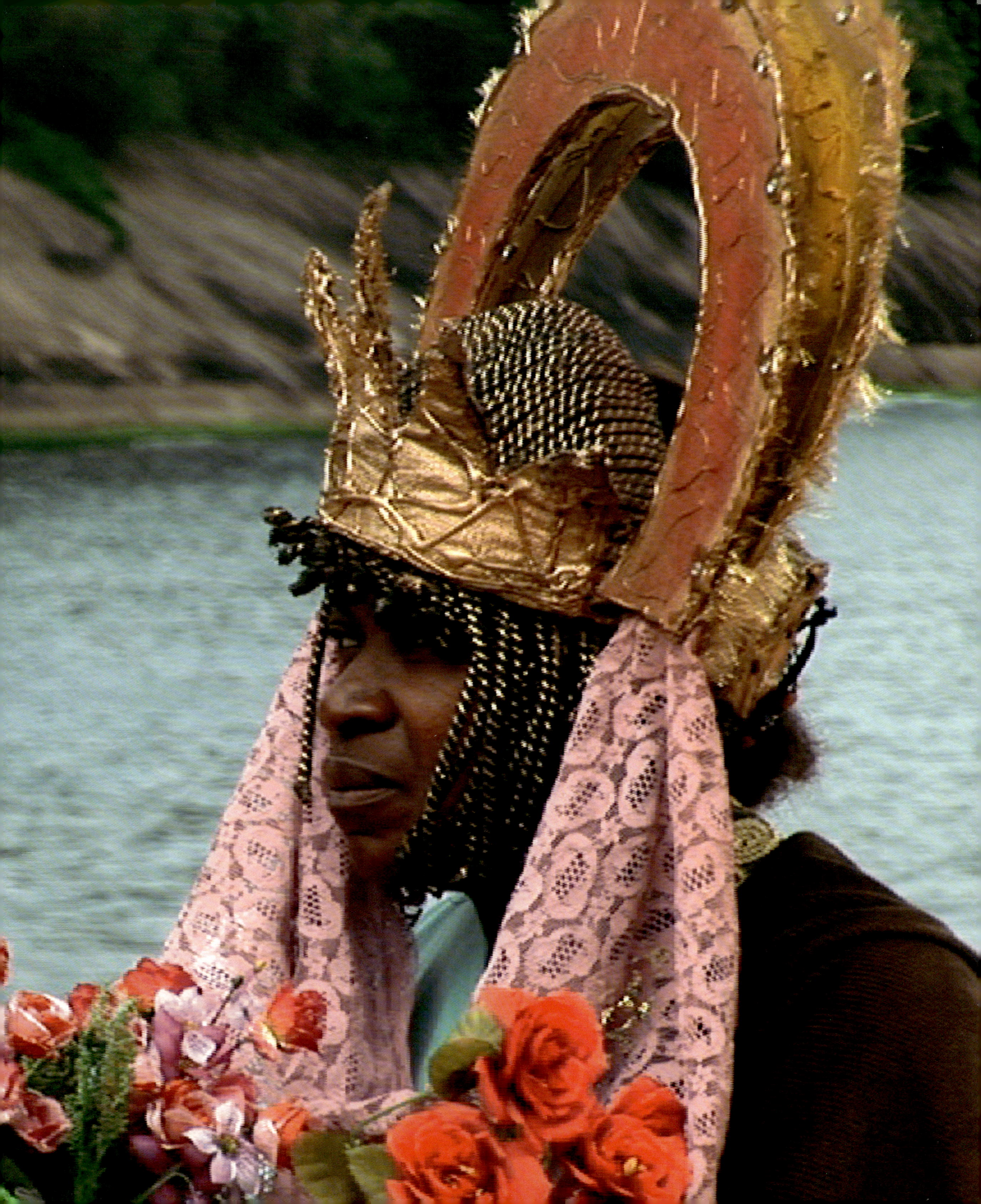

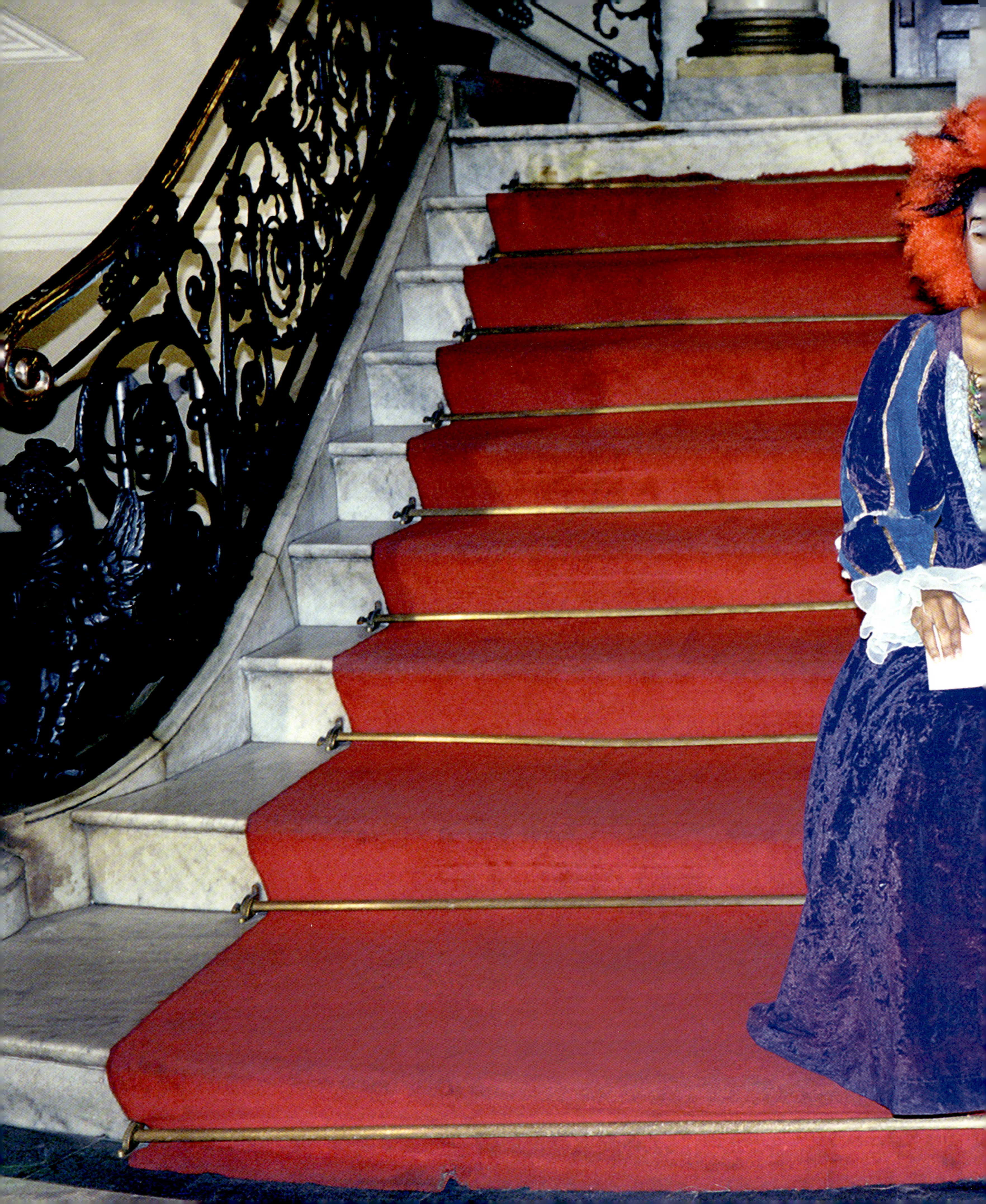

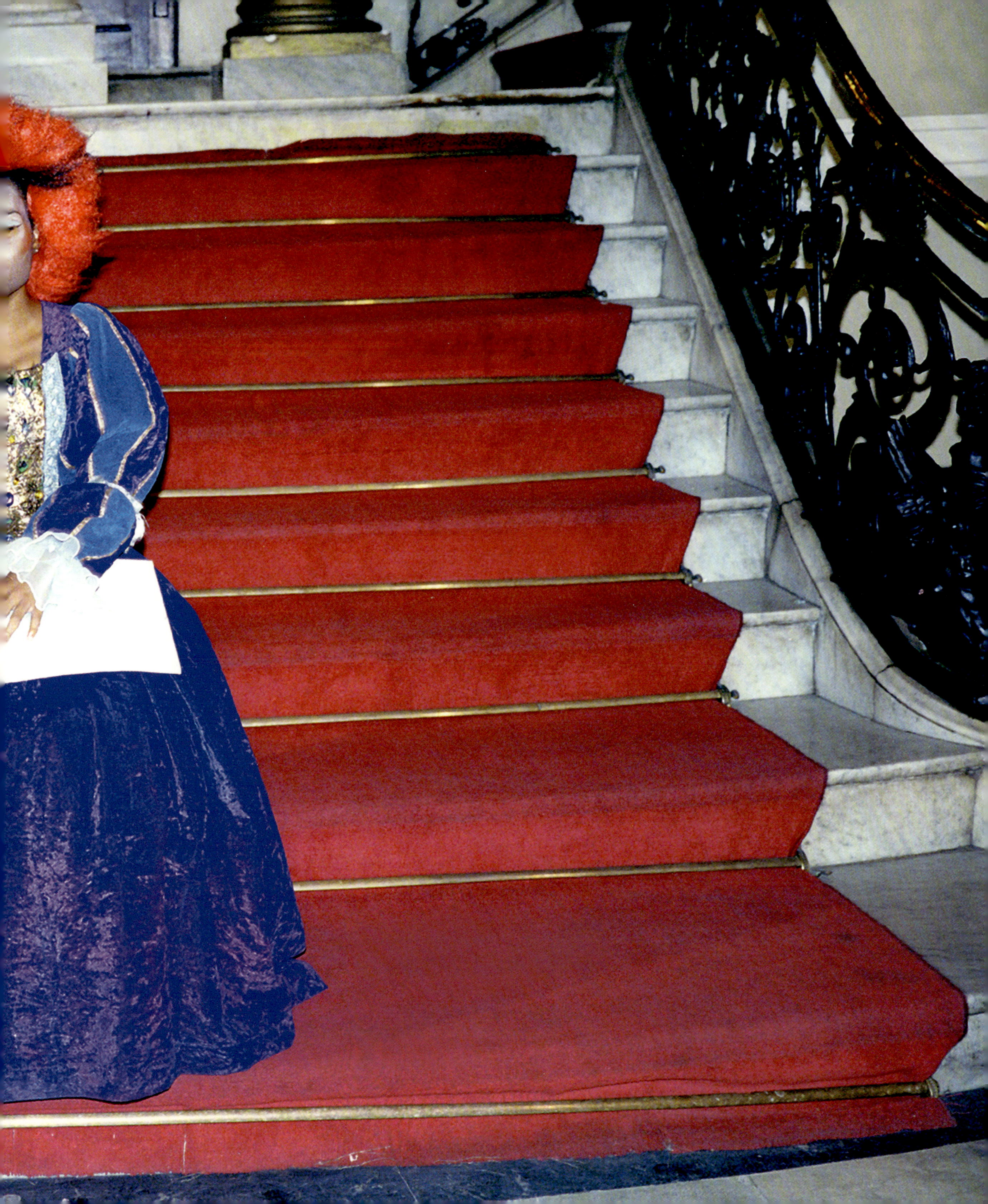

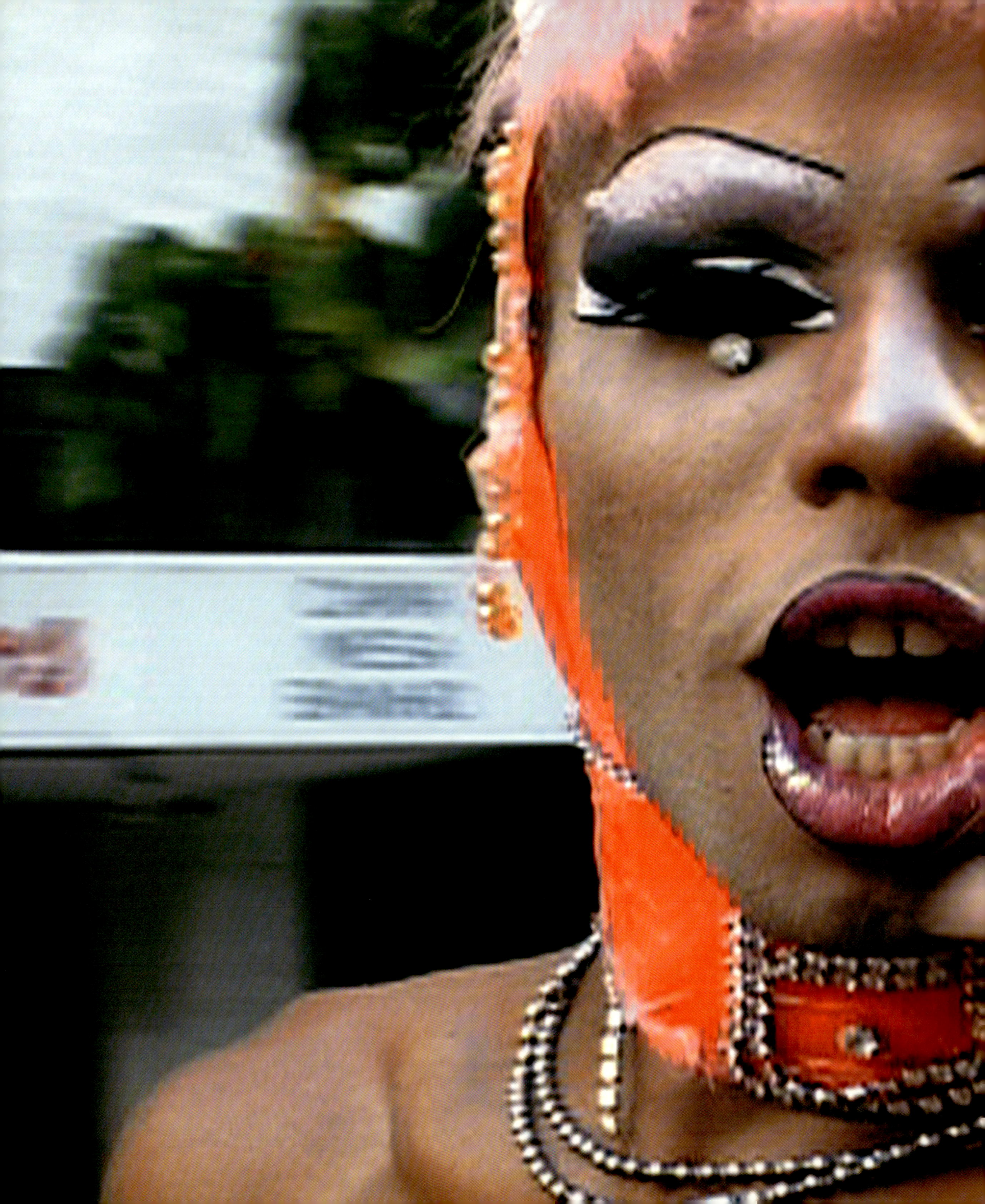

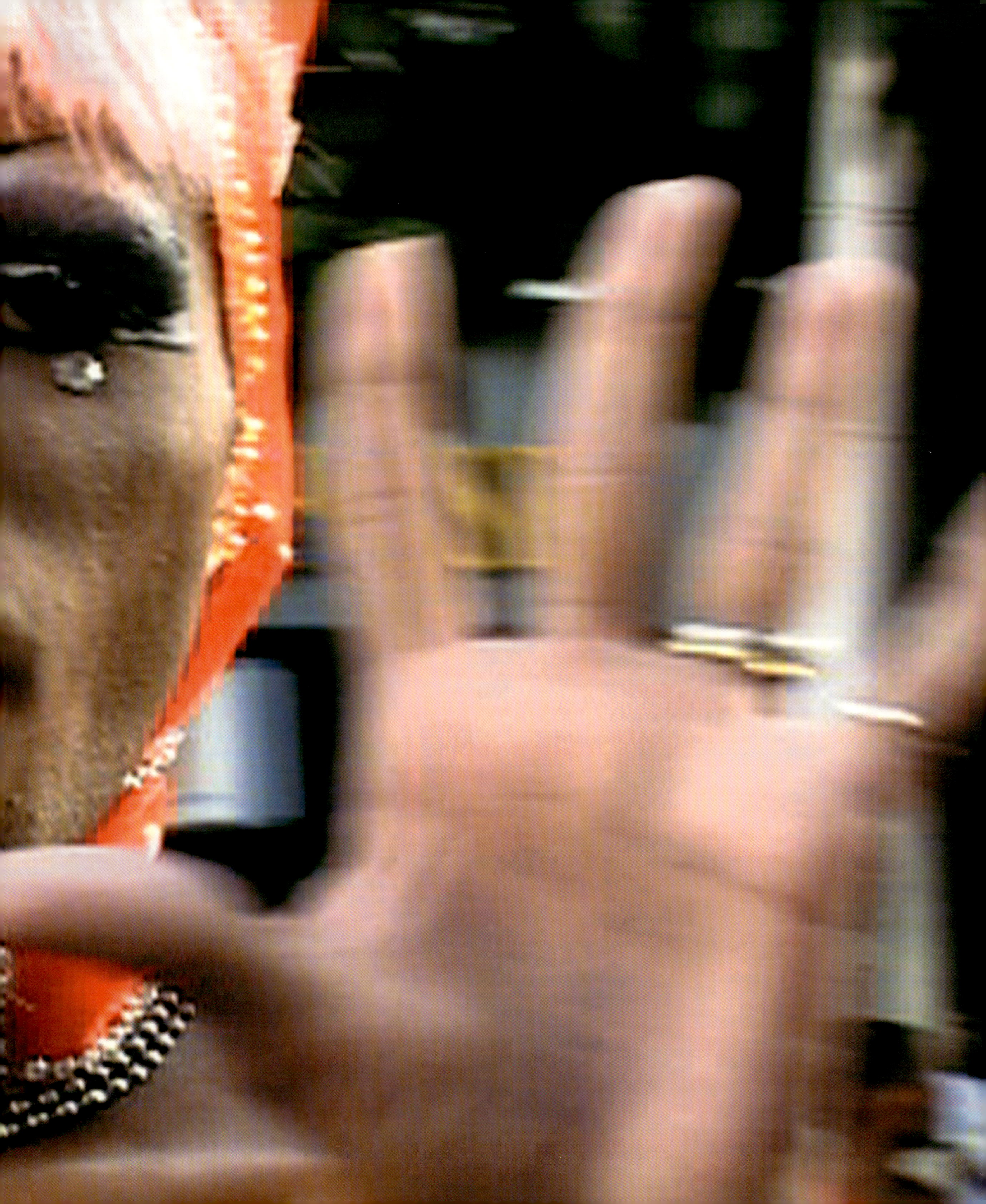

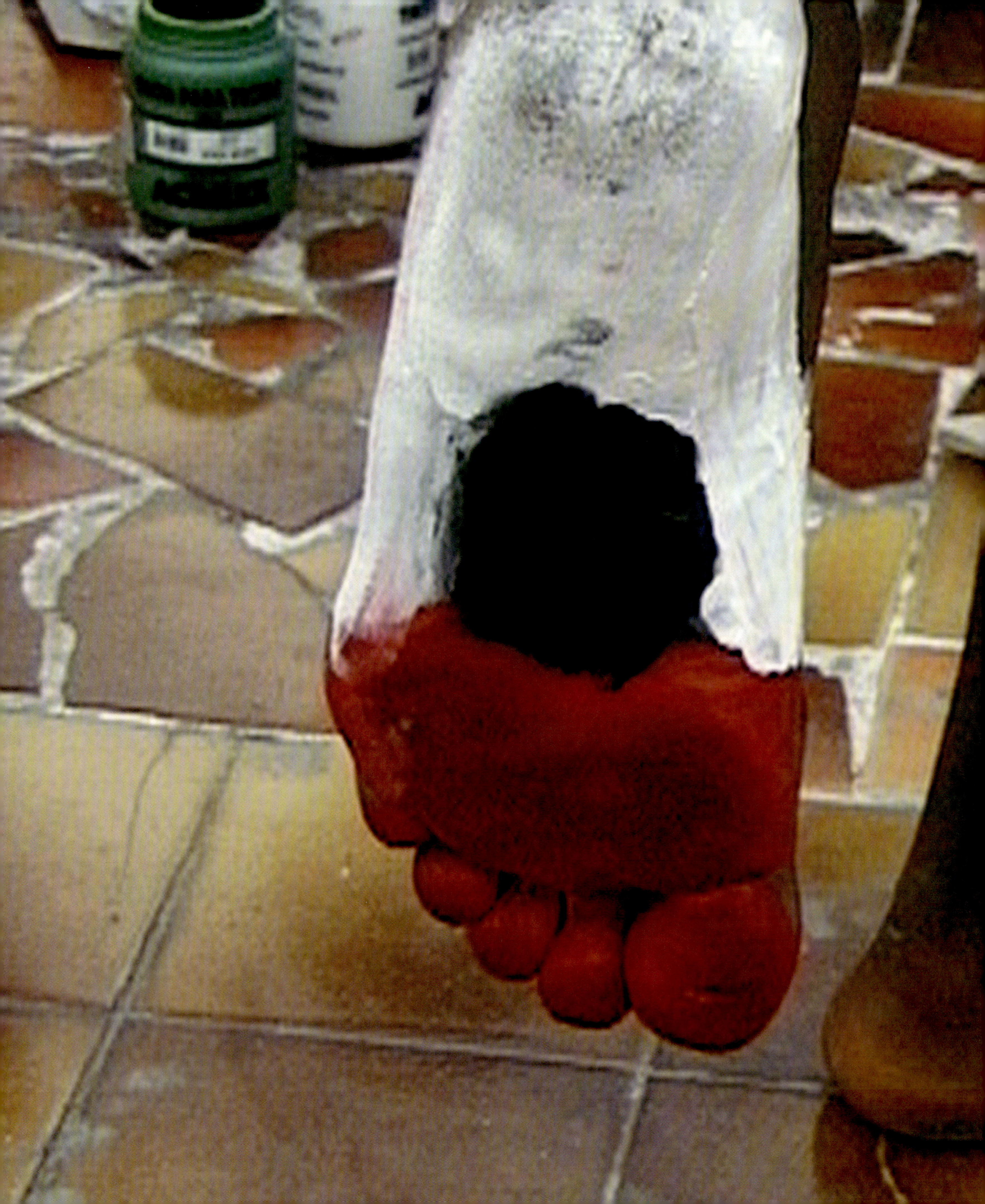

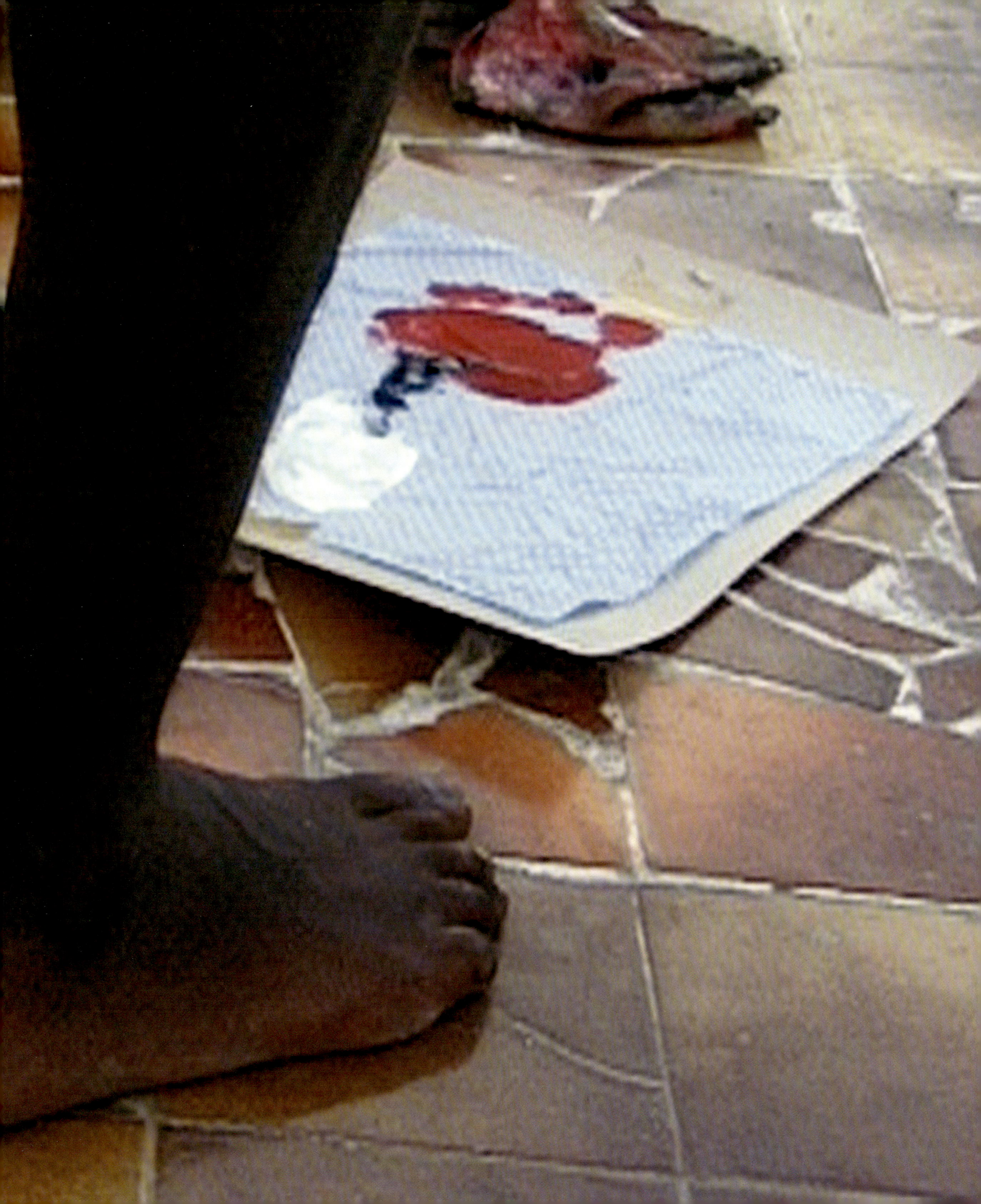

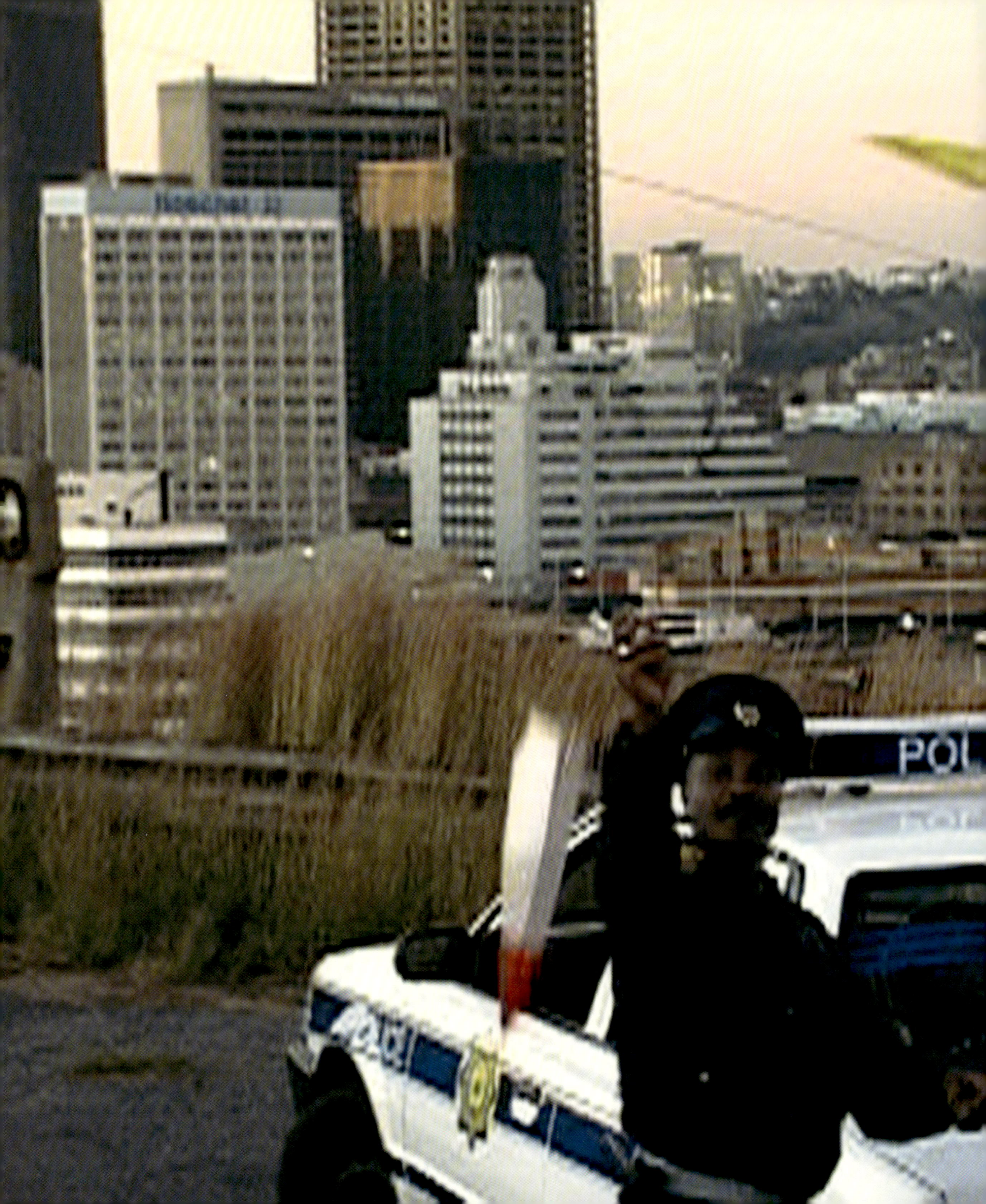

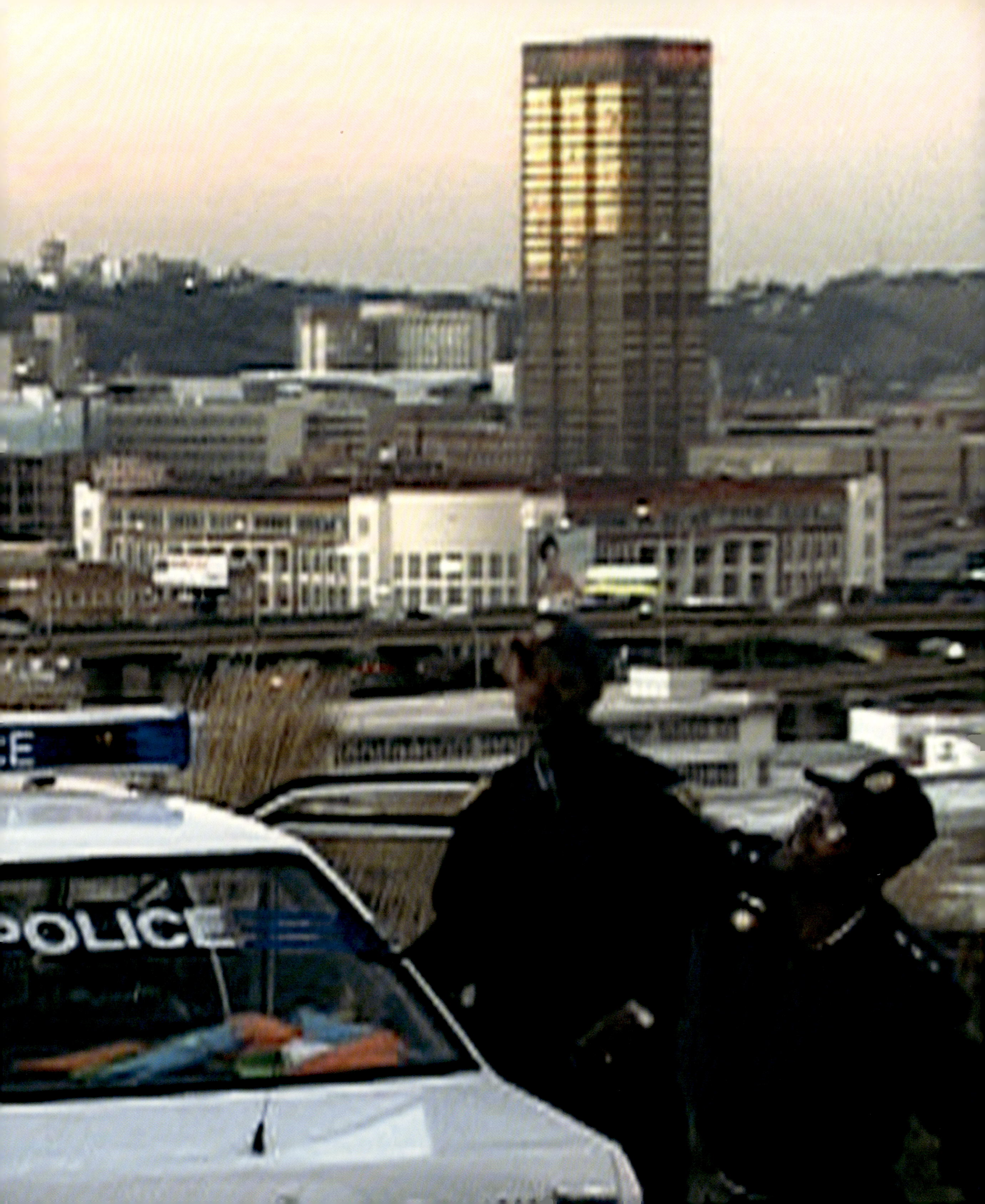
POLICE

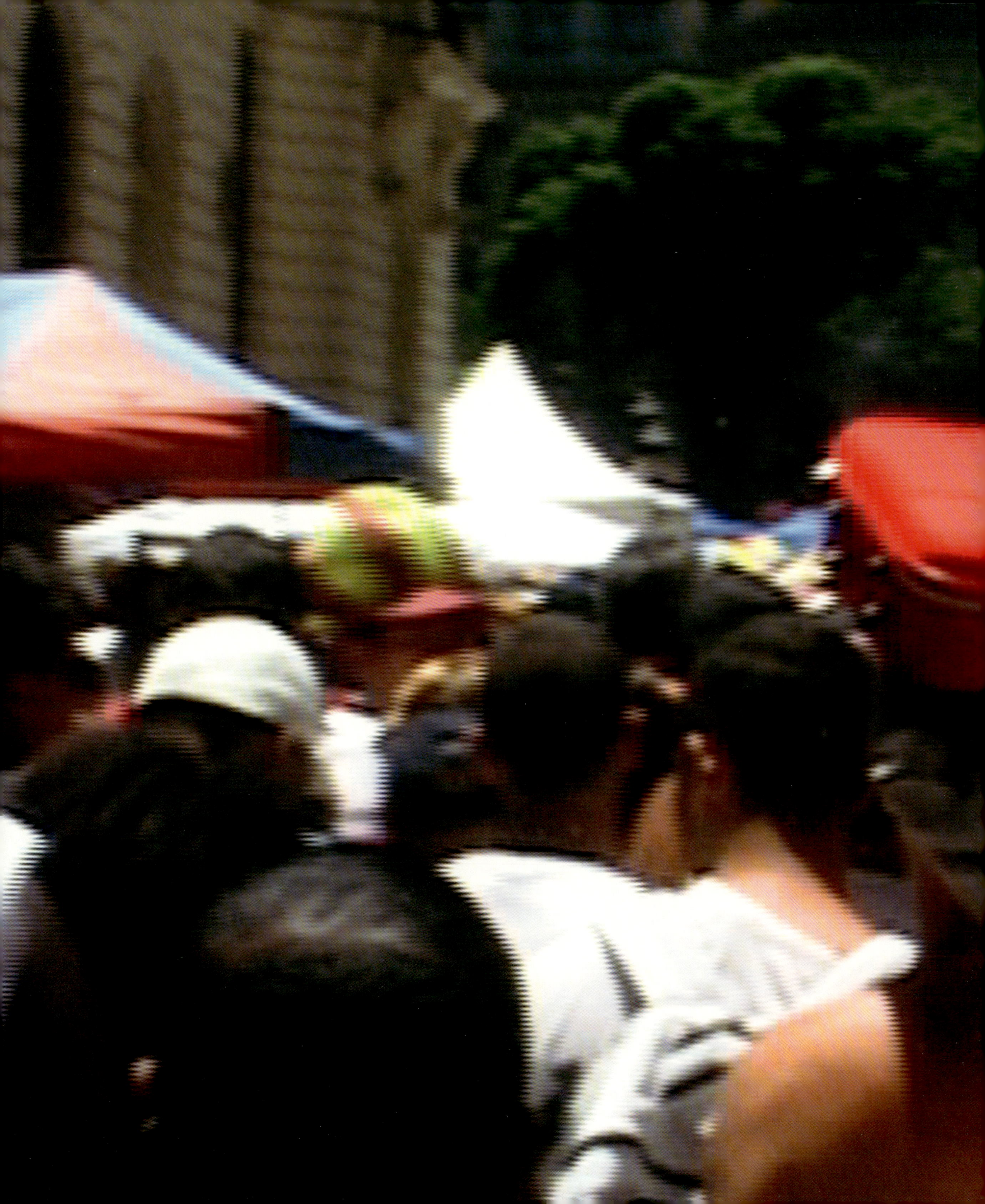

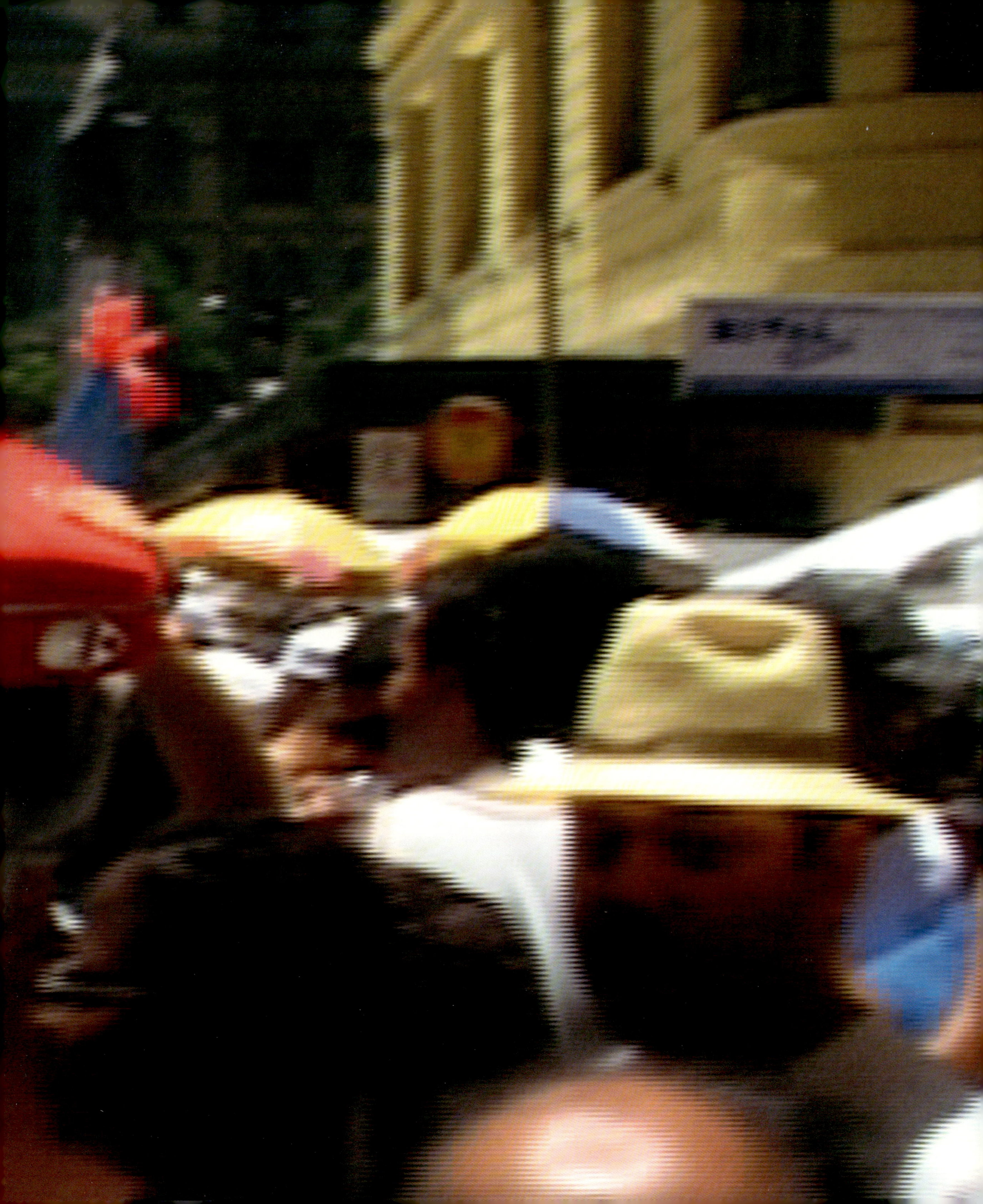

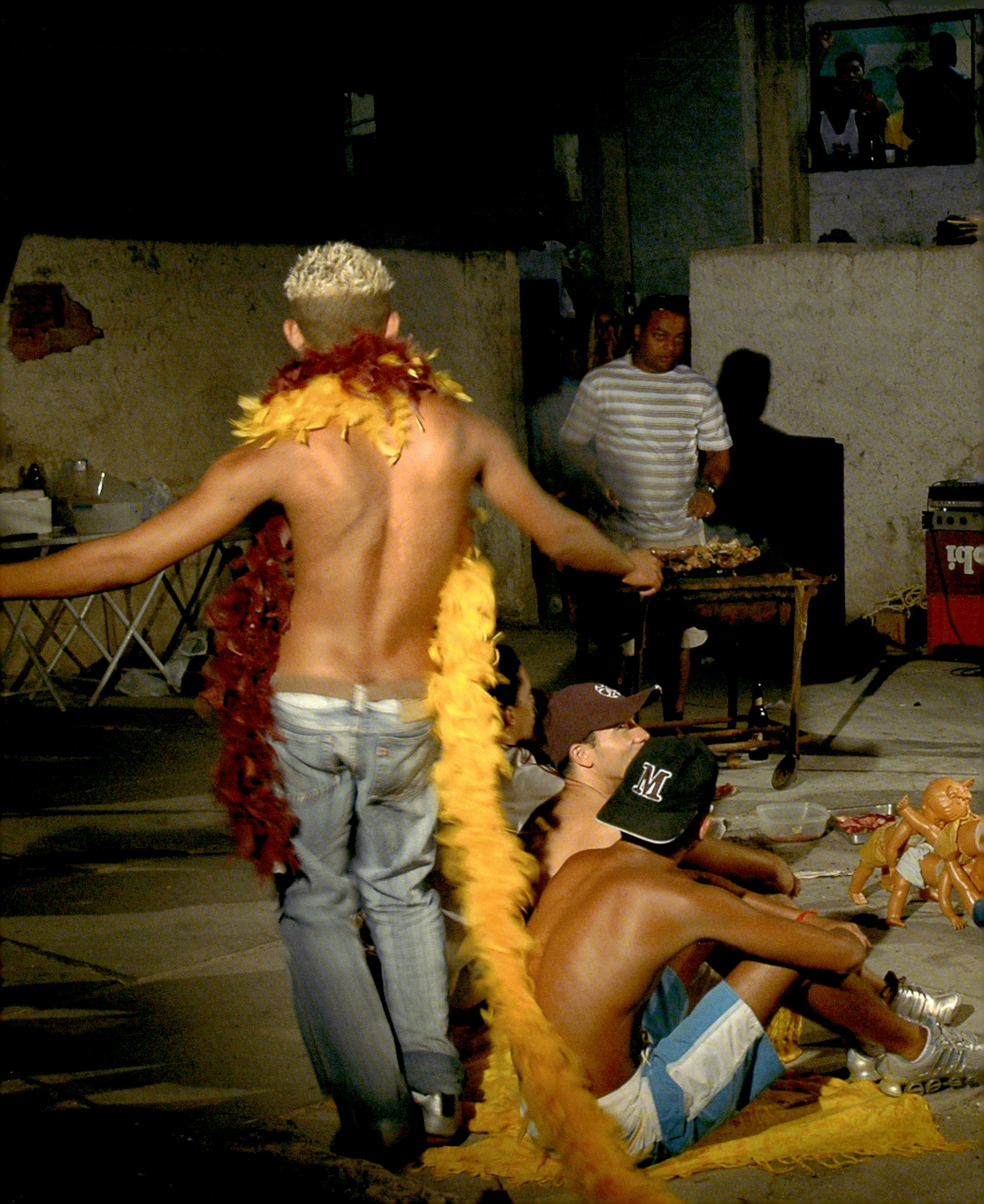

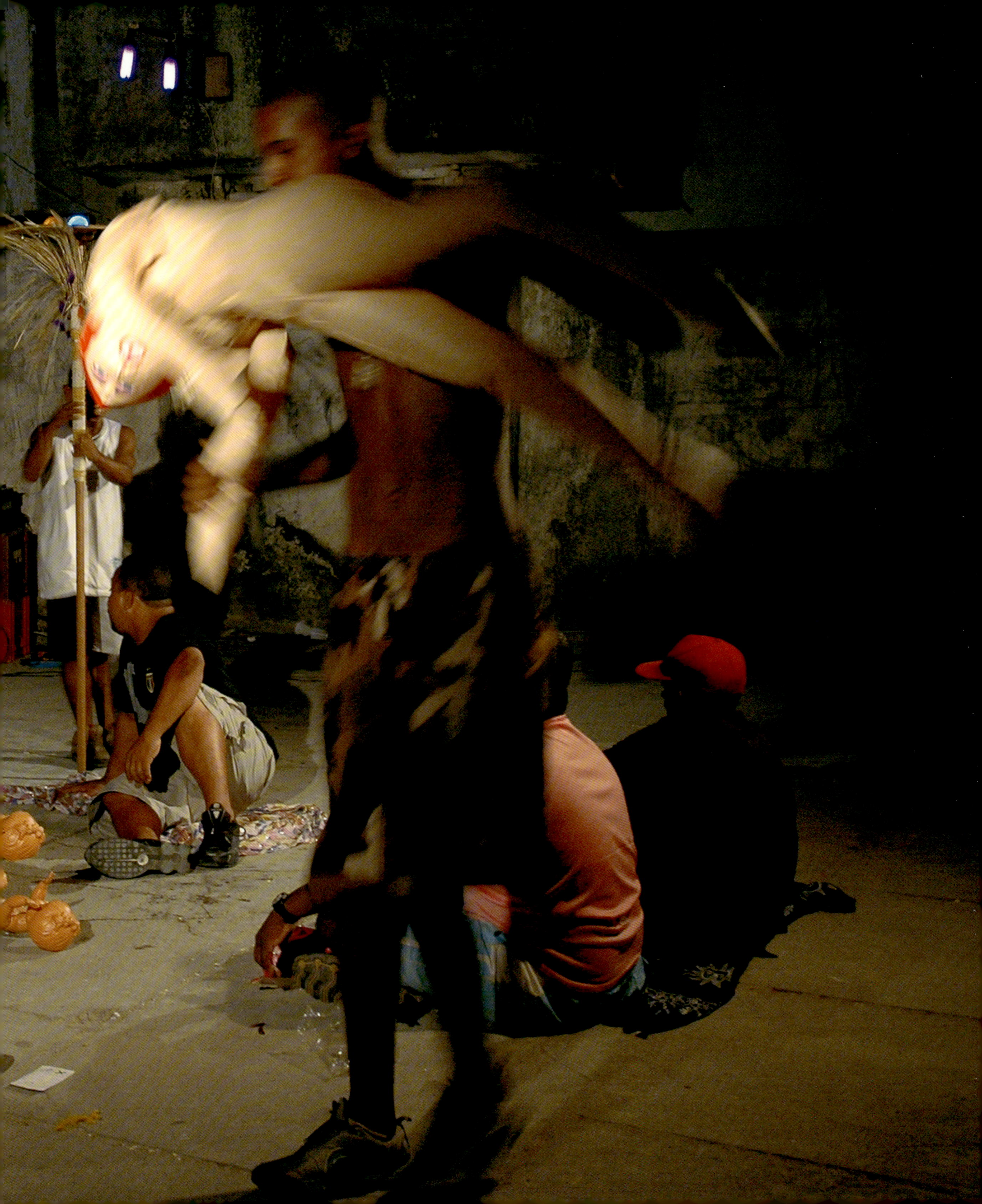

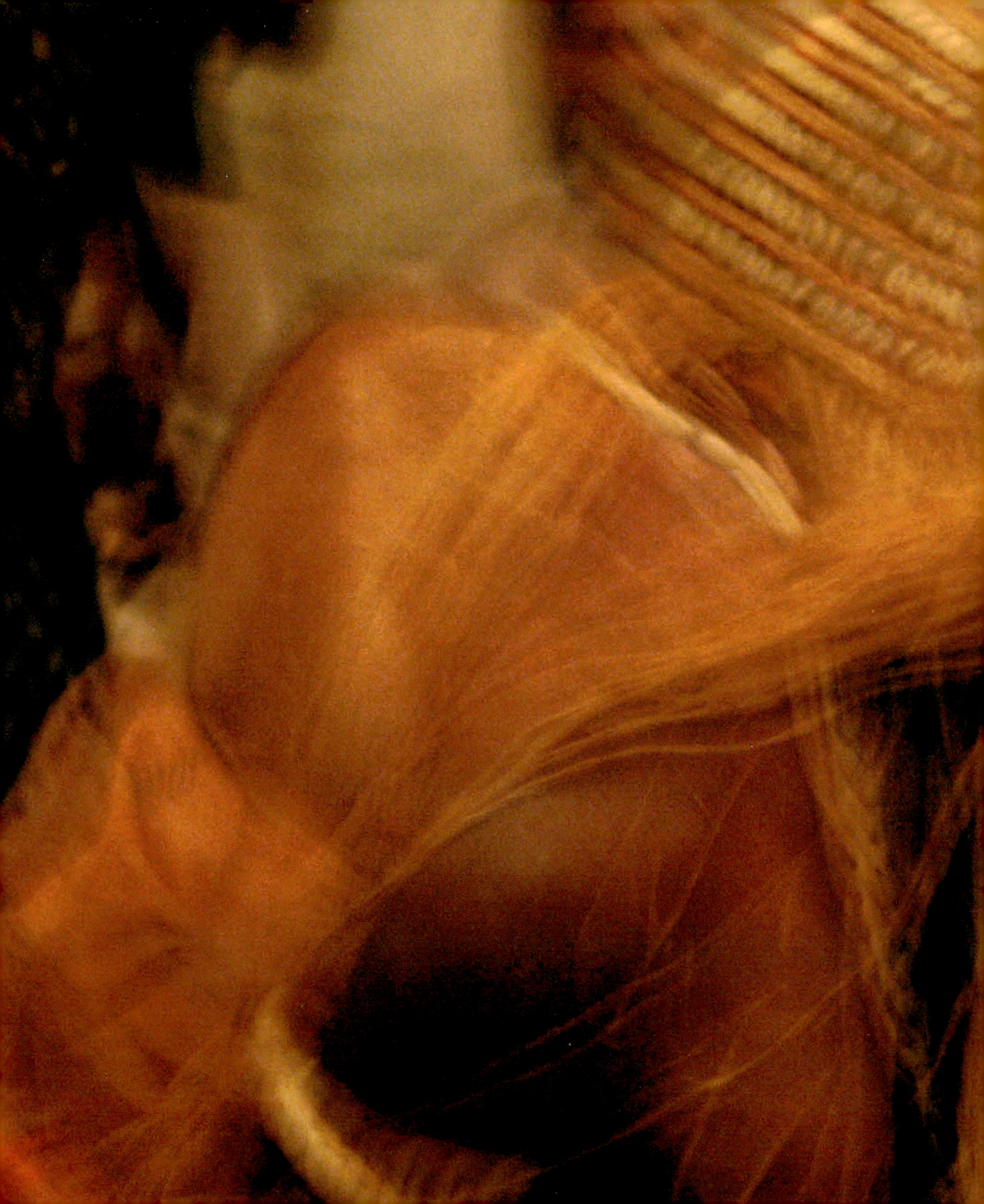

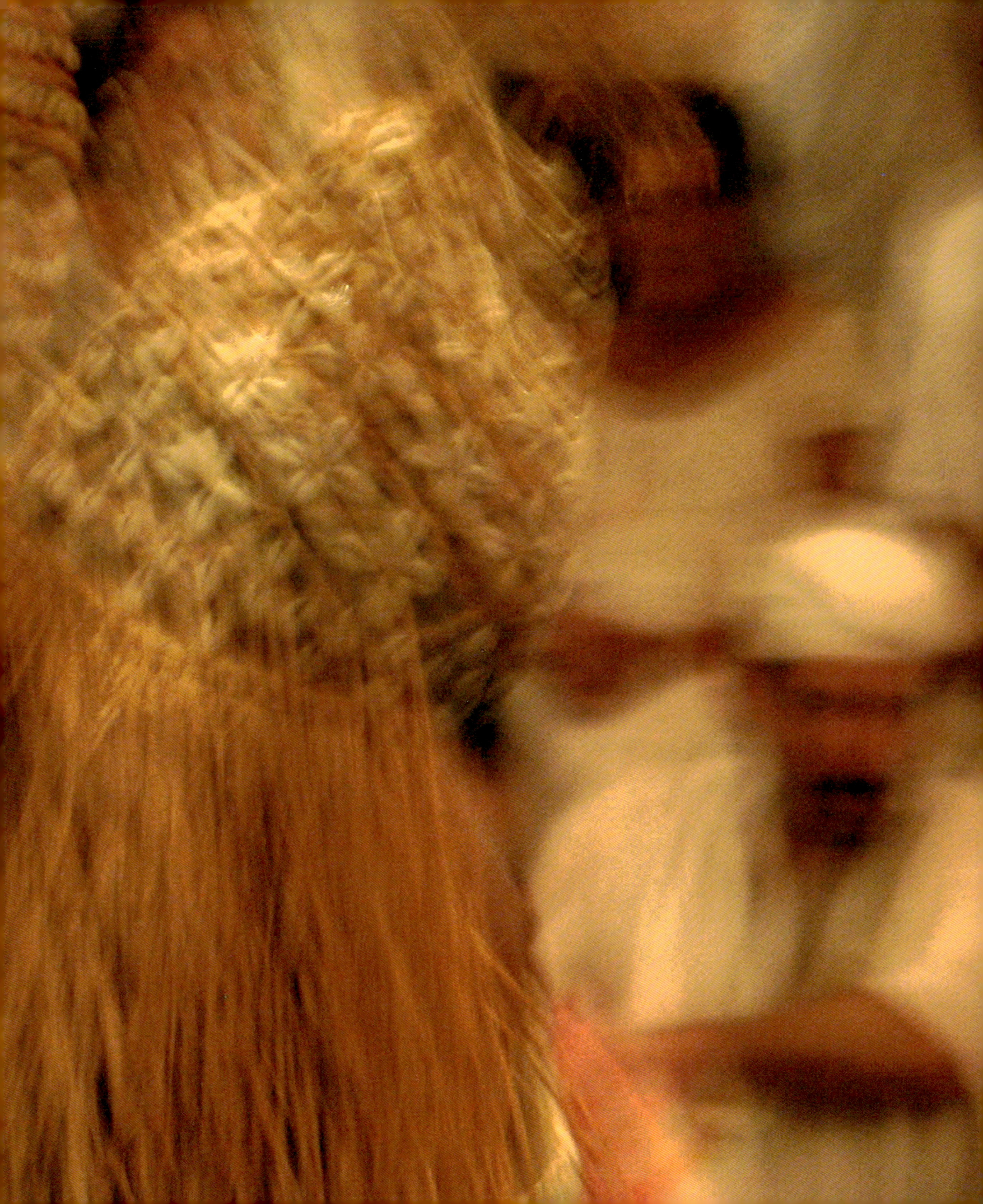

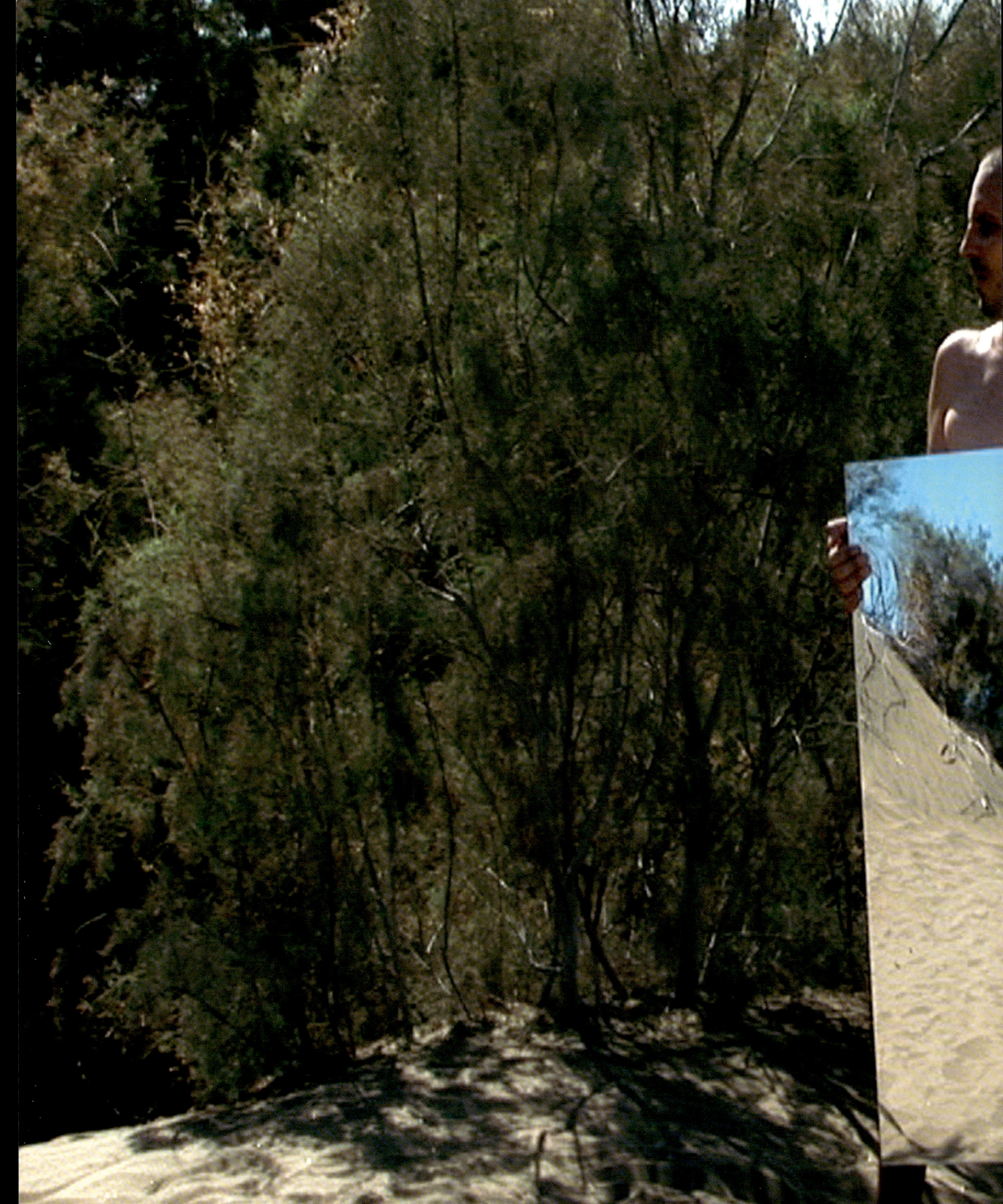

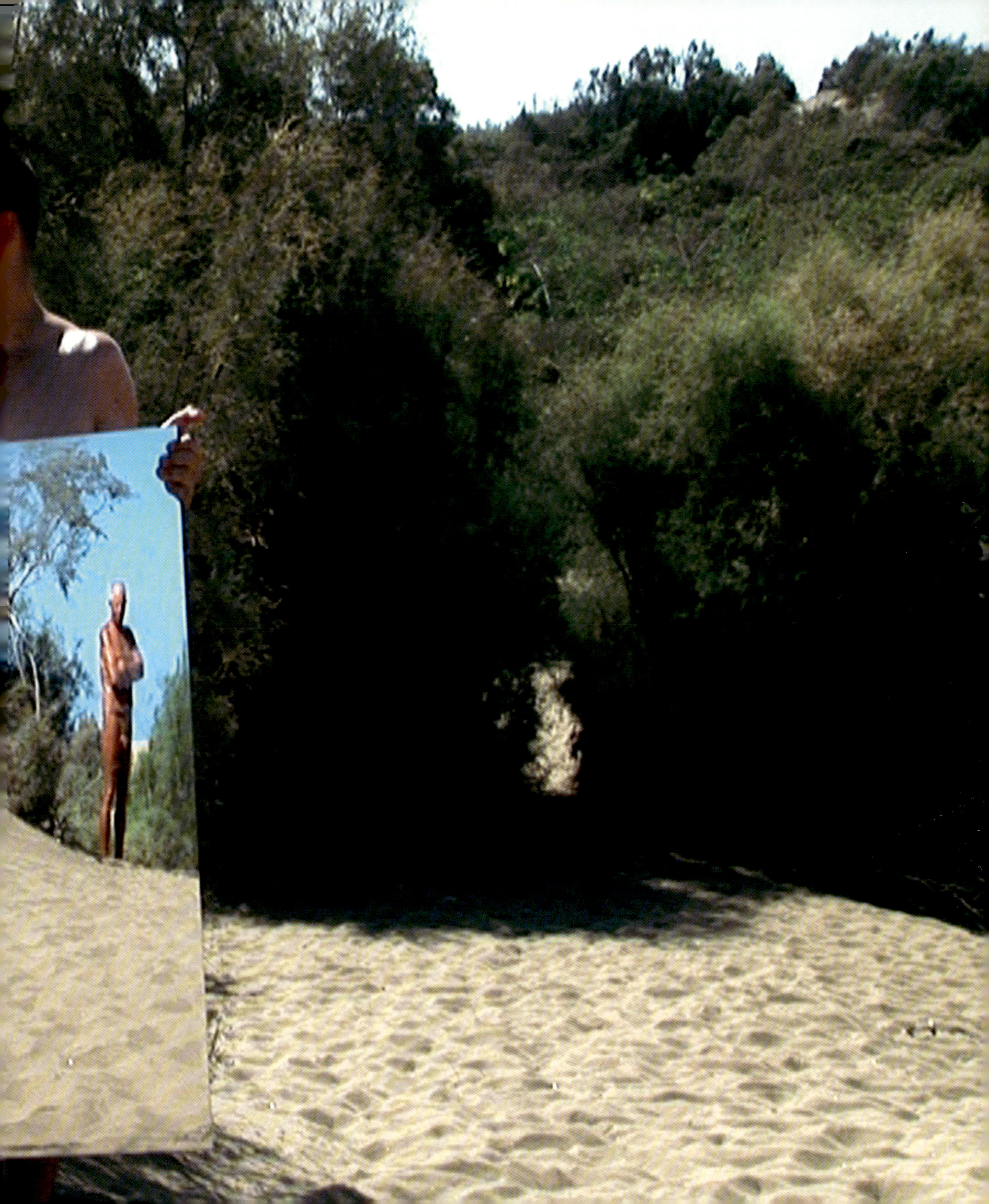

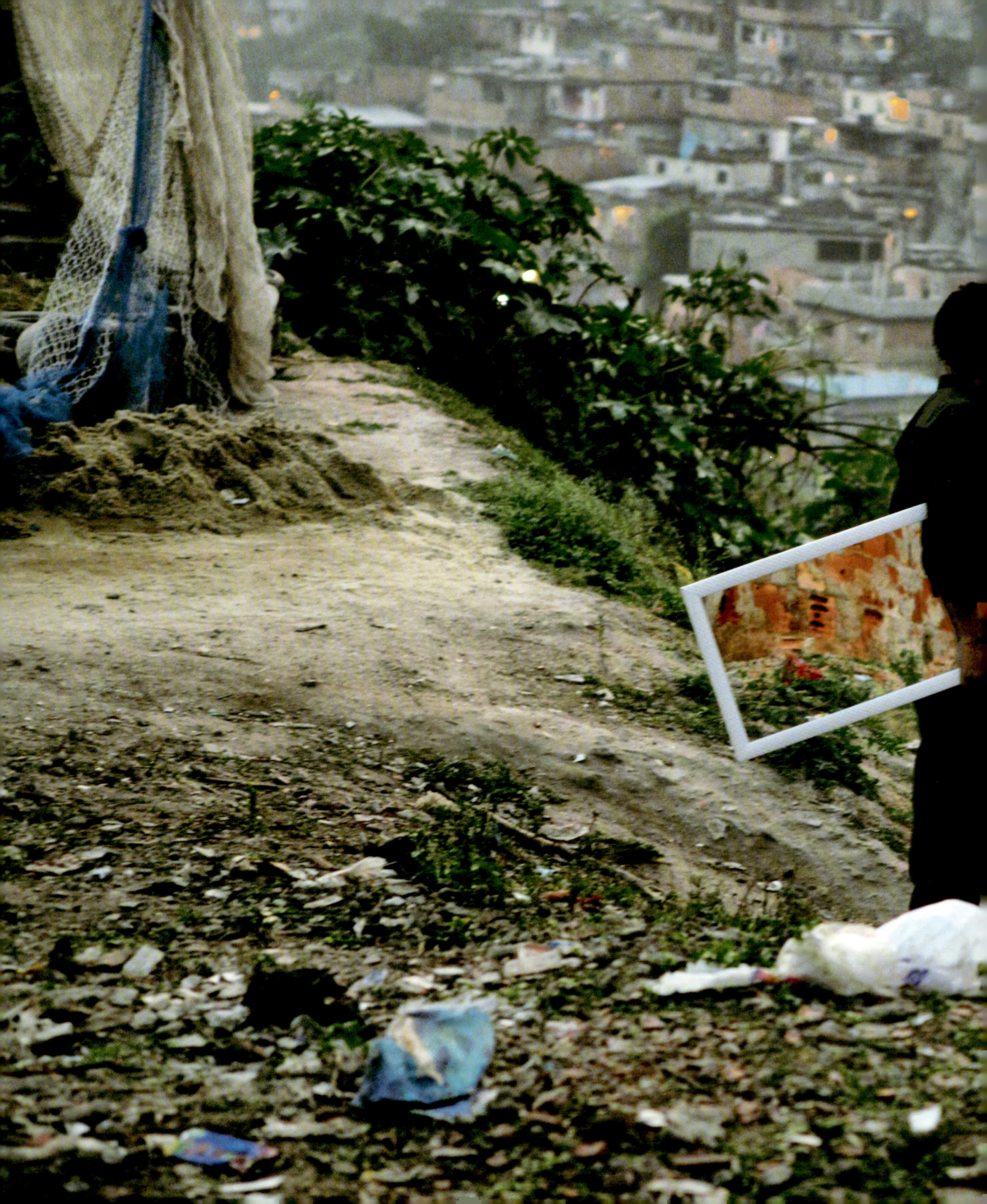

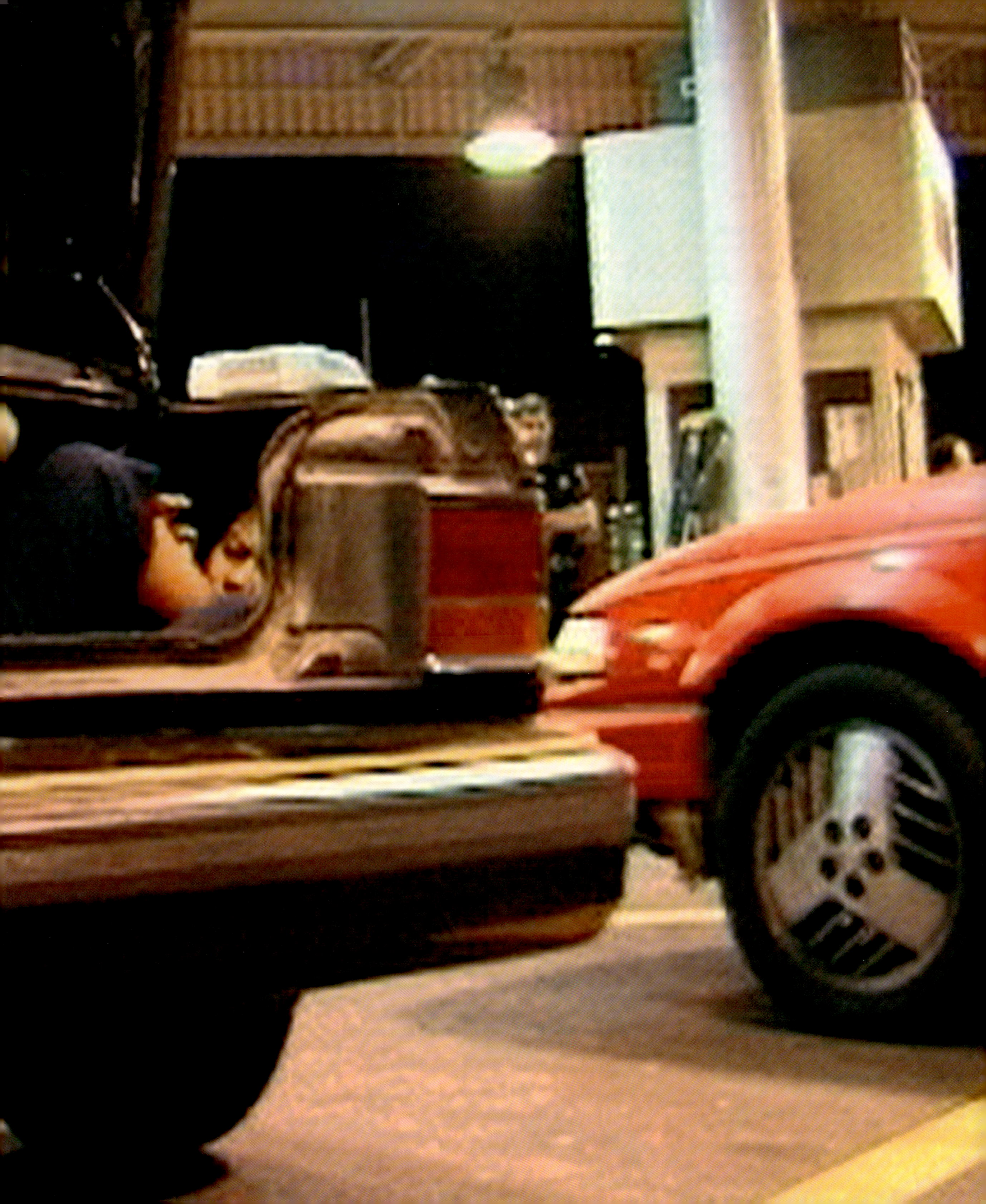

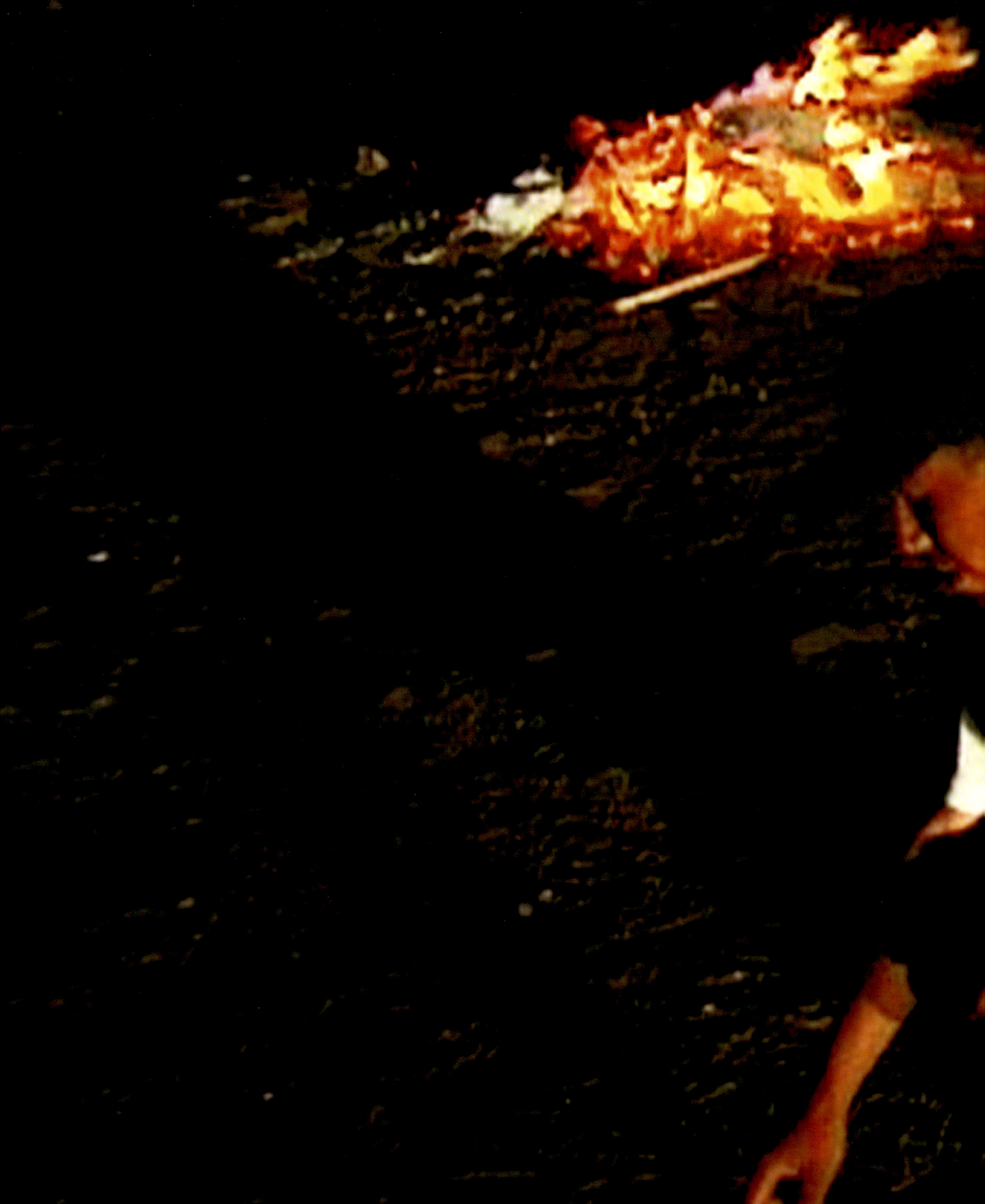

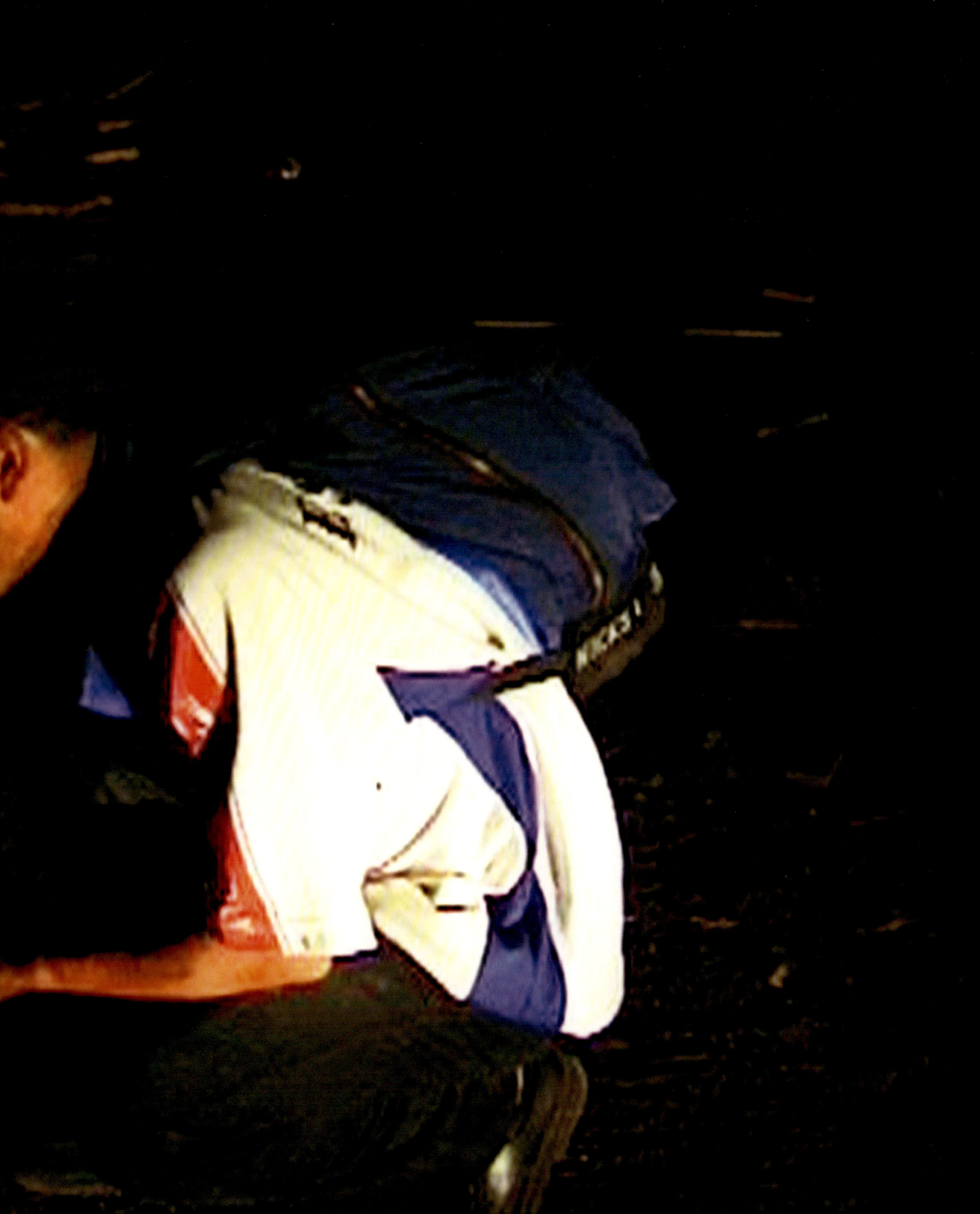

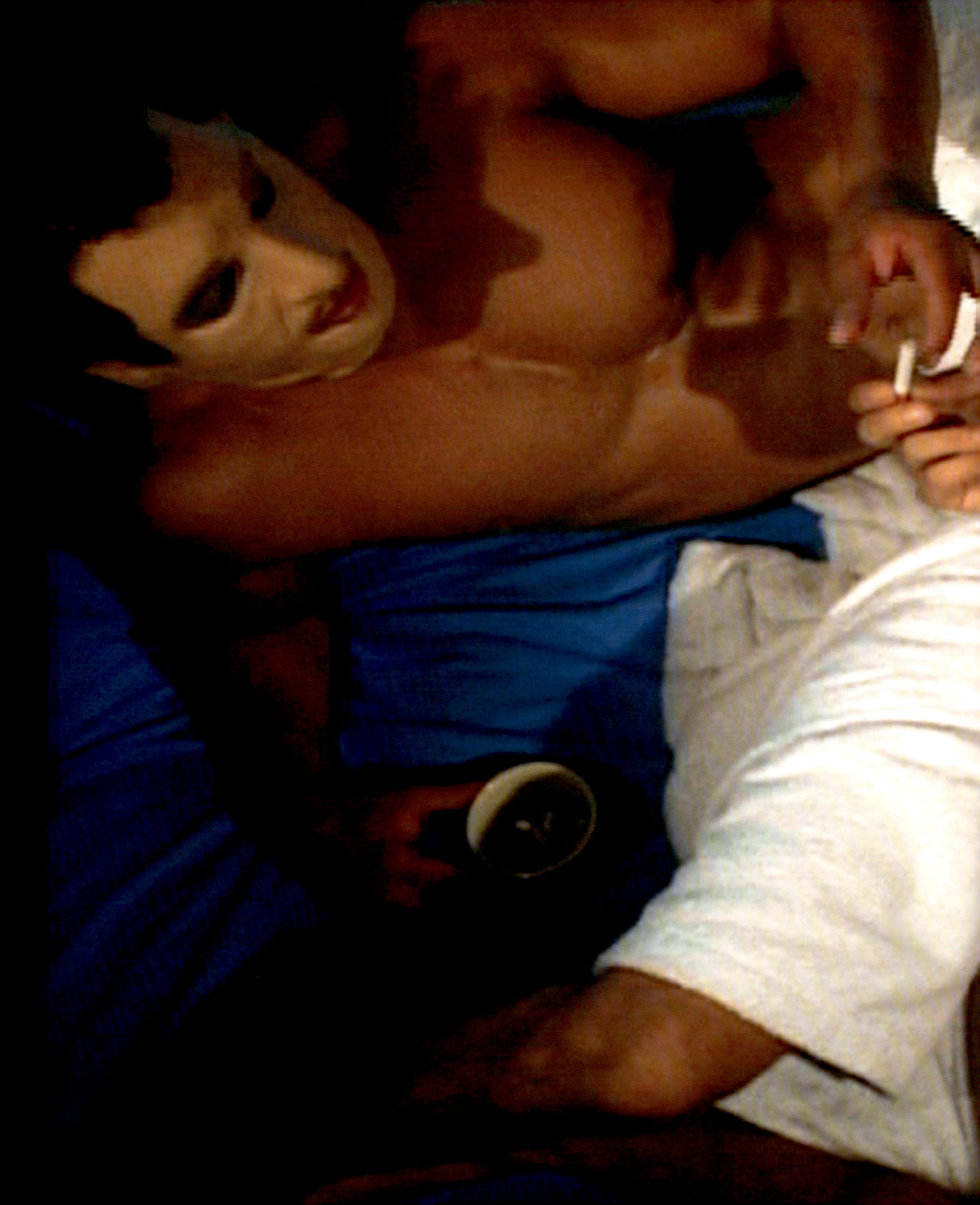

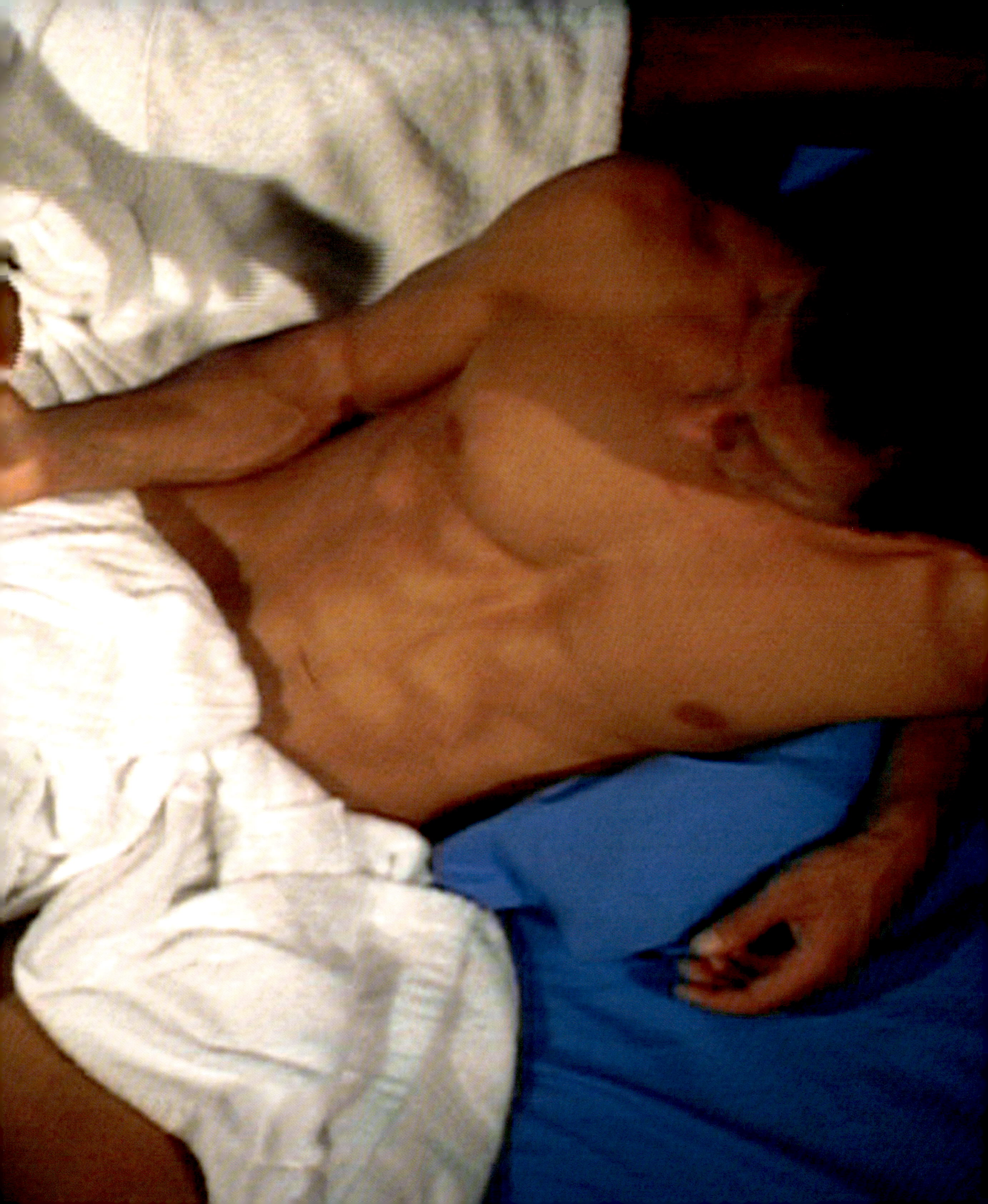

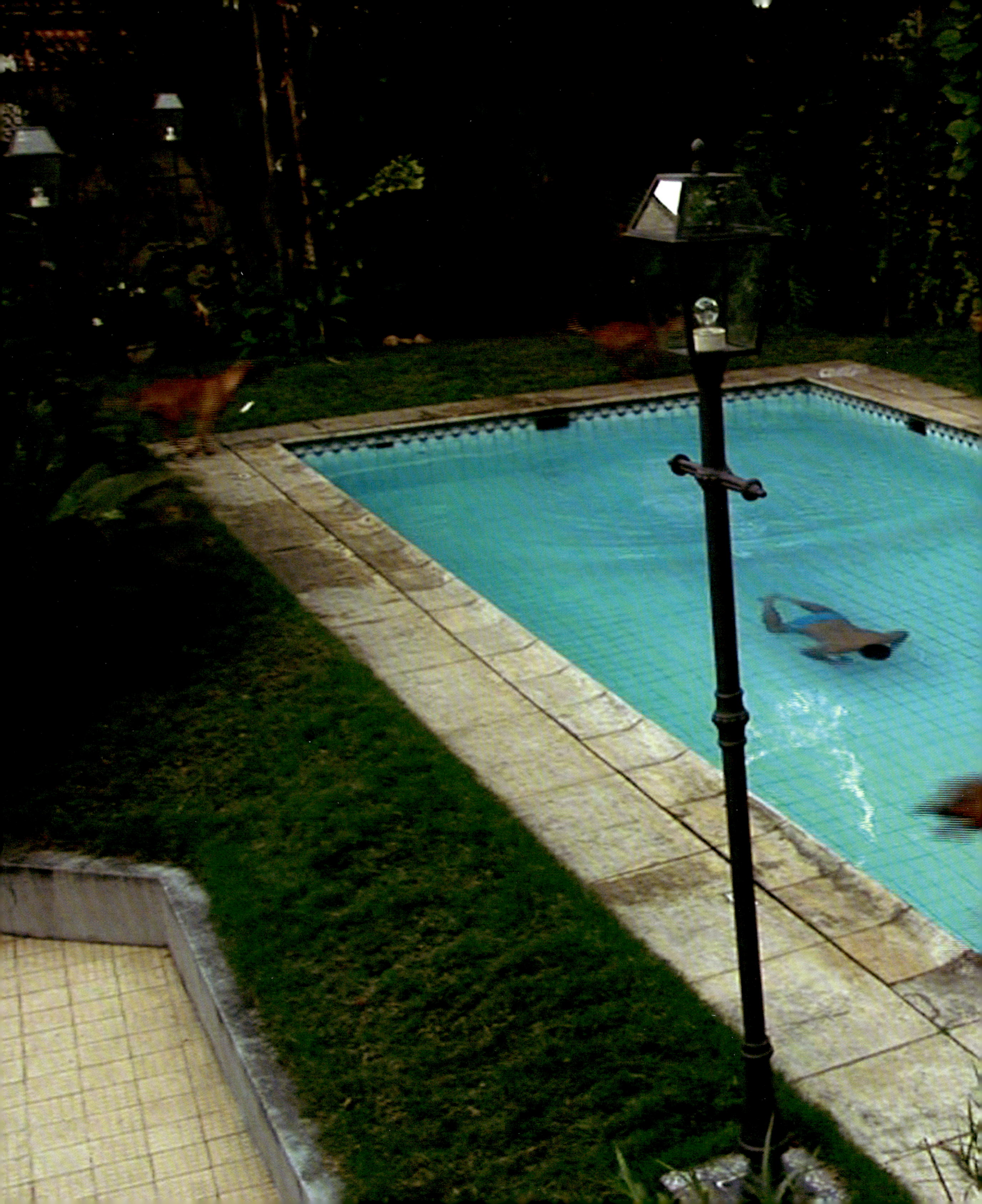

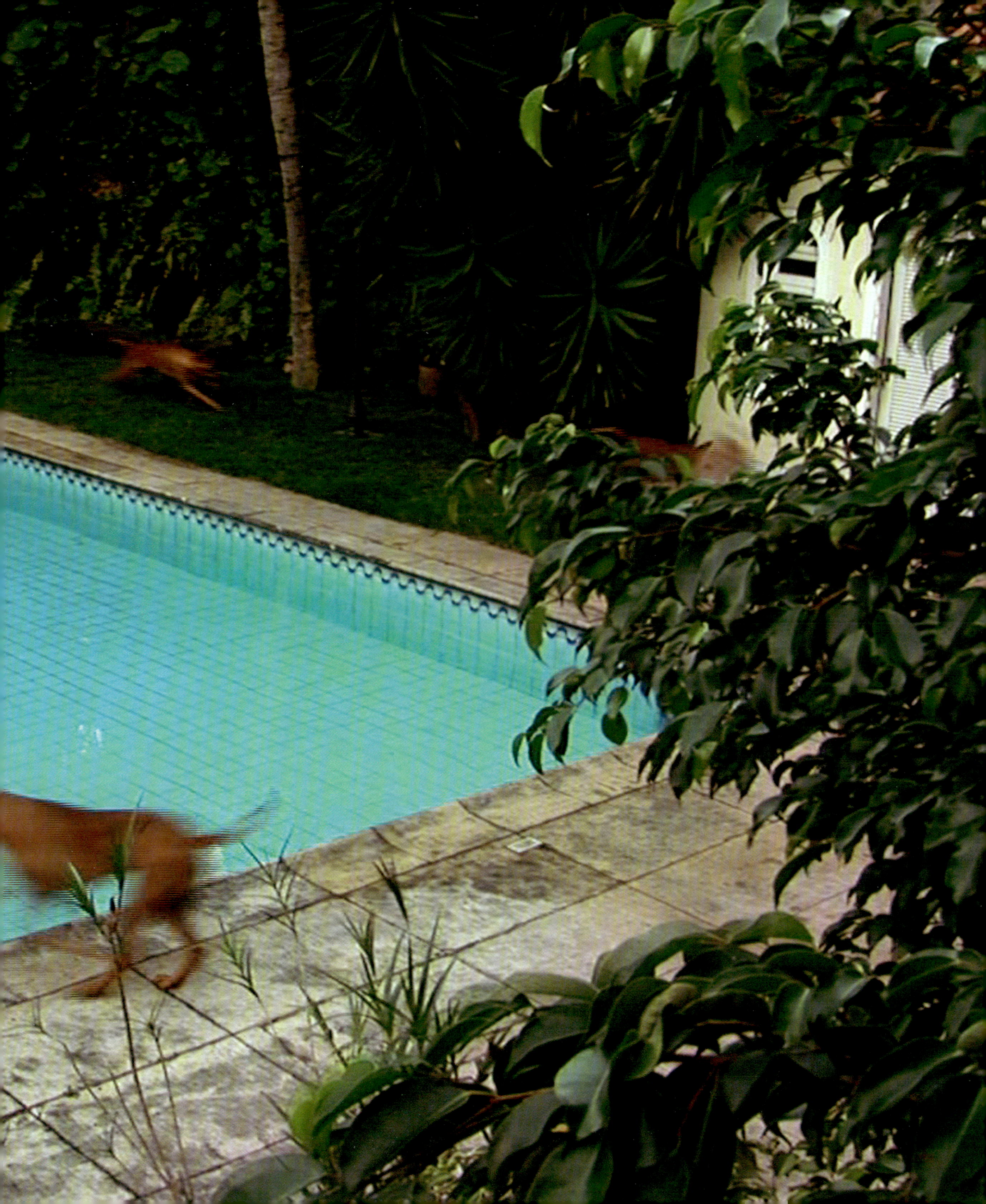

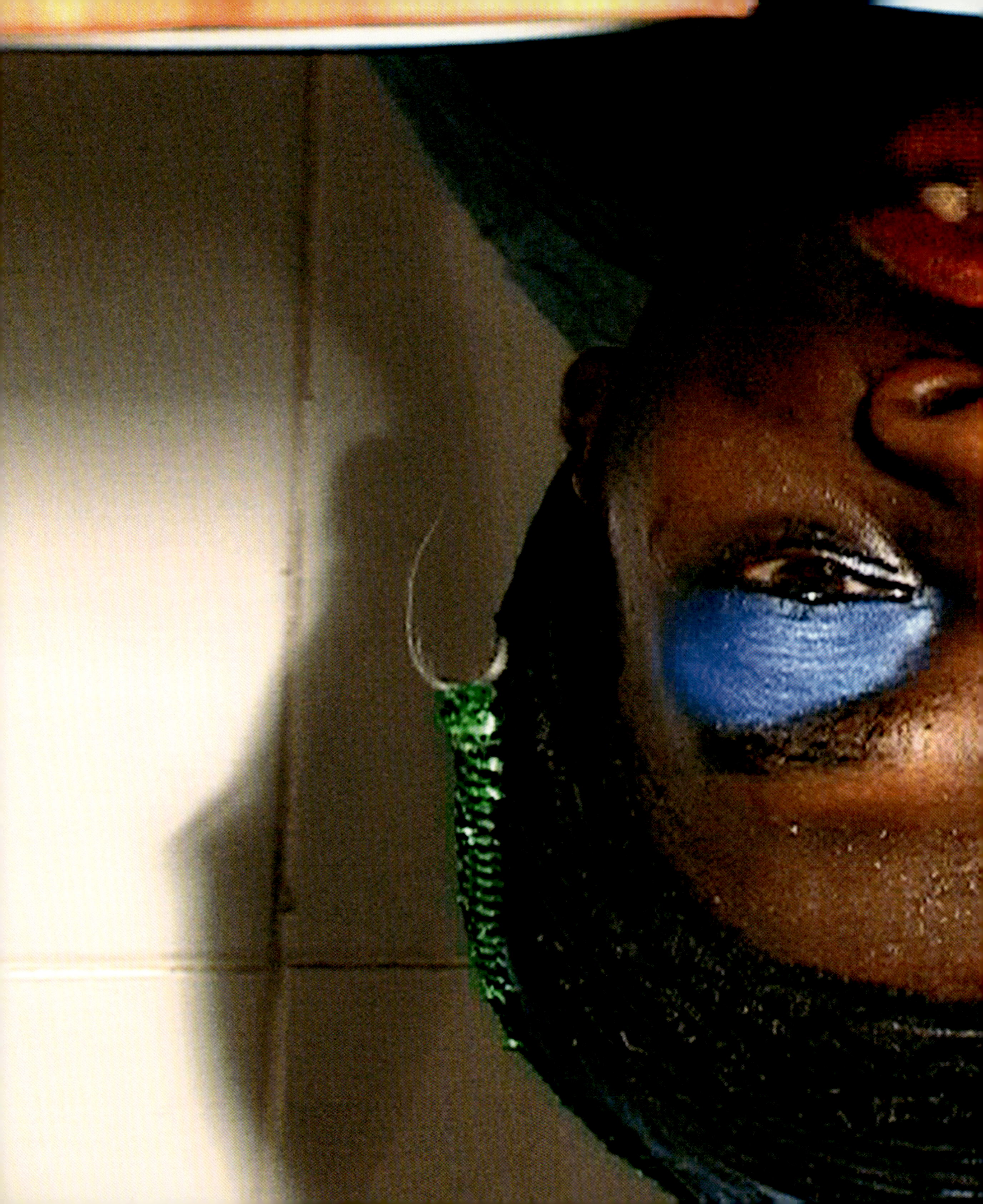

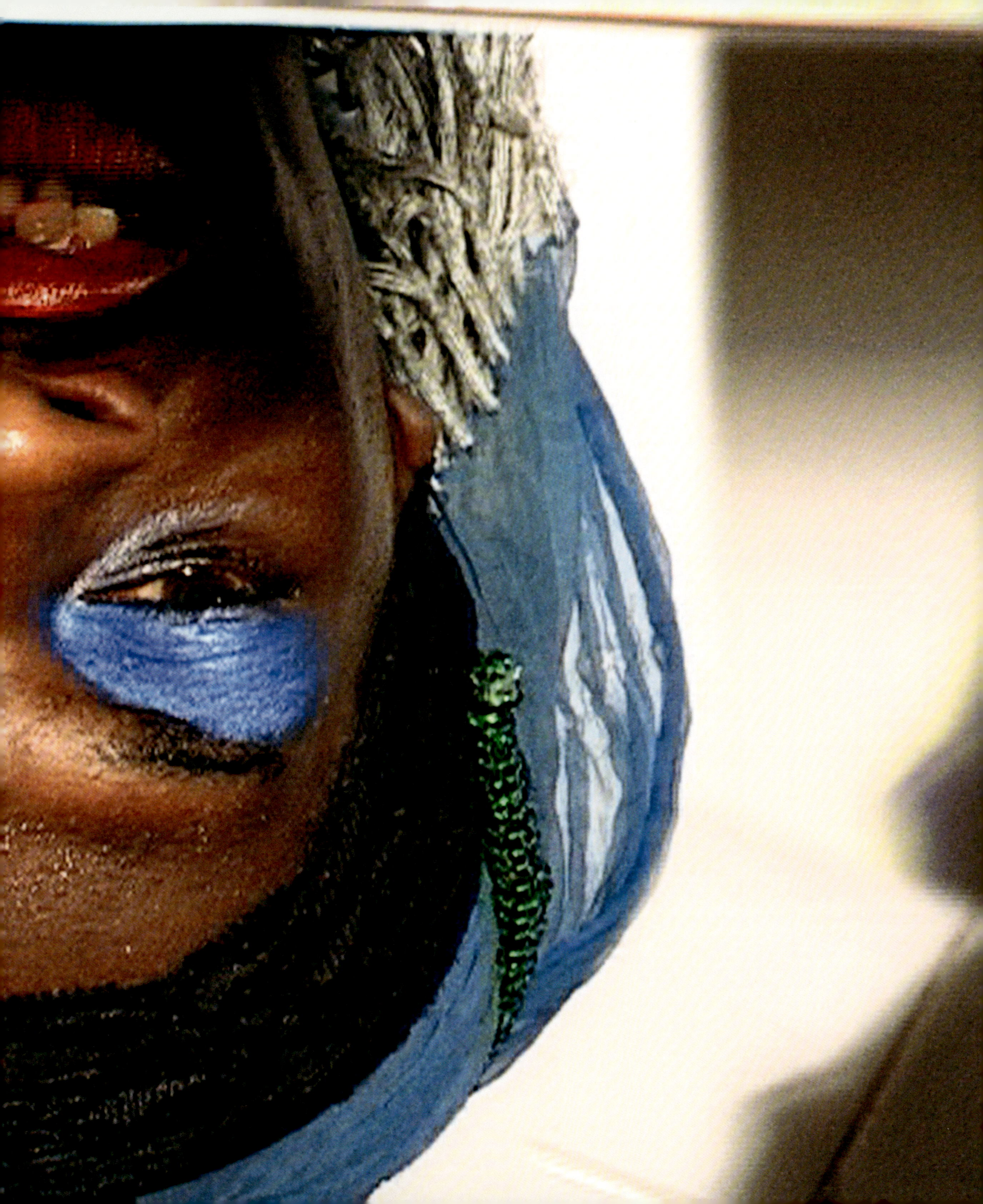

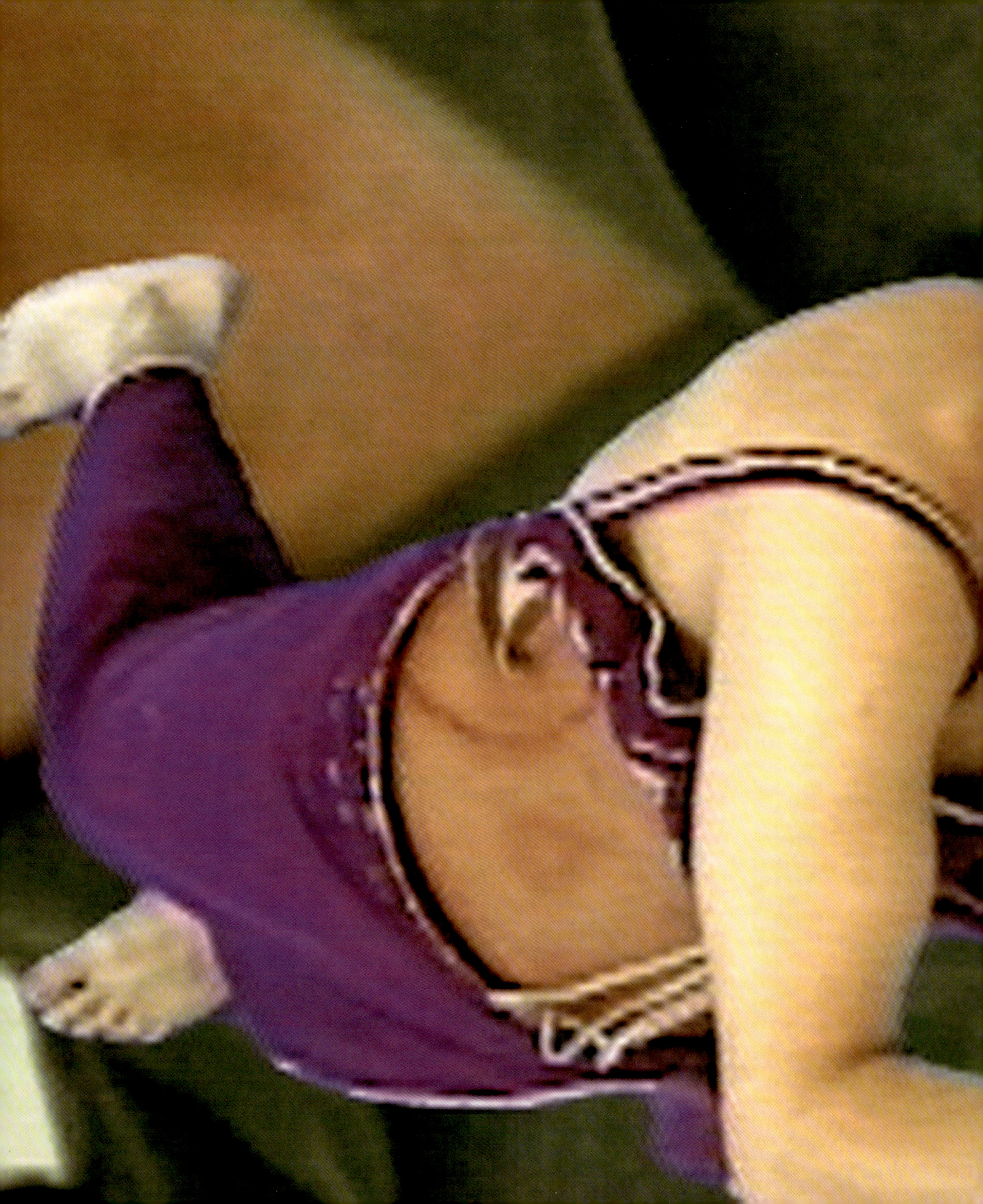

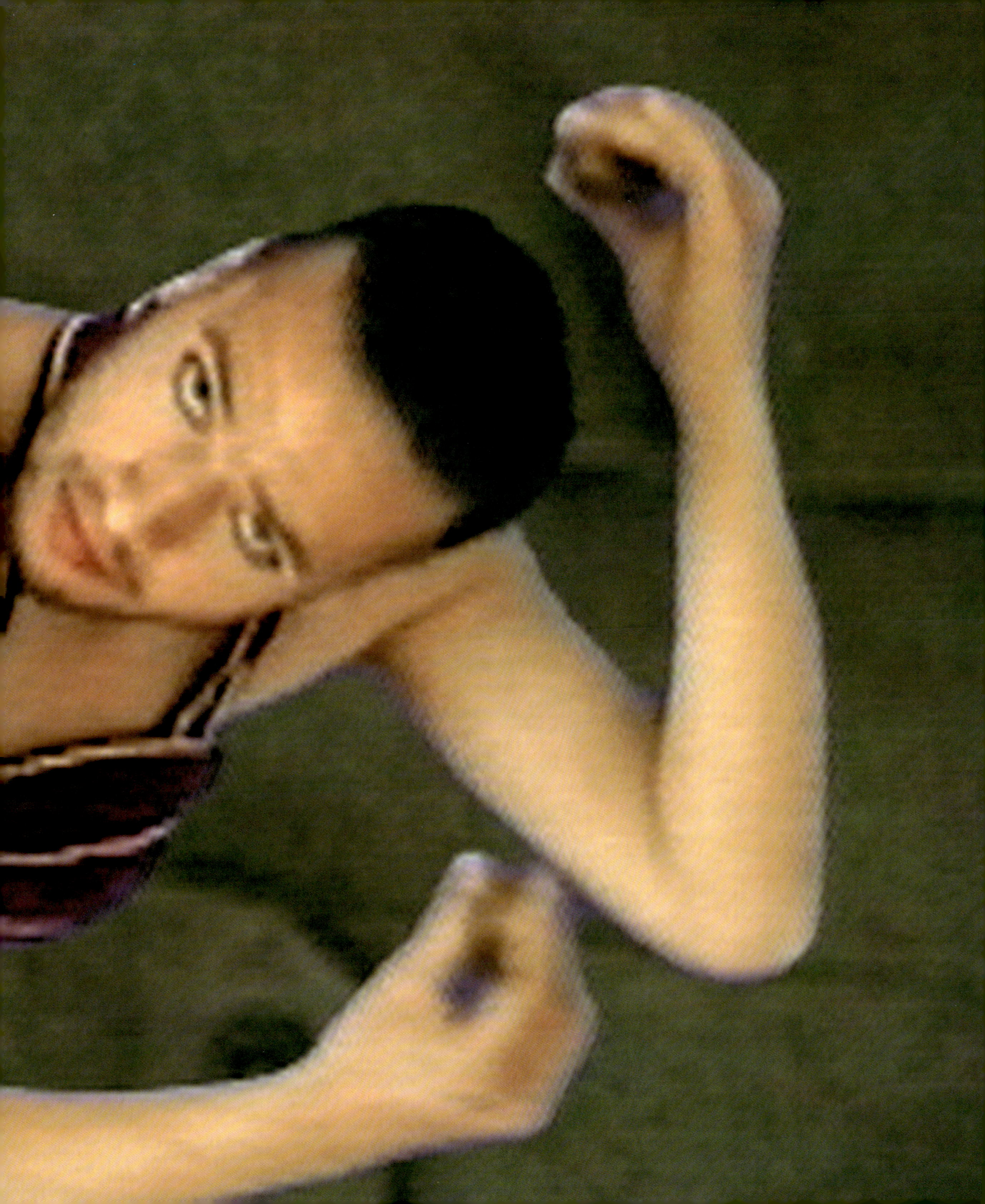

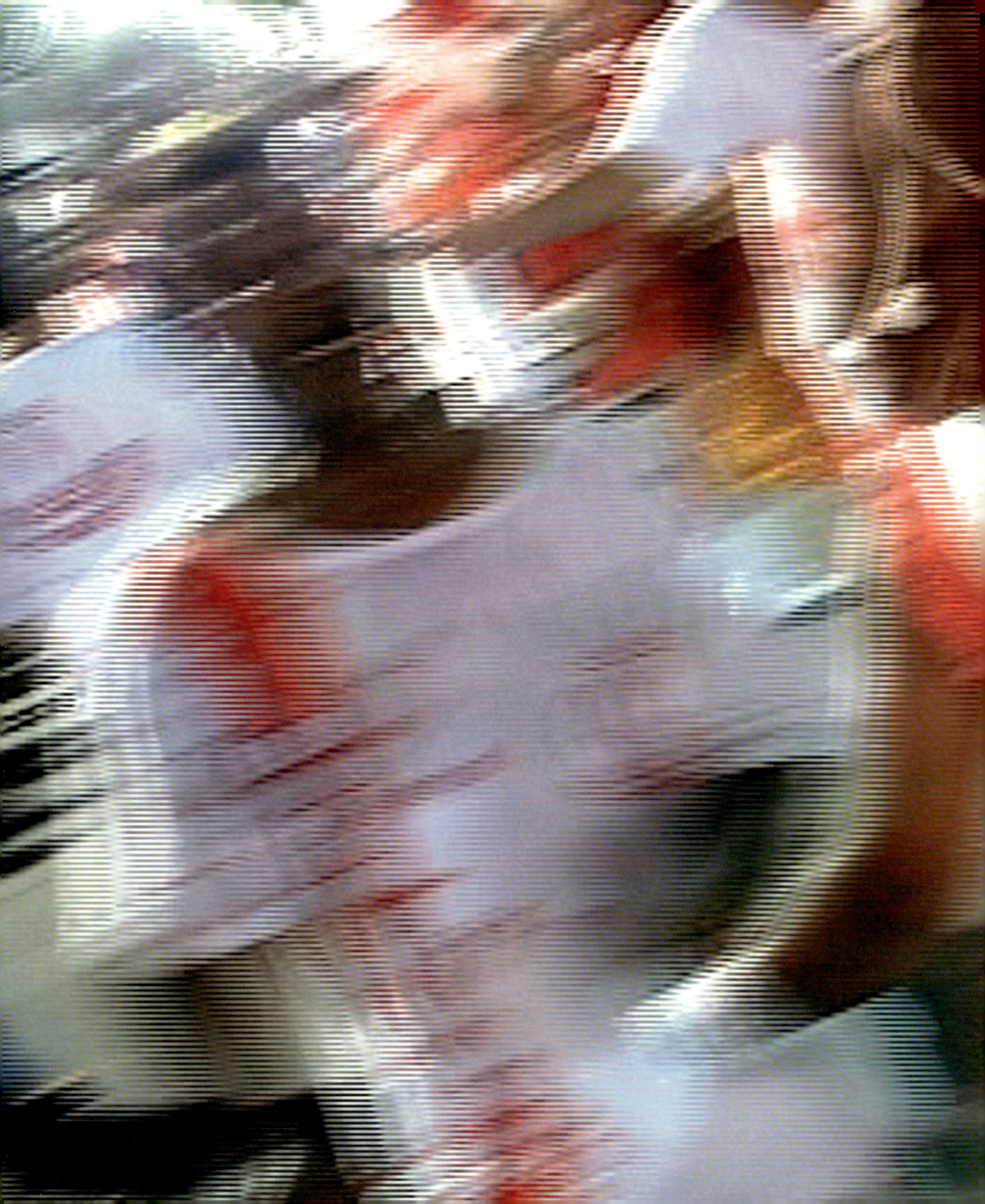

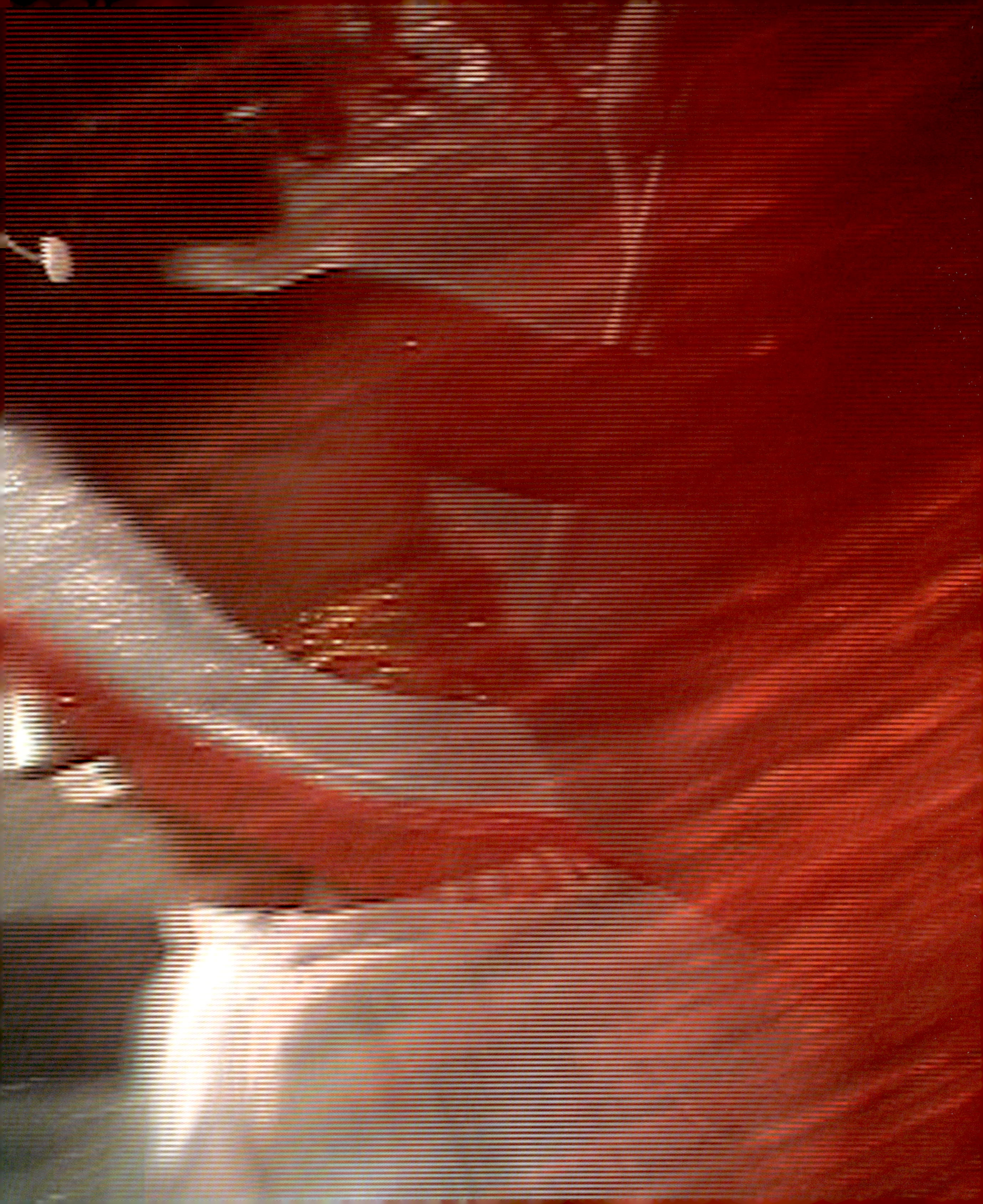

Table of Contents/Inhaltsverzeichnis

50
Being Native
Fanni Fetzer

56
Body to Body
Chantal Pontbriand

64
Homing Devices
Dieter Roelstraete

73
Chronology

126
Index of Stills

130
Being Native
Fanni Fetzer

136
Körper an Körper
Chantal Pontbriand

146
Heimkehrmittel
Dieter Roelstraete

154
Biography/Bibliography

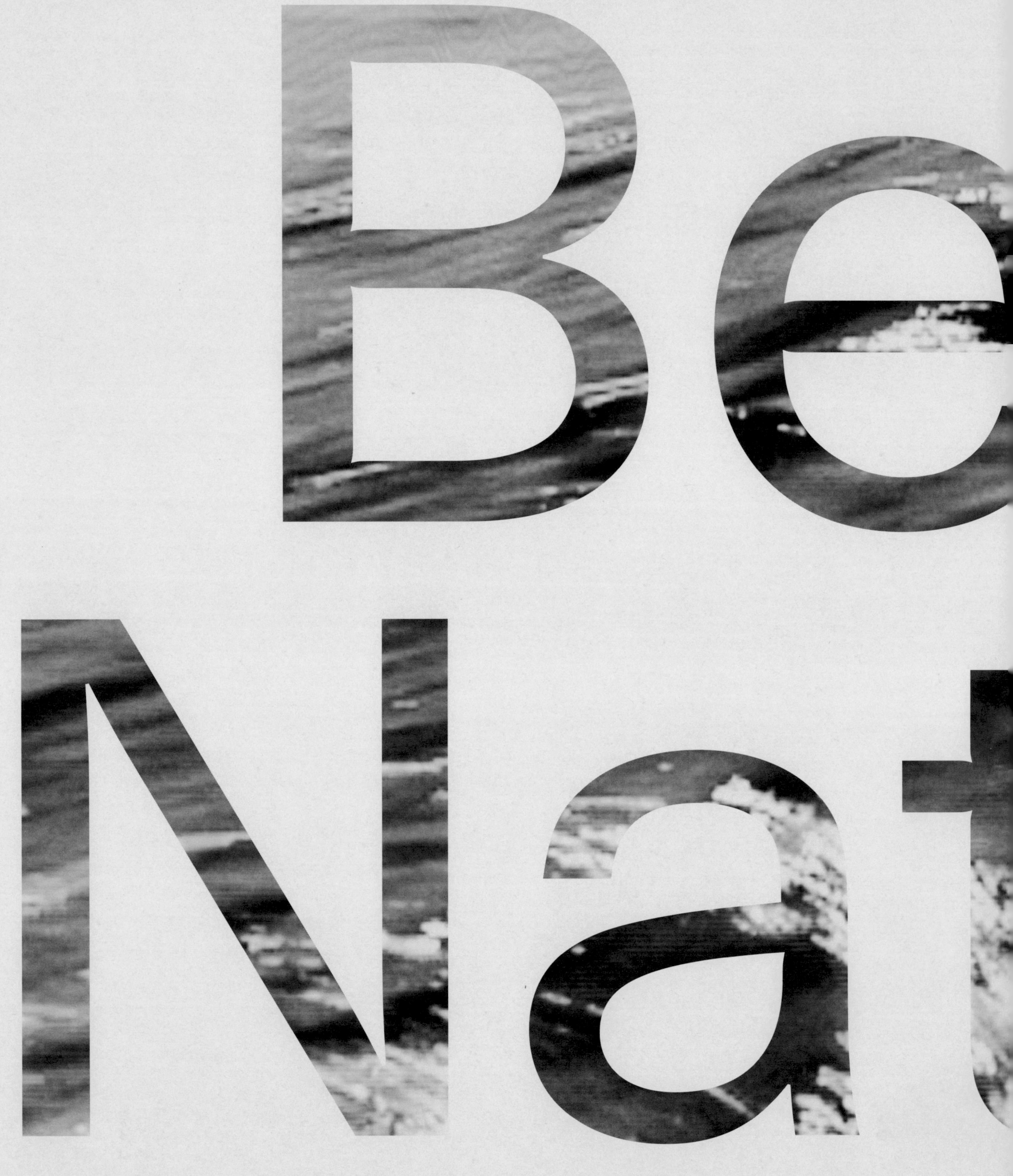
Be
Na

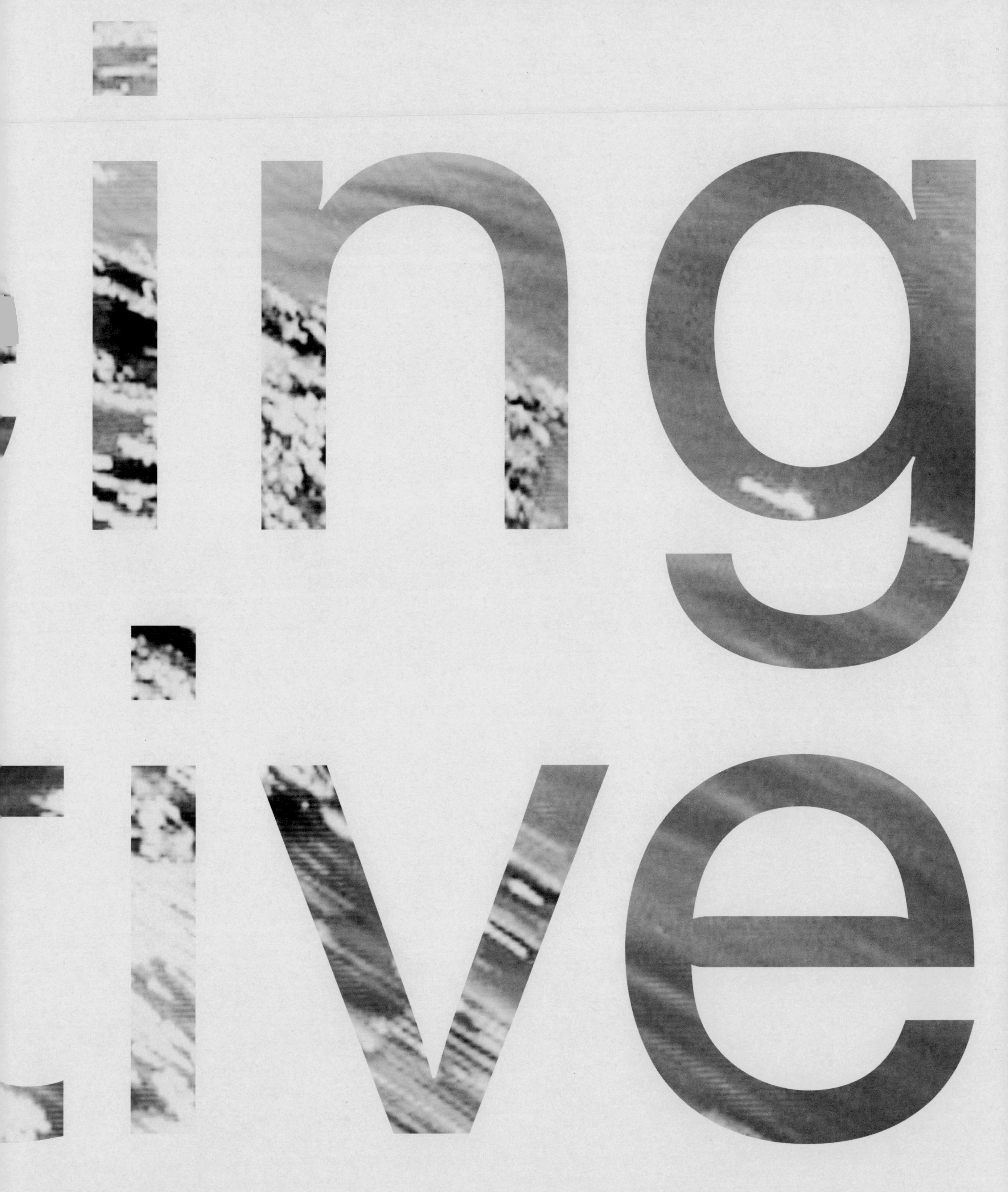

Dias & Riedweg are storytellers. But perhaps that term is not entirely accurate, because it is too narrow. In fact, Dias & Riedweg are story finders. Not inventors, but finders. They find their stories everywhere, but most of all from other people. In direct encounters with the artists there is not a single moment of tension. They immediately establish intimacy by telling stories: their own, stories about their current projects, their travels and ideas, but also about their lives, their origins, and their relationship. The artists speak candidly about how they met, what they are working on at the moment, the people they meet, how they live. In this quite natural account of their everyday lives, their house in Rio de Janeiro, their circle of friends, there is no shortage of coincidences, misadventures, rage, and joy. Their stories create an immediate closeness. The listener is involved in their daily life and invited to take part.

Storytelling is a means through which explicit and, more importantly, implicit knowledge is communicated in the form of a metaphor or a narrative. It is received by listening, and, in the case of Dias & Riedweg's videos and photographs, also by looking. The audience is involved in the story told, and so is more easily able to understand the contents of the narrative. The communicated knowledge is thus more strongly internalized, because stories are essential experiences: they determine how we behave, how we feel, and how we construct meaning from new experiences. Stories organize information about our lives, they form the perspective from which we consider it, our past and our future. Stories are central to our coexistence and well-being. But where do they come from, who tells them, and how are they told?

Dias & Riedweg address these issues directly in their videos. Early works arise more out of documentary research (*Mama & Vicious Rituals*, 2000; *My Name on Your Lips*, 2000), and provide the people involved with precise metaphors. In the workshops they undertook over several months with adult and juvenile prisoners for *Question Marks* (1996), the delinquents addressed their questions to the public via car registration plates (not the only setting for storytelling, which was continued by the authorities once the artistic project was over). In *All Venetians* (1999) people give an account of their own death, as if it was already behind them. A fine image for the sinking, eternally rotting city of Venice! But also a clear framework for what is to be recounted and what is talked about. In more recent projects the two artists encourage people to tell their stories in a much freer form. They do not give accounts of heroic deeds. They often take as their subjects loss (*Juksa*, 2006) or the construction of identity (*The Raimundos, the Severinos and the Franciscos*,

1998; *Exhausted Paradise*, 2009). Difficult areas such as migration, sexuality, and the home are not ignored, but rather explicitly made the focus of attention. Dias & Riedweg also succeed, with precise metaphors, to create both pleasurable and impressive images for trade and mobility (*Suitcases for Marcel*, 2006; *Moving Truck*, 2009).

In seminars on interviewing technique, whether in journalism or in the social sciences, one is taught that nothing is given to the interlocutor without at least the partial abandonment of the self. This applies equally, of course, to storytelling. How is someone persuaded to tell his or her story? The moment of telling is intimate. Attention is focused entirely on the teller of the story. Trust is produced by stories, although it is often betrayed. Your experience against my experience, your story against my story. This should not be understood in terms of competitiveness, but is a precondition for the loosening of tongues and mouths. Dias & Riedweg seem to have internalized this principle of giving and taking. The idea of abandonment might imply something unpleasant, but not in the work of Dias & Riedweg. For them it is more a participation than an abandonment. Not being participant observers like ethnologists, but being involved body and soul, as befits their art. They are part of the stories they transform into video installations that are as complex as they are atmospheric. It is precisely this closeness in *Funk Staden* (2007) that allows the artists to stage a parody of European prejudices from the 16th century toward the cannibalistic, sexually uninhibited savages of South America, featuring indigenous young people. The viewer is seduced by the rhythms of the music and the bodies, and unpleasantly moved by the dolls and hunks of meat. For the artists, on the other hand, the situation is not uncomfortable; they are a part of the culture under examination. It is for this reason that they can motivate their actors to play with prejudices and clichés in such an extraordinarily believable way. The unusual authenticity in Dias & Riedweg's work arises out of the very fact that they are at home in the stories presented.

This is not to say that Dias & Riedweg live in the favela, but it does mean that their contact with the people in the favelas is very intimate. So much so that these people willingly take part in their projects. This does not apply only to participatory projects such as *Devotionalia* (1994), *Sugar Seekers* (2004), and *God's Lips* (2002), in which everyone, in principle, can take part. It pertains equally to works featuring more awkward subject matter, in which the people involved either introduce personal and intimate details, or engage with prejudices about themselves, their origins, or their race. The artists are so involved in this that the projects seem to have neither a clear beginning nor a clear end. No distinction is made between art and life, work and privacy. For example, the people of *The City Outside Itself* (2011), the very first work in the series *Little Stories of Modesty and Doubt* (2011–ongoing), are so much a part of Dias & Riedweg's everyday life that the twins Vitor and Vitoria were unable to leave the artists once the filming was over. In response, Mauricio Dias decided to adopt the two children.

The house in Rio that features in the two works *The House* (2007) and *The Garden* (2008) is the residence of Mauricio Dias and the two children. It is here that Dias & Riedweg work with their assistants, and guests come and go, always warmly welcome. Here the stories, the artists' own and those brought by others, are condensed and shaped into gripping video installations. This house with its many rooms, historical details, and big garden, provides the ideal starting-point for artistic research. But it is also a place for the many people associated with Dias & Riedweg. They consistently allow us to participate in it; in *The House* and *The Garden* they lead us through this house and this garden. As they do so, we meet Walter Riedweg and Mauricio Dias: they look at us in duplicate, they walk in multiple forms around the pool and dance through the rooms. It is never entirely clear what is play, what is everyday life, what sort of a couple they are at any given time—but the small videos, shown on screens mounted in a prettily-drawn ground plan of house and garden, look extraordinarily private. This intimacy is seductive, we are already mentally moving in, perhaps we're undertaking part of the gardening work that needs to be done, or becoming involved in the house and studio. We want to be part of it, and identify ourselves to an inordinate degree with the interlocutor, the stranger.

"going native" refers to the anthropologist's or ethnologist's over-identification with the object of their investigation. Feeling at home, being native, and losing the critical distance necessary for reflection is a misdemeanor in the social sciences, because it runs completely contrary to academic criteria; notably to the principle that everyone can reach the same conclusions from the same objective viewpoint. The very tense of the verb "going native" implies that a motion of convergence is taking place. The field researcher is not originally native, local, indigenous, but becomes so in the course of their studies and participant observations. But what if the distance overcome in "going native" never existed in the first place? Much has been written, with reference to Dias & Riedweg's work, about the Other, the reflection of the Self in the interlocutor. This corresponds to our, the audience's, perspective. For the artists themselves, this

distance from the Other does not apply; both are part of the interlocutor, they do not become innate or indigenous, they already are. Dias & Riedweg are the Others, even if they do not live in the favela or work as rent boys. Being native is the attitude that makes the telling of stories possible in the first place.

We meet the artists, for example, quite directly on their blue-sheeted beds, in *Maximal Voracity* (2003), and once more in duplicated form. This time, however, the duplication of Walter Riedweg and Mauricio Dias is not a technical trick; instead, the artists lend their faces in the form of masks to male prostitutes who relate stories from their lives. The rent boys lie there half-naked, wrapped in white terry toweling dressing gowns, masked with Walter's or Mauricio's face, relaxed on a bed with blue sheets, talking to the artist whose face they have borrowed. Dias & Riedweg are not just responsible for the staging, they are part of the scene, and are also shown half naked in the picture. Being native: the artists do not allow any objective distance from the prostitutes, which means that voyeurism is impossible. The curiosity with which we now assume our seat as observers in the exhibition, on a blue-sheeted bed between the video projections, is benevolent and compassionate.

In the extensive work *Holy Body* (2012), starting with drawings of psychologically damaged individuals, Dias & Riedweg develop fantastical costumes that patients in a psychiatric hospital then put on for the video filmed by the artists. In this video, a good hour in length, these outlandish figures give such a stirring account of their feelings and their lives through music, dance, stories, and an excursion to the sea, that all distance from the audience vanishes. The encounter with the inmates of the mental hospital occurs so immediately that no room is left for sentimentalities such as pity, revulsion, or fear. Even the distinction between the viewer and the Other is no longer possible, because *Holy Body* is much too poetic and much too attractive.

This lack of distance generates an extraordinary authenticity in Dias & Riedweg's work. Astonishingly, despite their intense involvement, the two artists manage to remain critical, and to develop a multi-layered vision. Perhaps their incredible closeness to the actors is in fact a precondition for the development of the complex narrative strand—as if the artists were giving an account of people and their destinies that they had known for a long time, if not forever. In this familiar atmosphere we, the audience, come unimaginably close to the Other via the works. The characteristic immediacy of the artists allows us to lose distance ourselves, and to become the Other. To go native, in fact.

Dias & Riedweg's works are often made in South America, and indeed in Rio itself—but not exclusively so. They aren't

South American artists—rather they are native to everywhere in the world. For the series *Little Stories of Modesty and Doubt* they developed two additional chapters from Europe to complement the four from South America. They take us with them into their city, but also to Switzerland, a country to which at least one of the two artists is native, even though he emigrated a long time ago. Dias & Riedweg take us at night to a brightly lit football pitch (*Nocturnal Kick-Abouts*, 2011), to an amusement park (*Saturday Night at the Fairground*, 2011), through Rio as it changes from the center to its edges (*The Mirror and the Dusk*, 2011). The path of this last little story of modesty and doubt shows the metropolis as fragmented, and precisely for that reason shows the sense of life in the city in such an impressive way. The plot is simple, if not basic, but the metaphor is complex: a young man with a mirror under his arm walks from the city center up into his favela. The mirror reflects the surrounding city, the brightly colored alleyways. In any case there are always two pictures in the picture. Dias & Riedweg intensify the composition by overlaying the picture with two additional projections. The projected rectangle is not a single-channel, but a threefold projection. Recognizing the brightly colored fragments, the pictures in the picture, is demanding, confusing, and at the same time very sensual. His journey takes the young man with the mirror from the busy city center along the winding alleyways and up steep flights of steps into the favela high on the hillside with a view over Rio. In the process we can make out the urban-planning efforts to open up and tame the rougher suburbs with new steps. It is a work truly South American in its bright colors, and one that clearly reveals the artists' familiarity with the city of Rio. The two latest chapters in the series *Little Stories of Modesty and Doubt* were made for the exhibition at the Kunstmuseum Luzern. The short stories of Vreni & Fritz and Esther & Heinz recount, in *Two by Four* (2014), experiences of living together, of life in Switzerland, of the country and the city. Once again it is immediately apparent how familiar the two artists must be with their actors to be able to capture such closeness in the videos. Although "capture" has too much of a whiff of hunting about it; it is rather that the two artists create the space in which their interlocutors are able to tell their stories so openly. Because Dias & Riedweg are native to this place: Walter Riedweg grew up in this countryside, and chafed against the village structures, the pettiness of rural life, before moving out to study music, mime, and art. It was here in this city (Basel) that Mauricio Dias met him at the VIA (Video Audio Atelier Basel). They both set off to become native elsewhere. After years in Basel they changed continents, but preserved their friendships and family relationships.

This act of moving out into the world, but also becoming native everywhere, in themselves, and in their interlocutors, characterizes Dias & Riedweg's artistic work. They cross many boundaries, including their own, they shed their distance and engage, with remarkable sensitivity, with issues of identity, sexuality, wealth, education, and urban planning. In their work they demonstrate how much intensity we can gain if we abandon the distance from the Other, from Others. "Being native" always means we are involved, we are at home, indigenous, aboriginal, familiar with customs and habits, native. What if we understood "being native" in broad, global, comprehensive terms, beyond the continents, as Dias & Riedweg do? Because we are all native, here or there.

to B B B

Body
Body

Body to Body
Chantal Pontbriand

"Everything in the world began with a yes. One molecule said yes to another molecule and life was born."
–Clarice Lispector, *The Hour of the Star*

In his book *The Creation of the World or Globalization*, Jean Luc-Nancy puts forward the different meanings of the words *globalization* and "*mondialisation*" [world-making].[1] In French, both terms can be used, but Nancy brings nuances to them by differentiating the possible meanings of one versus the other. *Globalization* is seen as an abstract, totalizing phenomenon, from which a linear development can be predicted. *Mondialisation* is more concrete; it implies movement, fragmentation, and change. Here, language plays a role in defining world phenomena and in "incorporating" the different significations that these can take on. Language seizes only fragments of the real. It has a tendency to enclose the real in definitions, transformed into a norm by the dictionary or the encyclopedia. A philosopher's task is to question the normativity of language and to redefine words and unfold new meanings. Maurice Merleau-Ponty, however, one of a generation of philosophers who lived in the middle of a century that through the two World Wars saw violence and conflict inflate to an unprecedented scale, counted among those who could see the limits of philosophy. Merleau-Ponty thought that in the future one would have to turn to art to best seek meaning.[2]

Dias & Riedweg could be seen as present-day philosophers, philosophers who work with images rather than words, in a world taken over by the phenomenon of globalization. How can one situate the duo in the "globalization/*mondialisation*" conundrum? Before attempting to get a grip on this question, I shall return to Nancy, as his thoughts on the issue can be inspiring in this particular case. Quoting from the introduction Nancy himself wrote to the original French edition of the book:

> "The creation of the world or globalization": the conjunction must be understood simultaneously and alternatively in its disjunctive, substitutive, or conjunctive senses. According to the first sense: between the creation of the world or globalization, one must choose, since one implies the exclusion of the other. According to the second sense: the creation of the world, in other words globalization, the former must be understood as the latter. According to the third sense: the creation of the world or globalization, one or the other indifferently, leads us to a similar result (which remains to be determined). The combination of these three senses amounts to raising the same question: can what is called "globalization" give rise to a world, or to its contrary? Since it is not an issue of prophesizing nor of controlling the future, the question is, rather, how to give ourselves (open ourselves) in order to look ahead of ourselves, where nothing is visible, with eyes guided by those

two terms whose meaning evades us—"creation" (up to this point limited to theological mystery), "world-forming" [*mondialisation*] (up to this point limited to economy and technological matters, generally called "globalization").

Nancy sees the process of *mondialisation* as identical to that of the creation of the world, as one where the world is created. It is world-forming in the sense that the world is no longer a given, but it is to be processed or recomposed. This future is unknown to us as it is created. It can counter globalization, which is usually linked to the dominance of economy and technology. But, Nancy wonders, what is "creation"? Its meaning escapes us, it lacks clear guidance, all we can do is open ourselves in order "to look ahead of ourselves."

Dias & Riedweg are Brazilian artists, or rather artists that live and work in Brazil, in Rio de Janeiro to be more specific. Mauricio Dias is Brazilian, Walter Riedweg is Swiss. One was trained as an engraver, the other in theater and music. Working as a duo profoundly changed their art, as it became a common endeavor. But, as we shall see, being an engraver, being a performer, both these postures combined have created the specificity of the duo. The engraver seeks to work out a material imprint of the world,[3] the performer acts out tropes and situations arising in the world. Both have a bodily link to art making combined with world-forming.

In 2006 I was invited to the Henry Moore Institute in Leeds on the occasion of an exhibition about sculpture from Brazil.[4] I had just published an issue of *Parachute*, the magazine of which I was then editor, on São Paulo.[5] This research had led me to develop the "body-to-body" concept, which gave the lecture I was invited to give on this occasion its title. I had known Dias & Riedweg and their work for a few years by then, and it seemed clear that they too inscribe themselves in this particularity of Brazilian art that can be characterized as a body-to-body exploration. The work of Lygia Clark, Lygia Pape, and Hélio Oiticica, in particular, had driven me to develop that concept, but Tunga's work, as well as that of Cildo Meireles, also related to that trope in my mind. Dias & Riedweg have developed other ways and other means of working, but essentially their art pursues a certain tradition, or view of the world, which is all about the active process of world-forming. Underlying this process is a constant working out of the question of the Other.

Brazil lives on as the "New World." After being home to many immigrants from other continents for centuries, mostly from Africa and Europe, it is increasingly becoming a dynamic spot on the planet because of its booming economy and developing demographics. Comprised of diverse races and ethnic groups, its many megalopolises, including São Paulo and Rio de Janeiro, are laboratories of life on earth at this point. The situation today is one that forces us to "look ahead of ourselves," in an incomparable conjecture that stems out of the mixing of many worlds, many cultures, and all this in a region of the world that sits in an incredibly powerful natural environment. One that is being challenged by a boiling urbanization, which has to deal with the development of cities the size of countries elsewhere in the world. São Paulo now counts almost 12 million inhabitants, and Rio 7 million.

Rio, home to most of the artists mentioned here, and to Dias & Riedweg as well, is bordered by the Atlantic Ocean. The Atlantic here is a continual reminder that there is an "other" out there, constantly knocking at the door. A very large and breath-taking other.

Life is a challenge to these artists, who attempt to work out living conditions in their art. Dias & Riedweg have from the start addressed these questions as a collective speaking out to others. They constantly explore the issue of being-in-common, of what links one to the other, of how the common works, and this in the context of contemporaneity. Contemporaneity characterizes the present times, it envelops all of the many issues and ways of being that constitute our epoch, and defines what makes an event out of the times we are living through. But unlike historians or politicians, the artists accept the fact that contemporaneity is elusive, unfixed. Contemporaneity has to be worked out almost on a day-to-day basis. It has much to do with the process of democracy. Exercising democracy is to put in place processes that open up minds and possibilities, and foster change. This change is based on collective as well as individual input.

Let us look at some of the works produced since the 1990s. In 1994, Dias & Riedweg started a project called *Devotionalia*. They worked in Lapa in Rio de Janeiro (a thriving area with a youth culture expressed in music and bars) and went around with a mobile studio, interacting with children and teenagers, who were invited to make a cast of their hand or foot. These became ex-votos that were eventually exhibited as an installation in a museum. Ex-votos in churches are usually deposited there in order to express a wish or desire. Here the sheer accumulation of these casts of young living bodies formed a potent choir of voices invoking the realization of unspoken dreams.

The piece *The Raimundos, the Severinos and the Franciscos* (1998), pursues this interest in mixing the private and the public, the individual and the collective, and developing an ensuing artistic statement that could show the workings of the being-in-common. This piece is an "investigation" à la Dias & Riedweg that deals with doormen working in São Paulo, as it was conceived on the occasion of the XXIV São Paulo Biennale. Many of the participants came from Northeastern Brazil. They were asked to talk about their work in front of the video camera. They were chosen because they happened to bear the same first names: Raimundo, Severino, or Francisco. From the commonality of a first name could emerge the singularity of each one filmed. They talk of immigration, displacement, working conditions, relationships, giving an insight into the intermingling of their personal lives with the rapidly moving and bustling city. These janitors were also persuaded to participate in a collective fictitious final scene, for which they built the stage set with the artists, bringing their own real furniture and private objects. The set referred to the average size of their own living spaces and was, after the shooting, exhibited at the Biennale along with the documentary video revealing the protagonists' histories mixed with this acted-out final scene. Here again, the question of the Other is convened, and personal destiny is intermixed with collective interaction and empowerment.

Maximal Voracity, realized in Barcelona in 2003, is a major piece in the context of Dias & Riedweg's parcours. Here they not only come face-to-face with members of a community, but also literally with themselves. The faces in the resulting video of *Maximal Voracity* are in fact masks. For this work, eleven male prostitutes in Barcelona participated in making *Maximal Voracity*. They were asked to talk about their work, their personal history, their clients, their emotions, while lounging about in bathrobes on a bed, wearing with masks cast from the faces of Mauricio and Walter. Mirrors were installed in the room so as to generate images of front and back simultaneously. Multiplying Brechtian strategies, this intimate piece of theater coupled with the making of a video and the ensuing installation apparatus, spatializes the concerns and lives of a community that is still marginalized in today's society. The use of masks of the artists' faces introduces a particular angle to the question of representation. By multiplying the discourses around one subject–that of male prostitution–to questions of economy mixed with sexuality, Dias & Riedweg deconstruct the possibility of there being one master narrative overpowering the phenomenon that is being discussed in front of the viewer. The use of the masks inscribes the artists' surrogate presence onto the work, a presence that is normally absent (unseen). The piece speaks of power, more precisely of relationships in which there is a power dynamic–

between prostitutes and clients of prostitution. In the end it articulates the apparatus that is most often invested in this economy of sex. It enables other words and other images to emerge. It puts in place a counterpower in dealing with a situation that can be seen as extremely "voracious," eating away at self-respect and autonomy.

Playing one's own role and simultaneously distancing oneself from it is a strategy that is found in other works by Dias & Riedweg. *Holy Body* (2012), for example, takes another look at this strategy. The duo worked with patients in a psychiatric clinic (the Psychiatric Institute of the Federal University Hospital of Rio de Janeiro), inviting the patients to create free theatrical scenes, dressed in costumes inspired by paintings and drawings from the Prinzhorn Collection (assembled by the psychiatrist, art historian, and collector Hans Prinzhorn, in Heidelberg). The videos that were filmed during these "working through" sessions are shown along with the costumes.

Mirroring can be said to be one of the main strategies at the forefront of many of Dias & Riedweg's works. Mirroring and metaphor, like that employed in *Devotionalia*. Metaphor is a conceptual type of mirroring. It consists of the redoubling of meaning in order to expand one's consciousness of a situation, a feeling, or a sensation. In the realm of mirroring, one could also place history. History, as a discipline, interprets the past in different ways and often claims to mirror the past. Through different devices and strategies artists can reinterpret the past, together with the way history is made. Representation in history has also preoccupied Dias & Riedweg in their research. The piece they presented at documenta in 2007, entitled *Funk Staden*, addresses the creation of the meta-narrative that traditionally constitutes History. The installation is made up of three one-sided mirrors interspersed between three large-screen video projections. Hans Staden was a German soldier and adventurer from Kassel, who was captured by the Tupinambá Indians after being shipwrecked on the coast of what now is called Brazil. He was eventually released and wrote a book about his experiences, *True Histories and Description of a Country of Wild, Naked, Grim, Man-Eating People in the New World, America*, published in 1557. Claude Levi-Strauss was fascinated by this book, which is one of the first renderings of the European encounter with the Other. In *Funk Staden*, images of dances and rituals by young funk aficionados from Rio, the *funkeiros*, who constitute a real subculture in contemporary Brazil, contrast with renderings of 16th-century cannibalism and aboriginal rituals. The bodies of the viewers themselves, reflected in the surrounding mirrors, are added to those in the video. Hence past and present, near and far, recreate a fragmented, fantastic vision of history that destabilizes the myth of there being one canonic view of any history, or of any story. The eerie camerawork in *Funk Staden* contributes to a destabilization of the body, echoing rituals of the past and contemporary rituals.

It should be said, however, that any mise-en-scène created by Dias & Riedweg is at odds with the notion of "ritual" itself. A ritual is meant to be repeated, and is called upon to exorcize traumas, fears, and so forth. This work cannot be categorized so easily. Because of its deconstructive approach, it goes further than the Brechtian precepts in distancing the viewer/spectator from the issues at hand in any one piece. A ritual contains the notion of a collective gathering, and also addresses a question relevant to a specific community. This specificity is to be insisted upon, as we observe that in any given situation it is the particular context that is being addressed, together with the "actors" of that context, its main proponents. The actors in the piece are once again "real" people acting out their own daily lives. They are not playing prescribed roles that would make them something other than what they already are. It is each and every individual being that is addressed in the context of a community. This could be a definition of democracy in a world that has lost many of its illusions such as that of capitalism, communism, and nationhood.

Hence Dias & Riedweg continuously address the question of the Other in multifarious ways and contexts. The psychoanalytic process of "working through" replaces the mystifying notion of ritual.

In a piece such as *Exhausted Paradise* (2009), the duo staged a performance on a beach on the island of Gran Canarias. Two men walk along the beach without ever communicating; one is dressed in white, the other in black. The encounter represents an "impossibility," recorded by the camera, a fleeting moment of being-in-the-world which reveals the existential gap that is endemic to each being. Maurice Blanchot's "unavowable community" comes to mind, a notion of community that is always in progress, and never complete. At one point, a mirror appears, incongruous in this beach setting. The recurrent trope of the mirror in Dias & Riedweg's work appears again, this time in an intimate setting of only two people, whose face-to-face meeting reveals them to be one and the same person. (When the two men really meet, at the exact moment at which the video reveals the other [documentary part] in the reflection of a mirror, it becomes clear that the two men are played by the same actor.) Jacques Lacan claimed that the Other is the inverted mirror of the self. A constant loss is linked to being, a constant loss that is accompanied by an eternal quest for life and love. This piece is quite similar to *The House* (2007), another video installation in which the artists themselves appear. *The House* is a self-portrait in which the working out has to do with living and working together, and the visualizing of this relationship in the context of a place where a practice develops (in this instance the artists' own home in Rio). The filming and display of the resulting five videos further enhance the uncertainties and discrepancies found in the real, and in any attempt to define identity or relationships with certitude.

The mirror device is used once more in the series *Little Stories of Modesty and Doubt* (2011–ongoing). Started in Rio, this series of works consists of several individual pieces: *The City Outside Itself*, *Saturday Night at the Fairground*, *The Mirror and the Dusk*, and *Nocturnal Kick-Abouts* (all 2011); *The Sky and the Day* (2013); *One Way Walk* (2013); and *Two by Four* (2014), the last one first shown at the retrospective exhibition in Lucerne in 2014. This series initially brought together images of interactions between Rio's different communities. The first *Little Stories* reveal a Brazil of today, a Brazil inhabited by social and economic phenomena that develop in unprecedented ways, such as the rhizomatic favelas. The later works in the series recorded in Salvador da Bahia, Uruguay, and more recently in Switzerland, all comment on recent urban and architectural manifestations through the eyes of the artists and through local inhabitants. In both form and content, the series has become a continuous research into and working-out of the subject of modesty and doubt as supreme virtues of human subjectivity in these times of harsh global capitalism.

These micro-narratives, rendered in their mutiplicity by the different videos, show a world that can never be seized in its entirety, but in which the playing out of individual singularities is even more enthralling than that of the splendid view of Rio's famed beachfront, where the series began. Micro-strategies of empowerment are played out in multiple peripheral situations, as shown in the work. As the "globalized" Mexican art critic and curator Cuauhtémoc Medina, from another megalopolis, rightly says, "Brazil isn't a Brazilian question: it is crucial to the description of the world."[6] Dias & Riedweg's take on the wider world is informed by a keen attention to how Brazil is "performing" now (through an impressive array of performative strategies), and in this sense their work opens up doors to understanding "contemporaneity" today.

1
Jean-Luc Nancy, *The Creation of the World or Globalization*, State University of New York, Albany, 2007.

2
Maurice Merleau-Ponty writes, "My thesis: this decadence is inessential; it is that of a certain type of philosopher … Philosophy will find help in poetry, art, etc., in a closer relationship with them, it will be reborn and will re-interpret its own past of metaphysics–which is not past" (*Notes de cours*, 1959–60, p. 39, translation by Bernard Flynn). Ref: Bernard Flynn, "Maurice Merleau-Ponty," in Edward N. Zalta (ed.). *The Stanford Encyclopedia of Philosophy* (Fall 2011 Edition), http://plato.stanford.edu/ entries/merleau-ponty/ (last accessed April 2014).

3
See Georges Didi-Huberman, *La Ressemblance par contact*, Minuit, Paris 2008; *L'empreinte*, Éditions du Centre Georges Pompidou, Paris 1997.

4
Espaço Aberto/Espaço Fechado: Sites for Sculpture in Modern Brazil, Henry Moore Institute, Leeds, February 5–April 14, 2006.

5
Parachute 106, *São Paulo*, 10–11–12, 2004. See also Glória Ferreira, "Encounters with the Other: An Interview with Mauricio Dias and Walter Riedweg," *Parachute* 111, *Démocratie–Democracy*, 07–08–09, 2003.

6
"The Tropics Exists: Cuauhtémoc Medina Interviews Dias & Riedweg," in *Dias & Riedweg, Até que a rua nos spare (Until the Street Do Us Part)*, NAU/Imago Escritório de Arte, Rio de Janeiro 2012, p. 167.

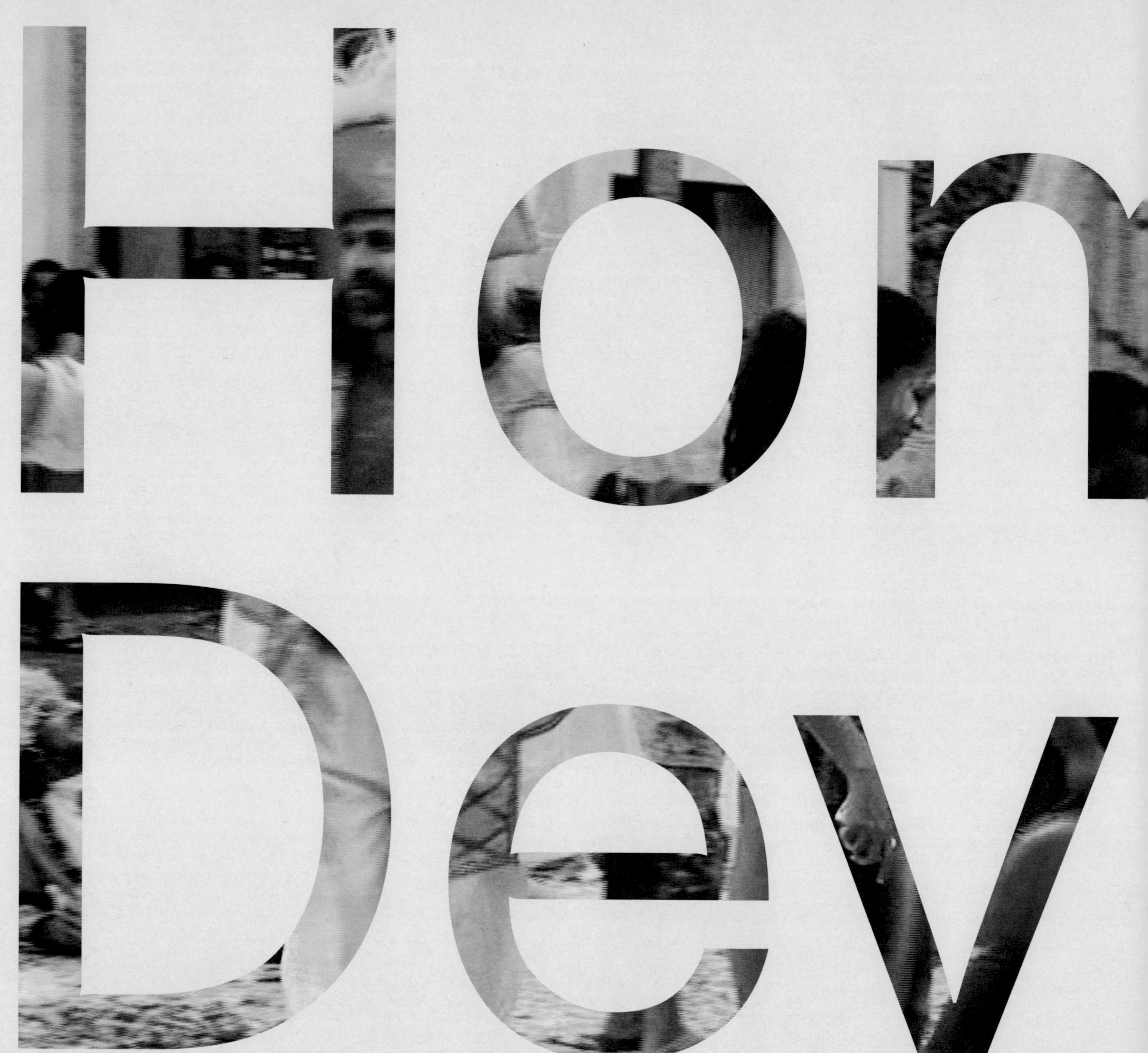

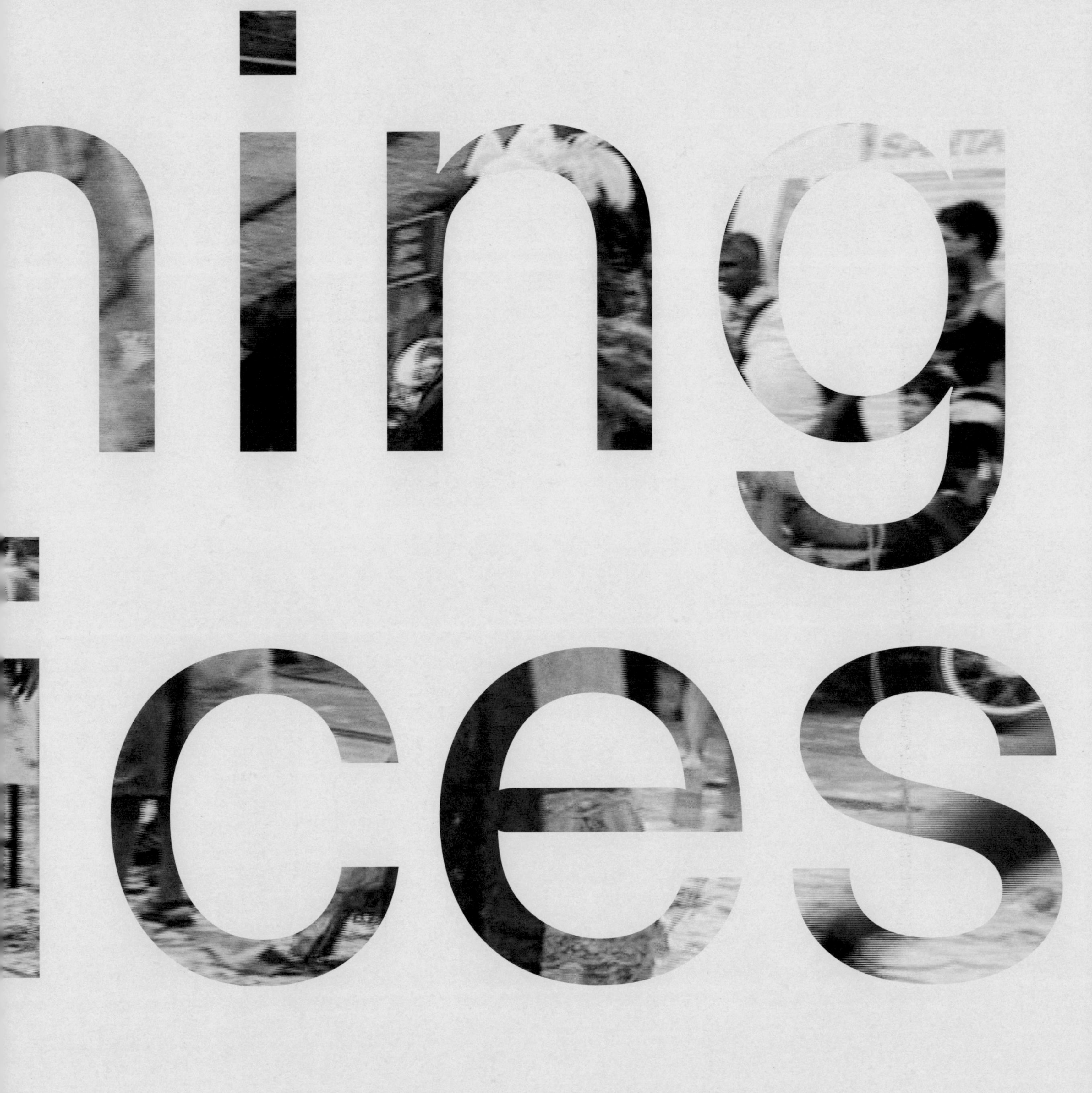

"Building as dwelling, that is, as being on the earth [...] remains for man's everyday experience that which is from the outset "habitual"–we inhabit it, as our language says so beautifully: it is the *Gewohnte*."
–Martin Heidegger, *Building Dwelling Thinking*[1]

In the early summer of 2012, while traversing Europe from one biennial to another, my traveling companion and I made a detour through the Black Forest region of Germany for a pilgrimage to what is arguably the most famous building in all of Western philosophy–Heidegger's hut in the tiny village of Todtnauberg, some 30 kilometers outside of the university town of Freiburg in Breisgau. It was a particularly miserable rainy day and we had forgotten both to properly map our route from Freiburg to Todtnauberg *and* fill up the tank of the car; we drove around for hours in the damp, rolling green countryside, asked around a couple of times (pensioners whom we imagined must have known "der Martin," and effectively had), but did not manage, in the end, to find and identify the most famous building in all of Western philosophy–the object of a special kind of architectural veneration. For a part-time Heideggerian who has made ample use, in his art-theoretical writing, of the various philosophical tools forged in this elusive, enigmatic hideaway (which, still in the possession of the Heidegger family, cannot be accessed, let alone entered, anyway), this was a predictably frustrating experience–a frustration we decided to wash away by paying a visit to the much more easily located villa Martin and Elfride Heidegger used to call home for the better part of their life in Southern Germany. Unlike the aforementioned hut, where the surly *Meisterdenker* hatched out many of the fundamentals underpinning his best-known works, the decidedly banal two-story house on a winding street in the leafy outskirts of Freiburg is not much of an architectural-philosophical destination. Heidegger himself, though a professed thinker of residence, location, and homeliness–a point we shall be returning to shortly–did not deign this domicile especially worthy of philosophical reflection; it was too closely associated, perhaps, with the distinctly anti-philosophical business of his Freiburg university career–the well-known low point of which concerned his affiliation with the Nazi party during his years as a rector there. For these reasons, his mundane brick-and-mortar residence seemed in many ways more real–and not just philosophically so–than the carefully cultivated, manipulative fantasy of the untraceable hut: the real home of 20th-century existential philosophy, along with its countless specters, phantoms, and ghosts, rather than the romantic rural fabrication in which the master's musings on identity and difference were cast in such fateful ways.

Why this long and winding path to arrive at the work of two artists–Mauricio Dias and Walter Riedweg–whose concerns seem impossibly remote from those of the troubled magus of Todtnauberg, and whose practice is so intimately bound up with a city–Rio de Janeiro–that in many ways represents the diametrical opposite of the pastoral, puritanical, and radically anti-modern idea-world of *Being and Time*? The work of Dias & Riedweg (the latter born, it should be noted, not so far from existentialism's troubled *Heimat*) is richly textured with a kaleidoscopic riot of memes, motifs, topics, and tropes, yet among these various thematic strands the decidedly Heideggerian tangle of "building, dwelling, thinking" stands out with enough prominence to warrant a concerted in-depth look—*inside* the artists' world, both built and unbuilt.

*

I should perhaps retrace my steps to the moment when I first met Mauricio Dias and Walter Riedweg—to be followed, soon after, by my gradual acquaintance with their work (it is not without significance, for the purpose of the current argument, that I met the people first, and the artists second). This first meeting took place in Rio de Janeiro in 2004, at their house in Santa Teresa. That this particular house, which to this day continues to function as their studio, was not like any other building—in a part of town that is not like any other carioca neighborhood—was immediately apparent. I was therefore not terribly surprised to discover, five years later, that Dias & Riedweg's home, the affectionately named Villa Laurinda—named after one Laurinda Santos Lobo, the leading Santa Teresa socialite of the day, a campaigner for women's rights and a key figure in the development of Rio's early 20th-century bohème—had effectively become the subject of a video diptych entitled *The House* (2007) and *The Garden* (2008). Consisting of five videos shown on TV monitors that are mounted on a schematic wall drawing, *The House* features a digital multiplicity of Mauricios and Walters going about their business—some of it decidedly less quotidian than other parts, and much of it positively comical too—in the beautifully manicured surroundings of the artists' living and working environment. Indeed, it seems telling that the most bluntly autobiographical work, arguably their most comprehensive self-portrait to date, in an oeuvre that is so deeply and programmatically preoccupied with "others" and the haunting question of otherness, should take on the form of an *architectural* fantasy centered on the artists' *home*—the proverbial labyrinth where *architectonic* categories such as "self" and "other" actually collapse and dissolve.[2] It is this process of doubling and obfuscation that renders the home unhomely, or, more accurately, *uncanny*, singling out the architectural equivalent of the most stable imaginable sense of self as the potential site of that same self's delirious undoing. As Anthony Vidler notes in his study

The Architectural Uncanny, with regards to "the most popular topos of the 19th-century uncanny […] the haunted house": "the house provided an especially favored site for uncanny disturbances: its apparent domesticity, its residue of familiar history and nostalgia, its role as the last and most intimate shelter of private comfort sharpened by contrast the terror of invasion by alien spirits."[3] In a sense—and fittingly enough for an artistic practice that time and again seeks out the very notion or act of an "invasion by alien spirits"—the alien spirits in Dias & Riedweg's *The House* and *The Garden* are the artists themselves (they certainly appear dressed for the occasion). Aliens in their own selves, intruders in their own home.[4]

*

Dias & Riedweg are not especially preoccupied, in their work, with architecture as such—but they are, in my view, with living conditions, both material and immaterial: with building, dwelling, habitation. In this sense, they are a quintessentially global artist duo: artists so well-traveled and at home in the world, so mobile and cosmopolitan, that is to say so (professionally) rootless and nomadic, that the dream of shelter ("home") frequently emerges as a major conceptual concern in their work—an observation compounded, obviously, by the fact that housing is a major political issue in their hometown of Rio de Janeiro, with its sprawling favelas, its reputation for what is sometimes euphemistically referred to as "informal" architecture (of the type, for instance, that framed the public art project *Mere View Point* from 2002), and the precarious circumstances in which millions of its inhabitants have to make a living day after day. The brute force of globalization, as the relentless centrifugal process of deterritorialization and dislocation, of travel, transfer, and trade, of migratory movement and ceaseless circulation, can certainly be seen to condition their work in its inclination toward the question of belonging, and alternative forms of rootedness and identification through disjunction and dislocation. These questions are clearly at the heart of some of their best-known works, as well as some of their lesser-known pieces, such as *The Raimundos, the Severinos and the Franciscos* (1998), the elaborately staged group portrait of 30 doormen and janitors hailing from the Brazilian northeast, the poorest part of the country and a major force field in the history of Brazil's internal migration, who at the time of filming all lived and worked in São Paulo; *David & Gustav* (2005), a double portrait of two protagonists of the swinging 1960s London art scene (David Medalla and Gustav Metzger) highlighting "the contrast between different perspectives that can significantly affect the construction of one's identity when one lives outside his or her homeland–the cosmopolitan and the exiled"[5]; *Juksa* (2006), a video documenting three different moments in the lives of three people on a small island off the coast of Norway who have seen their existences transformed over time by the changes wrought by the globalization of the fishing industry, once the island's sole dependable source of livelihood; *Exhausted Paradise* (2009), a "portrait" of another island (this one part of the Canary Island archipelago, known primarily for its sex tourism industry–a familiarly depressing side effect of the globalized economy's impact on migratory patterns) as seen through the eyes of an exile from yet another island, namely Cuba.[6] In some way or other, all these works–most emphatically so, perhaps, in *The Raimundos, the Severinos and the Franciscos*–confront the question of the home, of home-making, of shelter from the storm of worldly events, conjuring the futile dream of stability in a world ruled by the principle of (a very narrowly understood) mobility. In fact, it is not without significance that one of the artists' best-known public artworks is an ongoing project involving a moving truck, that most mundane and muscular of symbols of the global fever of mobility– of the messy tangle of desires, pressures, and requirements to always be on the move. (On a primary conceptual level, this work operates as a performative reflection on the origins and meanings of the very notion of "moving image"–it is worth remembering here that one of the Lumière shorts habitually associated with the very birth of cinema is the 50-second film *Arrival of a Train at La Ciotat Station* from 1896–and the artists have spoken about this particular work in the virological terms of contemporary image culture. The fact remains, however, that the moving truck, as a homing device of sorts, returns our experience of the work to the spatial terms of architecture and mobility, housing and moving.) The same symbology, finally, also serves as an undercurrent of another ongoing video installation project, namely *Suitcases for Marcel* (2006): a 12-part moving-image narrative in which we follow a suitcase's surreal odyssey through the city of Rio de Janeiro. The work combines art-historical reference–the object of homage being Marcel Duchamp's talismanic boîte-en-valise–with a broader reflection on the vagaries of moving image culture and its entanglement in the frantic production and consumption cycles of the global economy. Yet in many ways, the key to a fuller understanding of the work's relationship to the artists' daily lives can be found in a 13th video that is habitually projected on a nearby wall in which Dias & Riedweg themselves are shown picking up the 12 suitcases at an airport, typically that of a city to which they

have found themselves invited as visiting, exhibiting artists. In this faux-documentary afterthought, the artists are seen lugging around both the works of art and their own luggage, traveling from airport to museum and back again–the quintessential contemporary nomads for whom a suitcase literally becomes a home-away-from-home, as conveyed in the expression "living out of one's suitcase." And I should point out here that I have had the good fortune to exhibit this work in an exhibition I curated at the Antwerp museum of contemporary art M HKA in the fall of 2011–the culmination of a dialogue with the artists that started as far back as the summer of 2004, in their casa in Santa Teresa. This exhibition was titled *A Rua (The Street)* and took both the unique quality of carioca street life and the particulars of Rio's urban fabric as a point of departure for an in-depth consideration of the relationship between artistic practice and place or locale; in many ways *A Rua* looked upon the street as carioca art's primary home.[7] If the 12-part cycle that is *Suitcases for Marcel* can be viewed as a tribute to the streets of Rio de Janeiro, the artists' natural working environment, then the work's 13th-chapter-cum-site-specific-epilogue can be read as a slightly melancholy rumination on the contemporary artist's naturalized condition of a constant homelessness, of nostalgia– literally the painful longing for the homestead of yore–as embedded in the artists' mercurial way of life.

*

Being at home in the streets of Rio de Janeiro, just like Dias & Riedweg and the protean protagonists of their many video works, leads us back to the hut in Todtnauberg and the house in Freiburg, and the key insight contained in Heidegger's text "Building Dwelling Thinking" that the titular "dwelling," the "art of homing," has very little to do, ultimately, with the titular "building," with architecture. It is dwelling–the making-oneself-at-home, in frequently unhomely spaces, that is such a distinct topos of the works of Dias & Riedweg discussed in this essay– rather than building, the house rather than the hut, that, according to Heidegger, constitutes "the basic character of Being, in keeping with which mortals exist […] Man's relation to locales, and through locales to space, inheres in his dwelling. The relationship between man and space is none other than dwelling, thought essentially." This relationship, I argue here, is regularly at the forefront of Dias & Riedweg's work, partly determining the much more emphatic relationship between self and other– between identity and difference–which it is sometimes directly translated into. Heidegger's essay concludes with a reflection on the modern condition of homelessness that seems especially appropriate here, not in the least because of its relevance to a socio-cultural context (namely that of Rio de Janeiro) in which homelessness is both an acutely lived tragedy and a philosophical conundrum: "the proper dwelling plight lies in this, that mortals ever search anew for the essence of dwelling, that they must ever learn to dwell. What if man's homelessness consisted in this, that man still does not even think of the proper plight of dwelling as the plight?"[8] The work of Dias & Riedweg teaches us a thing or two about this plight; dwelling upon it, it teaches us to properly dwell—to be simultaneously homeless in ourselves and at home in others, in elsewheres.[9]

1
Martin Heidegger, *Poetry, Language, Thought*, trans. Albert Hofstadter, Perennial Classics, New York 1971, p. 145.

2
Here, a cursory return to Heidegger's hut seems apt–it was the site of conception, after all, of what Heidegger himself considered to be his most important philosophical treatise after *Being and Time*, namely the appropriately titled *Identity and Difference*, committed to paper in Todtnauberg in September 1957. In this text Heidegger asserts, "we think of Being rigorously only when we think of it in its difference with beings, and of beings in their difference with Being. The difference thus comes specifically into view." Martin Heidegger, *Identity and Difference*, trans. John Stambaugh, University of Chicago Press, Chicago 2002, p. 79. In a sense, this essay (really a coupling of two lectures, one "about" identity, and one "about" difference–one delivered, tellingly, in Freiburg, the other in Todtnauberg) marks the elusive source of the continental theorization of difference and otherness that would go on to have such a momentous impact on the postwar intellectual and cultural landscape.

3
Anthony Vidler, *The Architectural Uncanny: Essays in the Modern Unhomely*, MIT Press, Cambridge, Massachusetts 1992, p. 17.

4
It is worth pointing out here that a 1968 installation by Lygia Clark, the matriarch of Brazil's sensuous brand of conceptualism, was titled *A casa é o corpo* ("the home is the body")–a formula that programmatically conflates our current concern, namely domesticity and homeliness, with another key ingredient of Dias & Riedweg's practice, namely the politics of the body (consider such widely-discussed key works as *Corpo Santo*, 2012, *Funk Staden*, 2007, and *Voracidade Maxima*, 2003, for instance). Dias & Riedweg have referred to this particular work of Clark's on a number of occasions.

5
Dias & Riedweg, *… and it becomes something else*, Americas/Society, New York 2009. David Medalla was born in the Philippine capital Manila in 1942 and moved to London in the early 1960s; Gustav Metzger was born in Germany in 1926 to Polish-Jewish parents, and ended up in London as a child refugee in 1939.

6
The image of the exiled protagonist carrying a mirror as he crosses the island's arid landscape made up of windswept dunes inevitably brings to mind the reflecting game played in *The House*; the fraught image returns more literally in a video work from 2011, *The Mirror and the Dusk*, in which an inhabitant of Rio de Janeiro is shown carrying a mirror through the streets, squares, and alleys of the teeming tropical metropolis, focusing on the rapid urban development of one of Rio's notorious old favelas in particular. This is not the place for an in-depth exploration of the use of mirrors and mirroring imagery in the work of Dias & Riedweg; suffice it to say, for now, that the mirror is simply an archetypal symbol of the dialectics, dynamics, and mechanics of *reflection* that are so crucial to their practice and oeuvre as a whole.

7
One of the main sources of literary inspiration for this exhibition project was a reverie by the quintessential early 20th-century carioca litterateur João do Rio, whose text *A alma encantadora das ruas* (*The Enchanting Soul of the Streets*, 1908) was included in the exhibition catalogue. The ghost of João do Rio returned as a guiding light in Dias & Riedweg's solo exhibition at the Centro de Artes Hélio Oiticica in Rio de Janeiro in the fall of 2013, appropriately titled *Até que a rua nos separe* (*Until the Street Do Us Apart*).

8
Heidegger, *Poetry, Language and Thought* (1971), trans. and intro. Albert Hofstadter, Harper &Row, New York 1971, p. 155.

9
Same Time Else Where is the title of an exhibition of Dias & Riedweg's work organized at the Kunstnernes Hus in Oslo in 2008. In the main essay, curator Maaretta Jaukkuri singled out the question of *cohabitation* as one of the artists' primary concerns. In this text I have sought to narrow this question down to that of *habitation*.

Zwei aus Vier
Two by Four

Two by Four is a twin installation that follows the routines of two Swiss couples. The artists wanted to make a twin portrait of two couples, who could really only be Swiss, and yet still be very different one from another. In the end they did not have to look very far, and made two portraits, one of their best friend, the artist Esther Meier, and her boyfriend Heinz, and the other of Walter's brother Fritz Riedweg and his wife Vreni. As they expected, the two video portraits resulted in very different material, although there were also many similarities. The installation comprises two back-screen projections and two mirrored surfaces of the same size that join in the middle like an *X*.

This installation was on view for the first time at Dias & Riedweg's retrospective exhibition entitled *Little Stories of Modesty and Doubt* at the Kunstmuseum Lucerne, Switzerland, in 2014, celebrating 20 years of the duo's collaboration.

The *Little Stories of Modesty and Doubt* series (2011–ongoing) started as a collection of firsthand accounts accumulated on video, in photographs, drawings, and music. These are works that praise doubt and modesty as supreme virtues of subjectivity. At the same time they record the social and economic transformations that people go through. To optimize the visualization of their recent investigations on the synchronism and multiplicity of all things, the video installations in this series present a device with three superimposed channels showing images filmed at the same time, and in the same place, but from different angles and at different speeds, thus materializing the existence of a more complex reality. For each *Little Story* there is a video, a series of photographs, and a piano composition, this last element by Walter Riedweg alone.

- Two-channel video installation
  with two mirrored surfaces
  Loop, 20:00
  Dimensions variable

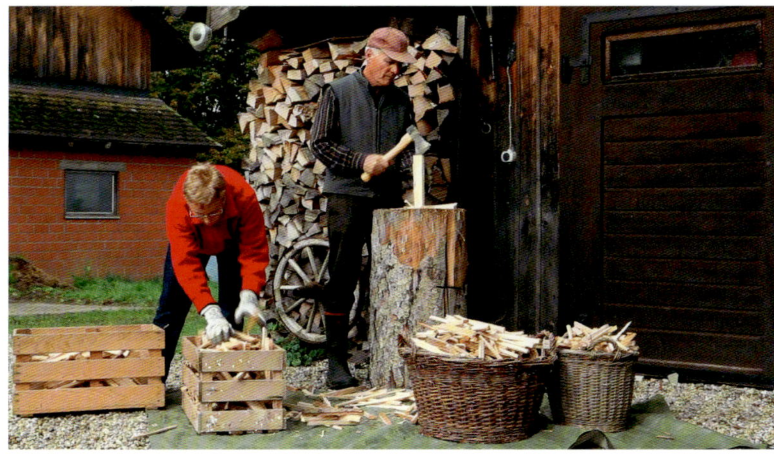

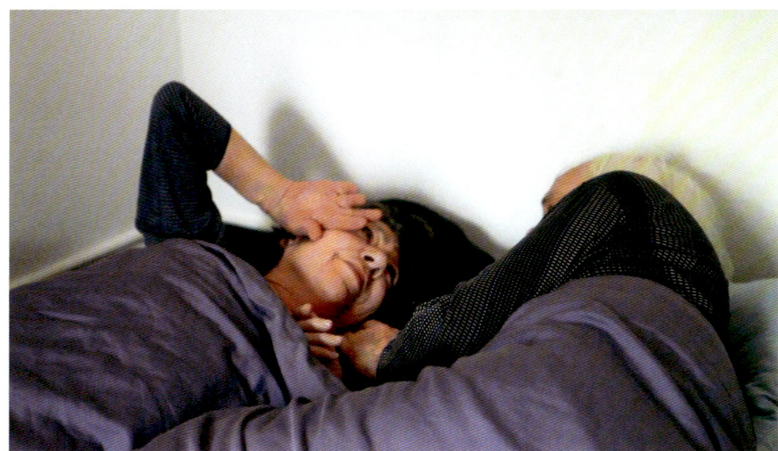

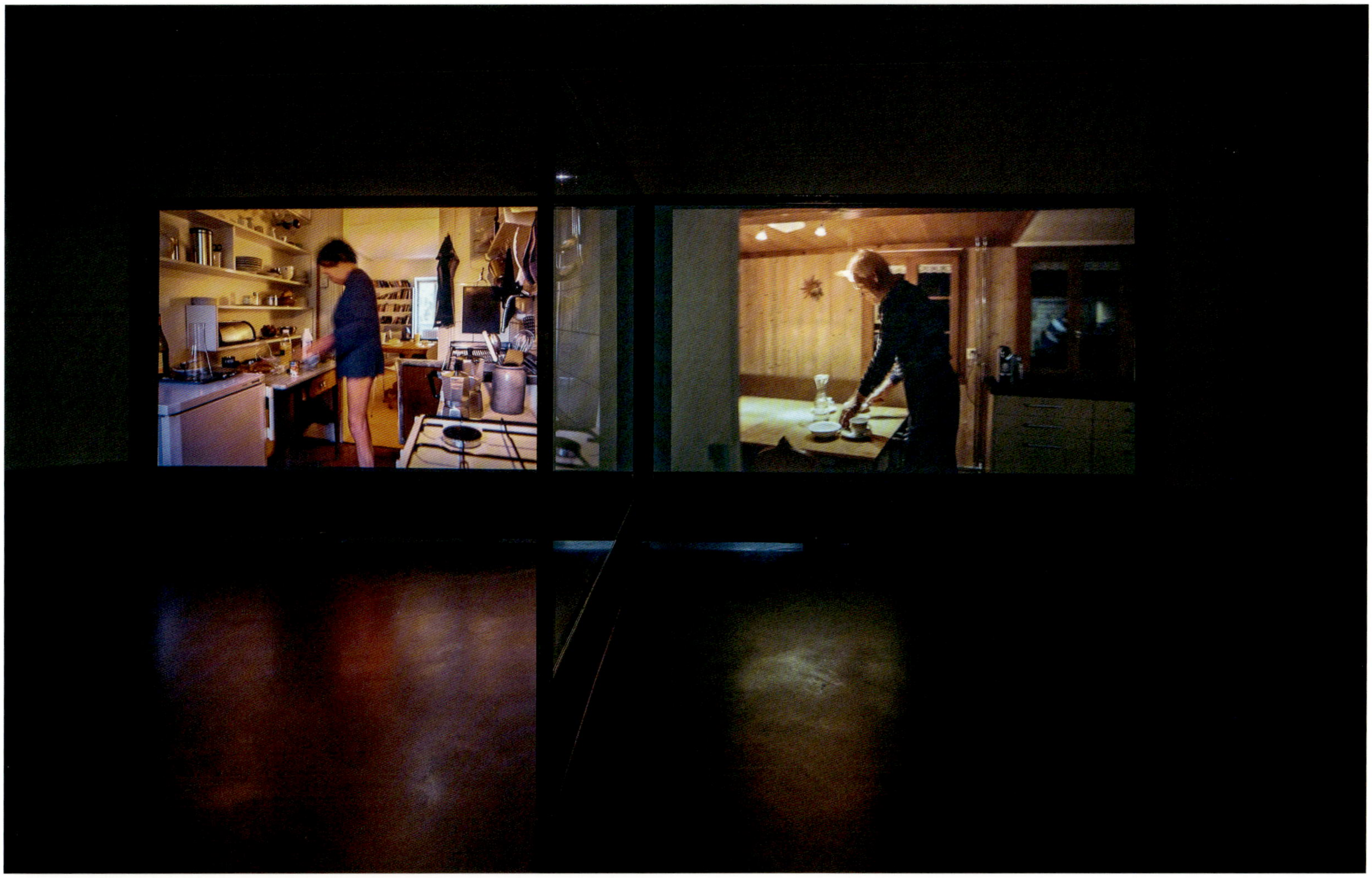

Amparo
Hope

Enrique and Susana met when they were at school, and immediately knew that they were strangely connected. They both grew up in the tiny village of *25 de Agosto*, near to the train station, and developed a special affection for trains from their early years. They became friends, but later, as adults, lost sight of each other, married, and had children. One day they took the same train to *25 de Agosto* and the connection started again. They have lived together near the train station in *25 de Agosto* for over 30 years now. The train stopped serving this village, and the couple built a model of the station inside their home. *Hope* allows the viewer into the universe of this couple, which is like a story.

On August 25, Uruguay's Independence Day, Dias & Riedweg went back *to 25 de Agosto* with the first edited version of the work, and staged a public screening on the tracks of the train station, to which they invited Susana, Enrique, and the few inhabitants of the village. They invited the German singer Marianne Schuppe (who also sang at the first screening of their video *Juksa* on the sands of Fugløya Island) to sing an aria by Purcell. Wearing the same red dress in both videos, she reincarnates a figure of nostalgia and the past in both narratives. As with *Juksa*, this event was recorded, edited, and added to the final video.

This project was realized for the Fotograma festival in Uruguay, during which the artists visited the country several times.

- Video installation
  Loop, 20:09
  Dimensions variable

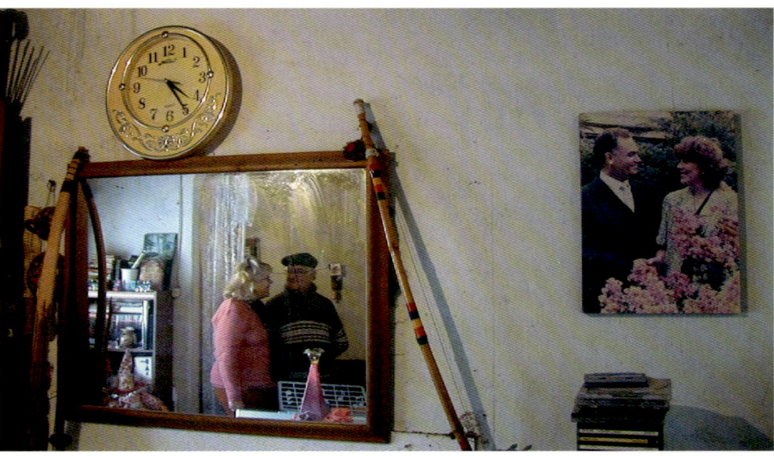

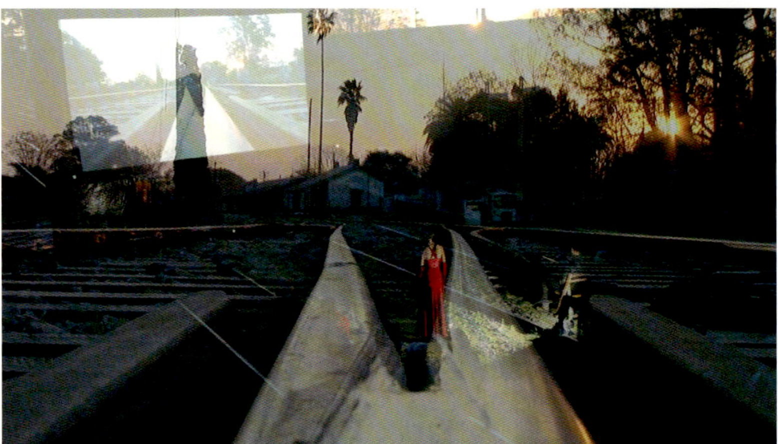

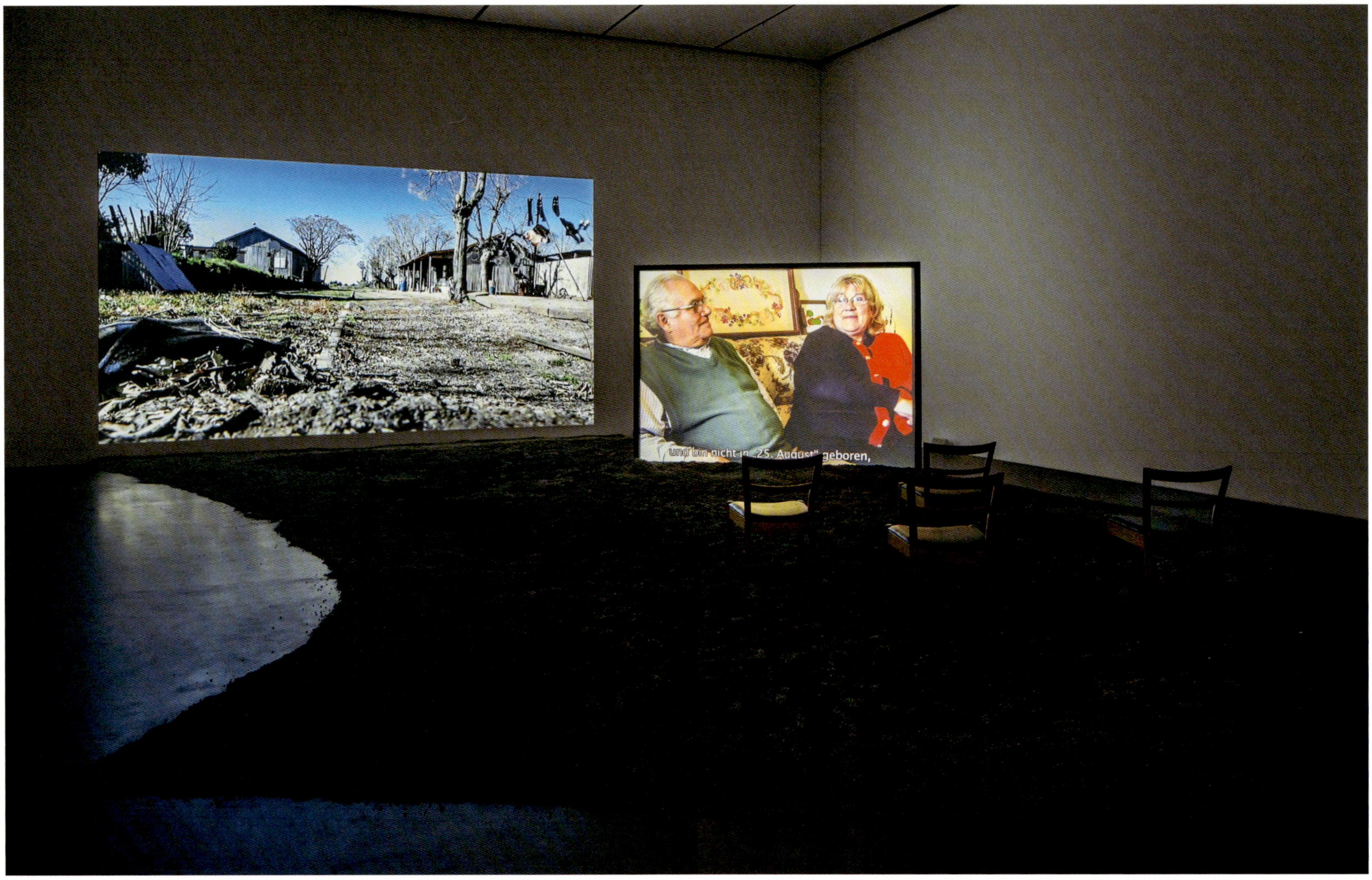

Desamparo
Desolation

This series of digital photographs portrays the abandon and decay of the railway system in Uruguay's flat and empty landscapes. From Montevideo, to the east, west, and north, the presence of a line south, which is no longer there, is felt. Clothes hang to dry on the platforms where people no longer take trains, but now live, and animals graze on plants on the train tracks where trains no longer run. The wind is visible in these scenes of timeless desolation.

→ See *Amparo/Hope*, 2013, p. 76
• Series of 74 photographs
  Dimensions variable

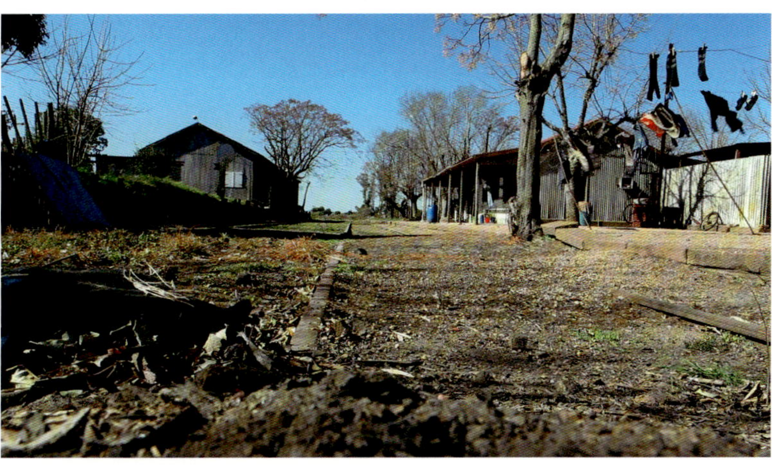

Caminho sem volta
One Way Walk

A man walks along an abandoned railway line in the desert plains. There are no longer any trains. He looses a shoe but finds another further on. He puts it on and continues walking. He does not talk. Asked where he is going, his only answer is to point straight ahead without a word. Further on he comes to another train station, which also seems abandoned. The video's soundtrack is original music by Walter Riedweg.

→ See *Amparo/Hope*, 2013, p. 76
• Single channel video
  Loop, 6:35
  Dimensions variable

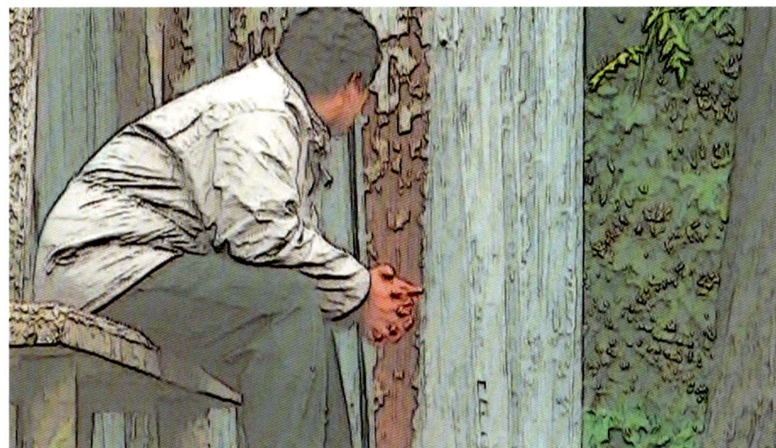

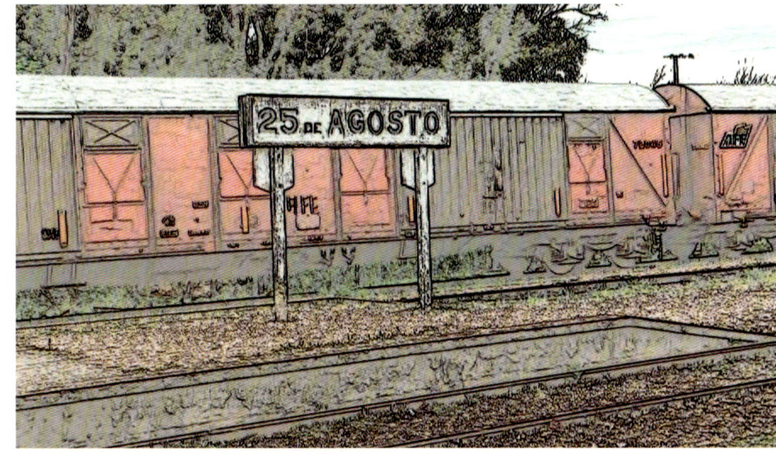

As aparências enganam
Appearances Might Fool

Things that are, but do not look like what they are, and things that are not, but might be. The same interest in the boundaries between documentary and fiction, between inner and outer worlds is explored in this ongoing series of photographs, which demonstrates the artists' interest in a formal approach. A small mushroom may appear gigantic, and a dog may be green. Appearances might mislead. Things are not always what they appear to be.

• Digital phoptograph;
  Tint jet HP12 on Canson rag paper
  142 × 60 cm each

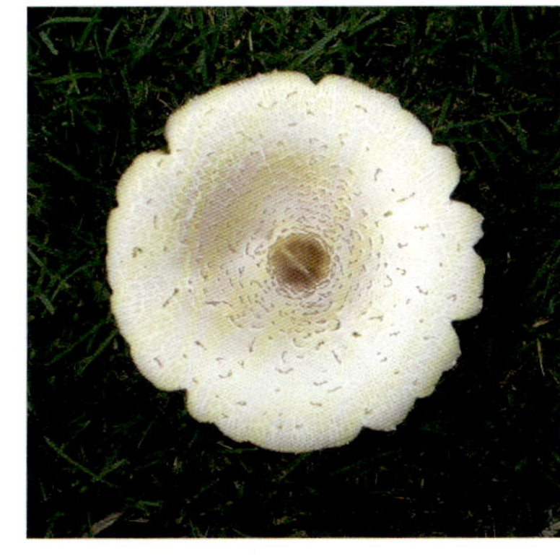
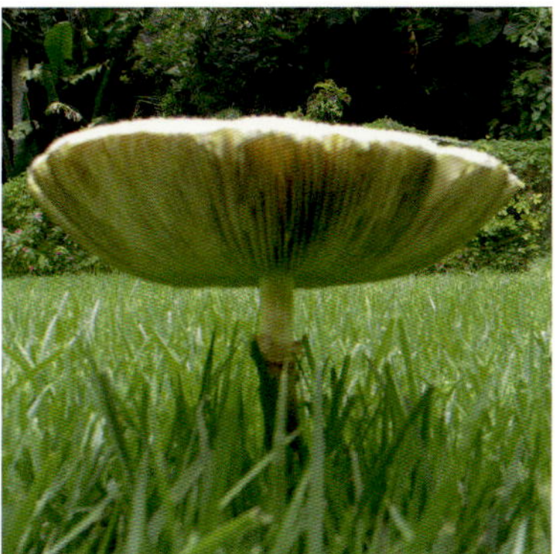
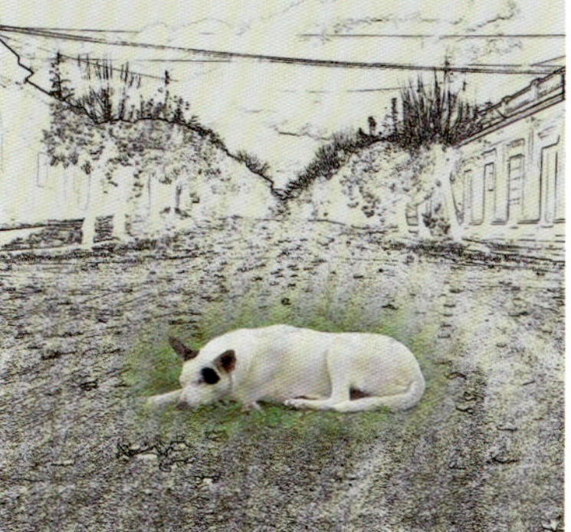

Crime Master

Crime Master was made after the series of photographs and the video installation entitled *The Mirror and the Dusk* (2011), which were shot by the artists with the same protagonist, Cleiton dos Santos, in the vast Complexo do Alemão slum in Rio de Janeiro, in 2011. The person in the photographs again appears to be involved in a dream, in which he steals a photograph of his own image from an exhibition in an art gallery, and takes it back to his home in the slum.

The insoluable dilemma of artistic representation of the Other in the field of contemporary art and the moving image is highlighted in this piece as a particular territory between a potential crime and artistic authenticity in the relationship between the artist and the protagonist.

- Video
  Loop, 09:57

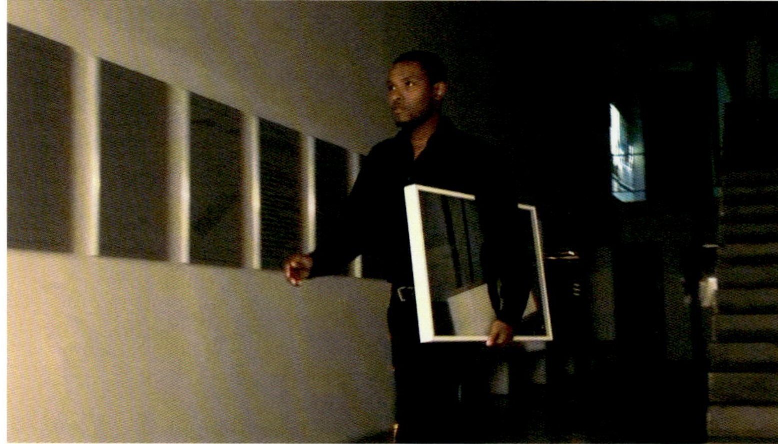

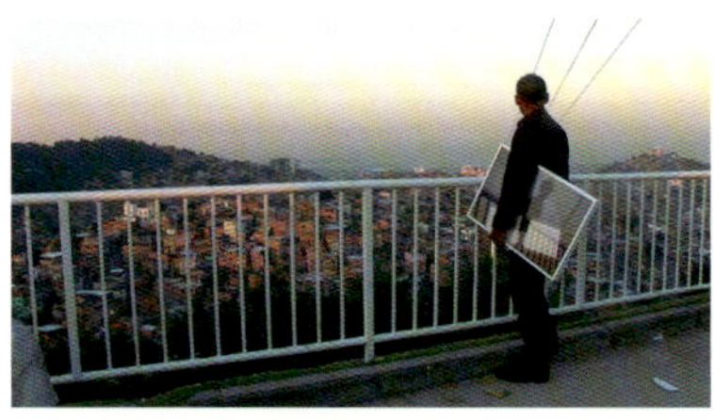

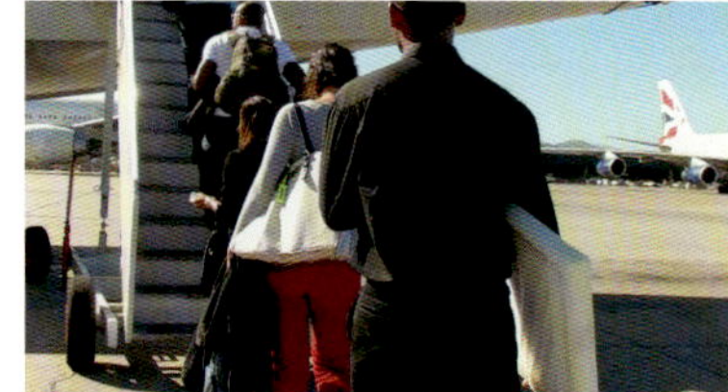

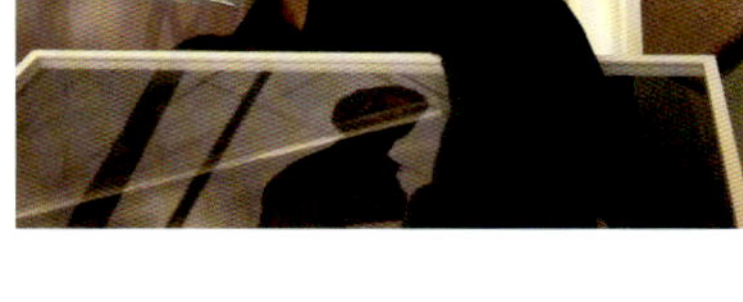

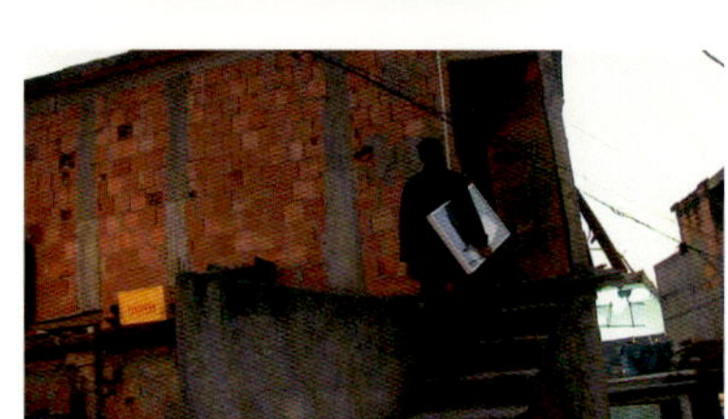

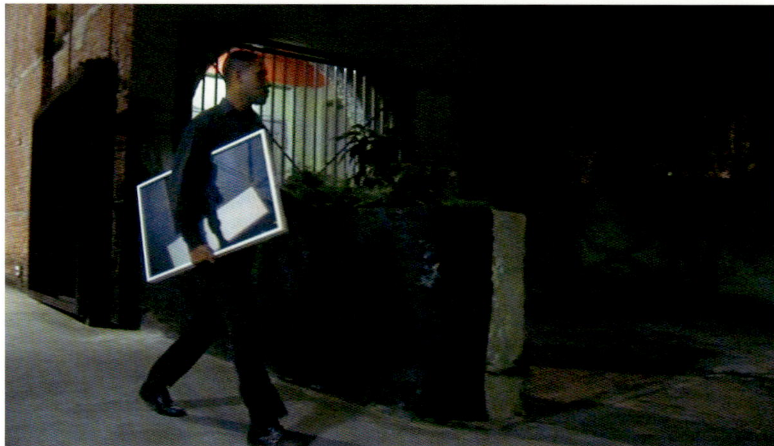

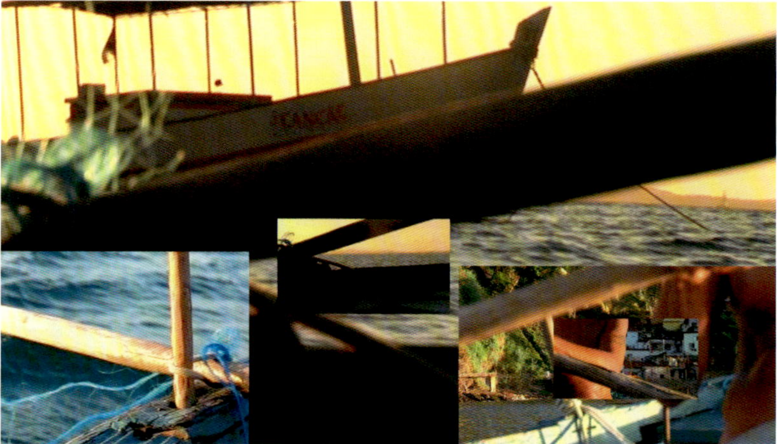

O ceú e o dia
The Sky and the Day

Recorded from dawn to dusk on board his small boat, this video shows us a day in the life of fisherman Raimundo, son of fisherman João, on the blue waters of the Bay of All Saints, in Salvador da Bahia.

Edited in three convergent shots and with a soundtrack of a piano composition by Walter Riedweg.

→ See *Zwei aus Vier/Two by Four*, 2014, p. 75
- Video installation
  Loop, 5:30
  Dimensions variable

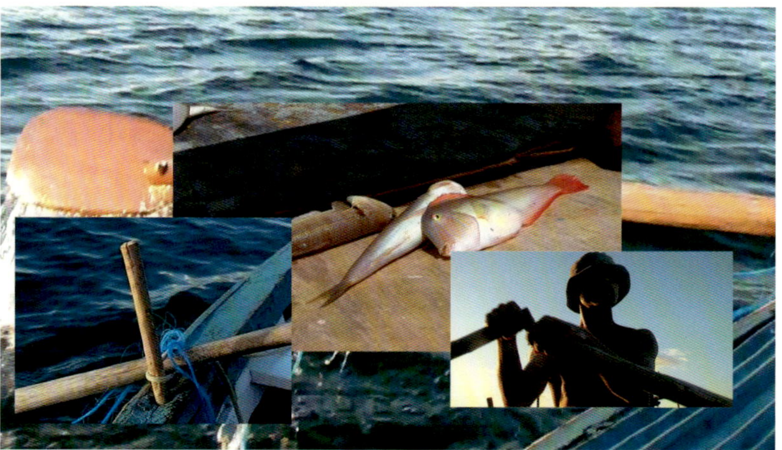

Corpo Santo
Holy Body

Commissioned by the Prinzhorn Collection in 2011, Dias & Riedweg chose to work with a group of patients from the Psychiatric University Hospital of Rio de Janeiro over the period of a year. They conducted a series of workshops in the clinic's old theater, which is called Qorpo Santo, named after the Brazilian dramaturge, who himself spent most of his life in a psychiatric hospital. In a newly built "theater dressing room," these patient participants changed from their drab and impersonal patient gowns into costumes inspired by and derived from the works of the Prinzhorn Collection, and freely improvised scenes and songs from their own inner worlds. The act of dressing up to animate a "lunatic's" costume somehow injected a new vital energy into their bodies. The costumes and an over-sized dressing table, in which the mirror was replaced by a video-screen, gave form to the video installation.

Doctors and jurists who followed the workshops at the Psychiatric University Hospital in Rio de Janeiro attested to the medical improvement among the patients. Further art projects have been incorporated in order to assist patients, the Qorpo Santo Theater building is currently under renovation, and patients are again allowed access to mirrors inside the clinic. The video installation was integrated into the Prinzhorn Collection in 2012.

- Two-channel video installation
  Loop, 60:00
  Dimensions variable

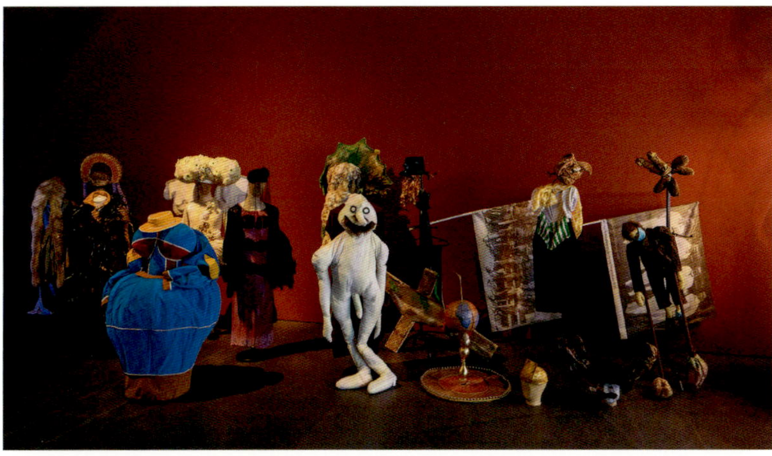

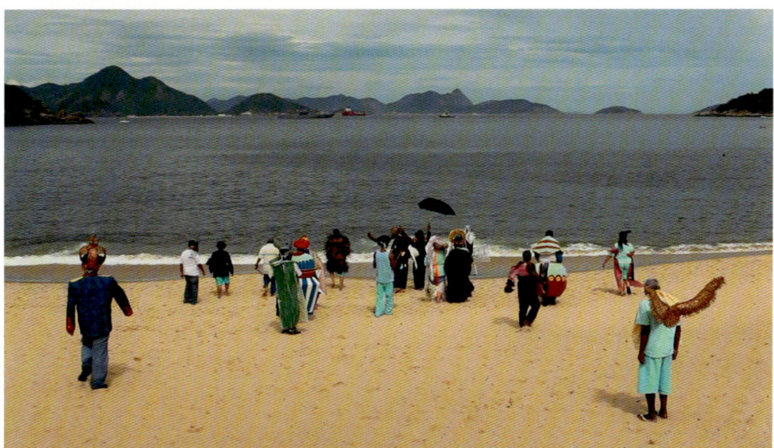

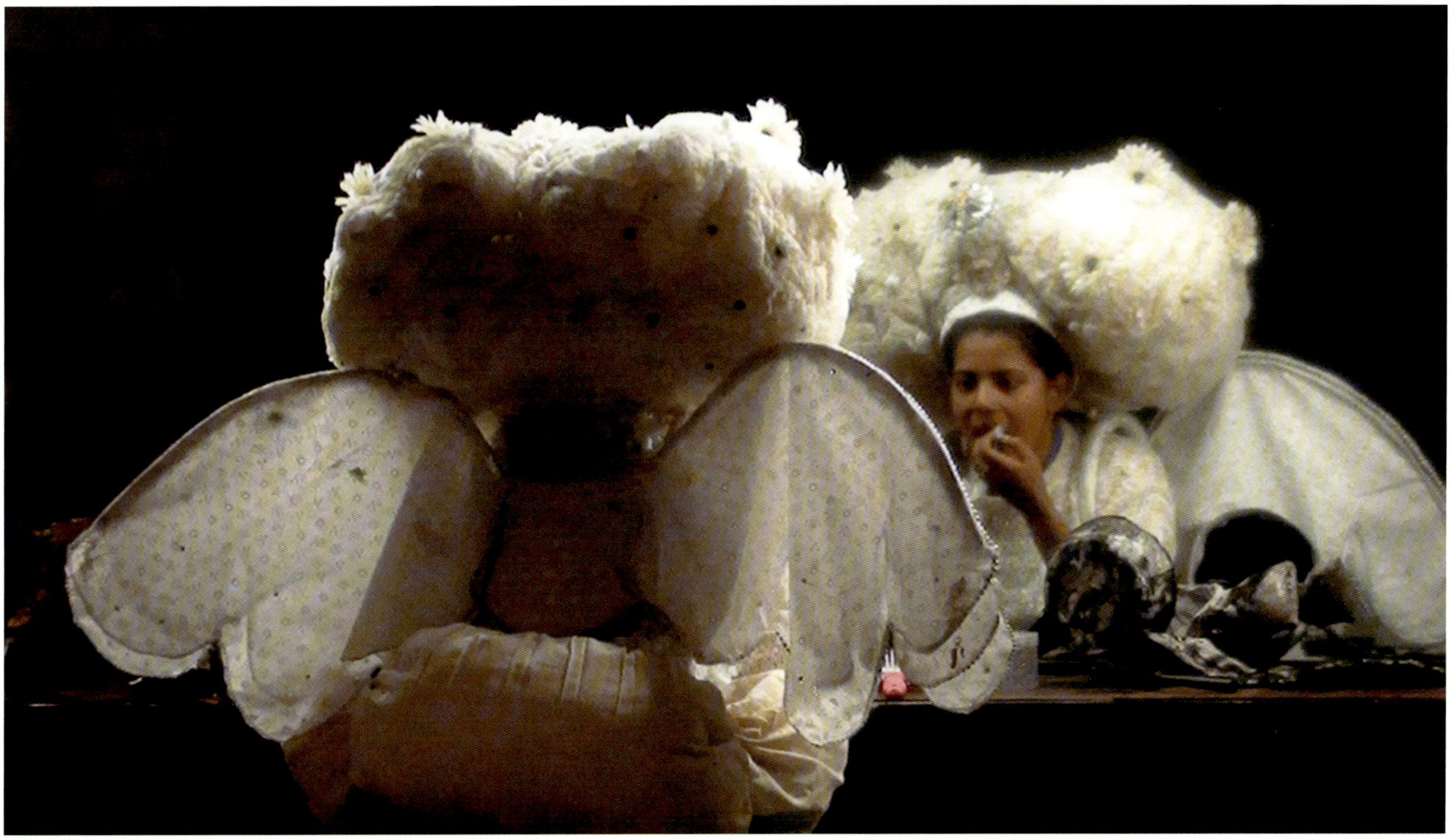

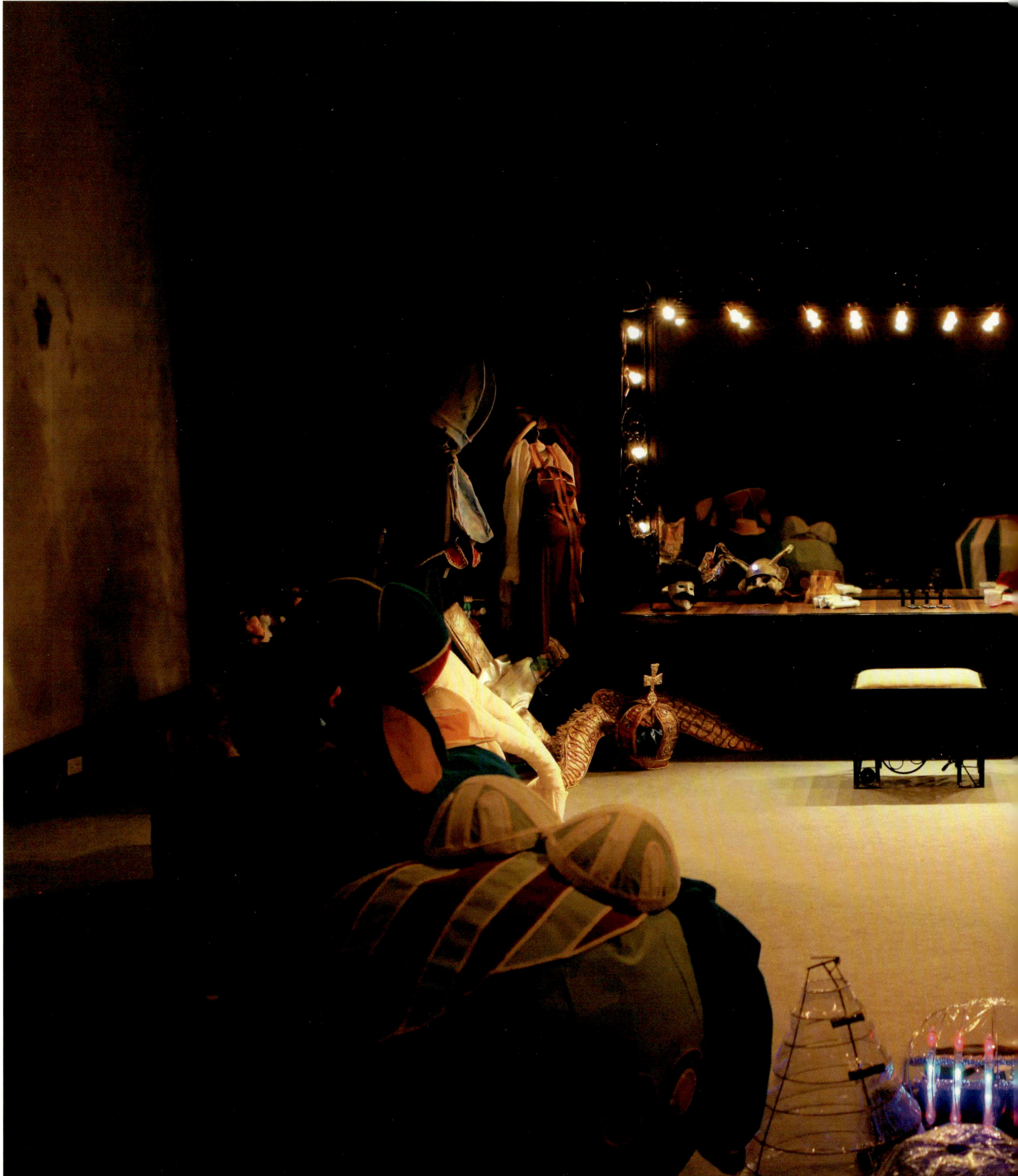

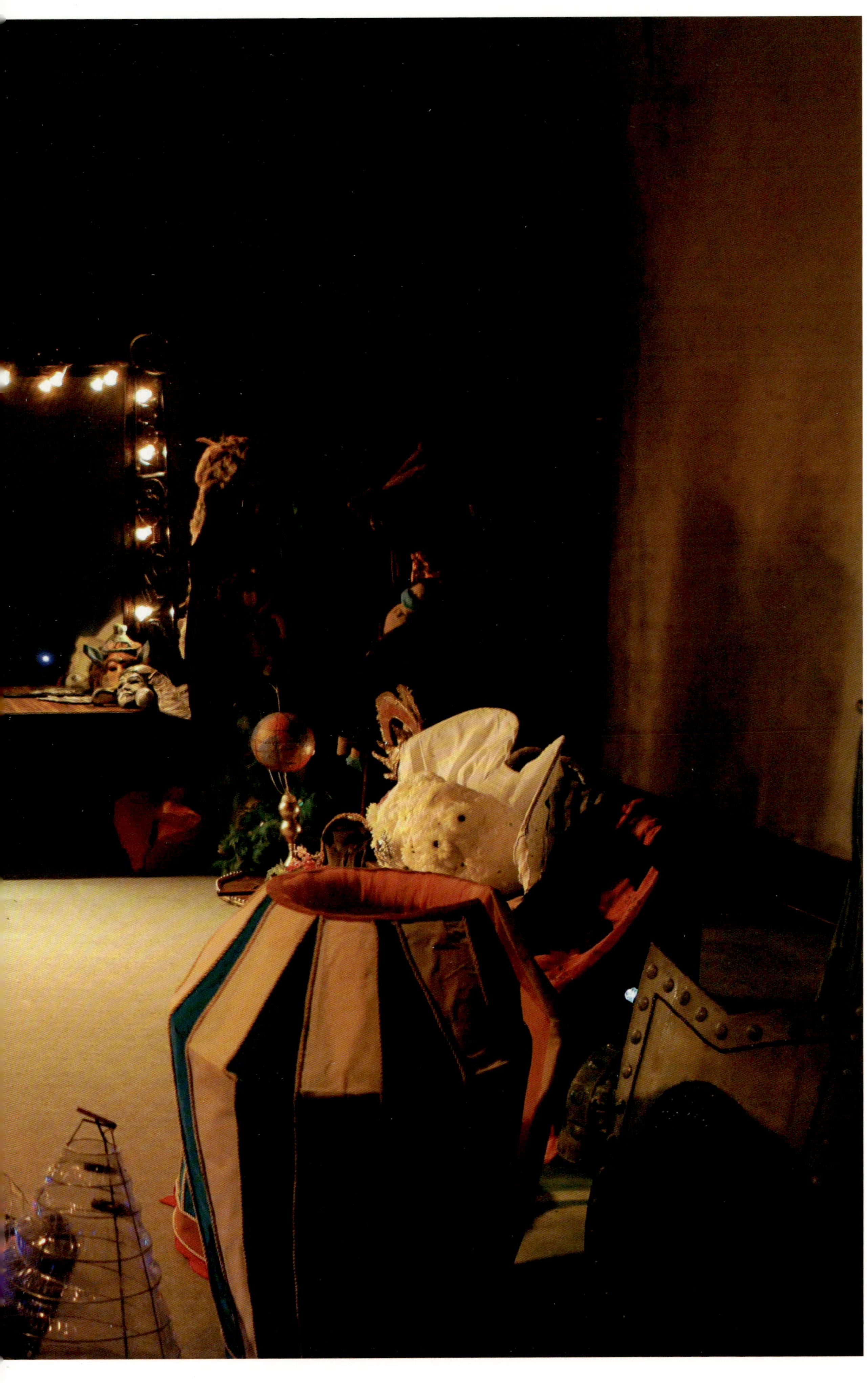

Água de Chuva no Mar
Rainwater in the Ocean

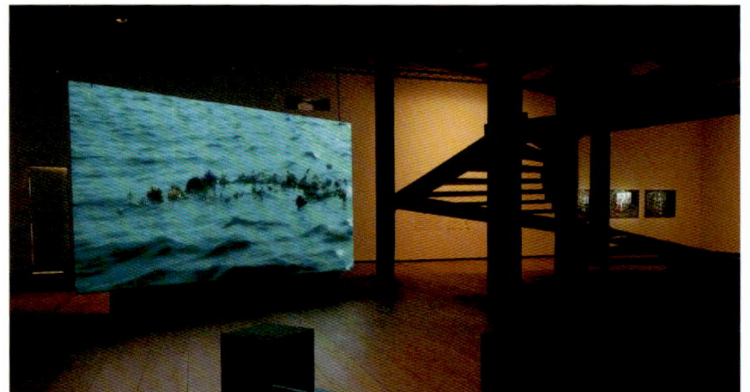

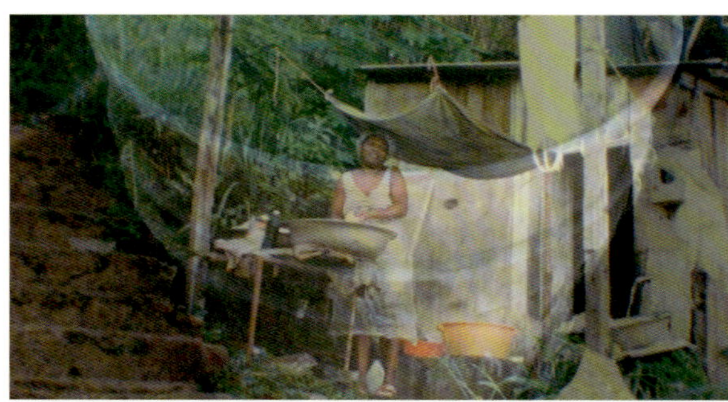

Rainwater in the Ocean focuses on a group of older black washerwomen at the favela Solar do Unhão, Salvador, who have spent most of their lives washing clothes for the city's whitish middle and upper classes, and have, thus, insured that their own children can go to university. Peppering the narrative are scenes from the *Feast of Iemanjá* (Goddess of the Seawaters), in which flower offerings in little boats are set sail in the blue waters of the Bay of All Saints from dawn until dusk, lending a universal and poetic dimension to the women's accounts.

Commissioned by the Museum of Modern Art of Bahia, Dias & Riedweg retrace the water cycle as a source of livelihood, revealing how invisible toil has, in fact, been a structural pillar of the class disparities at the heart of Bahian society for centuries.

- Single-channel video installation
  Loop, 20:00

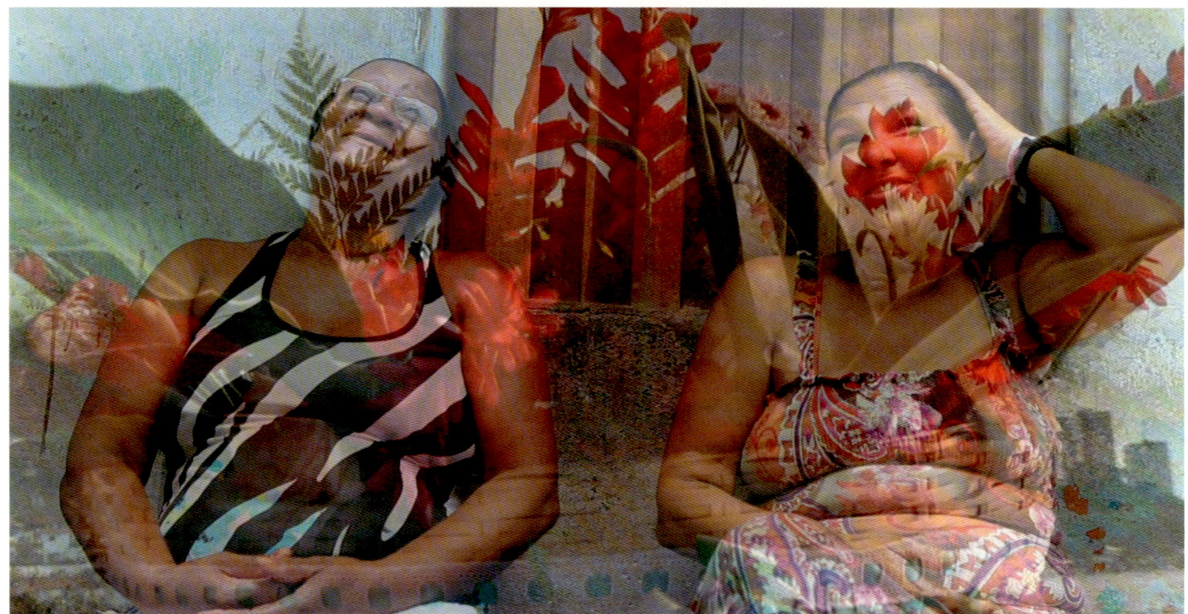

Peladas Noturnas
Nocturnal Kick-Abouts

Fenced-in sports courts, still visited by stray horses and pigs, are more like light-filled satellite stations out of context. The dozens of children and teenagers that descend upon these places from all corners each night seem to justify these strange boxes glowing in the landscape. At last, a football sailing through the sky replaces the stray bullet in a new daily ritual.

→ See *Zwei aus Vier/Two by Four*, 2014, p. 75
- Three-channel video installation
  Loop, 3:57
  Dimensions variable
  Series of 6 digital photographs
  Inkjet HP12 on Canson Rag 310g cotton paper,
  147 × 57 cm

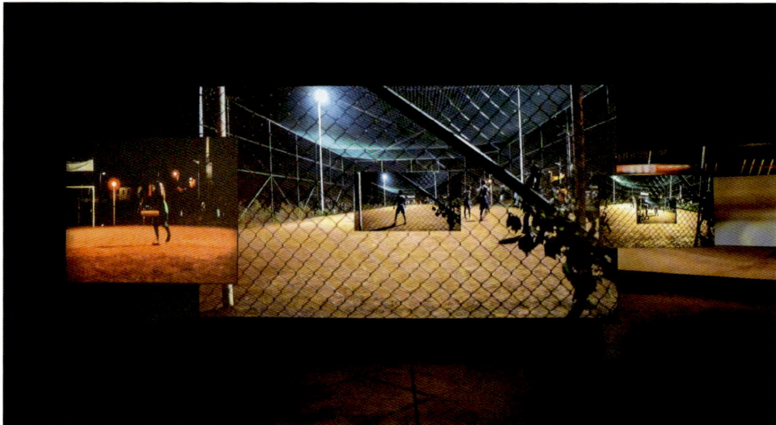

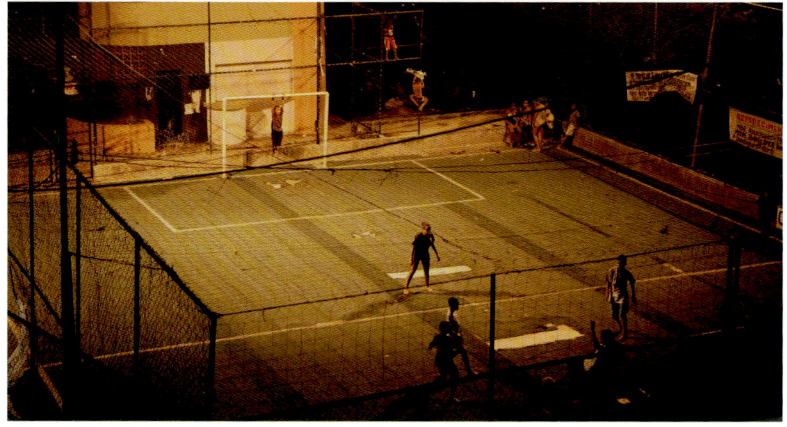

O Espelho e a Tarde
The Mirror and the Dusk

A resident carries a mirror through the avenues, alleyways, ghettos, and squares of the recently transformed favela Alemão Complex, revealing the same old problems in the new urban spaces. The reflections in the mirror complement the details of this strange new landscape at nightfall.

→ See *Zwei aus Vier/Two by Four*, 2014, p. 75
- Three-channel video installation
  Loop, 7:03
  Dimensions variable
  Series of 6 digital photographs
  Inkjet HP12 on Canson Rag 310g cotton paper
  2 photographs 100 × 150 cm
  2 photographs 66 × 100 cm
  2 photographs 45 × 66 cm

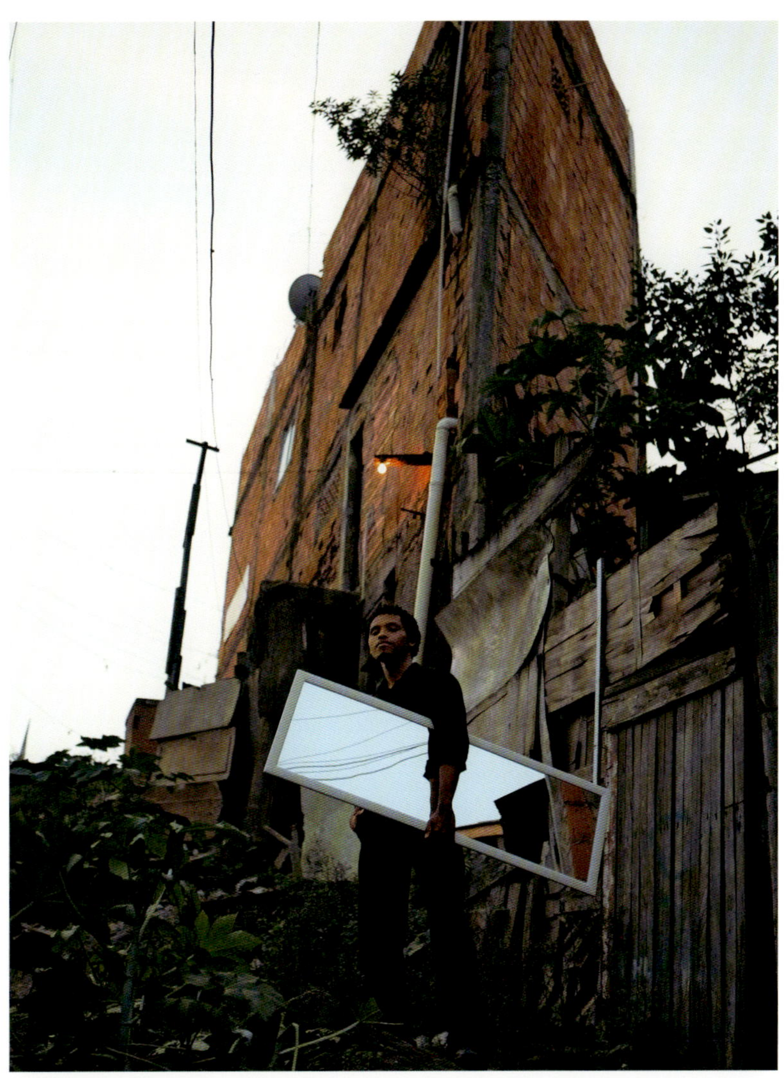

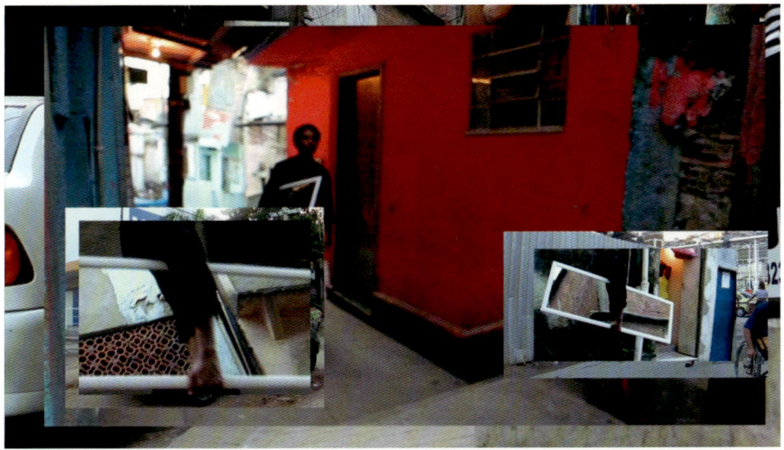

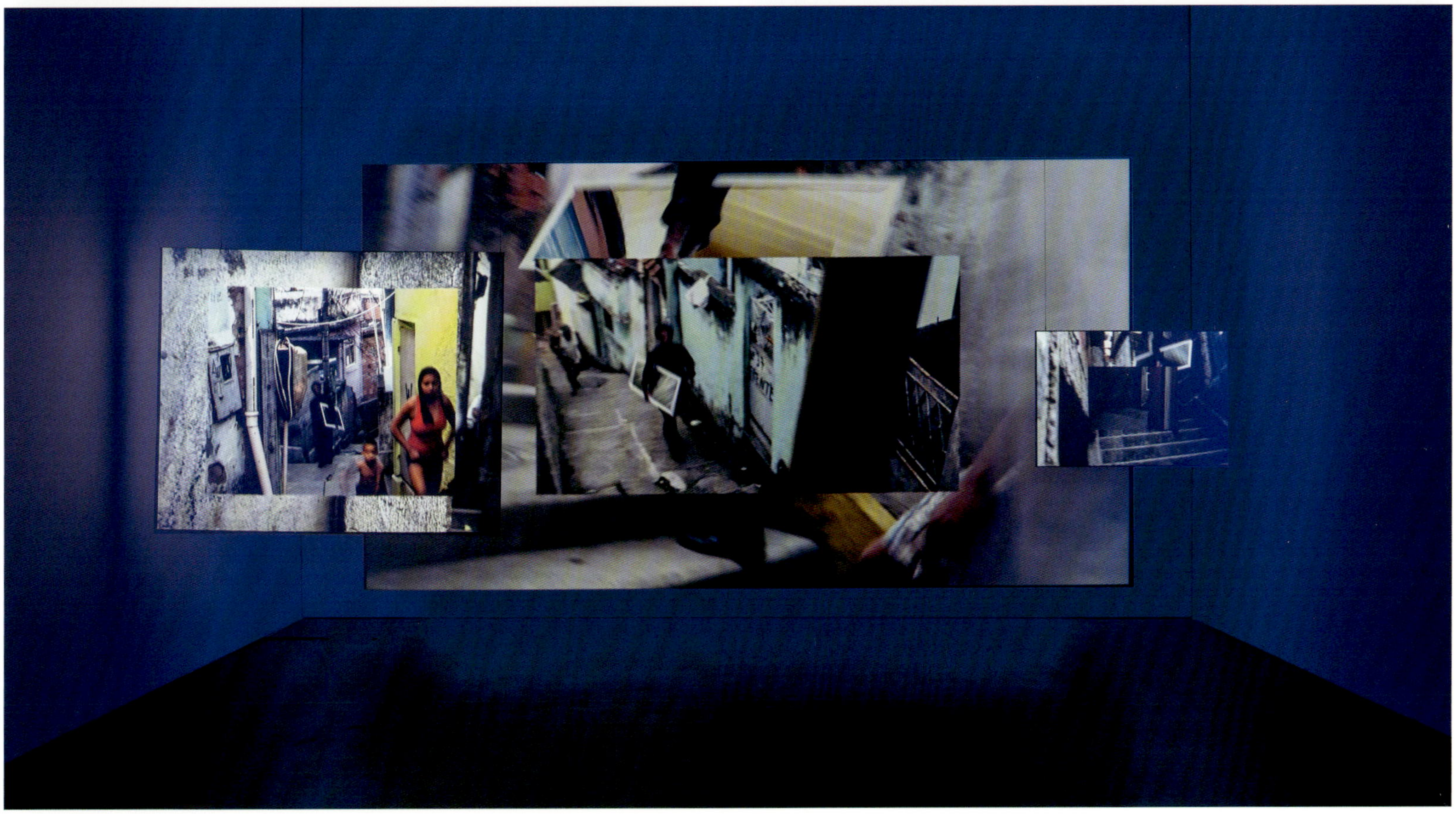

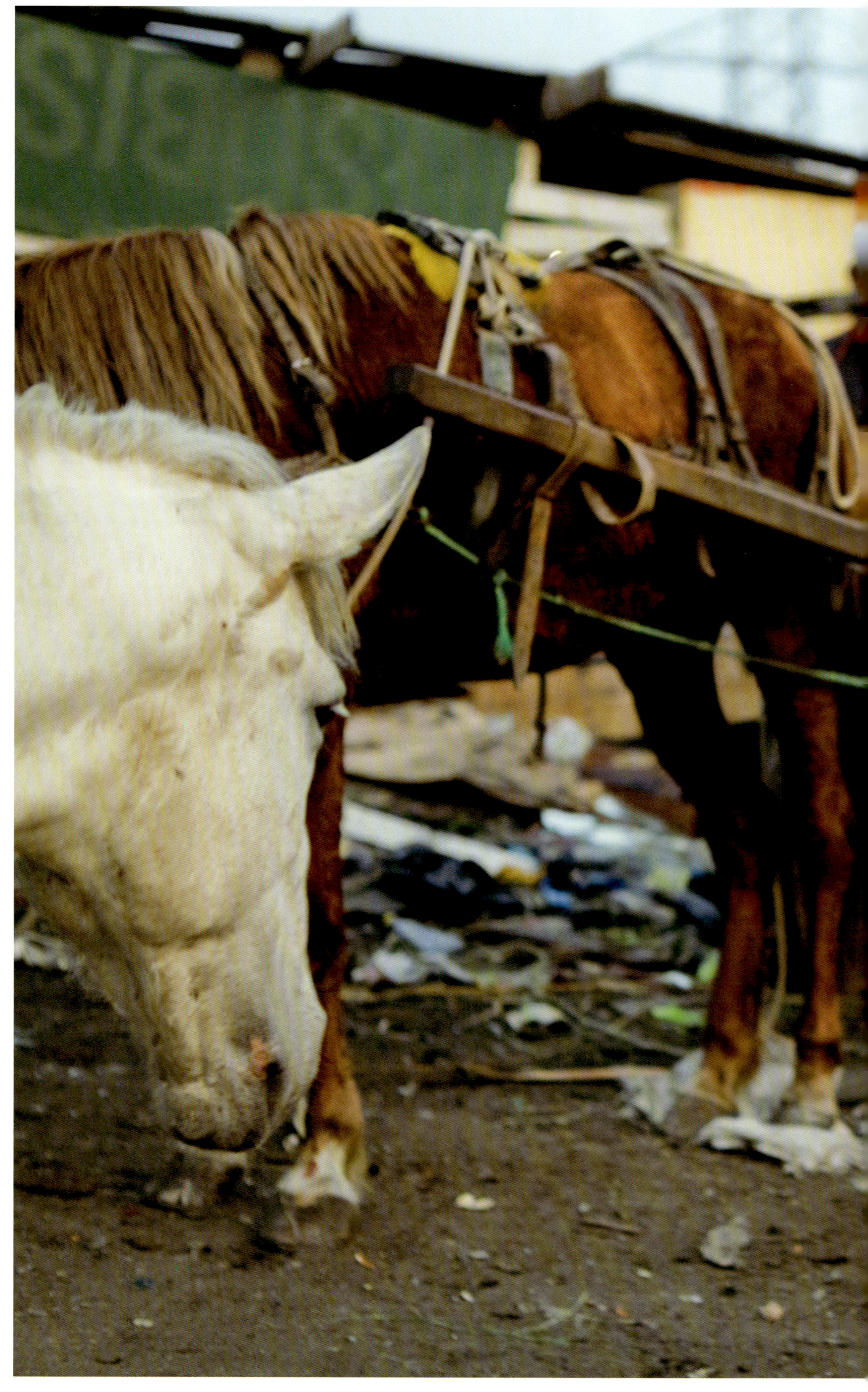

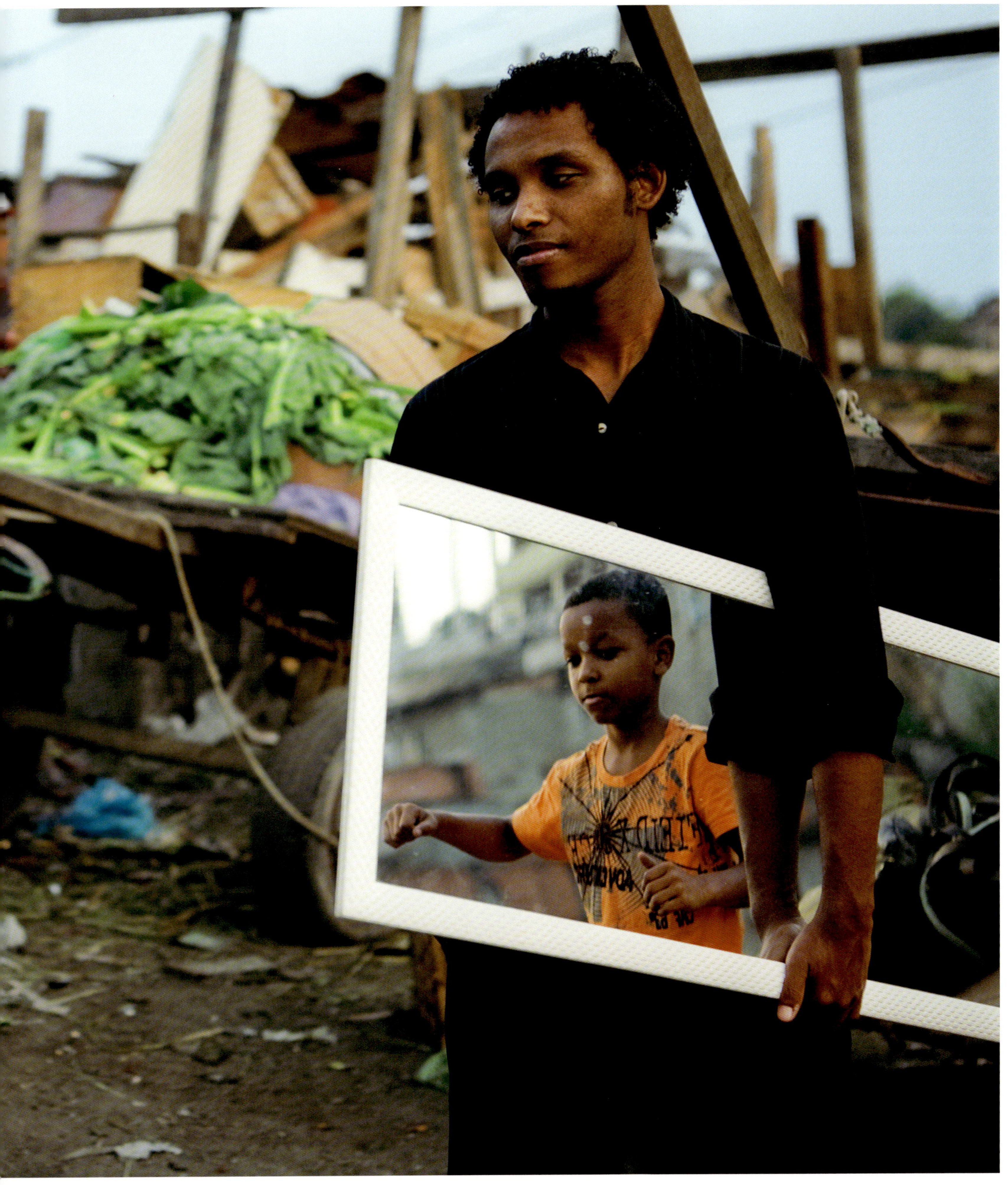

Sábado à noite no parquinho
Saturday Night at the Fairground

Bustling nighttime shots of a rickety old fairground jammed between the Falete, Fogueteiro, and Coroa favelas in Rio's city center, reveal moments of simplicity and fun on trampolines, merry-go-rounds, and slides. It is a colorful, geometrical ballet of the rusty cogs of children's carrousels and giant roller coasters.

→ See *Zwei aus Vier/Two by Four*, 2014, p. 75
- Three-channel video installation
  Loop, 8:42
  Dimensions variable
  Series of 12 digital photographs
  Inkjet HP12 on Canson Rag 310g cotton paper
  42 × 30 cm

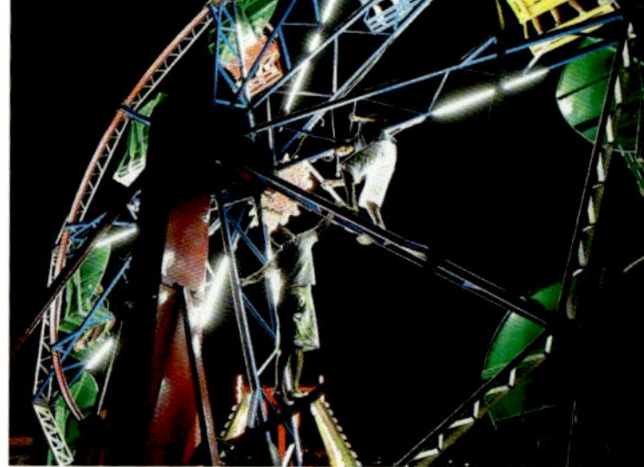
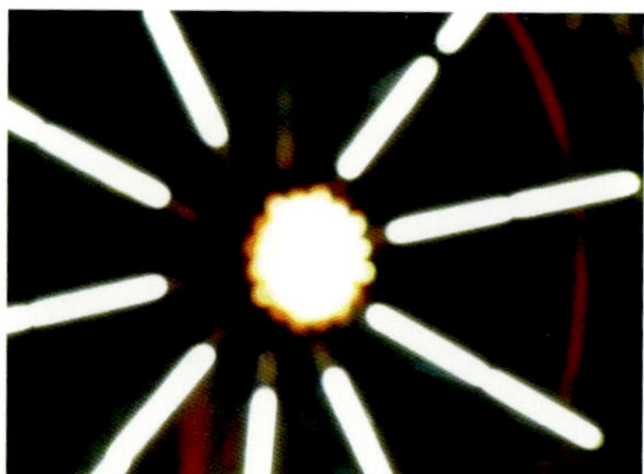
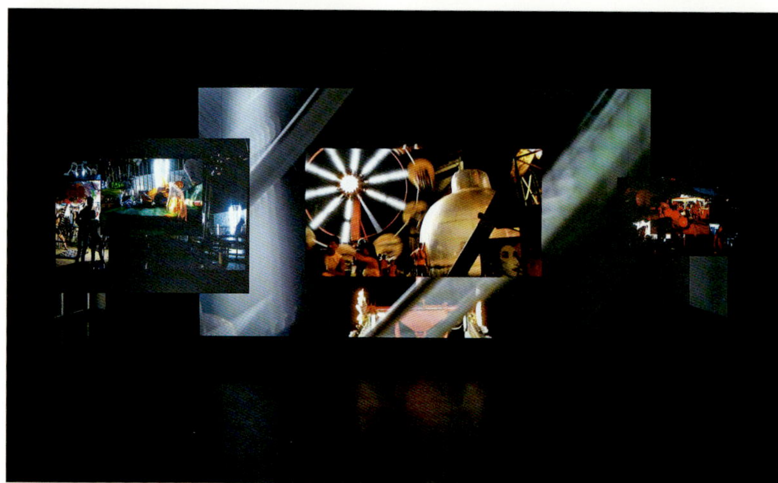

A cidade fora dela
The City Outside Itself

The piece shows the city of Rio as seen from the inside out–from the vantage point of its least known and most stigmatized parts. The picture-postcard sights of Lagoa, the Sambadrome, Brazil Central Station, and the Corcovado are here seen from the windows of favela bars. The shots are superimposed and mixed: windows and headlights begin to glow beneath a sky still full of kites. Little by little, night falls behind anempty beer bottle on the windowsill of one such bar, where a game of pool is being played.

→ See *Zwei aus Vier/Two by Four*, 2014, p. 75
- Three-channel video installation
  Loop, 8:18
  Dimensions variable

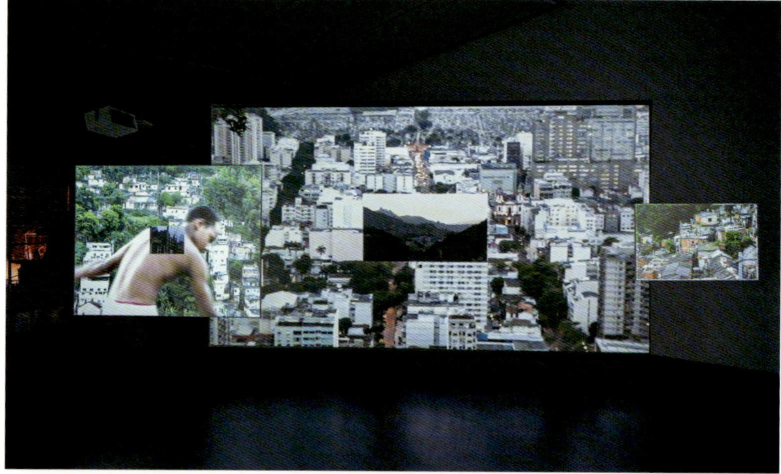

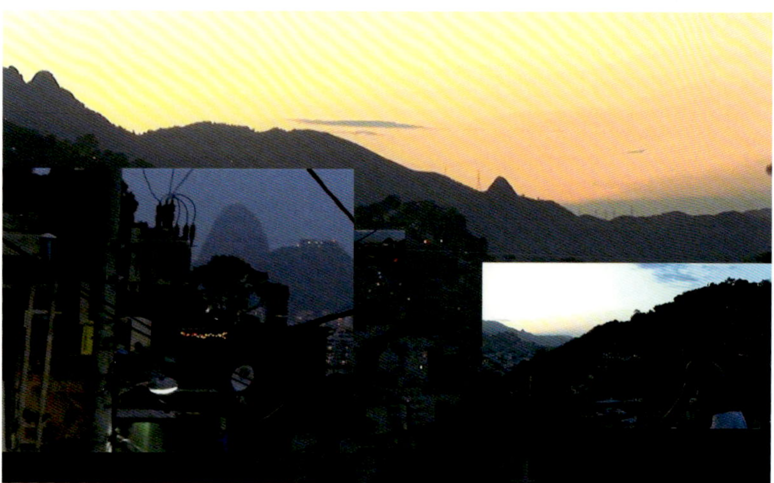
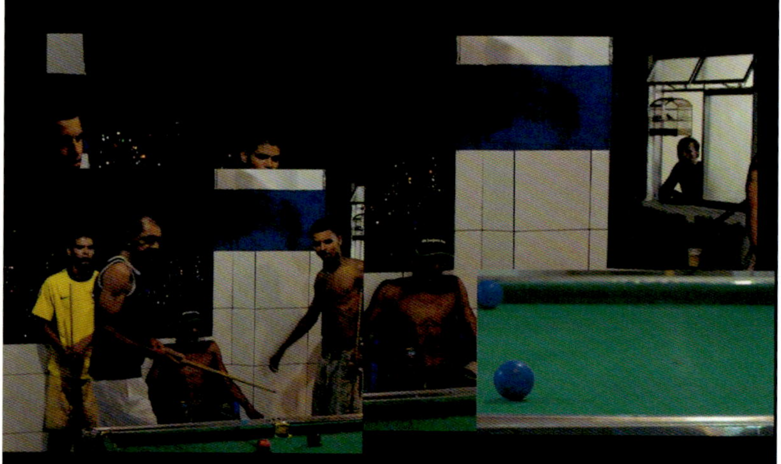

La Giselle

This video is made of only two images that slowly flow into one another over the duration of almost seven minutes: the canopy of a palm tree seen from below and a snow storm battering the windscreen of a moving car. While only these two imperceptibly changing images are seen, the Candomblé leader La Giselle can be heard talking about how the meaning of God differs between the Northern and Southern hemispheres, and about the possibility of trance as an extended and uncontrolled form of alterity.

Gisèlle Cossard was born in Marrakesh, in 1923. She first experienced the tropics in her childhood spent between fine French furniture and the exotic African gardens of her ambassador father.

This was renewed when she married a French diplomat and again lived in African countries. But it was only years later, in Brazil, when she was taken by black employees of the Embassy in Rio to a Candomblé ceremony in a favela, that she fell into a trance and was initiated into the rites of Candomblé. She went back to Paris where she became a doctor in philosophy under the guidance of Roger Bastide, and met Pierre Vergé, with whom she traveled back to a new life in Brazil. Today she is the only white, foreign Mãe de Santo (Candomblé leader) in Brazil, and is an unparalleled expert in the secrets of these religions in this country.

• Single-channel video
  Loop, 6:50

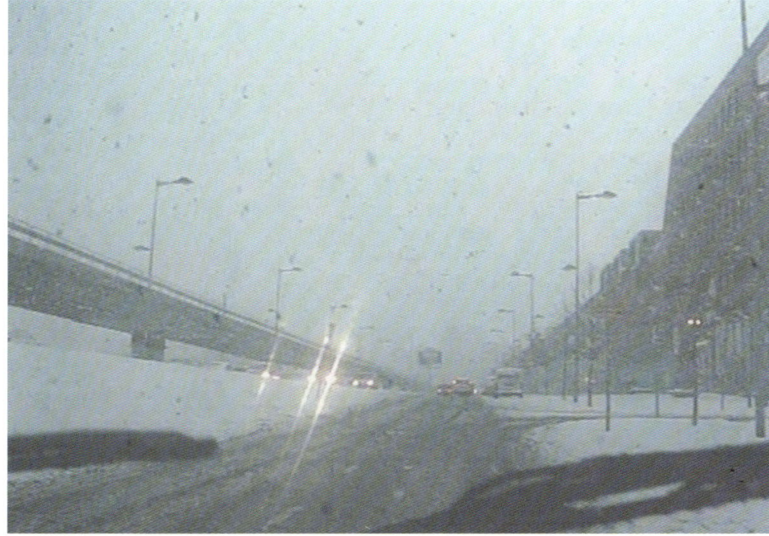

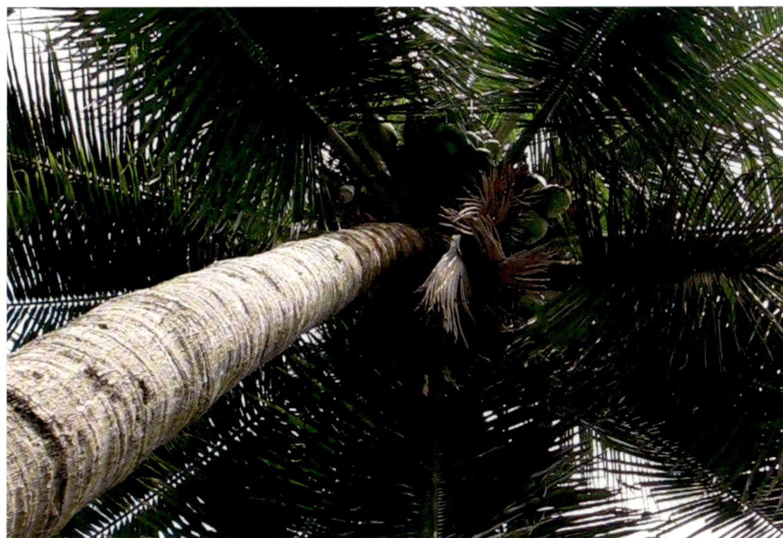

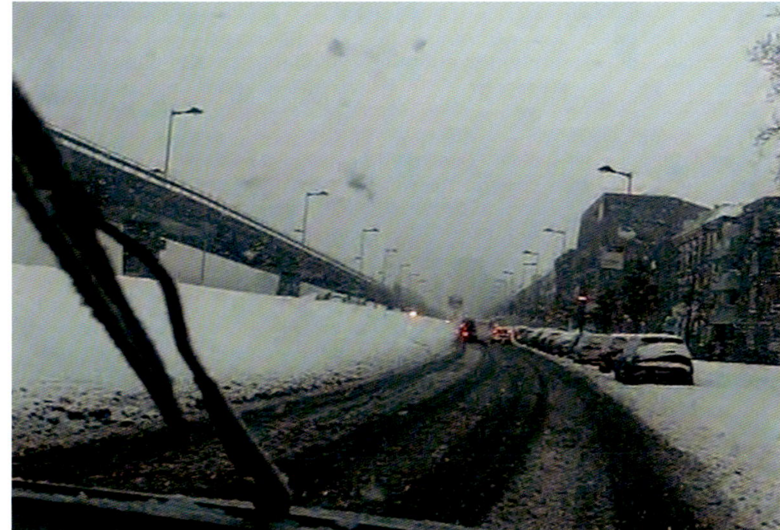

Cold Stories

Dias & Riedweg conceived this piece—made with images exclusively collected from open archive images that deal with the political and geographical history of the world from the Cold War to Global Warming—in reference to their fragmented personal memories of growing up in front of a TV set, like many of their generation. The installation has four large back-projections inside a huge cube placed in the exhibition space and four old used travel cases, each one containing a puppet of a major figure of our political history and its respective video, animated by Rio's marionette artist Marco Nogueira. The four figures chosen are exponents of the Cold War period, whose acts directly and indirectly contributed to the phenomenon of global warming in which we live today. The figures chosen are Che Guevara, Mao Tse-Tung, John F. Kennedy, and Nikita Khrushchev.

The metaphorical use of floating color circles reminiscent of soap bubbles as the visual support to present historical archive pictures, and the use of puppets to present historically crucial figures of this period, indicate how ephemeral, how manipulated and manipulative the so-called "facts" that build up our history actually are. In this piece, some of the most significant historical facts come from an unseen puppetteer, and are mixed up with images from advertisements and TV series; getting bigger and bigger, they fill the installation screens before blowing up and disappearing just like soap bubbles.

• Eight-channel video installation
  4 synchronized rotating projections and 4
  adapted travel-cases each containing a puppet
  and a video monitor
  Dimensions variable

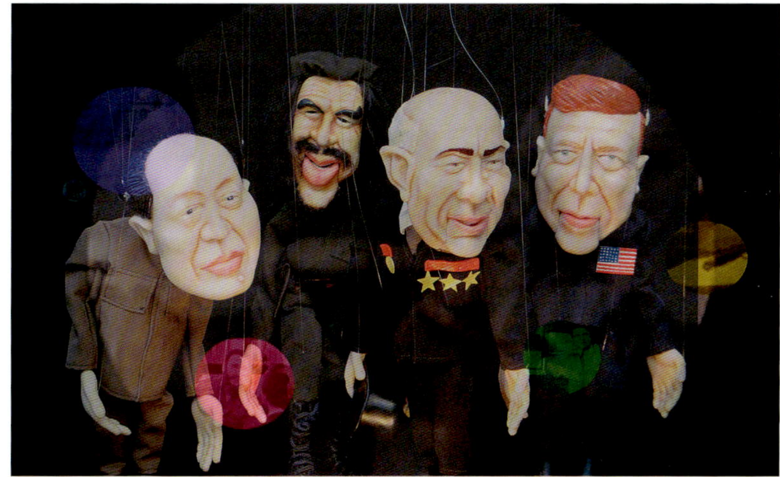

Padre y Hijo
Father and Son

Two squares, one a white monochrome, one black. On closer inspection it is possible to make out Antonio and his father, the controversial singer Manoel Agujetas, each framed in a square of color, black and white, father and son.

Manuel Agujetas is recognized as one of the greatest Flamenco singers, with an international career behind him. However, he now lives alone out in the Andalusia vineyards, and is hated locally as an over-ambitious man, because he left his children behind–seven of whom are deaf-mute–for his career. Antonio is one of the two children who can speak, and he sings for his father in this video.

The *Flamenco Suite* series deals with the evolution of tradition: based on rituals, these are not simply chronological, but cyclical. When religion no longer serves as a cement to bind people in space and time, these rituals become rare and are less and less practiced in contemporary life. However, certain regions, such as Andalusia in Spain, have built up a definitive and charismatic resistance to this loss. Artists have always been fascinated with this subject. Commissioned by CajaSol, Dias & Riedweg found a focus of interest for their work in the small city of Jeréz de La Frontera. Flamenco is no longer a regional tradition, but a musical style played worldwide. However, its pure, traditional manifestations are now rare; they survive in modest social circles and small spaces known as *peñas*. The artists realized four pieces in the *peñas* of Jerez.

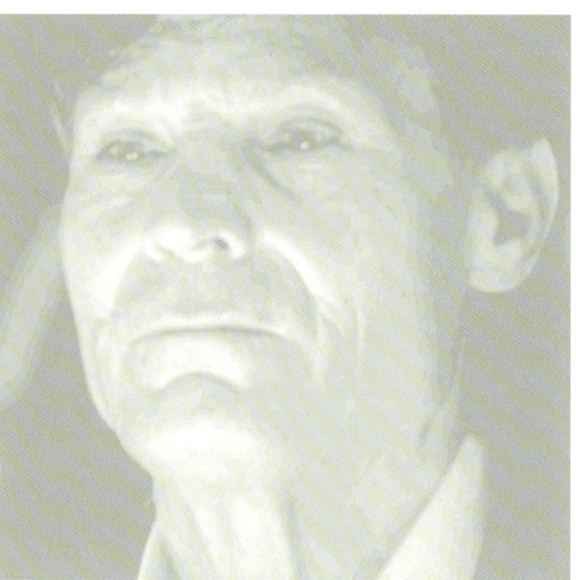
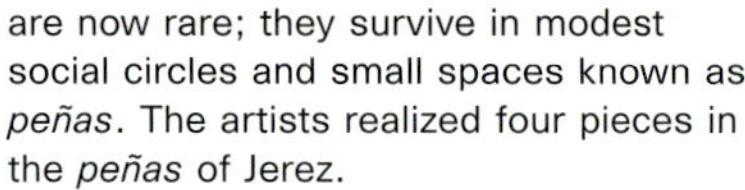

- Digital photograph
  Tint jet on Hahnemüller paper
  83 × 83 cm

Antonio

Antonio Agujetas, the son of Manolo El Agujeta and grandson of Agujeta El Viejo, is the third generation exponent of the most brilliant family of Flamenco singers. In this video, Antonio speaks about his deaf-mute mother, and the difficult relationship he has had with his artistically powerful, but pitiless father throughout his life. He also talks about how he went to prison for 16 years, where he became heroine addict and contracted AIDS. In spite of his evident fragility, he speaks directly to the camera, and every time he is lost for words, he sings very sad pure old Flamenco *seguiriyas, martírios*, and *marteletes*.

→ See *Padre y Hijo/Father and Son*, 2010, p. 88
- Single-channel black & white video installation
  Loop, 17:00
  Dimensions variable

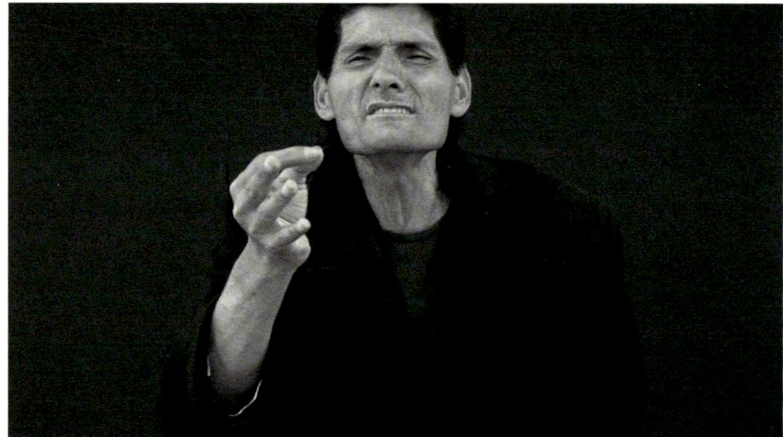
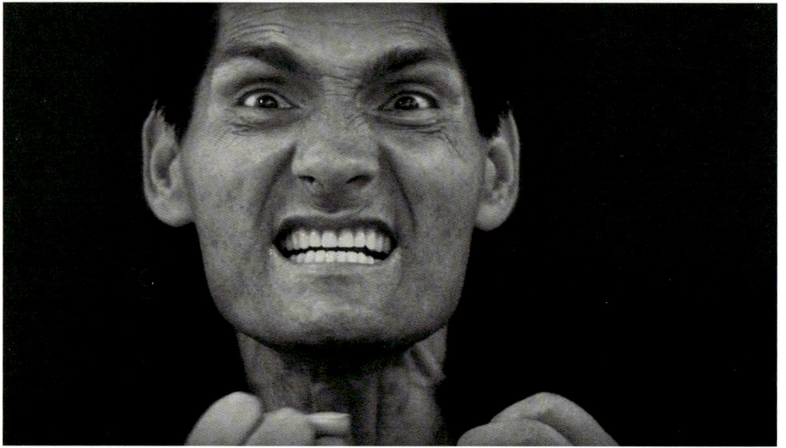

Cuarto de Cabales
Chamber of Cabales

The artists staged the encounter of guitarist Alberto San Miguel and singers Diego Agujetas, Jose Mendez, Paco Peña El Gasolina, and Juan El Zarzuelita, in Jerez de la Frontera, in the very same space where the installation was first shown. The musicians, who had never all been brought together before, played, sang, and drank for hours around a table with a few friends. Dias & Riedweg recorded this encounter with two cameras that were placed at the table, at the same height as the participants and the same distance from them. The sound, also entirely recorded live, was captured from four equidistant directions departing from the center of the table. This was reversed in the four corners of the installation space, thus unfolding the intimacy and the artistic strength of this encounter in a four-channel stereo sound system.

Chamber of Cabales is the name given to the gathering of traditional flamenco musicians, when they get together in small groups to play and sing flamenco in its most traditional forms for an entire night. A cabal is the final version of the *siguiriya*; which literally means honest, exact, complete. The *siguiriya* is the heart of the *cante jondo* (deep song); it expresses anguish, lament, and despair.

→ See *Padre y Hijo/Father and Son*, 2010, p. 88
• 2-channel black & white video installation with 4 audio channels
Loop, 21:00
Dimensions variable

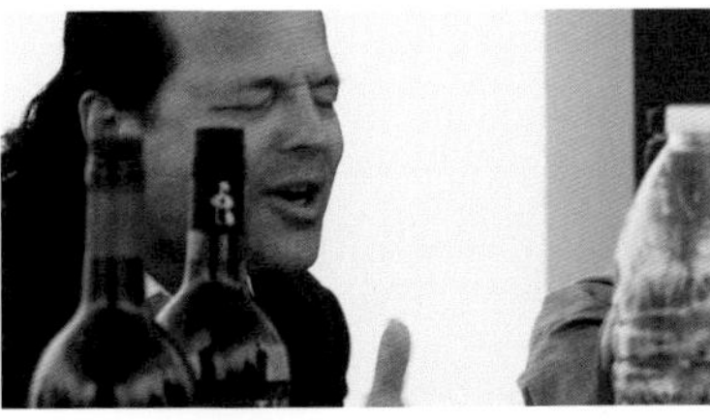
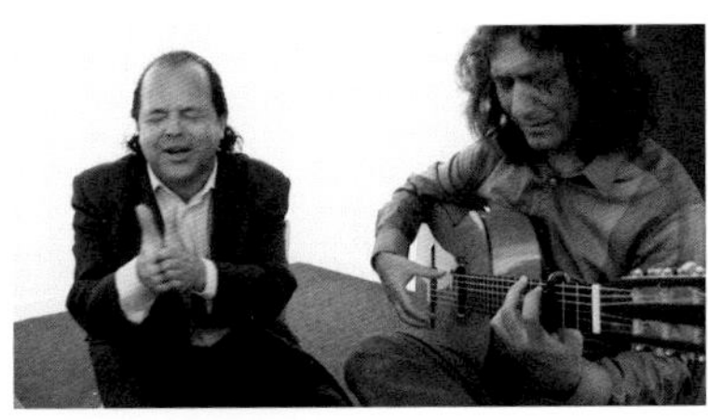
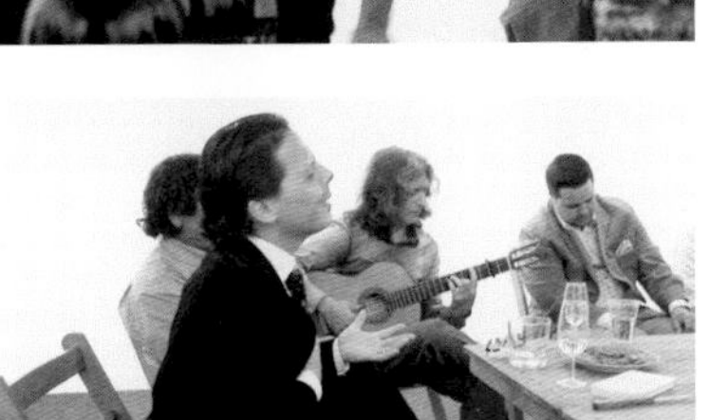
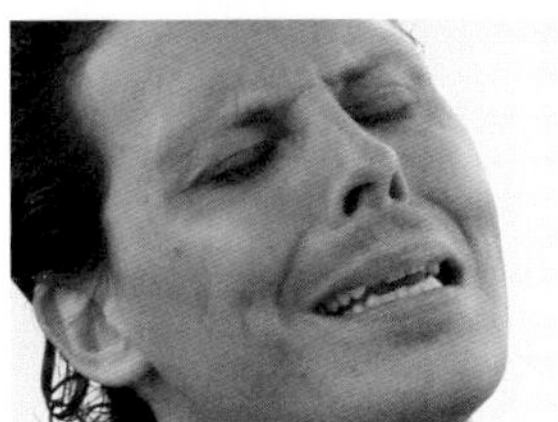

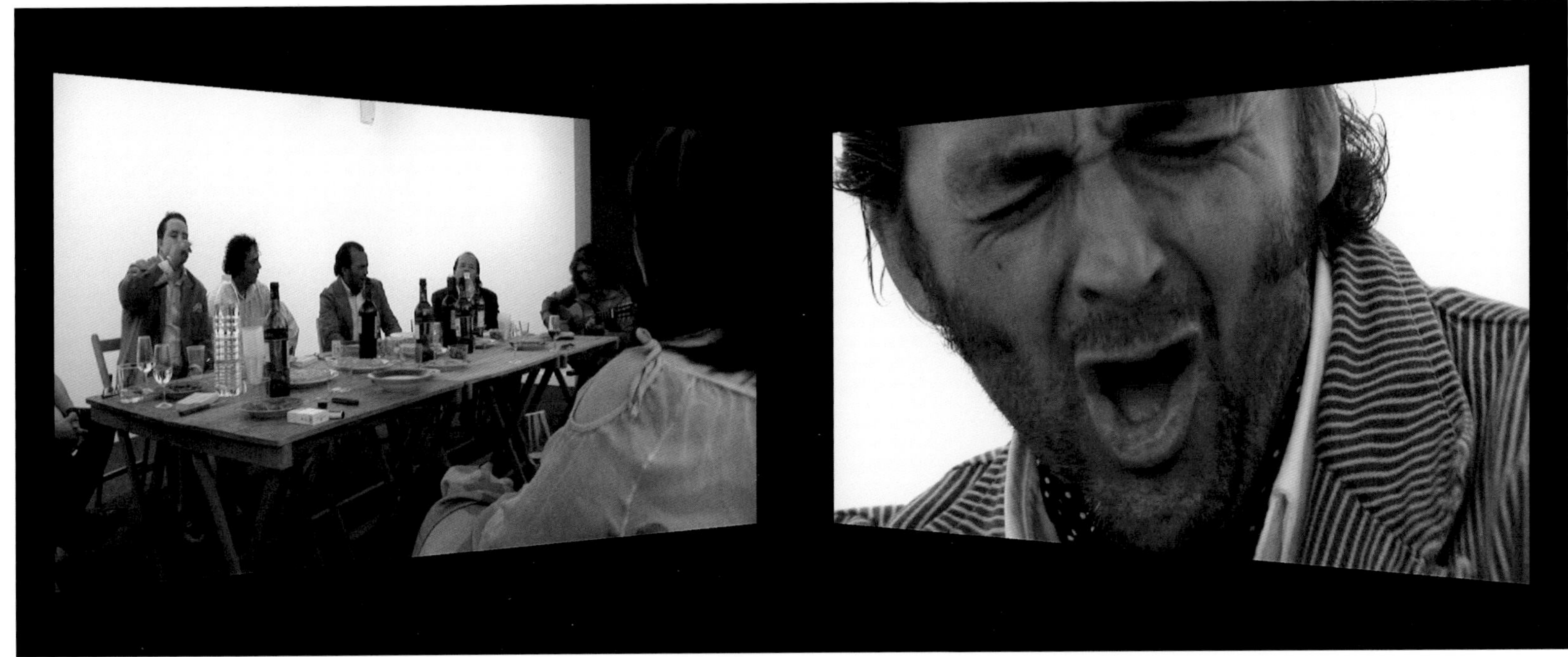

Peñas de Pena
Parties of Sorrow

Seventy-four photographs that, looked at together, give an impression of the walls of the flamenco *peñas*, which are often covered with photographs of their idols—musicians, singers, and dancers. Dias & Riedweg printed the same photographs twice, once in color on cotton paper, and then again in black & white with only 10% opacity on adhesive vinyl of the same size. The vinyl sheets were stuck directly onto the wall, partially obscured behind the color photographs, thus doubling the images like ghosts of themselves, so underlining the past and nostalgia of the subject.

→ See *Padre y Hijo/Father and Son*, 2010, p. 88
• Series of digital color photographs
  Tint jet HP12 on Hahnemüller paper 320g repeated
  in 10% saturation black & white on adhesive vinyl
  Dimensions variable

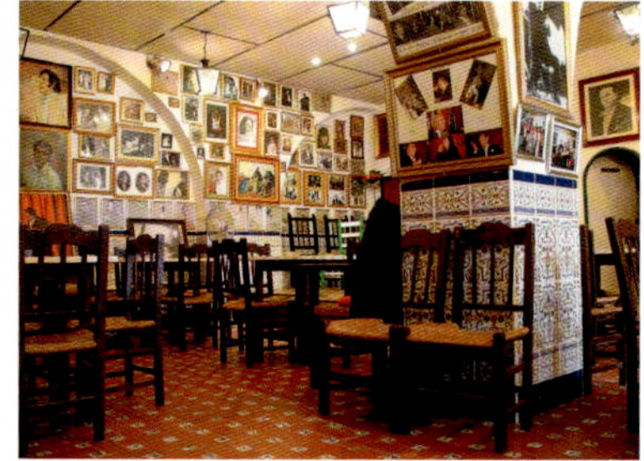
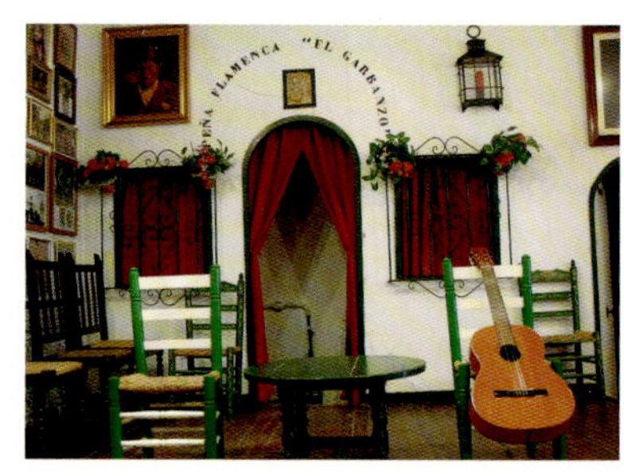
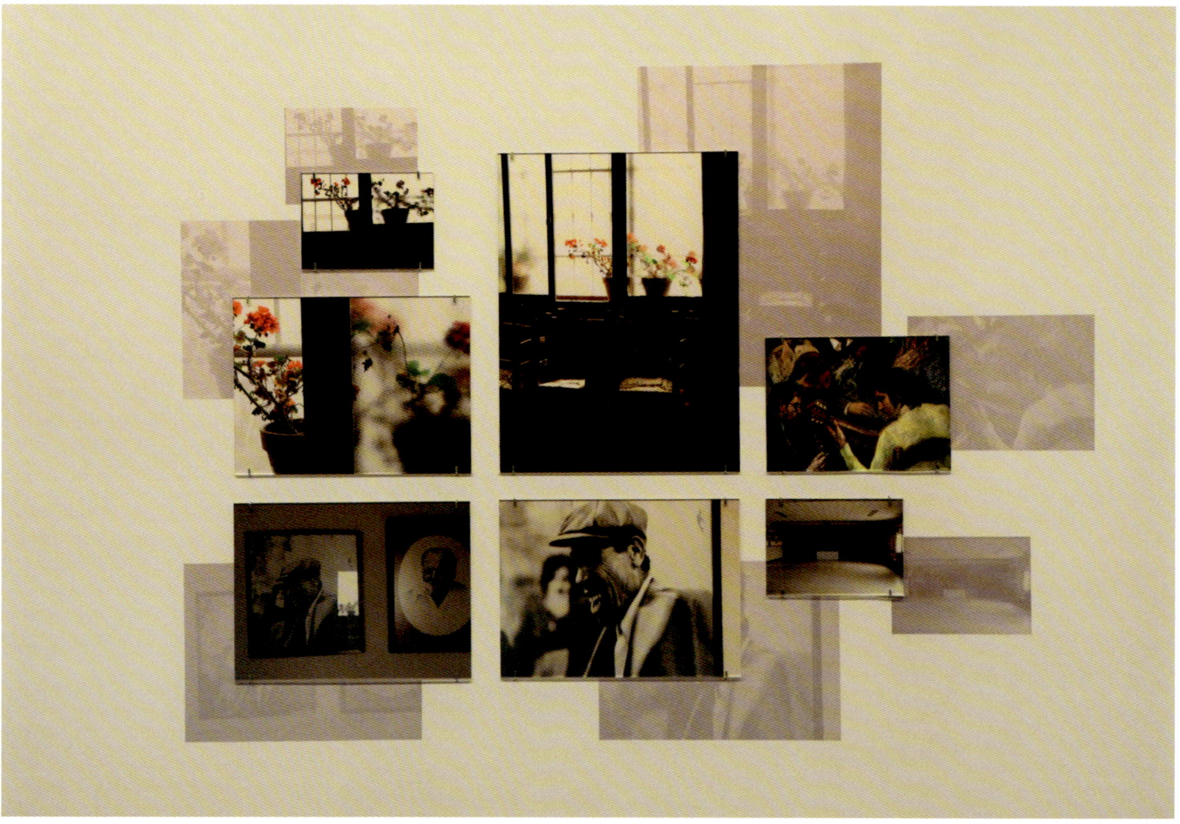

Chaque chose sa place. Autre place, autre chose
Each Thing Has its Place. Another Place, Another Thing

All nine parts are different but very similar. They all present shots of suitcases used in the work *Suitcases for Marcel*—orderly sets on the shelves of a luggage store, photographed from the same distance and viewpoint. The displacement of Dias & Riedweg's finished video—*Suitcases for Marcel*—back to the sale shelf of a suitcase store subverts Duchamp's concept that every object can become an art object. In this case, the art object becomes a mundane object.

Although the ensemble of the nine parts is quite geometric, it immediately gives the impression of singularity and repetition. One of the nine parts is repeated, thus remaking a sort of *game of hidden differences*, like those often printed in magazines and newspapers for children and adults. This piece synthesizes the artists' belief, apparent in many of their works, that everything is similar but never the same, and that a simple displacement is enough to change something or someone.

• Photograph in D-Sec
  9 parts, 45 × 60 cm each

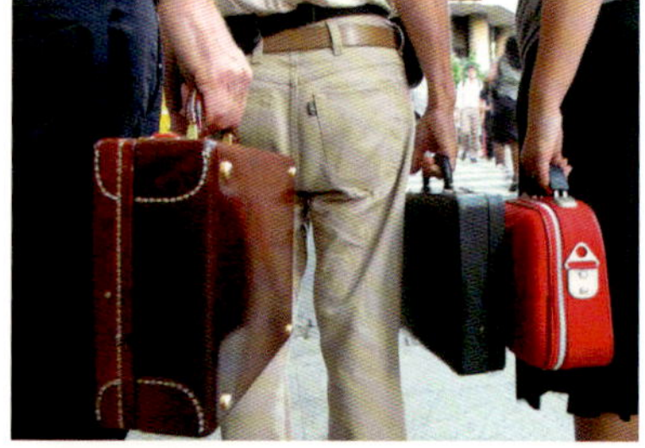
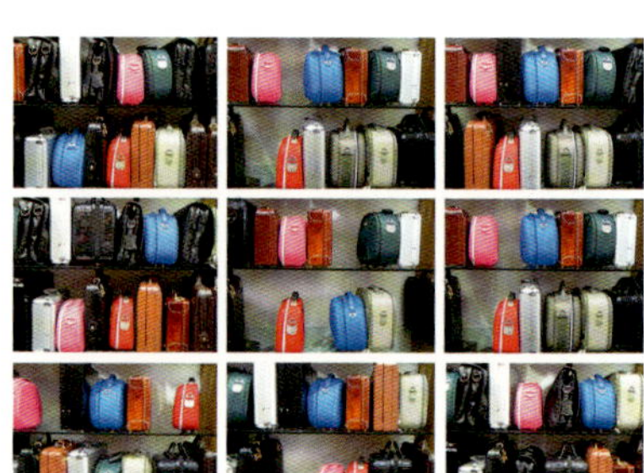
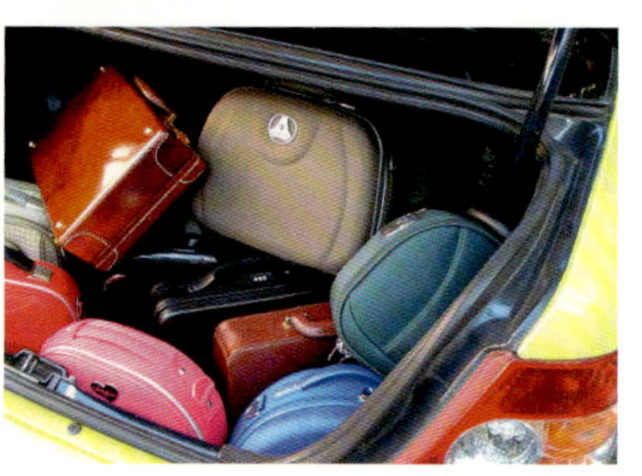

Caminhão de Mudança
Moving Truck

Ongoing since 2009, this long-term project consists of a series of six interventions in city traffic, in which videos were projected from the interior onto the back of moving trucks. The first intervention took place in the *Kunstenfestival des Arts* in Brussels, followed by others in New York, Lisbon, Mexico City, Houston, Copenhagen, and Rio de Janeiro. A first video was made of a moving truck as it drove through city streets. This footage was then projected onto another truck, making its way through another city, footage that was, in turn, projected onto yet another moving truck in yet another city, and so on, until the original footage was no longer visible under so many layers of images of trucks on trucks. After the last intervention in public space, a miniature truck was made to be driven by viewers inside a gallery space, with a LED screen presenting the moving images with all the moving trucks, all moving one inside another, on the back of the truck.

This project contextualizes in space the fate of every *moving image*: erasure by a newer image. All the trucks used were removal trucks, and the six interventions were all made in transit, with the vehicles moving through traffic.

- Public art project on moving trucks in six cities; video installation
  Loop
  Dimensions variable

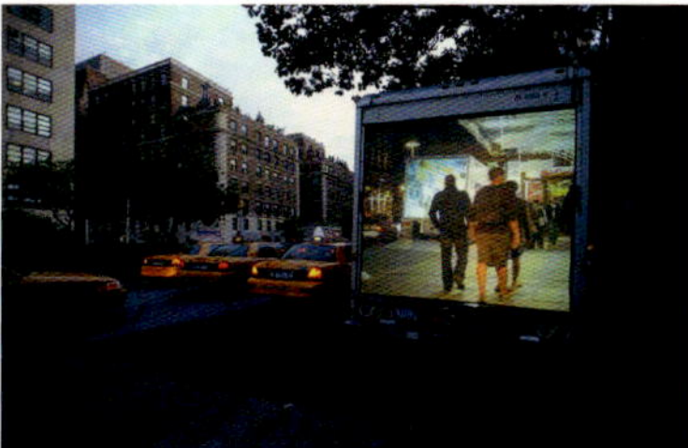

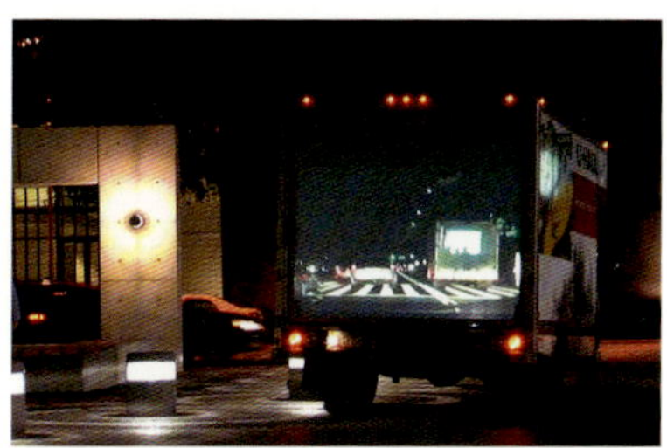

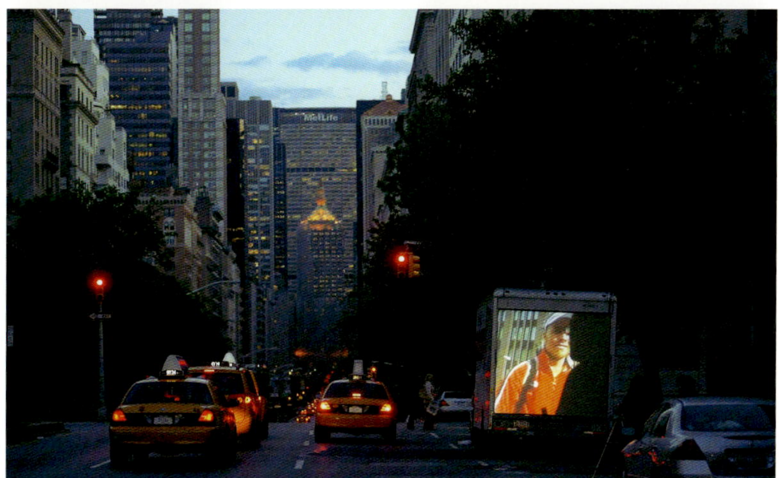

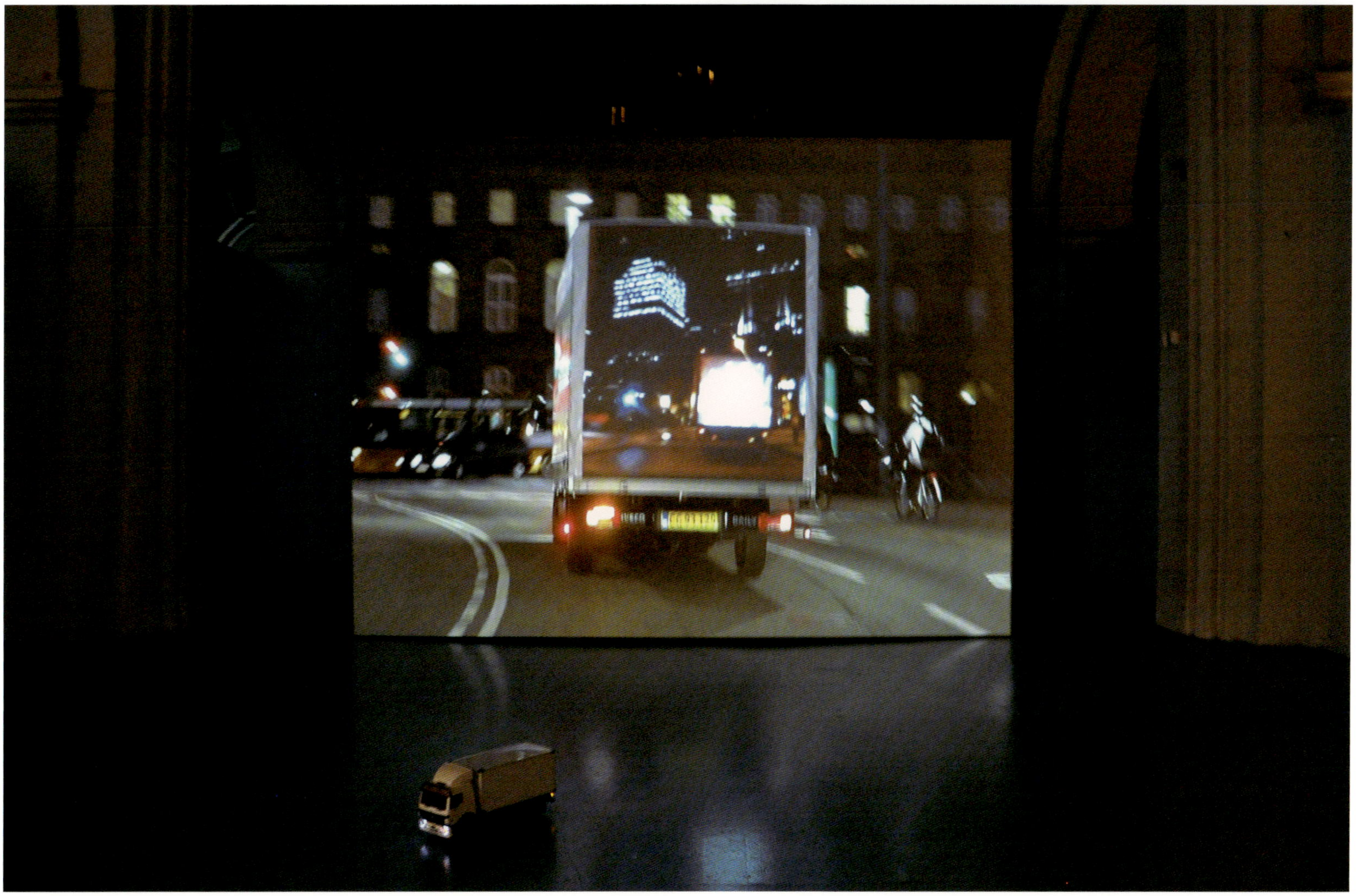

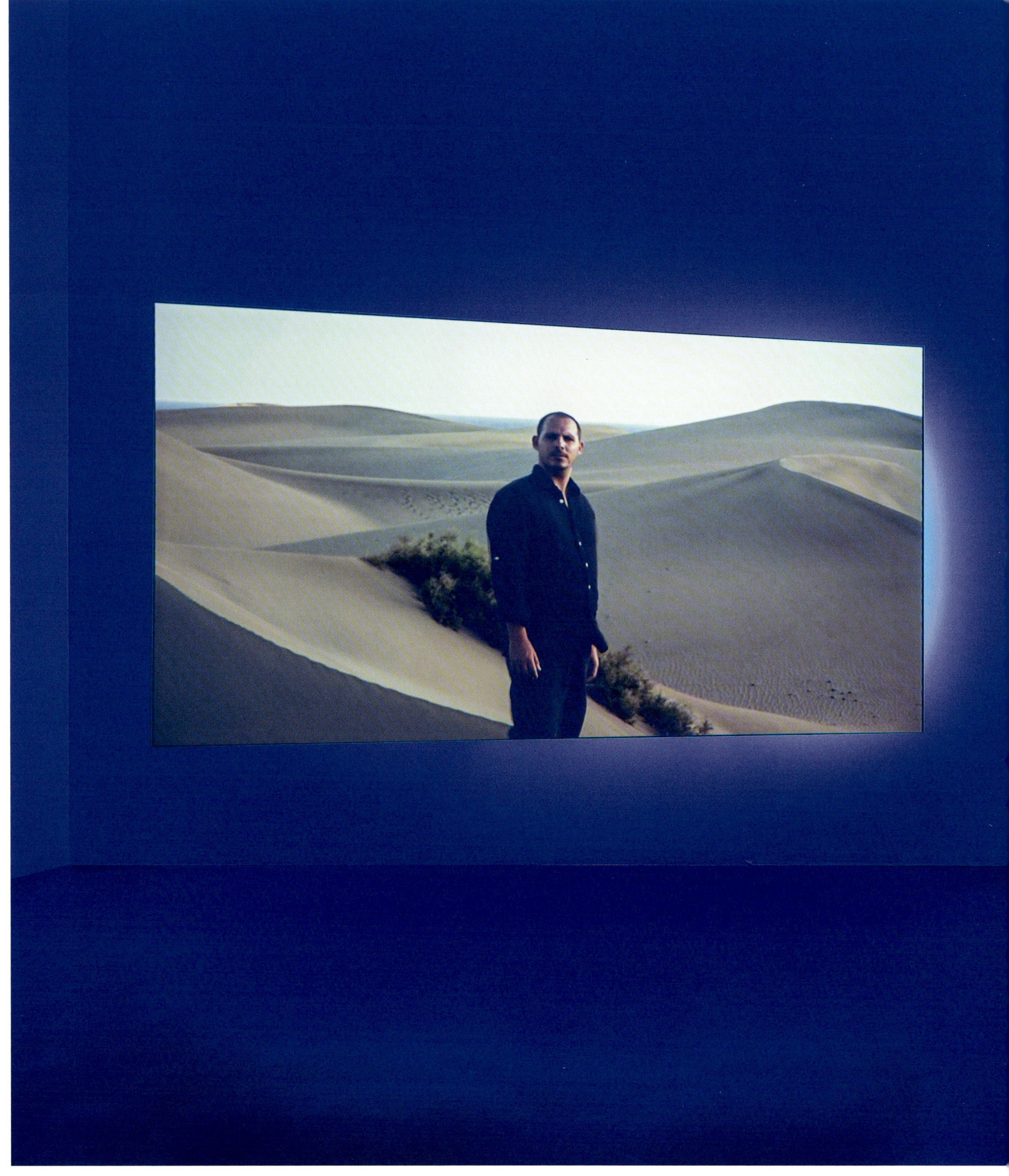

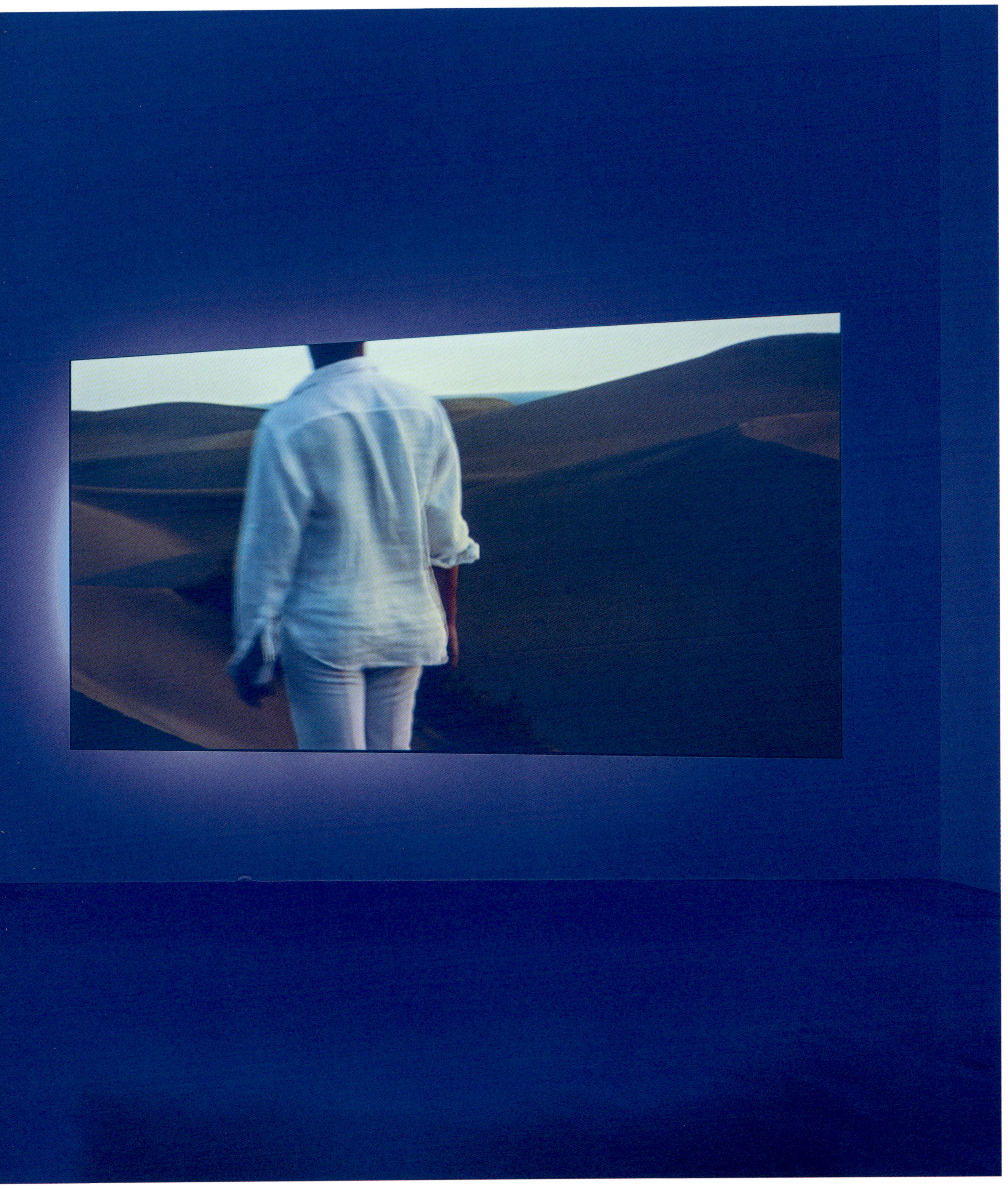

Paradiso Cansado
Exhausted Paradise

Two men, one dressed in black, one in white, walk symmetrically across sand dunes. They see each other. They walk toward each other. They pass each other. Again they walk toward each other. Again they pass each other. They walk behind each other. They see each other. They stare at each other, but do not communicate. Desire is palpable, as well as impossibility. The sun is the only witness beside a mirror and the ocean behind. The two men are one and the same.

Commissioned for the 2nd Biennale of Gran Canaria, Dias & Riedweg met Eduardo Garcia Gonzalez, a Cuban refugee and inhabitant of the island, and invited him to play the role in the video, although he is not a professional actor. The piece was entirely recorded on the dunes of Maspalomas, a beach known as a cruising ground by international gay tourists. A mirror is carried by the protagonist through the landscape; the juxtaposition of real and reflected images allow the insertion of documentary material into the territory of fiction.

- 2-channel video installation
  Loop, 7:34
  Dimensions variable

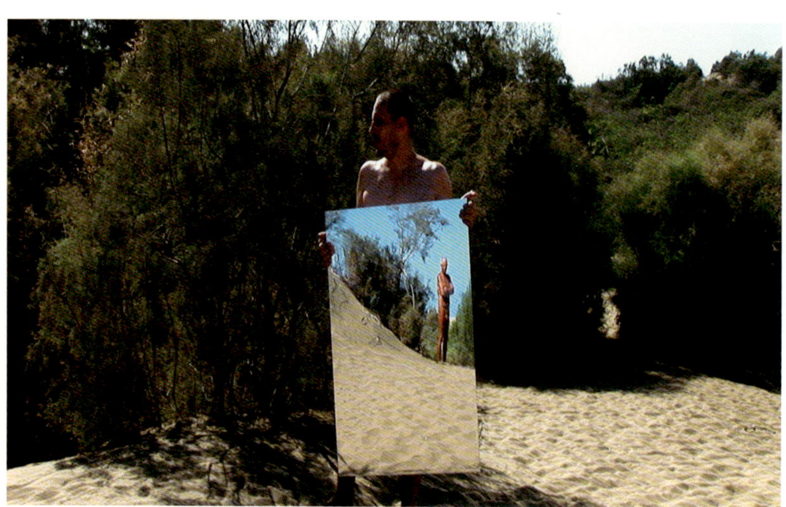

Dona Marta
(Diurno e Noturno)
Dona Marta
(By Day, By Night)

Two sets of twin photographs made at the *Favela Santa Marta*–two in the daytime and two at night.

- Digital photograph
  2 parts, 75 × 115 cm (each part)

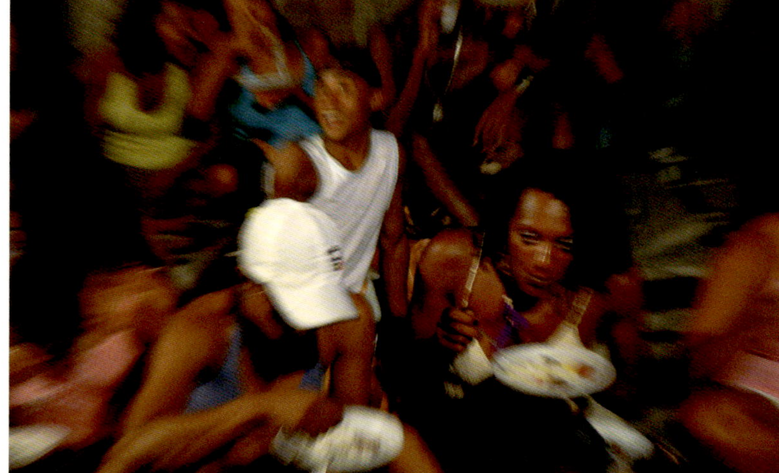

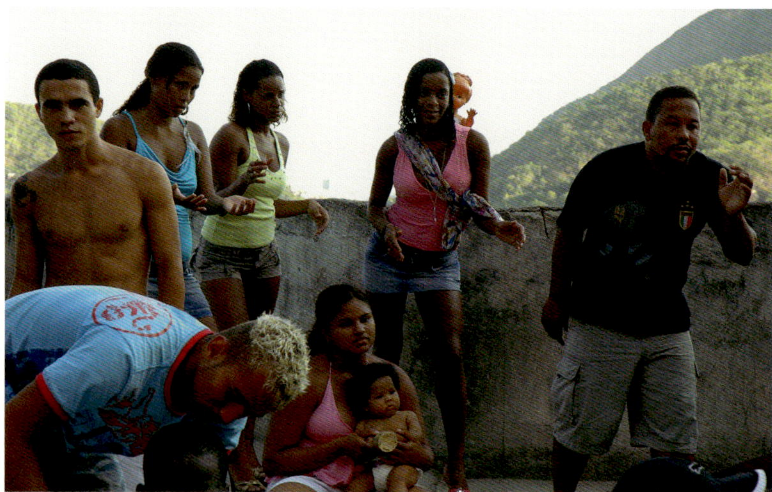

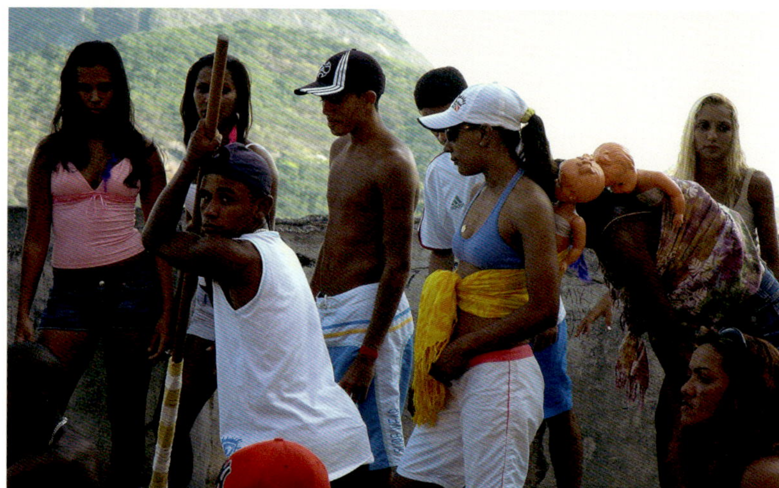

O Jardim
The Garden

The overlapping images of lenticular printing recreate the illusion of movement that reveals a rather humorous crime involving two of the characters from Dias & Riedweg's piece *The House* (2007). In *The Garden* some of these figures reappear (and disappear) in a haunting fiction.

• Series of three lenticular photographs
  110 × 78 cm (each photograph)

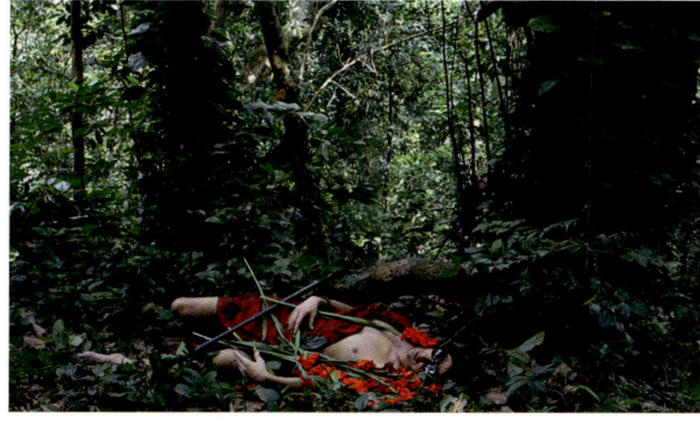

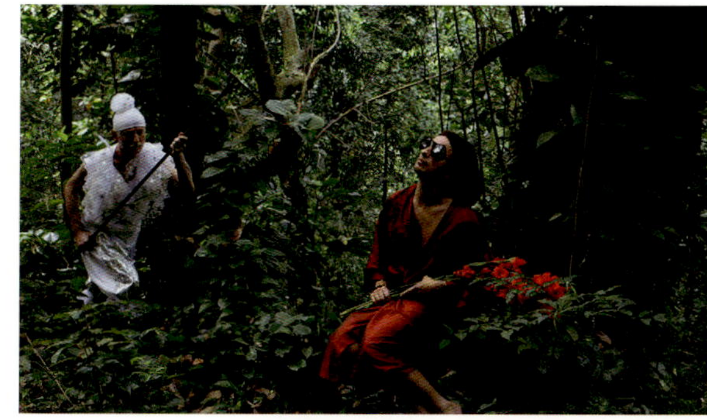

Do Universo do Baile
Of the Universe of the Ball

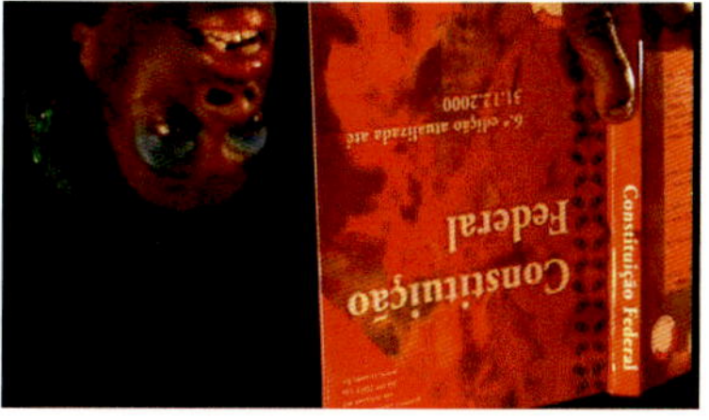

Though local histories and official records disagree vehemently in their accounts, they address the same globalized capitalist economy. One of the many existing expressions of this disagreement is funk, which has become as popular and as present as the local—and likewise unofficial—realities it represents. *Of the Universe of the Ball* points toward the mechanisms of social exclusion, and the exoticization that takes place within image culture. Three national symbols are confronted with their civic ineffectiveness: the Brazilian flag, which hangs inert, despite the blades of a fan swirling in the background; the Federal Constitution, read aloud by a drag queen who can barely read; and the National Anthem, played backward to the frenetic rhythm of Rio funk. The floor in front of these three projections is covered by a checkerboard of bathroom scales covered in green and yellow, creating a sort of dance floor. Visitors can walk across this floor and see their weight oscillate as they watch the three screens.

Do Universo do Baile/Of the Universe of the Ball, *Livro/Book*, *Xilogravuras/ Woodcuts*, *Funk Staden*: between 2006 and 2008 Dias & Riedweg visited the funk ball scene (a new musical genre developed in the favelas of Rio de Janeiro since the 1990s) and four works stem from that research: the video installations *Funk Staden* and *Of the Universe of the Ball*, the series of five photographs *Woodcuts*, and the single-channel video *Book*. These four works developed out of the meeting of two contexts. Hans Staden's book *True History and Description of a Country of Wild, Naked, Grim, Man-Eating People in the New World* (1557) served as a script for recording images from the Rio funk ball scene. When the two contexts—separated by 450 years—are juxtaposed, they allow for a critical rereading of (the) history (of perception), revealing mechanisms of cultural domination, and the perpetuation of European (mis)conceptions of the tropics (the imagined paradise of the New World), as well as the implementation of certain policies, still culturally prevalent today, that legitimized the genocide of Brazilian Indians, and usurpation as a governmental methodology during the colonization of the American continent. The images and sounds of the contemporary, ghettoized world of funk in the Rio shantytowns serve as an analogy for the heroic and cannibalistic war cries of the Tupinambá Indians, showing how the processes of exclusion pursued by globalized capitalism has its roots in the mercantile practices of the 16th century.

• 3-channel video installation with 550 bathroom scales covered with yellow and green vinyl
  Loop, 5:47
  Dimensions variable

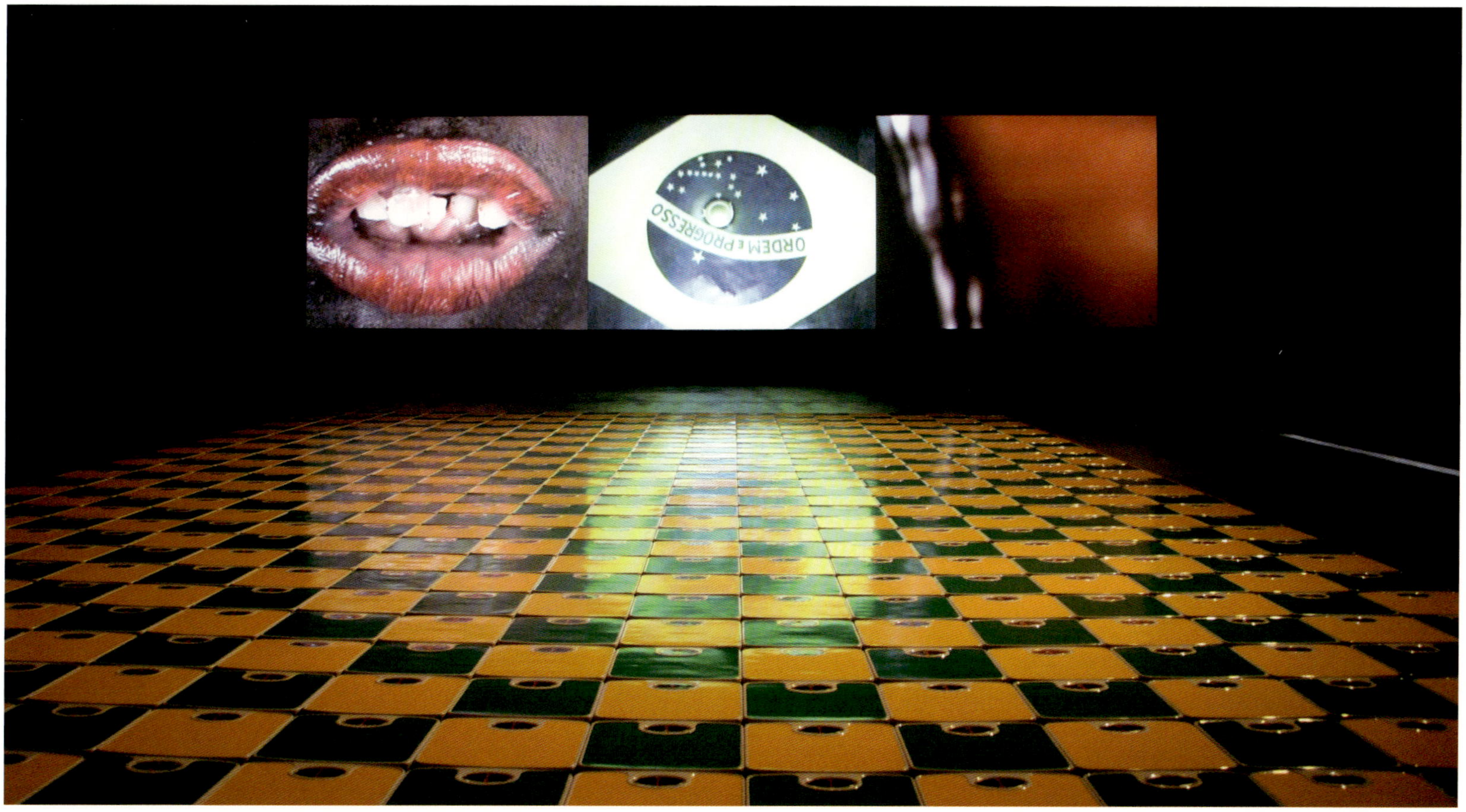

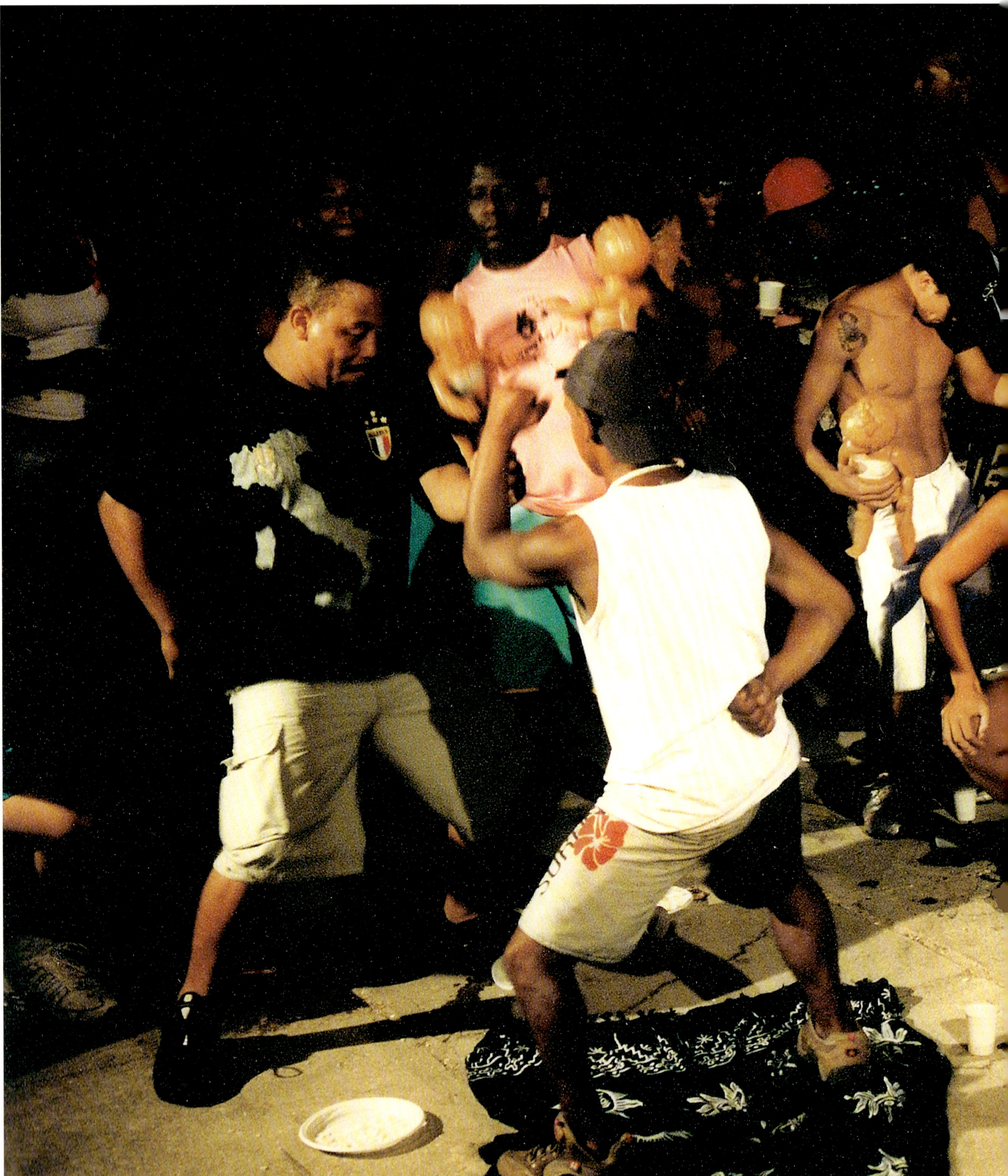

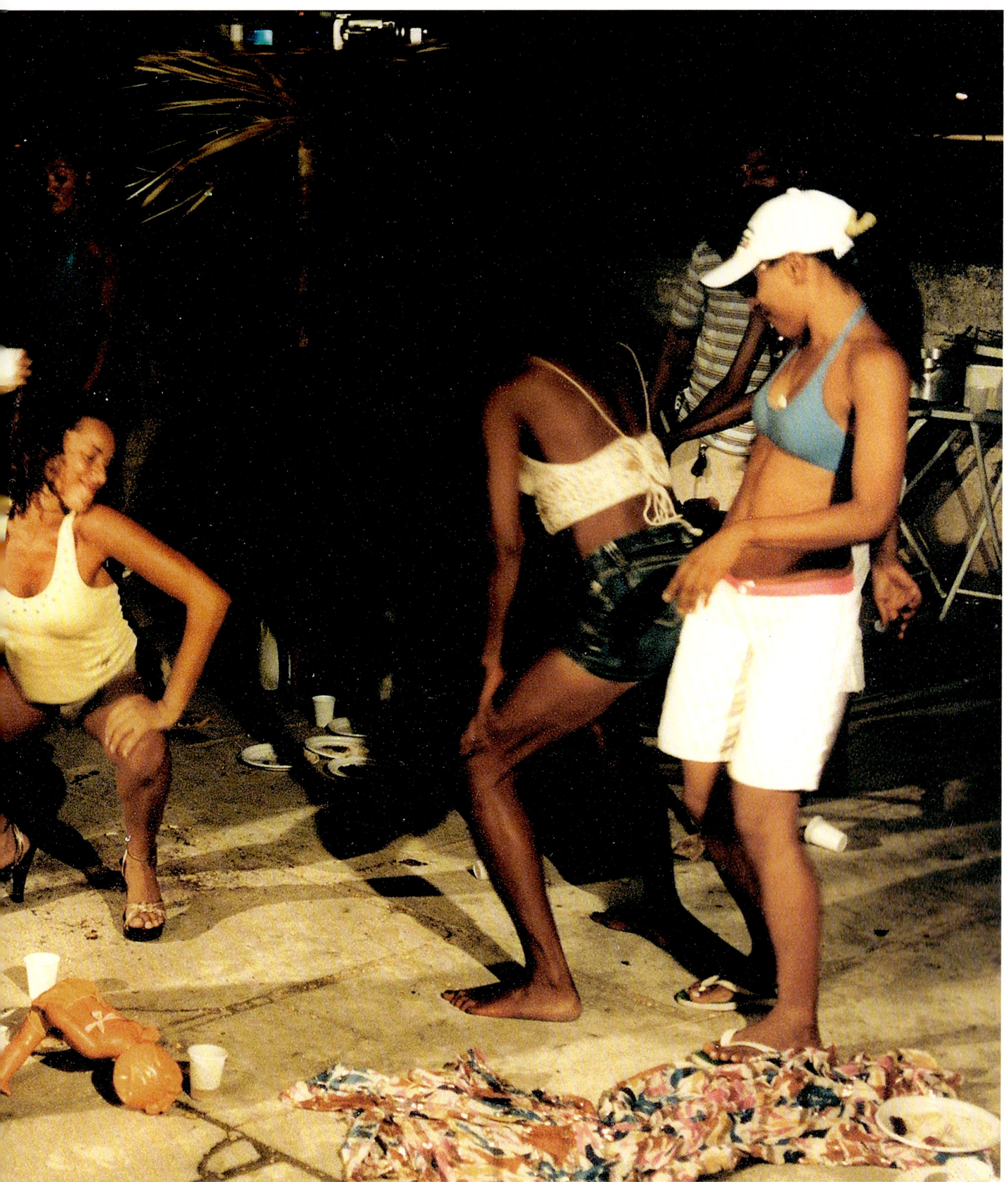

Livro
Book

The Other and the culture of the Other have always been—and always will be—officially recognized through the mere exercise of perception on the part of those who legitimize them and turn them into historical fact. The single-channel video *Book* shows that, when ghettoized, this Other and its culture are misunderstood, deliberately reduced to the exotic. Exoticism is the product of a manipulated or incomplete alterity.

→ See *Do Universo do Baile/Of the Universe of the Ball*, 2008, p. 95
• Single-channel video installation
  Loop, 5:30

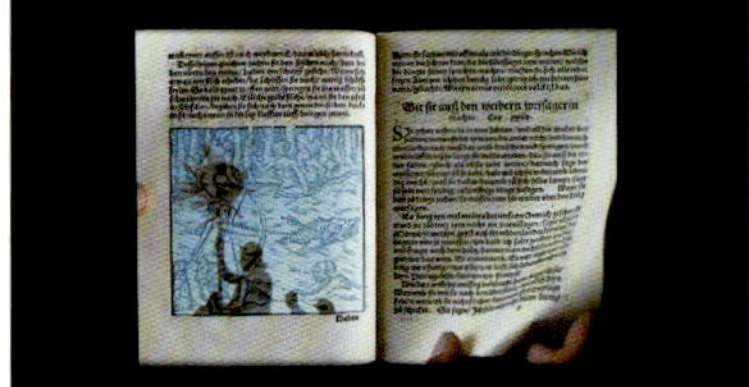

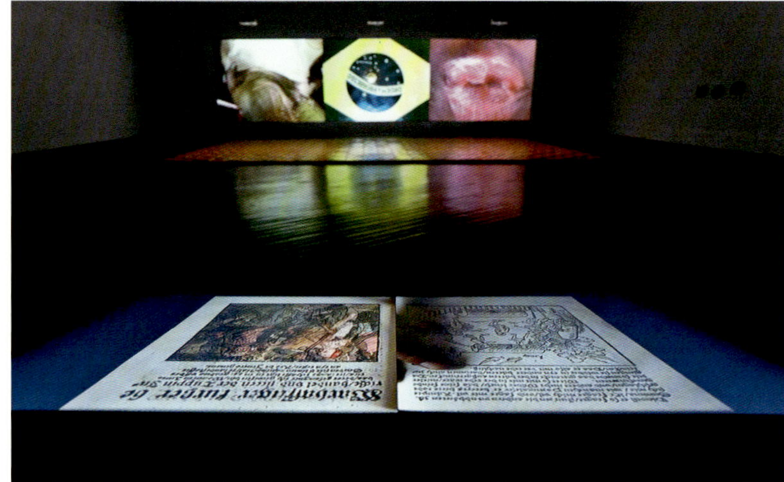

Xilogravuras
Woodcuts

Five of the original woodcuts from chapter 29 of volume 2 of Hans Staden's *True History* show Indians preparing a cannibalistic feast. These images were allegorically re-enacted by funk dancers and photographed during a rooftop barbeque in Santa Marta in Rio de Janeiro.

→ See *Do Universo do Baile/Of the Universe of the Ball*, 2008, p. 95
• Analog photographs printed on Kodak Endura paper
  160 cm × 135 cm × 10 cm each

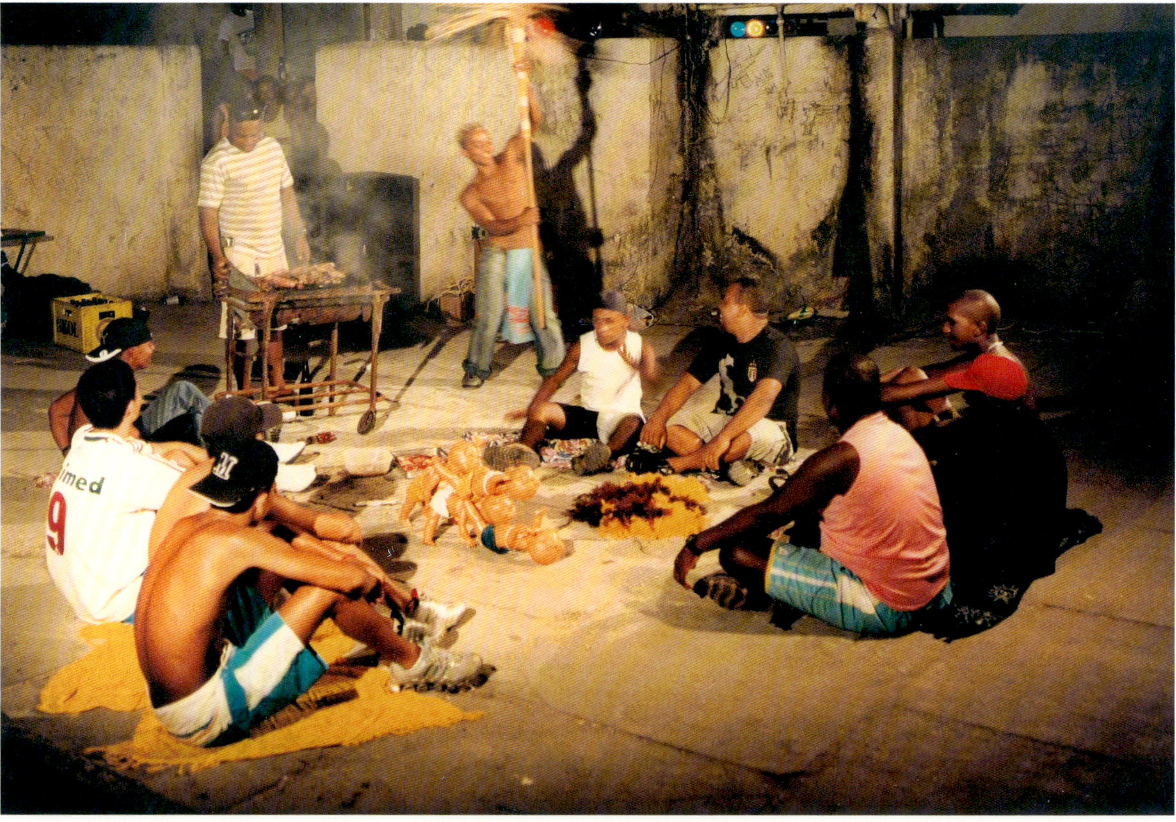

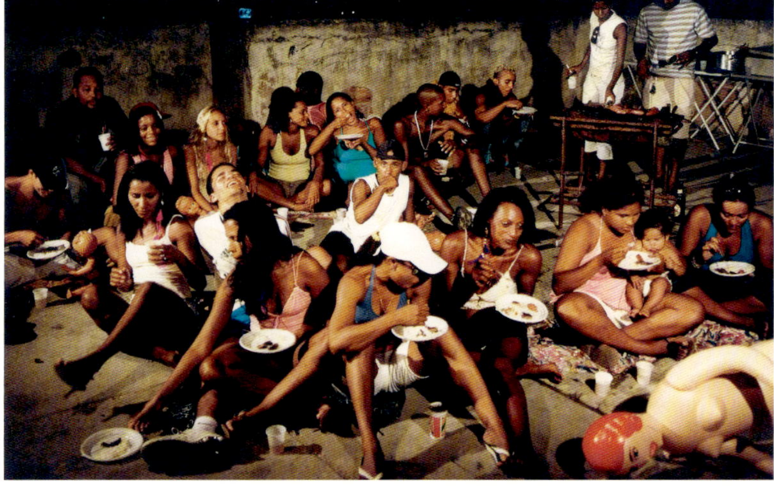

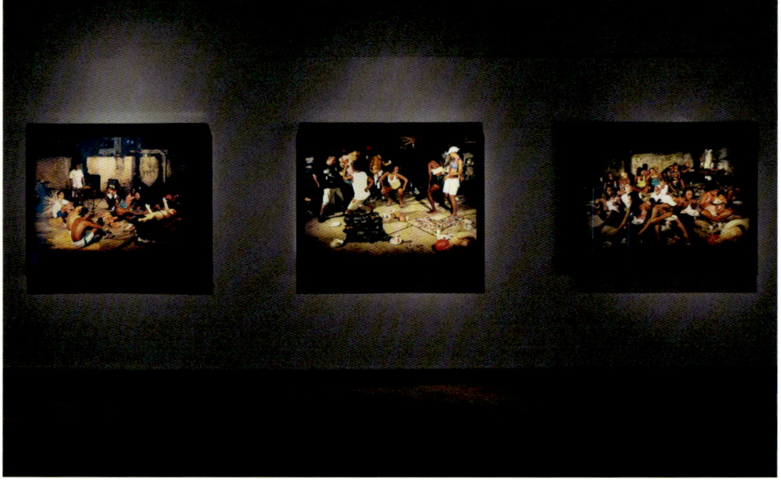

A Casa
The House

This work is an exploration of the self-portrait through video. Following the Other as the main focus of the piece, the artists multiply their own images in each of the five videos through the introduction of many *Mauricios* and various *Walters*, all recorded in everyday activities around the house in which the artists have lived and worked for over a decade. In this piece, the self is transformed into the sum of many others.

The visual repetition of the artists in each video removes the possibility of recognizing a single, real identity. The artists take us to the border of reality and fiction, without revealing which territory they operate in.

- Five-channel video installation on a plotter panel
  400 × 300 cm
  Loop, hall 1:40; studio 1:58;
  library 2:03; facade 3:06; pool 1:30

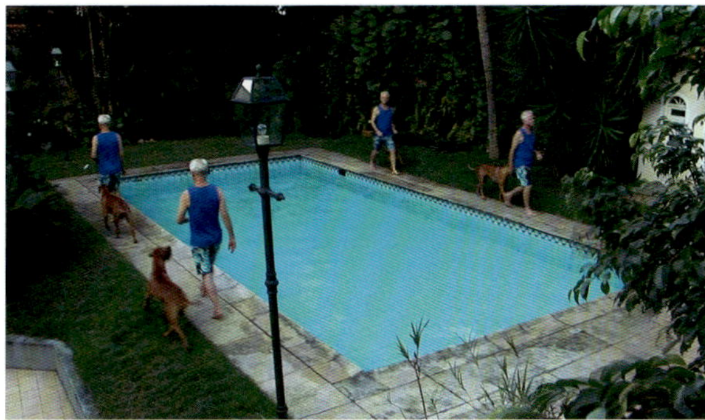

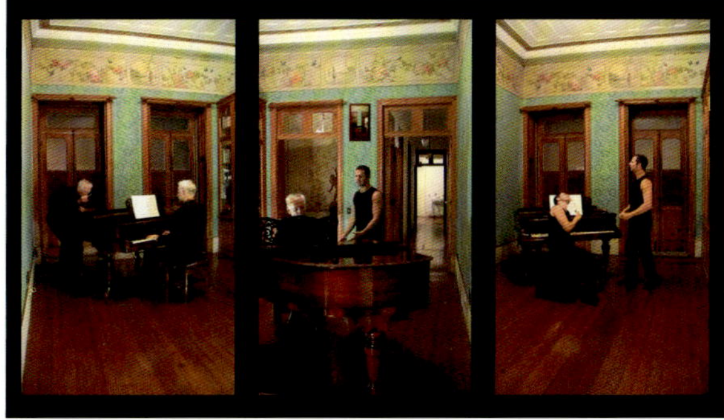

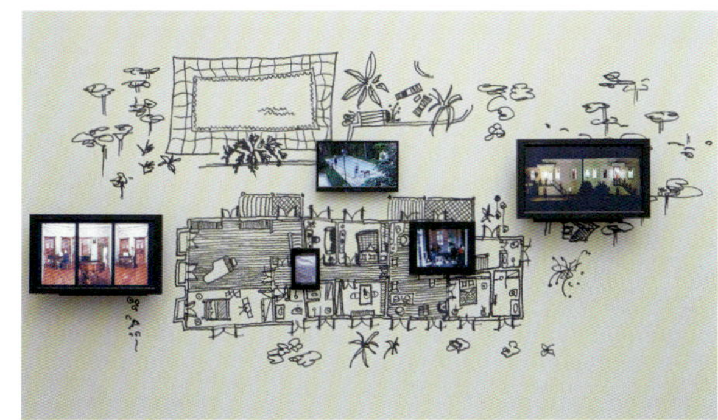

Funk Staden

Hans Staden was born in the Kassel region in the 16th century. He was shipwrecked and washed up on the coast of what would soon be named Brazil, where he was held captive by the Tupinambá Indians for two years. He later published *True History*, an illustrated account of this adventures, which became largely responsible for establishing an image of the tropics as infested by savage cannibals in the European consciousness, fueling a cliché that would be used to legitimize violent colonization. Dias & Riedweg re-enact this universe within the aesthetics of *funk carioca*, a genuinely contemporary cultural expression from the Rio favelas, and present it in a video installation in which three screens are alternated with three mirrored surfaces, thus recreating an octagonal arena that involves viewers in a kind of *anthropofagical pot*.

→ See *Do Universo do Baile/Of the Universe of the Ball*, 2008, p. 95
- 3-channel video installation
  Commissioned for documenta 12, 2007
  Loop, 14:32
  Dimensions variable

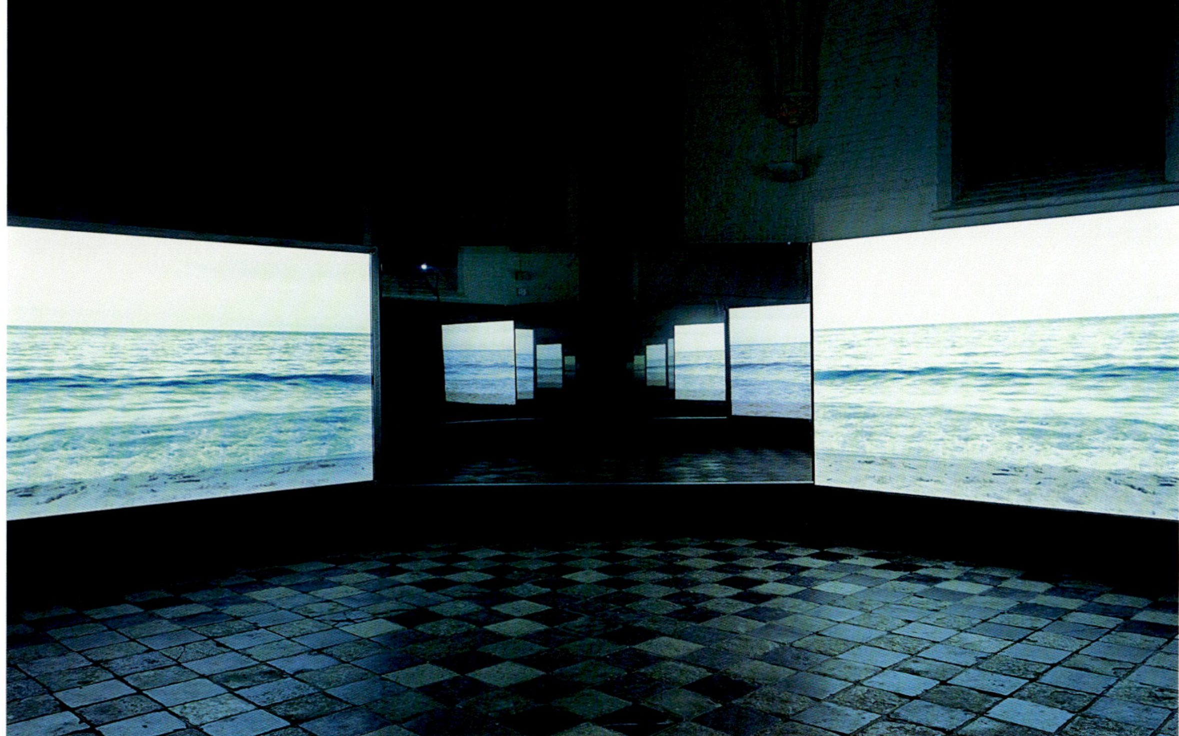

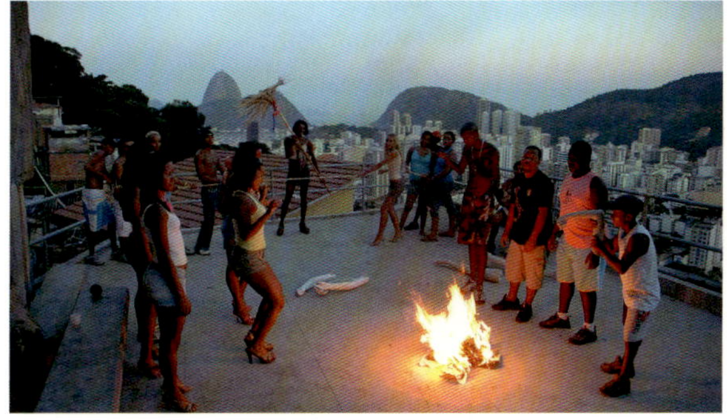

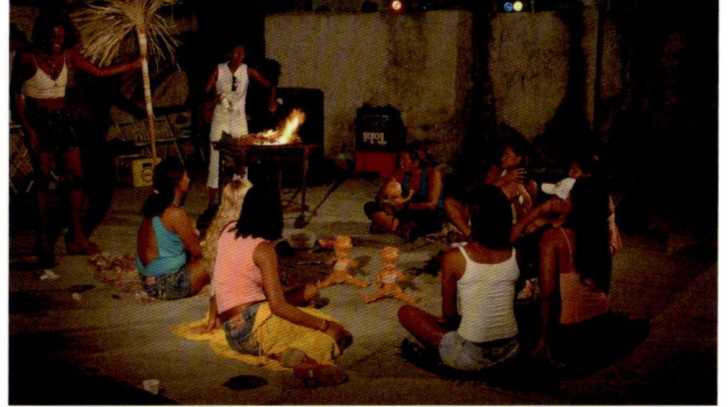

Não sou eu quem me navega
Not Me Who Navigates Myself

Overexposed shots of people dancing in a trance, wearing masks and costumes made of straw through the dark long night of a Candomblé ritual, become no more than impressive colorful fragments of bodies in very extended movements that characterize rituals of possession.

Candomblé is a religion of African origin practiced mainly in Brazil since the times of slavery and trade across the Atlantic Ocean. Its beliefs and practices involve ancient African languages and rituals of trance, possession, sacrifice, and offerings of the initiated by the *Orixás*, the pantheist Gods of the *Yorubá* traditions. To fall into a trance within *Candomblé* is somehow *to be the Other*, a possible form of alterity.

- Series of 10 photographs in D-Sec
  120 × 90 cm each

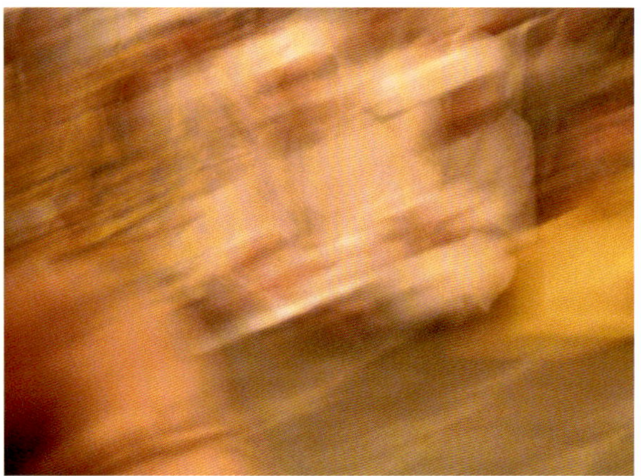
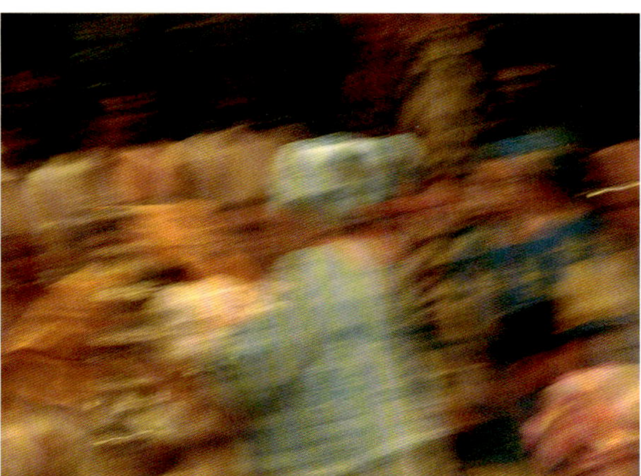

Malas para Marcel
Suitcases for Marcel

A series of 12 suitcases reconfigured as video-objects as a tribute to Marcel Duchamp's series *Boîte-en-valise* (1935–1940). These video-objects migrate from hand to hand, context to context, season to season through the city of Rio de Janeiro over the period of a year.

Viewers can recognize the city and the time of year in which the suitcases have traveled, but the videos are non-narrative. What counts here is the periphery of what is visible.

- 12 suitcases adapted with portable video players
  Loop
  Dimensions variable

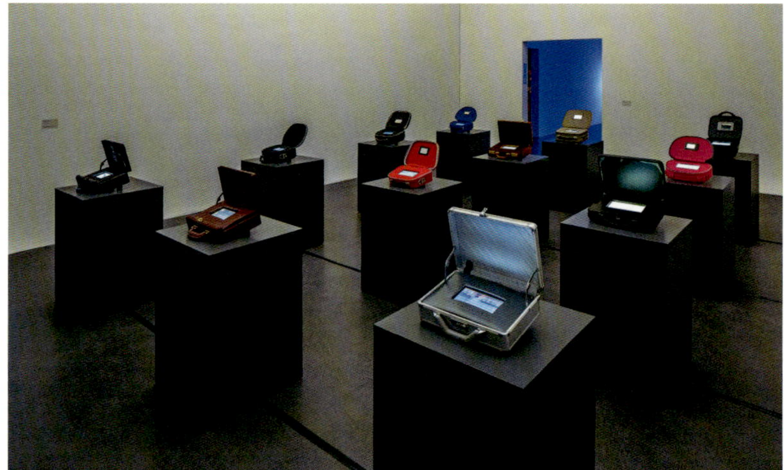

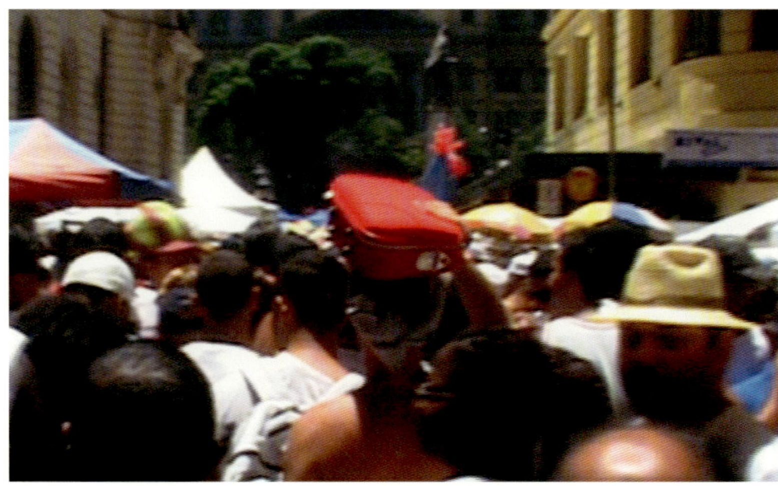
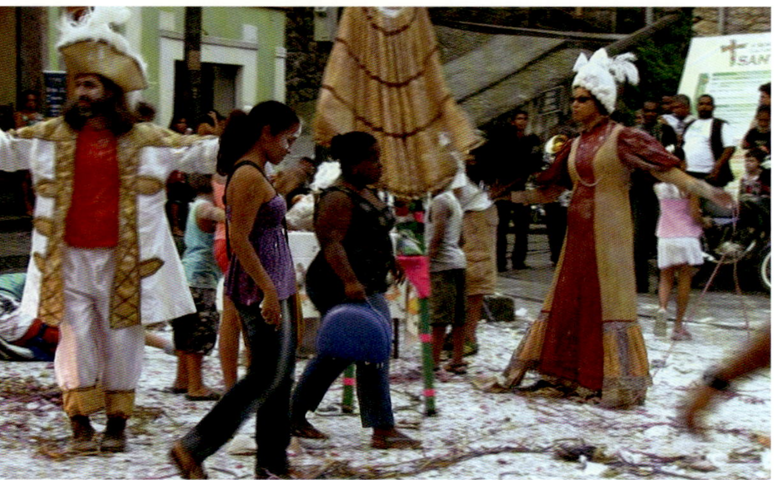

Promenade

Commissioned by Galeria Filomena Soares for Frieze *Outdoors*, this series of photographs were shot and displayed in Regent's Park in London. The lenticular technique allows a humorous sequence of a fictive crime staged and shot right on the spot where it was later exhibited. The work explores the possible relationship between fiction and everyday life in public space.

- Lenticular photographs on outdoor panels
  130 × 110 cm each

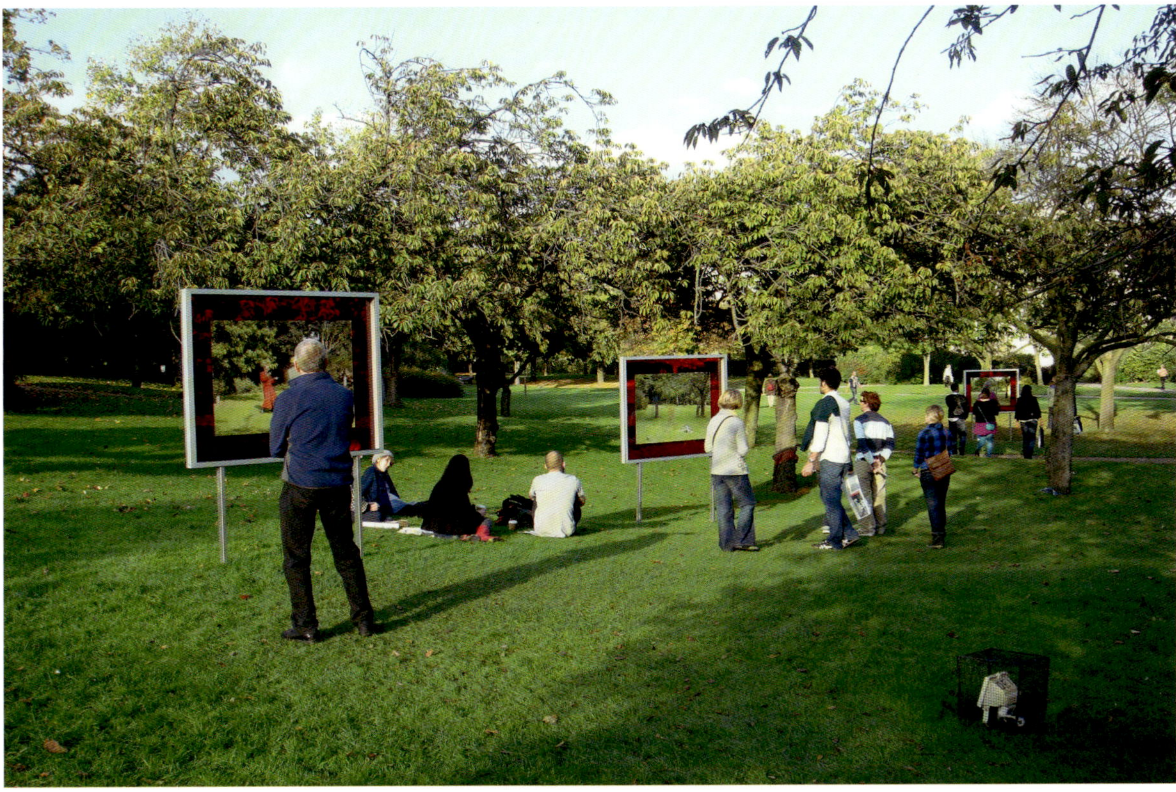

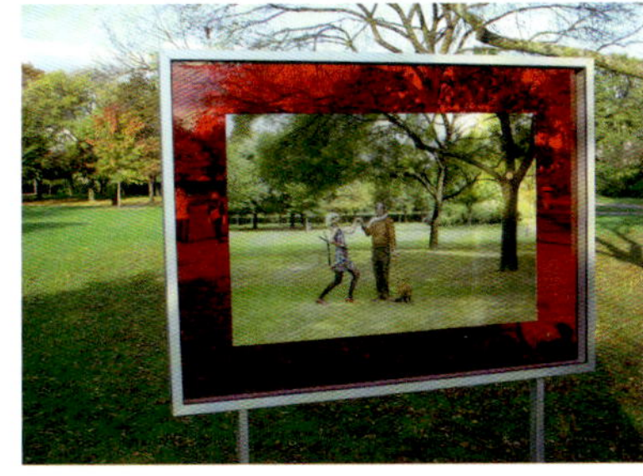

Juksa

Commissioned by Maaretta Jaukkuri for the Lofoten International Art Festival, *Juksa* shows three different moments in the lives of three people on the tiny island of Fugløya off the Norwegian coast, almost at the North Pole. The artists asked the same questions that were posed by Norwegian TV in 1976 to the same three people: Berentine I., Bjorn P., and Hanne T., workers in the fishing industry that has slowly died out in this region. Accompanying the video's first screening, the singer Marianne Schuppe sang the aria *The Plaint* by Henry Purcell (1659–1695) a cappella to the three participants on the sands of Sørfugløya. This scene was later integrated to the final version of the work.

Using archive images from Norwegian TV as a starting point, and having encountered these three people three decades later on this beautiful but now uninhabited island, Dias & Riedweg provoke universal reflections about time, and about aging both of people and of places. The Viking word "Juksa" refers to the oldest way of fishing in the world.

- 2-channel video installation with three chairs,
  the bottom image shows the installation indoors
  Loop, 29:40
  Dimensions variable

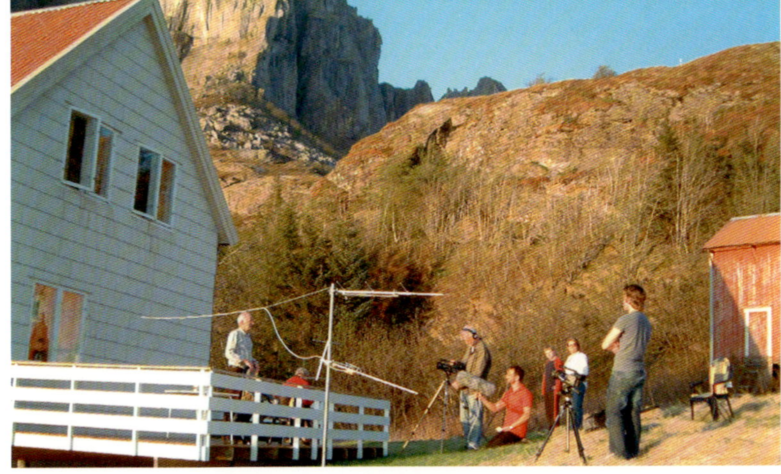

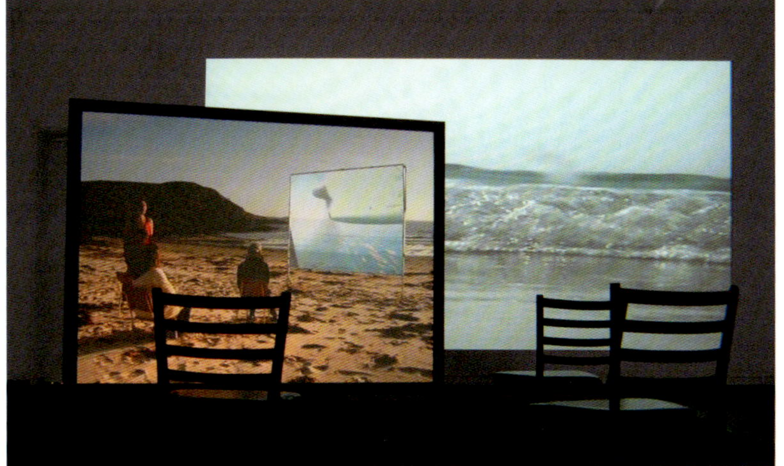

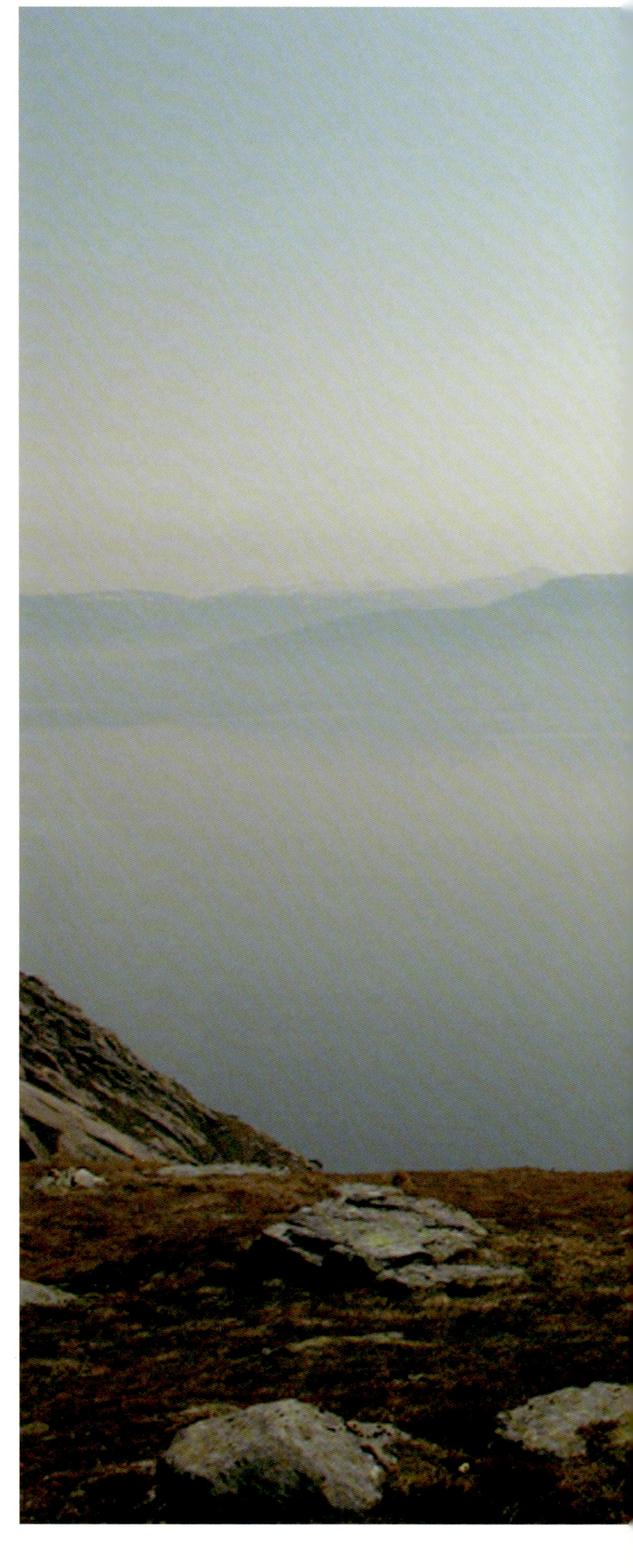

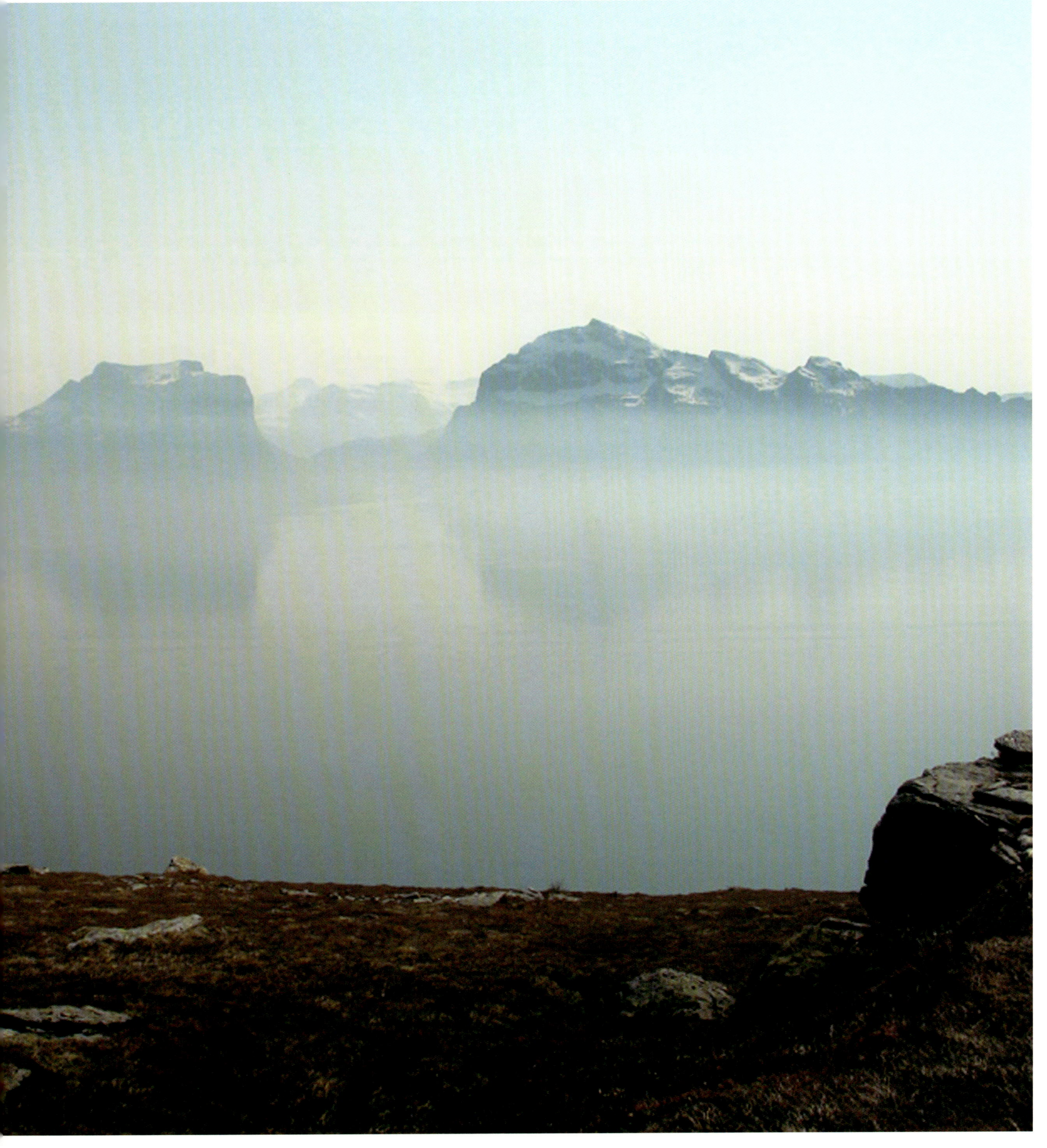

Labeur
Labour

Labour focuses on whose hands are in fact sewing pieces of haute-couture, preparing gourmet cuisine, and doing much of the work which invisibly contributes so much to the international lifestyle of contemporary Paris.

Commissioned by *Festival d'Automne à Paris* for the collection of the *Fonds régional d'art contemporain* – FRAC Ile de France, Dias & Riedweg reintegrated archive material from the Institut national d'audiovisuel on the workers' strikes of the 1960s and 1970s, including Sartre's activist speech to the workers; their own cameras focus on close-up shots of laboring hands. The piece reveals the very high percentage of immigrant people whose lives are woven into the social history of France.

- 2-channel video installation
  Loop, 21:14
  Dimensions variable

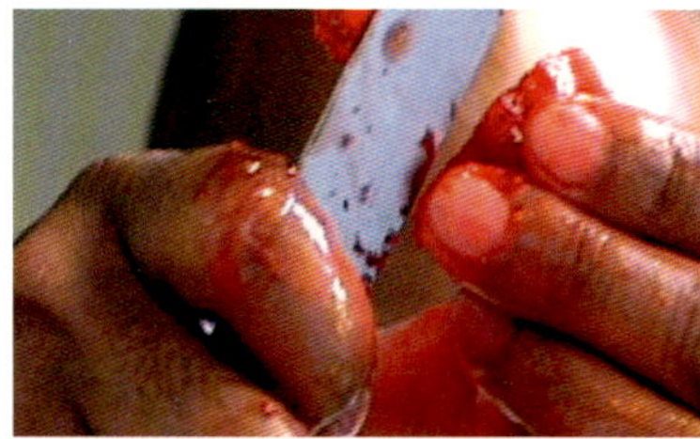
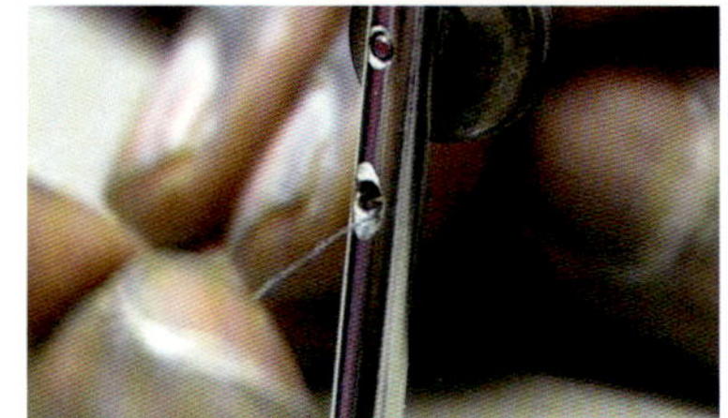
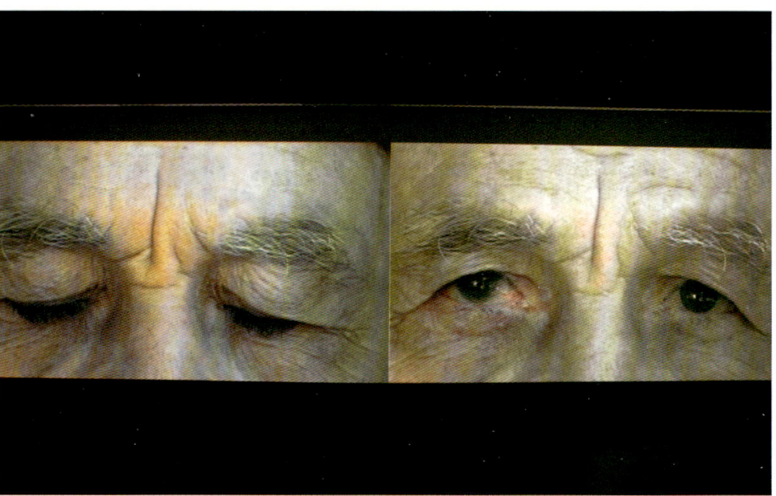

Parcours

Using street furniture as the starting point of their game, youngsters are seen trying to walk while balancing on the iron railings on the sidewalks of Paris–the objective being to keep their balance for as long as possible. Placed on the iron railings, the video camera is at foot level with the protagonists, whose feet come closer and closer until they invariably fall.

Created on the occasion of the artists' solo show at Le Plateau in Paris, the aim was to involve teenagers from the school opposite the exhibition venue. This piece metaphorically evokes the risks and challenges in growing up, as well as the often depreciated presence of youth in urban contexts. Curiously, *"parcours"* also became the name of a specific sport training discipline, developed from military obstacle course training, and popular among young people today.

- Video; series of outdoor photographs
  Loop, 5:34
  Dimensions variable

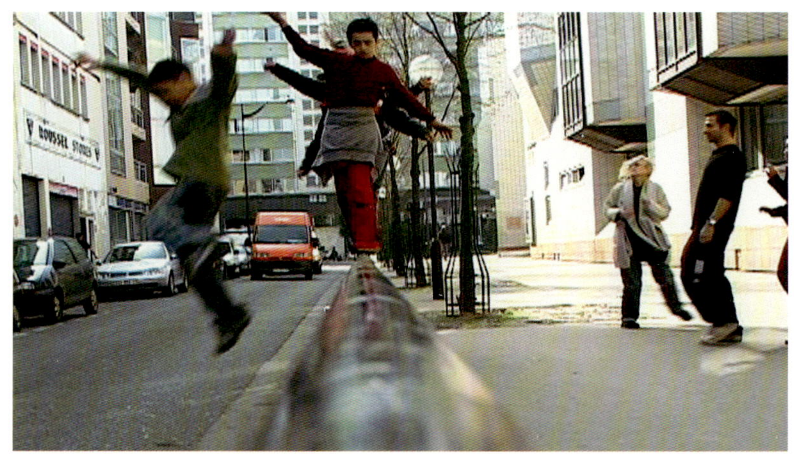

Flesh (Mustafa's Feast & Slaughter house)

Flesh is a two-channel video installation showing two videos. The first one, *Mustafa's Feast*, shows a three year-old boy, using only gestures to recount how his Egyptian father will decapitate and quarter a lamb following the religious tradition of the *Bayram*. The second video, *Slaughterhouse*, documents automated slaughtering in the Swiss food industry, where the animals are killed and hung in rows according to Western standards, recreating another sort of ritual. The videos are projected, facing one another, on phosphorescent boards.

The consumption of flesh appears directly related to cultural and economic backgrounds in this work. The *Bayram* is a very popular religious holiday in Islamic countries, and relates to the episode of the Old Testament, and therefore to the Christian and Jewish religions as well, in which Abraham, who is supposed to sacrifice his oldest son in accordance with tradition, receives permission from an angel to kill a lamb instead of his beloved child.

- 2-channel video installation
  Loop, 6:42
  Dimensions variable

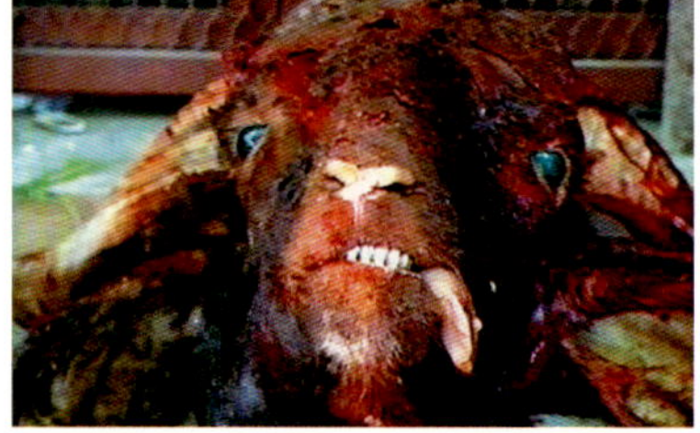
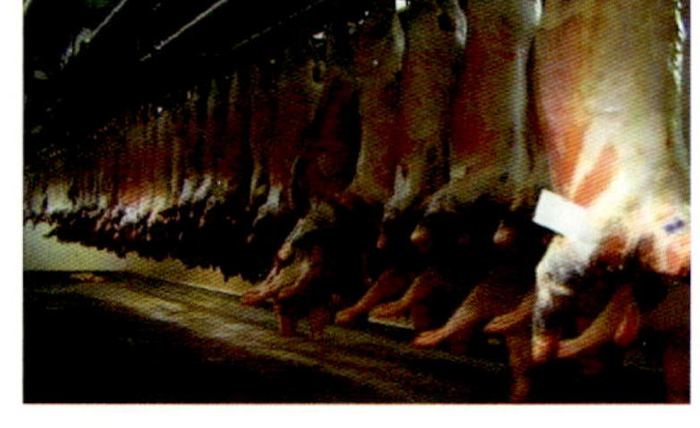
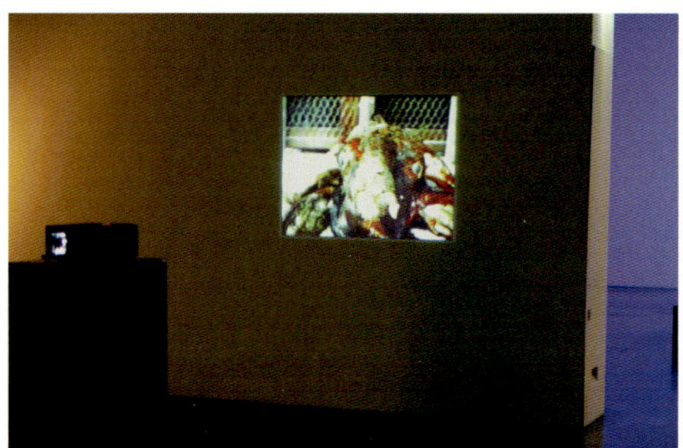
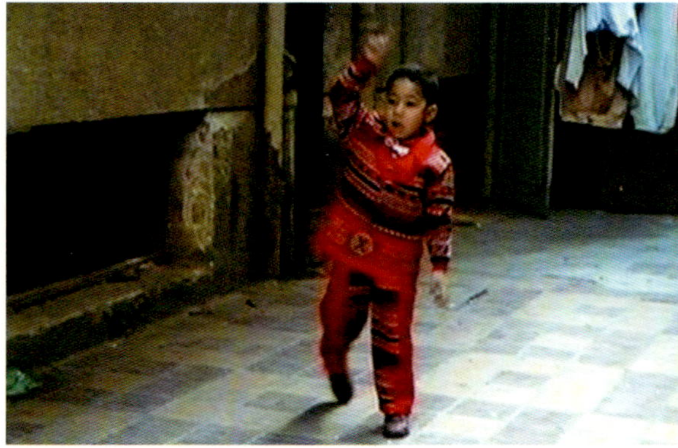

David & Gustav

An imaginary dialogue takes place between the artists David Medalla and Gustav Metzger, who share many similarities and an artistic reputation, but who relate to their histories and identities in very different ways.

David Medalla, a renowned Filipino poet and visual artist based in London since the 1960s, constructs his identity as a cosmopolitan citizen of the world, one who chooses to live outside his native country. By contrast, the equally famous Gustav Metzger, a modernist painter and survivor of a concentration camp, also resident in London, sees himself as existing in permanent exile. The piece highlights the contrasts between different but radical perspectives that significantly affect the construction of identity and the production of distinct and brilliant artworks.

- Video
  Loop, 13:28

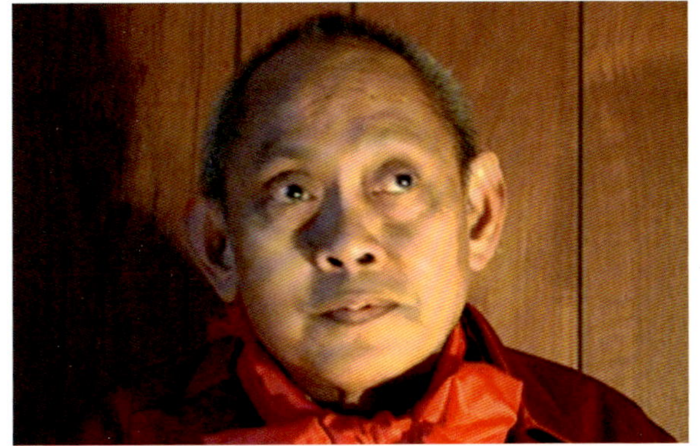
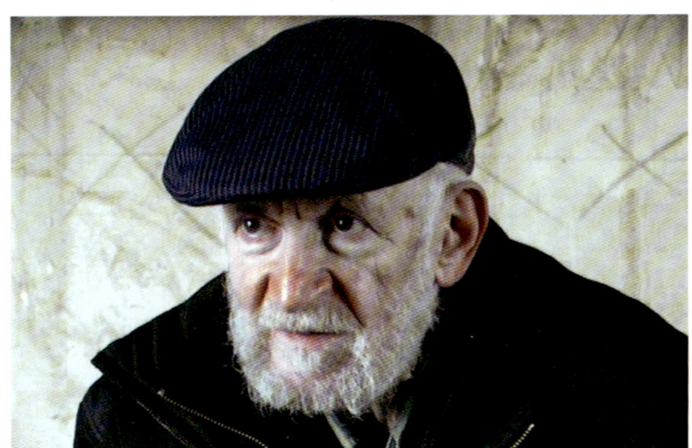

Throw

Powerful images evoked by the slow-motion effect of people throwing objects directly at the camera lens were later projected on a huge scale. Dias & Riedweg combined these with edited archive images in black and white of diverse political demonstrations that had taken place in Finland during the 20th century. The images were projected for the first time on the facade of Kiasma, the Museum of contemporary art in Helsinki.

After Pieter Sloterdijk in *Sphere III* (2004), the act of throwing something marks a significant development in the history of *Homo Sapiens*. When primitive men learnt to throw things, they initiated the idea of communication over distance. Before the existence of language, in order to communicate with others without physically moving, objects were thrown to attract their attention. In fact, throwing is still a social tool of communication and protest.

- Video installation
  Loop, 39:19

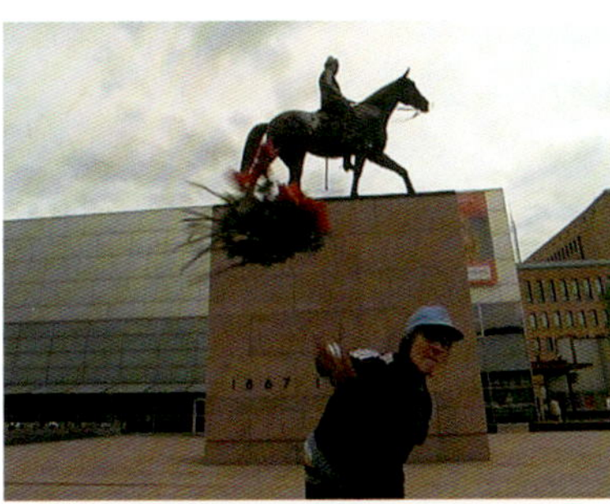
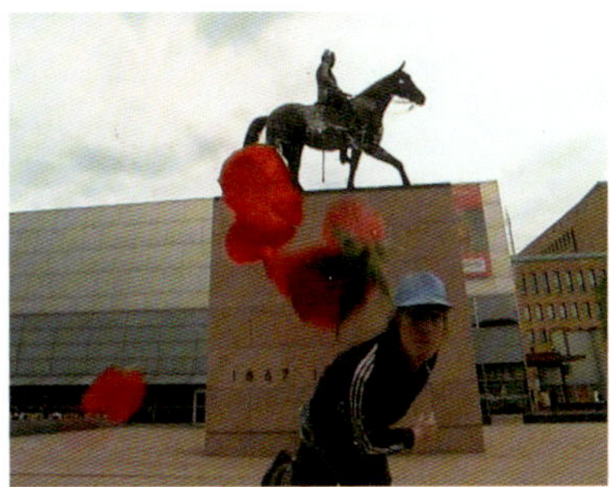
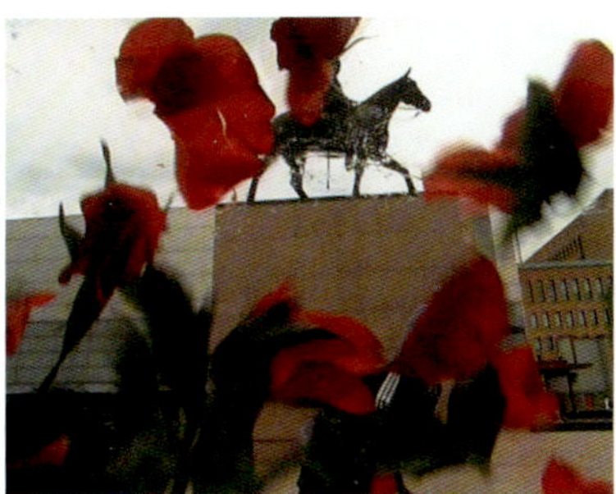
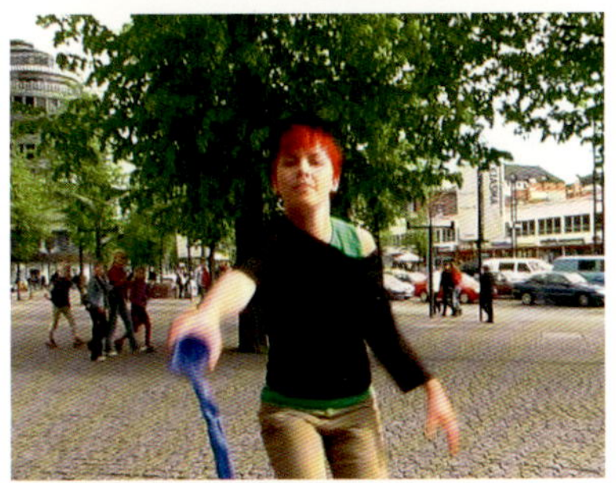
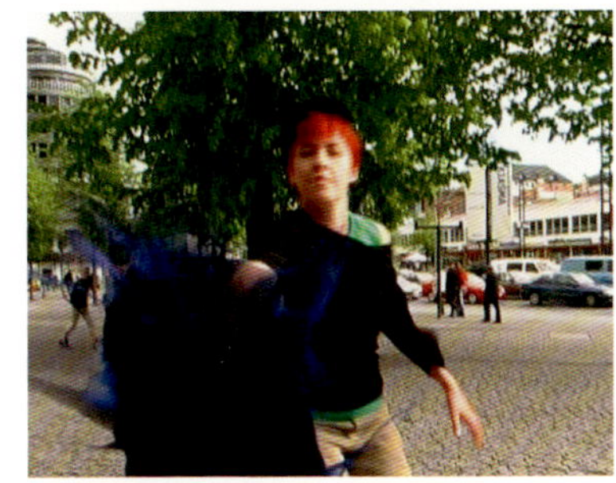
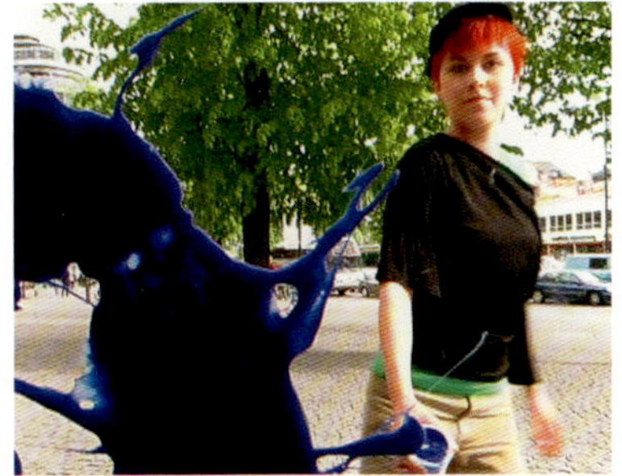
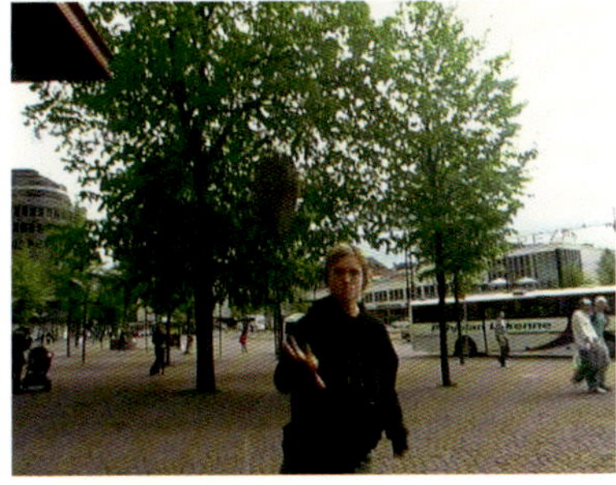
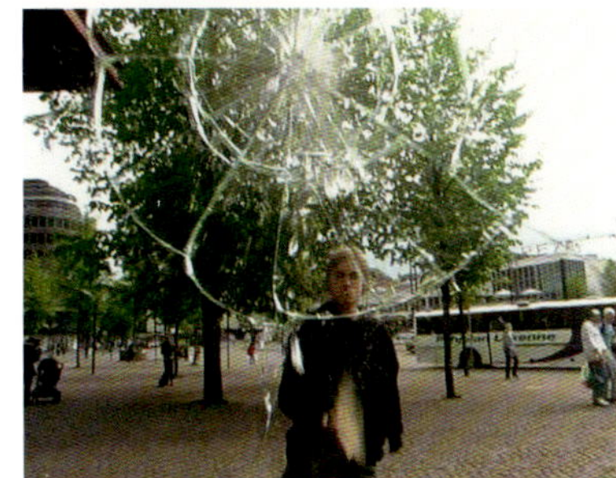
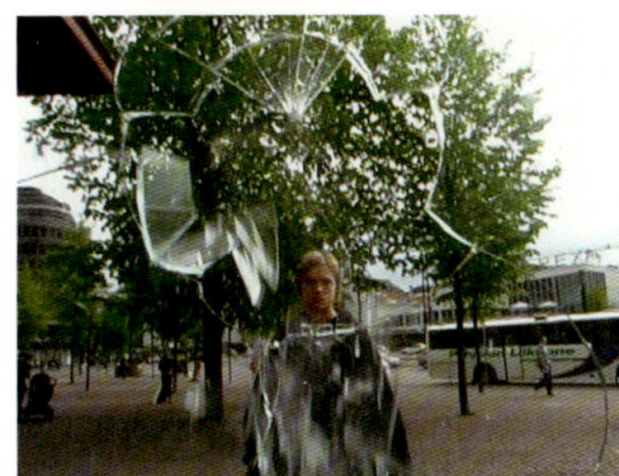

Sugar Seekers

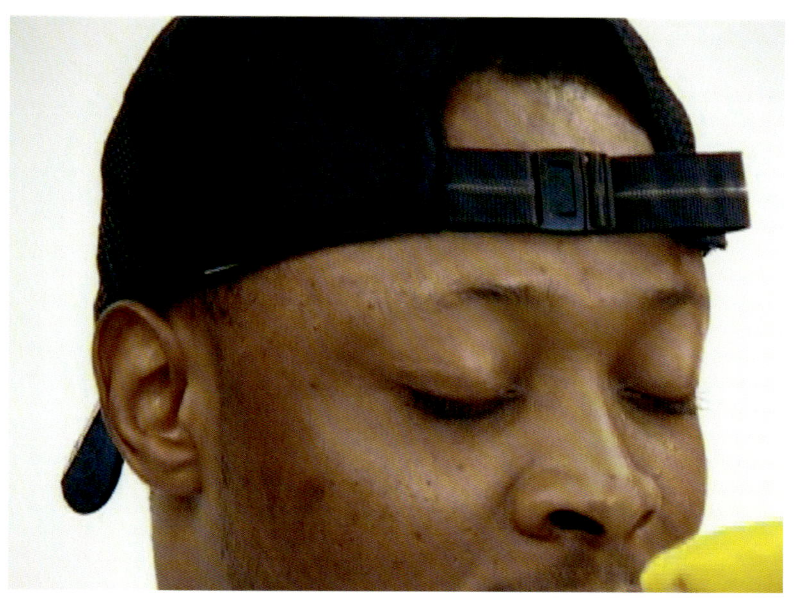

The nine participants held cameras at all times. Evoking memories through sensorial workshops, collating documentary-style footage of group discussions, interviewing other migrants, and compiling image archives from Internet word searches, they worked intensely with the artists in the execution of every step of the project. The resulting 4-channel installation does not set out to document stories; rather it opens up new definitions of the language of migration. The viewer adds a further layer of interpretive possibilities when they interact with the work: a touch command triggered by key words activates a new set of images and changes the narrative flow of the video. *Sugar Seekers* investigates the ways in which the global economy and local politics relate to each other and how they do not. The piece offers a broader comprehension of immigration as an urgent human right beyond the dominance of the current capitalist global economy.

Commissioned by FACT and Tate Liverpool for the 4th Liverpool International Biennial, *Sugar Seekers* continues the artists' ongoing exploration of the rights of the individual within the arena of immigration and emigration. The starting point of these investigations is Liverpool, a city that has historically played an important role in the global pattern of migration. The young people with whom Dias & Riedweg created *Sugar Seekers* are at different stages in the lengthy asylum-seeking process that categorizes them in terms of risk; their personal desires and needs for a new life are negated within this system. Only an individual who has economic and political power can achieve the degree of freedom necessary to migrate at will: the desire to travel is not itself a humanitarian right.

- Public art project and 5-channel interactive video installation
  Dimensions variable

Câmera Foliã
Sambing Camera

Sambing Camera is a four-channel video installation with eight audio channels. Dias & Riedweg built a "camera-object" and filmed several streets of Rio de Janeiro during the carnival: four cameras were set onto a rotating structure, which was lifted above the heads of the crowd. This object turned and filmed the carnival without the controlling presence of the artists' eye, as they could not look through the cameras' viewfinders. The movement of the cameras echoed the carnival dancers around them, thus recording the festival in the same way as the samba dancers see it from the floats.

The installation presents four large-scale rear-projection screens that envelop the viewers in the surrounding panorama of the images and sounds of Rio's carnival. The continuous movement of the images recreates a very physical experience of the subject. Although all images here are actually documentary in nature, the uncontrolled manipulation of the rotating camera distorts them, and the resulting impression of vibrant, colorful abstraction expands the boundaries between documentary and fiction.

- 4-channel video installation
  Loop, 18:54

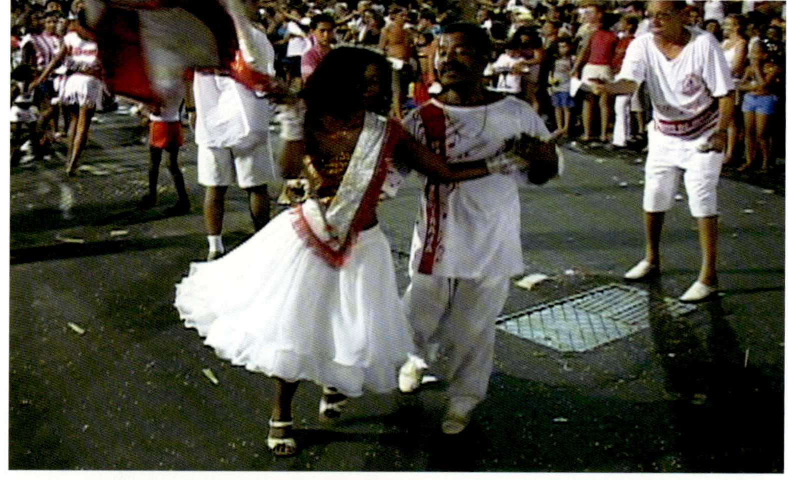

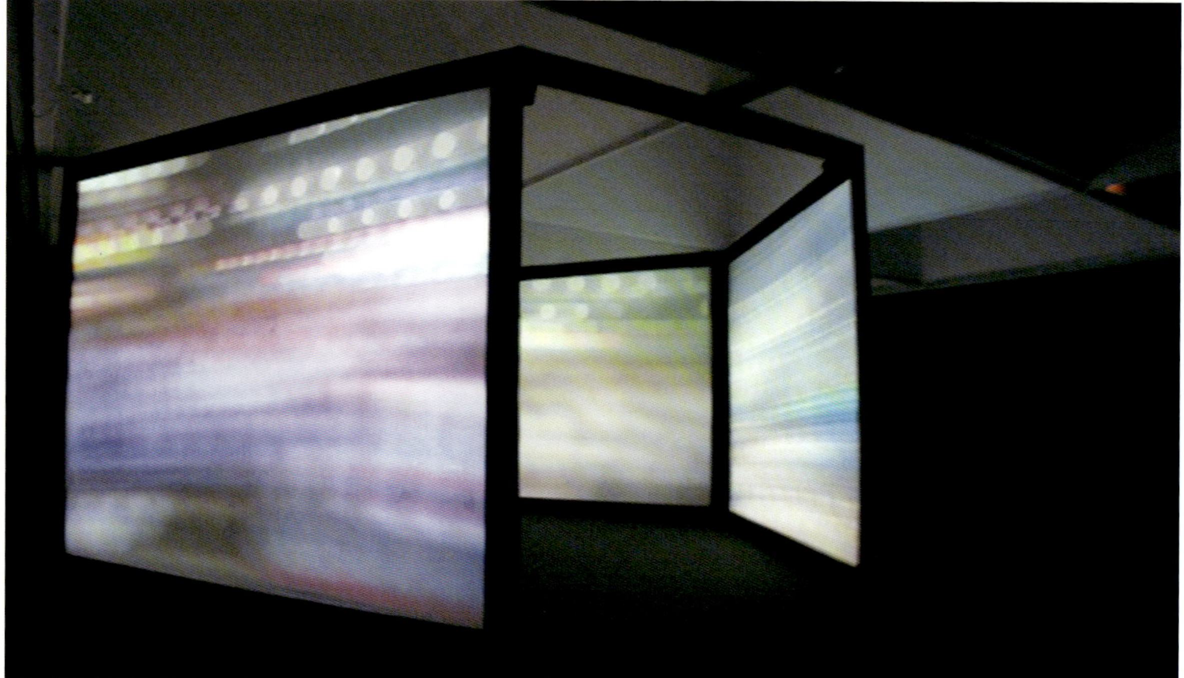

Voracidad Maxima
Maximal Voracity

Eleven young men, all sex workers in the city of Barcelona, were filmed by two cameras placed between two parallel mirrors on a double bed in a hotel room. Talking one at a time with the artists, who were both dressed in the same minimal clothing, the conversations assumed an intimate tone. Molded latex masks of each of the artists' faces covered the hustlers' faces and hid their true identities throughout each conversation. The parallel mirrors multiplied the faces–both the artist's face and that of the hustler with his face covered with a mask–assigning a unique visual identity to interviewer and interviewee, who could only be differentiated by their speech. The first shot in the installation shows the eleven men lying naked on the white letters of the words *Maximal Voracity* that have been painted on the street, waiting to be chosen by the audience in the final installation as if from a voyeuristic electronic sexual menu.

Commissioned by the Museum of Contemporary Art in Barcelona, Dias & Riedweg created a work inspired by Jean Genet's novel *Journal d'un voleur* (*The Theif's Journal*, 1949), which was writen in the Barrio Gótico where the museum is now sited. Focusing on gay male sex workers, the piece explores the relationships between sexuality and the economy. The work investigates the motivations of both the sex workers and their clients, both in terms of financial needs and each individual's subjectivity in a non-moralistic, theatrical, and almost therapeutic approach.

- Public art project and video installation
  Loop, 70:19
  Dimensions variable

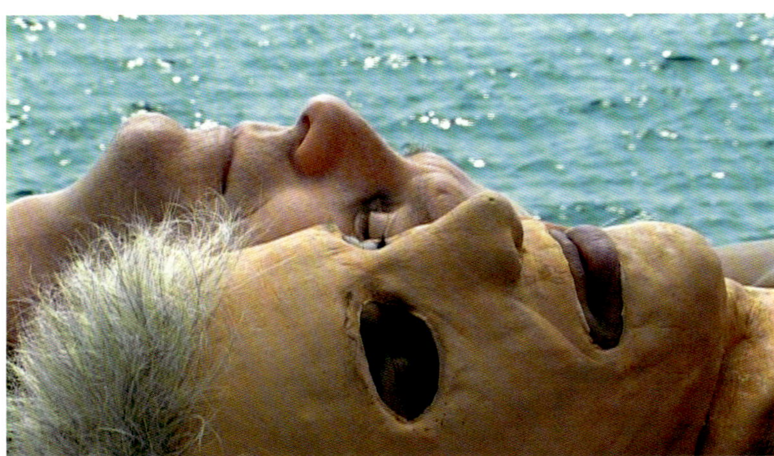

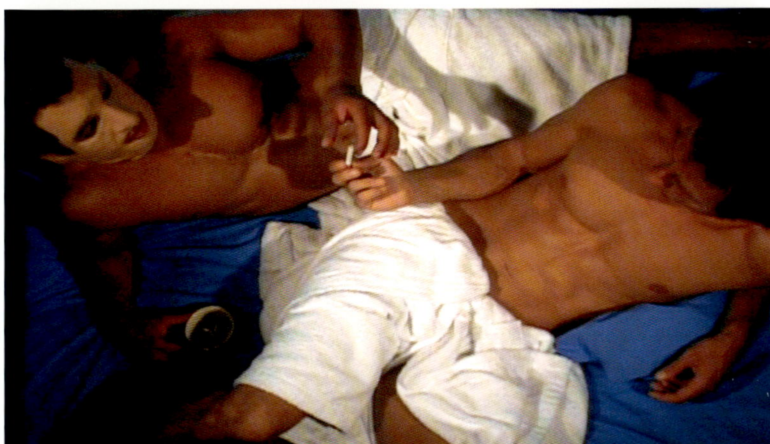

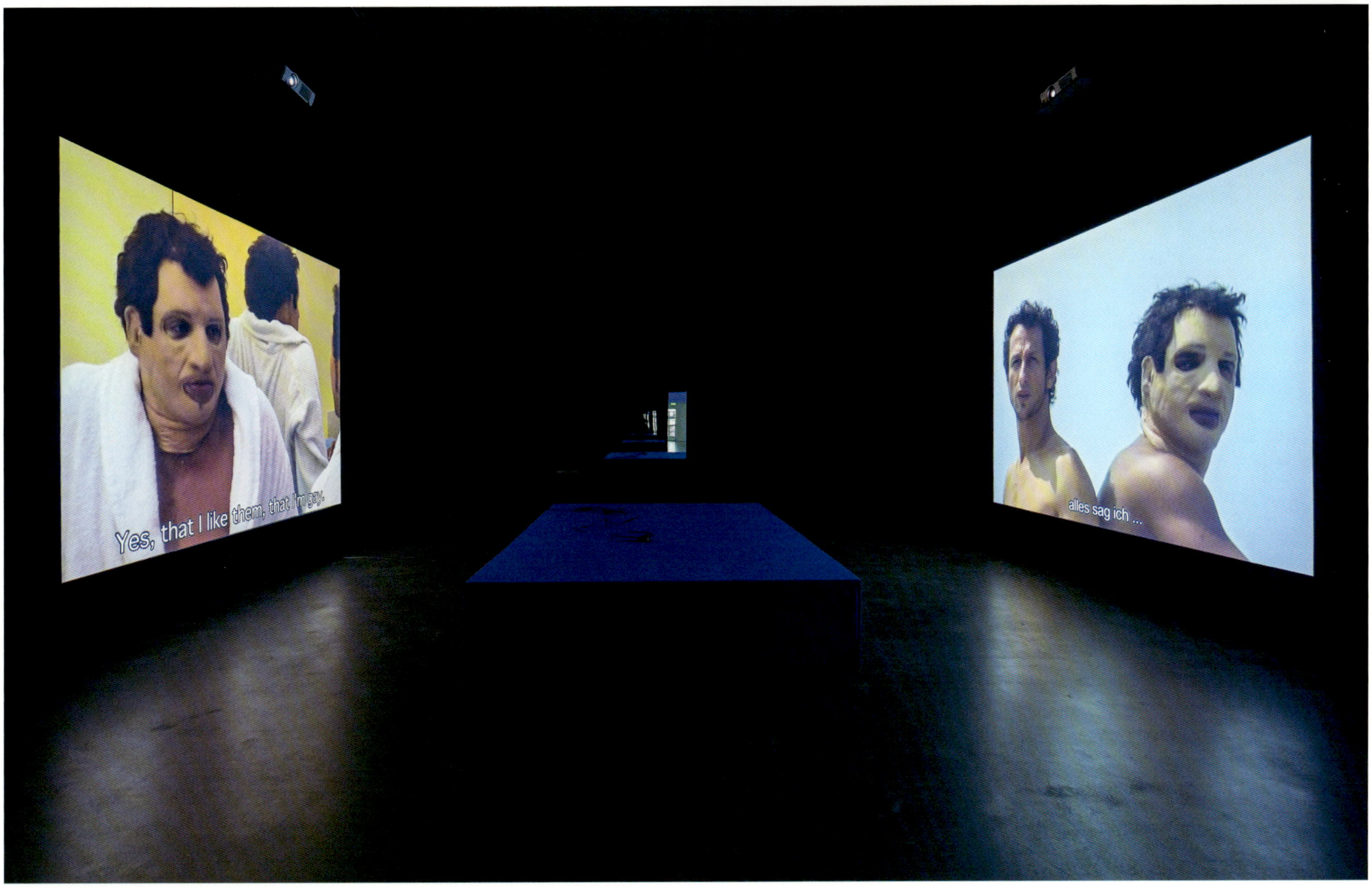

No estábamos hechos para los mismos caminos con el Grupo Recolectivo/ We Were Not Made for the Same Ways with the Group Recolectivo

Sixty performances that contradictorily expressed private situations in public space were realized by the Group Recolectivo, founded by Dias & Riedweg, on board the public bus system in Córdoba, Argentina, during rush hour. These actions varied from drying wet clothes, pealing potatoes, offering manicure and hair dressing services for free, to asking people to contribute to a dictionary of *urgencies.* The project took place in 40% of the city buses and was reported in the local media. Large posters with phrases written by Ionesco and Beckett were stuck on the sides of the buses, and placards with quotes from the Argentinean authorities were placed on sidewalks. The event took place during the country's severe economic crisis.

The idea of the bus (called *Colectivo* in Argentina) was born in Buenos Aires, as a mutation of the taxi, and became a social invention by this country in the early 1930s. In Córdoba, Argentina's second city, public transport was quite bad in 2002, and the main target of criticism and dissatisfaction among the local population. Dias & Riedweg founded a group of artists known as *Recolectivo*, who developed a series of performances and videos that took place on buses throughout the city. The form of the work itself materialized the political crisis and the fragile economic transformation that Argentina experienced over several years.

• Public art project and urban intervention

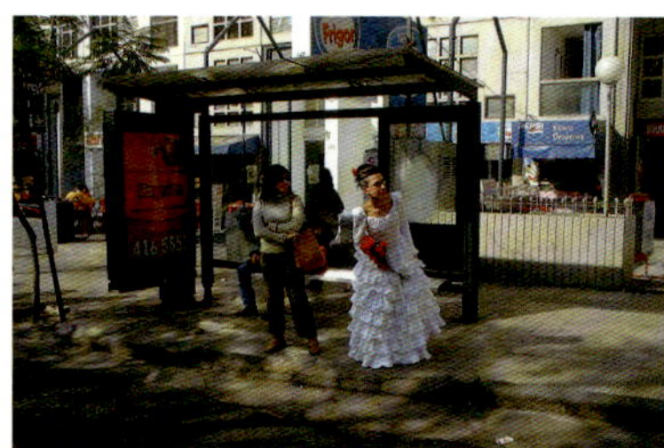

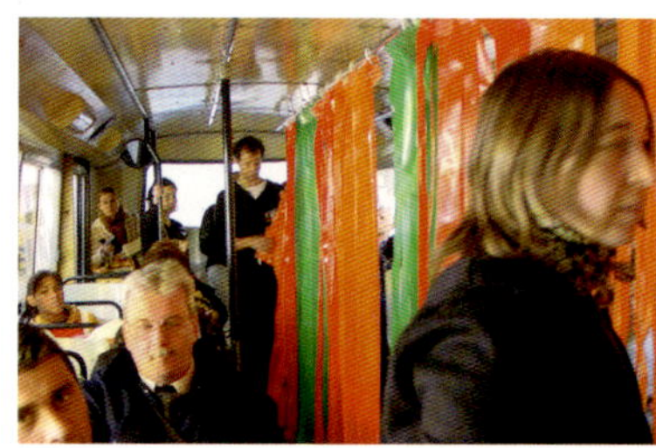

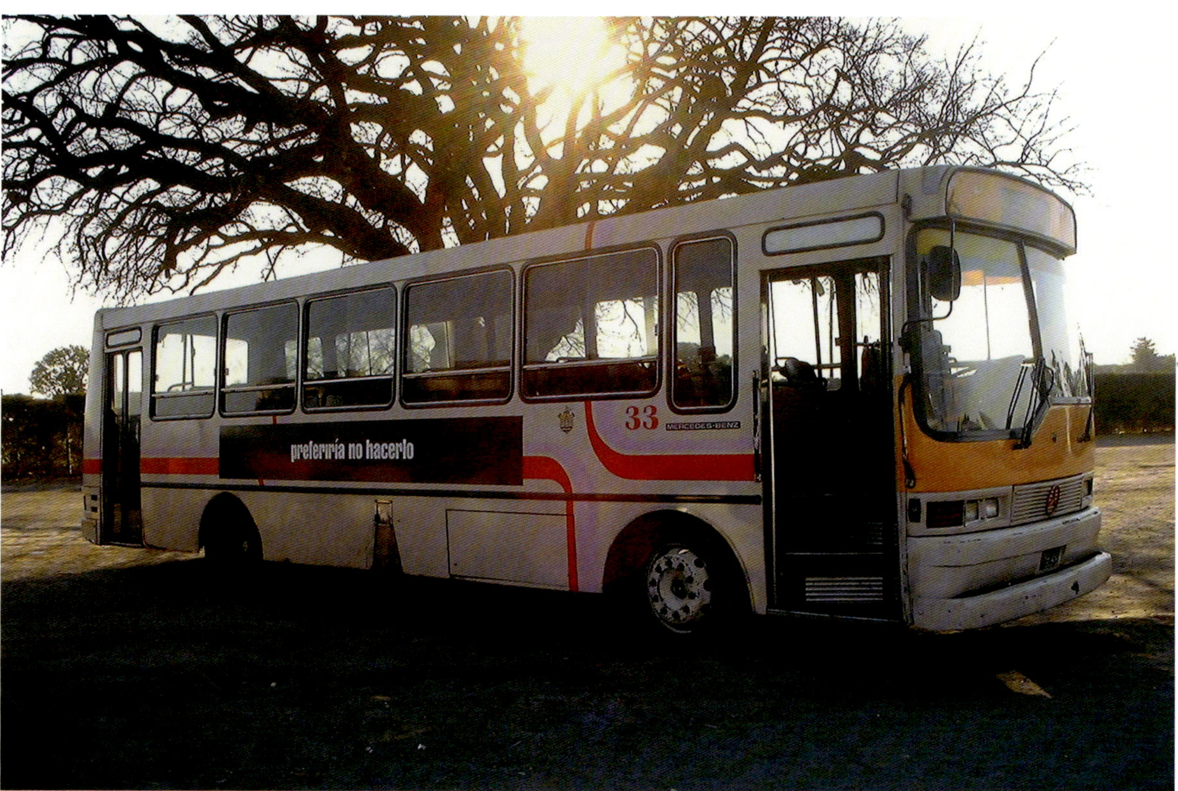

Deus é boca
God's Lips

The video installation proposes 44 definitions around the word "god," all of them using four letters, on four panels, such as God's Love, God's View, God's Fact, God's Half, God's Good, God's Cold, God's Fate, God's Game, God's Word, God's Lips, while documentary images show people frantically using their mouths and words to persuade others. Priests, politicians, teachers, judges, vendors, preachers … Videos of diverse people who make their living out of words are projected onto glass panels set together to form a glass case, in which a performer from time to time plays bingo live. The piece proposes the troubling and surprising possibility of the existence of God as a concept of persuasion above all other.

Faith moves mountains, but there are mountains of things that move faith. The manipulation of the individual need for faith by the diverse interests of power and politics has always resulted in the decay of individual belief and religious practices in society.

- 4-channel video installation on glass panels with a live performance in a glass case
  Loop, 16:00
  Dimensions variable

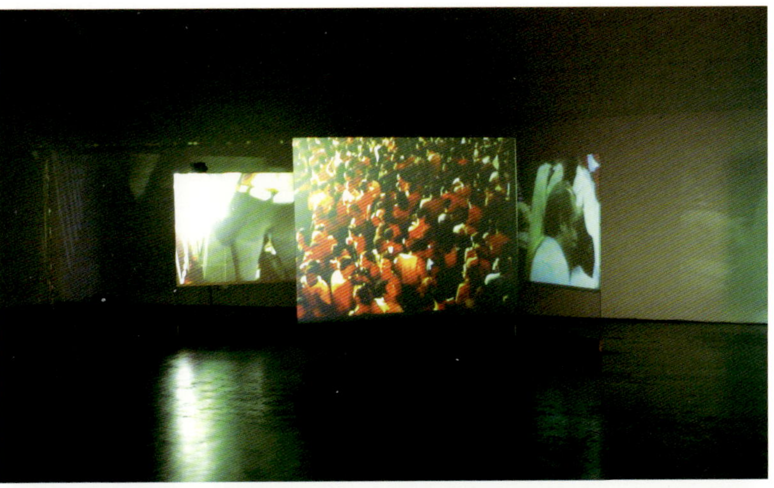

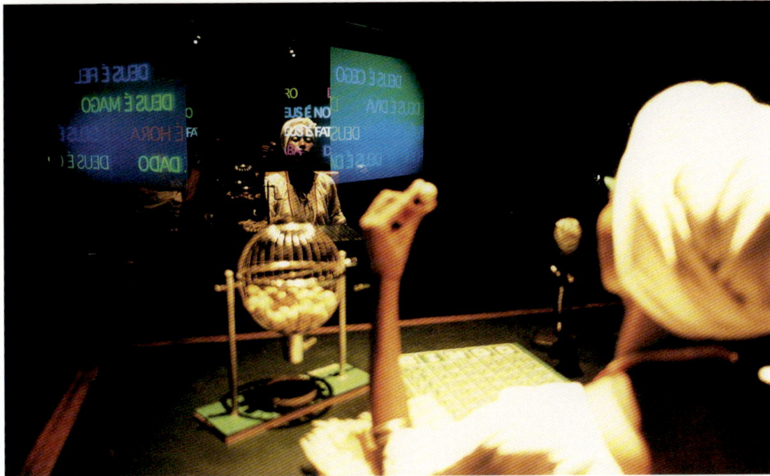

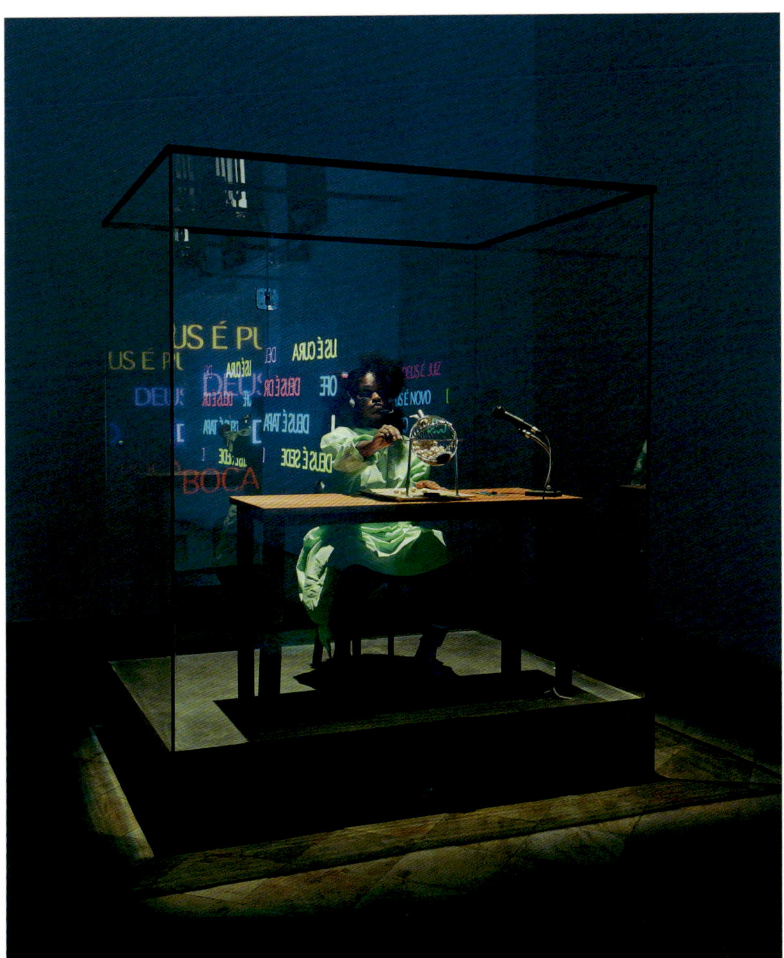

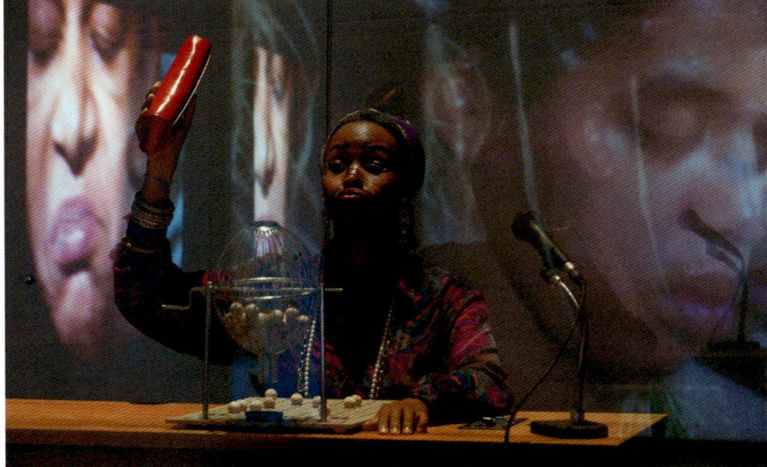

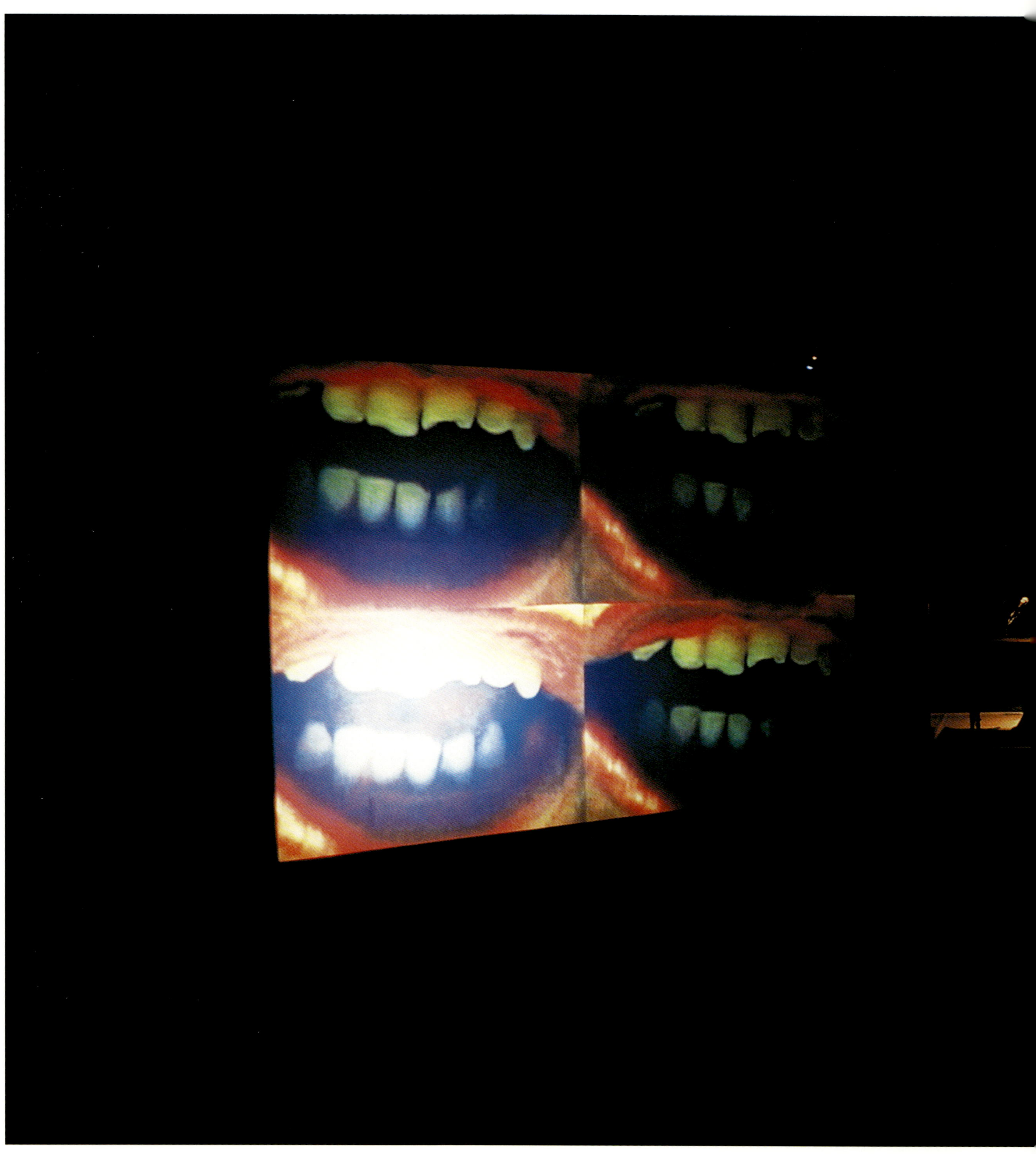

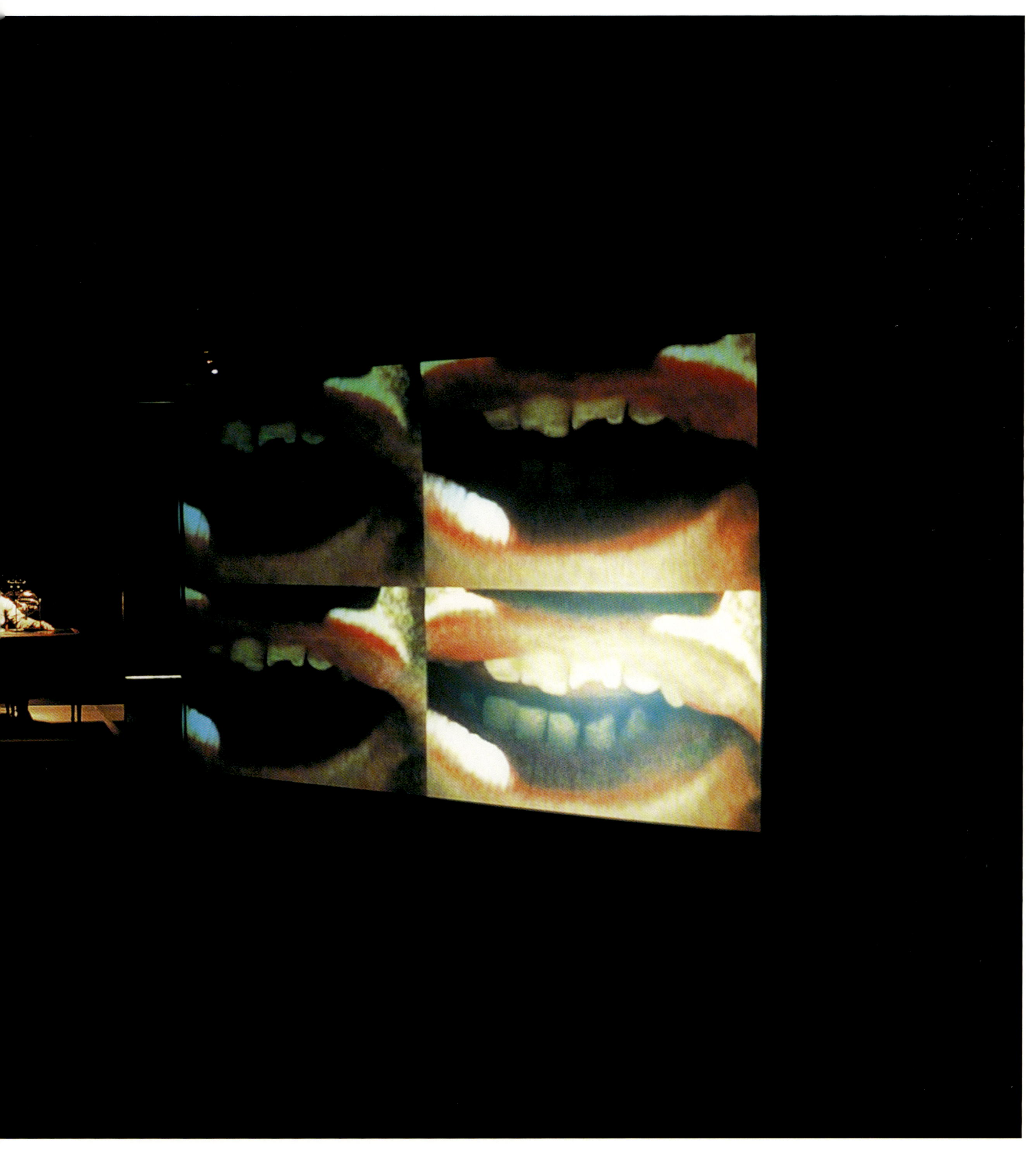

Marmorstein und Eisen bricht
Marble Stone and Iron Break

Commissioned to make a piece for a new school building, Dias & Riedweg worked directly with a group of children who would be the first to attend this school, believing them to be the primary focus of attention in the function of the new building. Around 500 objects and images, all connected to stories told by children who attended a series of workshops run by the artists, were digitally photographed. The images were printed onto transparencies that were later displayed as backlit photographs and functioned as ground-level lamps in the courtyard and the corridors of the Center for Special Education of East Munich. In addition the artists collected drawings and words, which were digitally enlarged and engraved with sand jet onto the windows of the glass facade of the building. These drawings and fragments of handwriting of the children who would attend the school in the building some years later, were thus inscribed onto the new architecture before their arrival.

The area of Riem, formerly Munich's airport, was intensively used by the Nazis and heavily bombed during World War II. At the beginning of the 2000s the area was entirely demolished and reconstructed to create a new neighborhood. *Kunstprojekte Riem,* curated by Claudia Buttner, had the difficult task of commissioning art within the context of this reconstruction. The artists' decision to use drawings to leave the spelling mistakes in the handwriting on the school's glass facade provoked strong reactions from the architect, the department of education, and the city administration, and generated a tense public debate. The artists and the curator eventually won the legal right to maintain the intervention with the original contributions of the children untouched.

- Public art project at a new public school building in Riem, Munich
  Floor backlight lamps and sand-jet drawings on glass facade

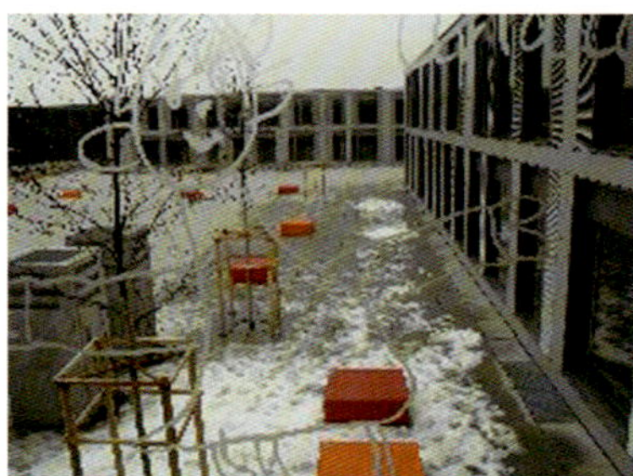
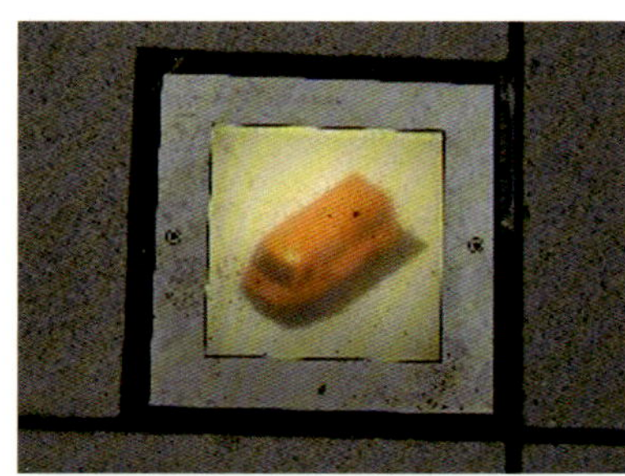
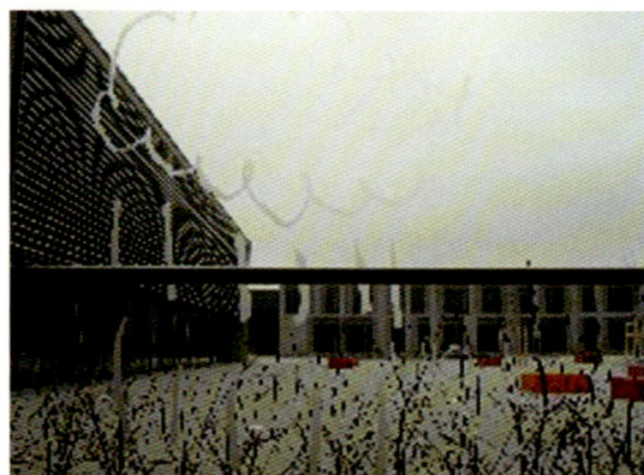
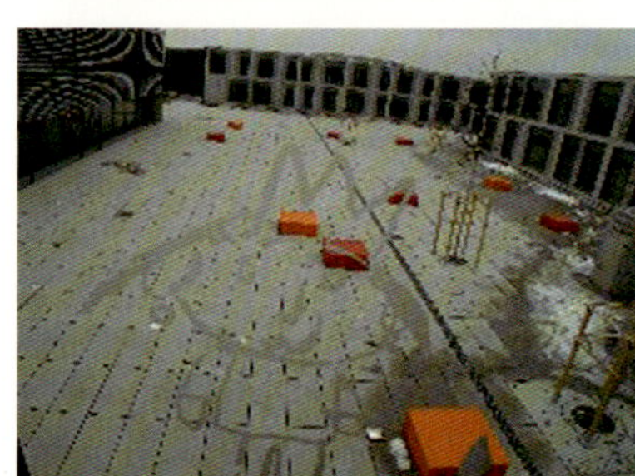

Belo é também aquilo que também não foi visto
Beautiful Is also that which Is Unseen

A series of videos shot in workshops during one semester with a group of 16 blind adults who attended the Benjamin Constant Institute for Blind People in Rio de Janeiro. The workshops directly debated the subjects of vision and blindness taking a philosophical approach, and their social consequences among people who see and people who do not. The videos introduce powerful and surprising definitions given by people who do not see for simple things such as colors, materials such as metal, wood, water, ground, noise, light, and for feelings, culminating in possible ideas of what a mirror can be. The artists also recorded one of the participants, disguised as The Hierophant (an archetypical figure from the Tarot deck who reads the truth from a book), reading texts in Braille by Homer and Borges—writers who also suffered from blindness—about mirrors.

During the 25th São Paulo Biennale, visitors were overwhelmed by the intense bright light when they entered the installation space and found themselves projected in a time delayed mirror, layered with other projections of the blind reading about the mirror. Replicas of three pieces of furniture from 1888 reveal 240 drawers each containing a map of Brazil in low-relief used by blind people to learn Brazil's geography at the Benjamin Constant Institute for Blind People, which was established in Rio in the 19th century.

- Public art project and video installation
  Commissioned by Alfons Hug for the 25th São Paulo Biennale
  5-channel video installation with delayed projection of images recorded live with a security camera alongside
  3 replicas of a chest of drawers containing maps of Brazil in bas relief from 1888
  Loops, 09:14/14:53
  Dimensions variable

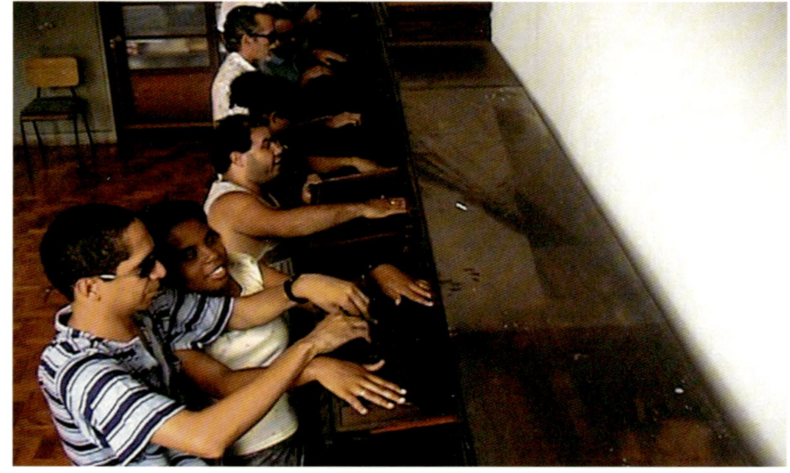

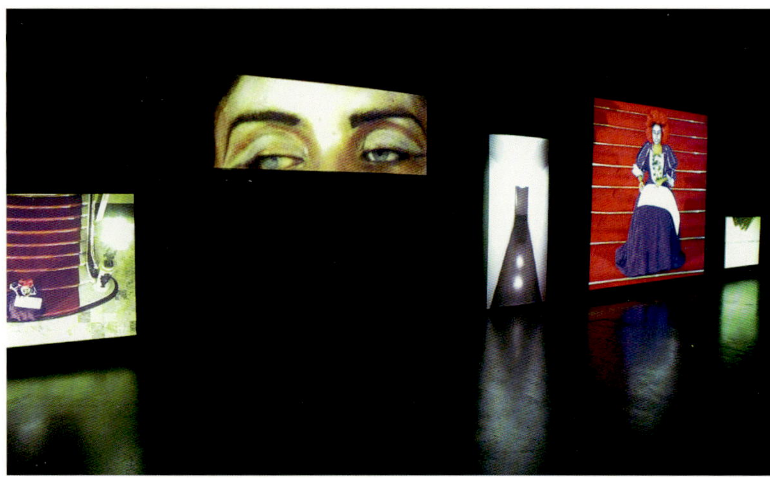

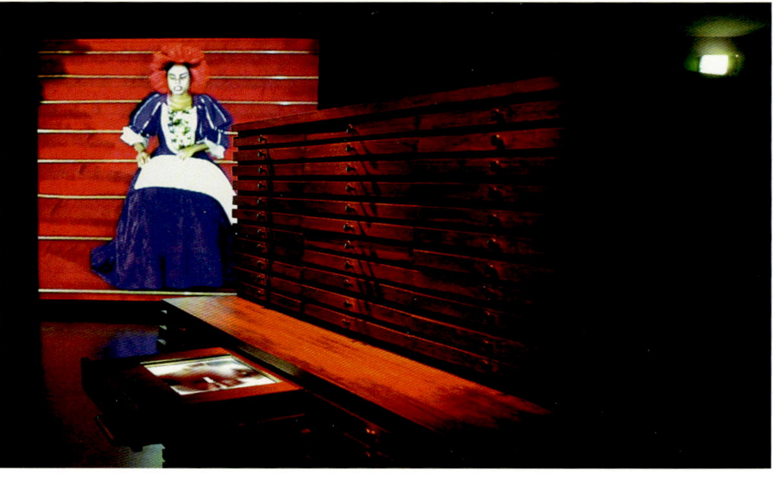

Mera Vista Point
Mere View Point

Thirty-three minute-long videos were made in São Paulo about 33 street vendors in the popular Concórdia Square market. A six-meter-high tower was erected in the middle of the square's tents, and a stand that sells little snacks was situated on it. A larger video monitor was placed on this stand, which was like a pleasant terrace above the bustling market. It was nicknamed *Mere View Point* because the whole square below was visible from this vantage point, as were the 33 large, black & white plotted canvases with portraits of the vendors who participated in the project. The intervention was completed with the distribution of 33 sets of monitors and DVD players to the 33 vendors who had taken part. Their videos were continuously screened on monitors on the stands where they sell their goods, and in this way a direct publicity video of their products was displayed at the point of sale.

Initially populated by people who had lost their jobs and started to sell cheap items on the streets for survival, Largo da Concórdia quickly became Brazil's largest concentration of informal street vendors, and very popular as an open-air shopping mall. In the videos shot by Dias & Riedweg, the 33 vendors talk about the products they sell—miniatures, imitations, kitsch objects, cheap junk—most of them costing about a dollar. The items reflect the consumption of a large part of São Paulo's poorer population: small, cheap, colorful things, often quite ugly and with no use, copies that imitate or allude to the original products promoted by the mass media. Alongside the videos and the photographs of the vendors plotted onto canvases displayed above the stands of the huge market in Concórdia Square during the months of *Arte Cidade*, the videos were simultaneously ironically broadcast as commercial

spots on open TV channels. Thus the videos became popular and attracted a wealthier crowd to the square. A longer version of the videos was produced and distributed to the vendors. They were not on sale through art galleries or at this market, but were given by the vendors as a bonus when people at the market bought their cheap products for higher prices. Anyone who bought products from street vendors for more than a certain sum received a video from the project as a gift. Sales increased by more than 300% during the months of the intervention.

- Urban intervention
  Commisioned by Nelson Brissac Peixoto and SESC São Paulo for Arte Cidade 4
  Urban intervention with iron tower, 33 photograhs plotted onto canvases, and 33 video monitors exhibited in 33 street vendors' stands and broadcast on TV

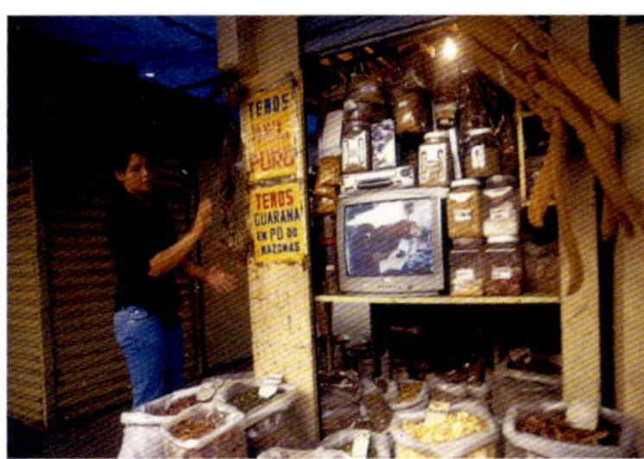

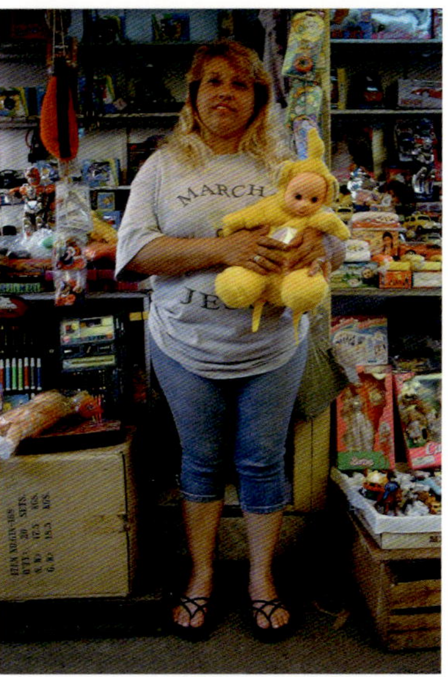

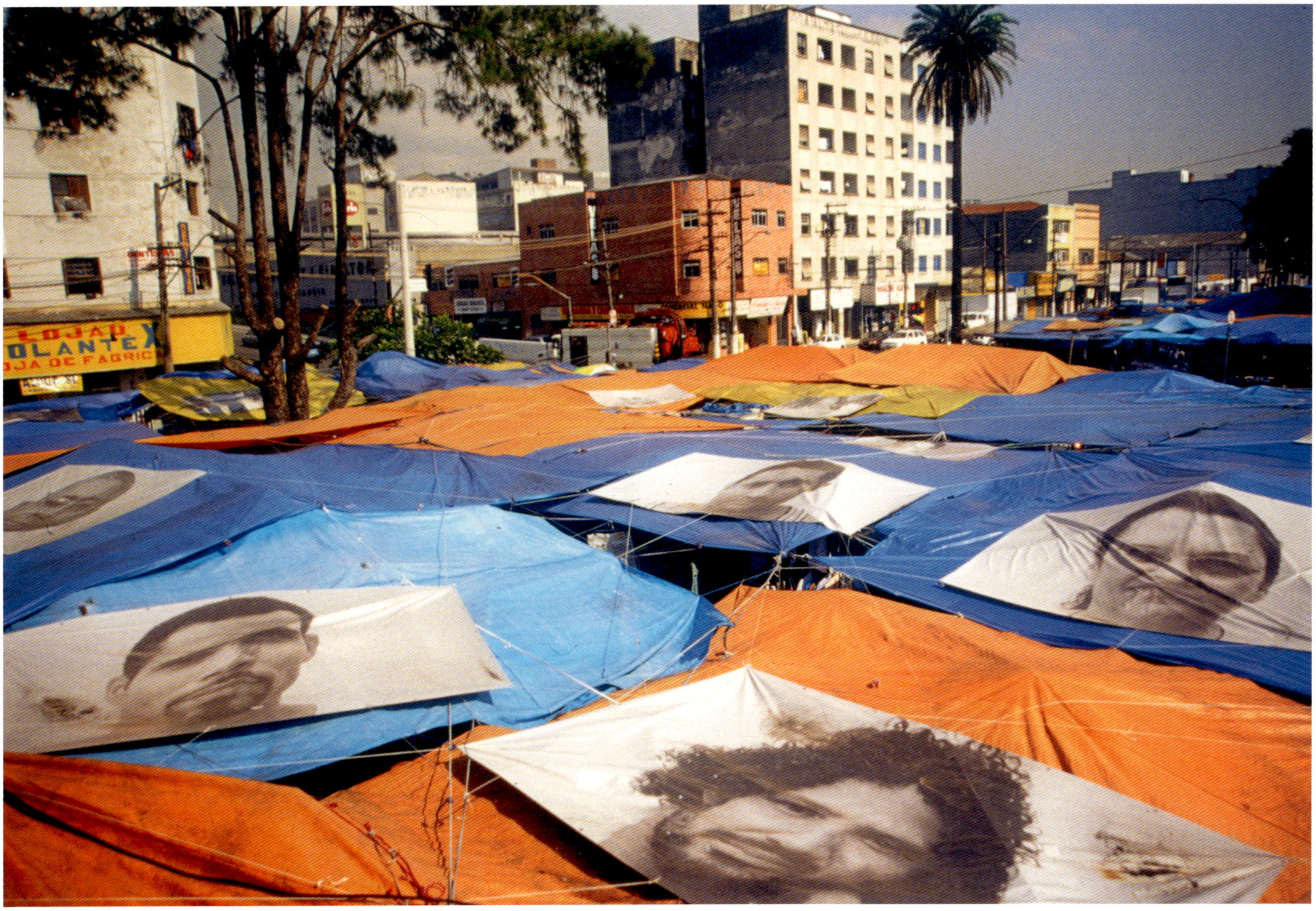

Porque eu poderia perder
Because I Might Lose

Under the theme of "The Body at Risk" Dias & Riedweg prepared twin video projections to be screened one facing the other on the edges of a "dance floor" made out of a large inflatable mattress. The work was situated in the open air in the Lapa Square in downtown Rio de Janeiro, where around 10,000 people usually hang out at the weekend.

Realized for the Festival of Contemporary Dance in Rio de Janeiro, the installation drew mixed crowds of youngsters, night-hawks, and the local street population of prostitutes and transvestites to interact with the music and the instable "dance floor" between the two projections that showed bodies in situations of risk.

- Open air public intervention with 2-channel video screening and live electronic music on inflatable air mattress 10 × 5 m, Lapa, Rio de Janeiro
  Commissioned by the Festival de Dança Contemporânea
  Loop, 33:09
  Dimensions variable

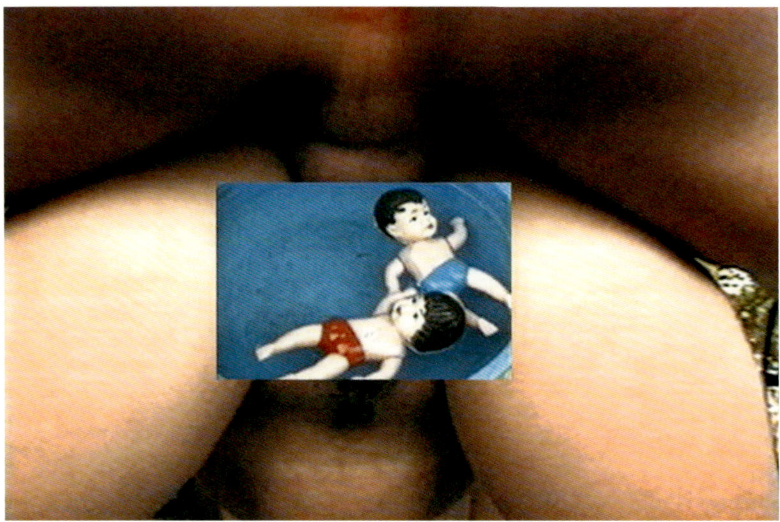

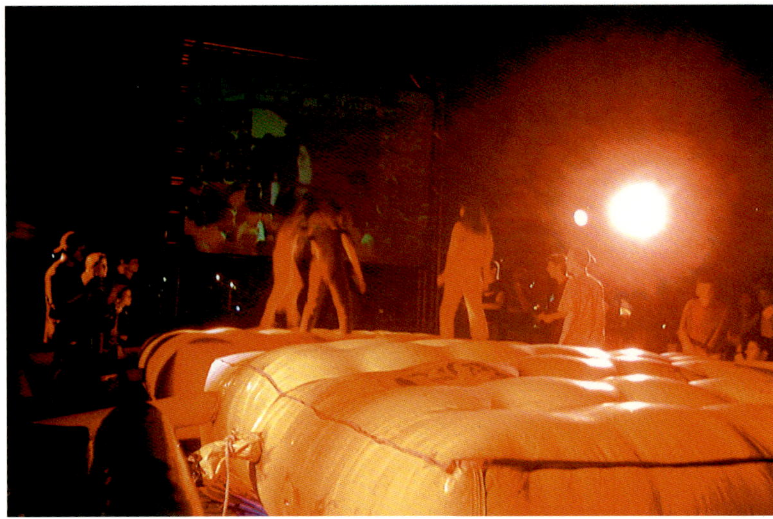

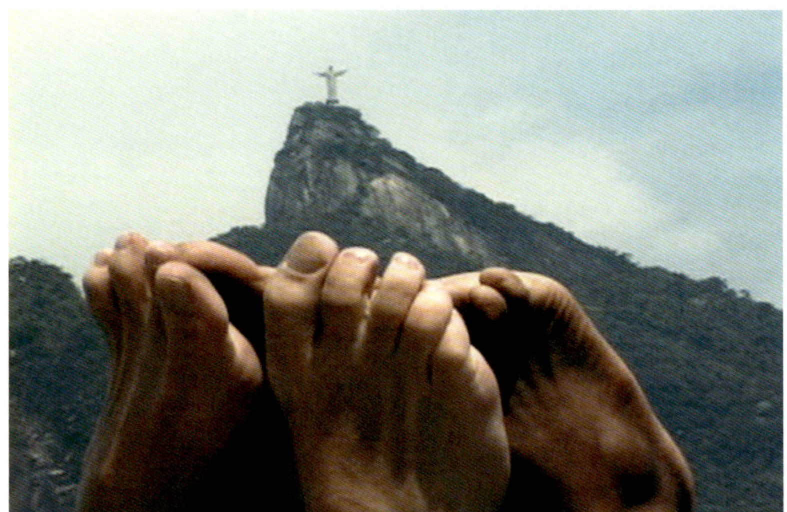

The Game of Black or White in Colour

The work comprises two chairs, their feet connected at the base so that their movements are inseparable (when one chair is pulled back, the other necessarily moves forward and vice versa) and a chess table were the support for six "video-cans" in which color videos were displayed on small screens at the bottom of six cans, with the audio output on the lids. Each video was named after a different area of Johannesburg, and revealed the racist structures that still exist in the city's routines and architecture.

The Game of Black or White in Colour, Video Wall, Night Shift: Dias & Riedweg received a Pro Helvetia residency grant in South Africa where they were invited to participate in the public art program of the Johannesburg Art Gallery, for which they realized three new pieces. The first post-apartheid years were clearly marked by political optimism as well as extreme social differences and blatant racism, which are strongly represented in this group of works.

- Multimedia installation with chess table, 2 chairs, and 6 "video cans"
  6 videos, loops of 2 to 3 minutes
  Dimensions variable

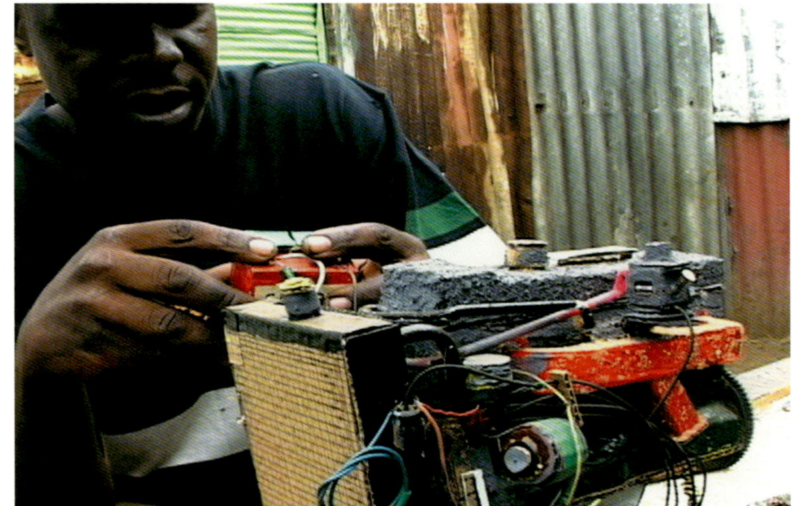

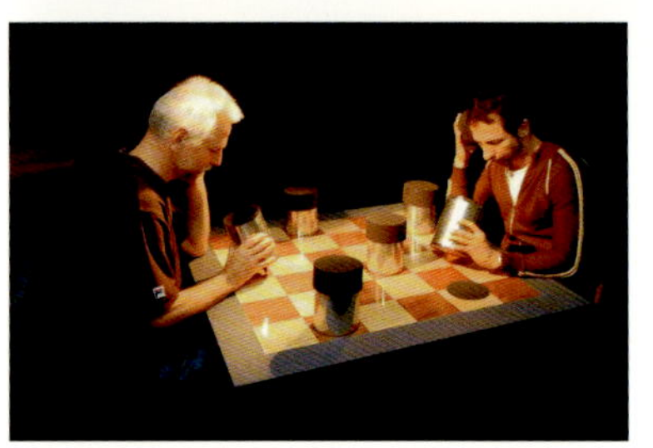

Video Wall

A video camera filmed people coming and going in front of a commercial video panel made of 16 monitors at Johannesburg Central Station. The passersby between the camera and the panel attest to the contradiction of South Africa's white-dominated publicity and the majority black population. Fifteen stills were later made out of the artists' new video, and printed to the same dimensions as the video panel, forming a meta work about the commercial video wall recorded at the station.

→ See *The Game of Black or White in Colour*, 2001, p. 114
• Video installation with monitor and 15 video stills on backlit panel
  Loop, 5:43
  Dimensions variable

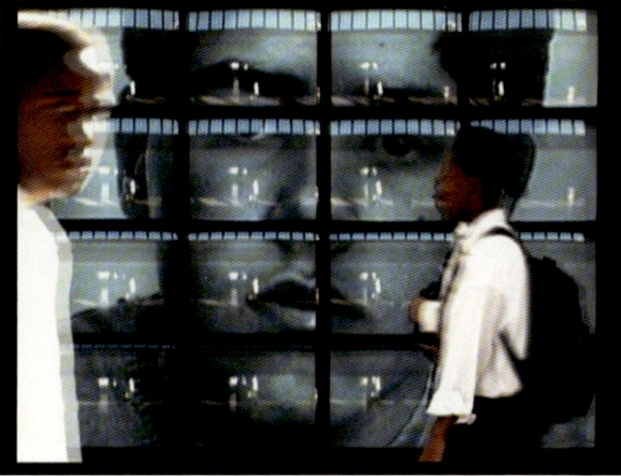
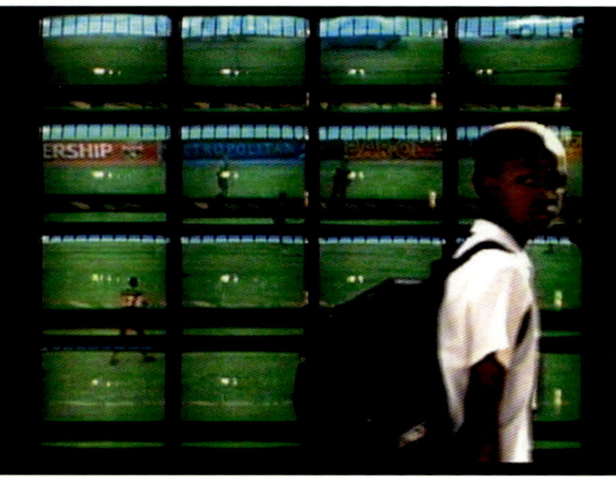

Night Shift

The streets of Johannesburg were recorded from inside a police car during a night shift. The real policemen Pau, Macachuca, and Mocotini attend diverse SOS calls that come through the car radio, and thus drove Dias & Riedweg through the city, revealing the danger and seduction of the ghettos, clubs, and brothels of the nightlife of the biggest African metropolis, until an unexpectedly innocent dawn at the Top Star Drive-In Cinema, and a typically urban documentary video, suddenly slide into fiction.

→ See *The Game of Black or White in Colour*, 2001, p. 114
• Video installation
  Loop, 13:28
  Dimensions variable

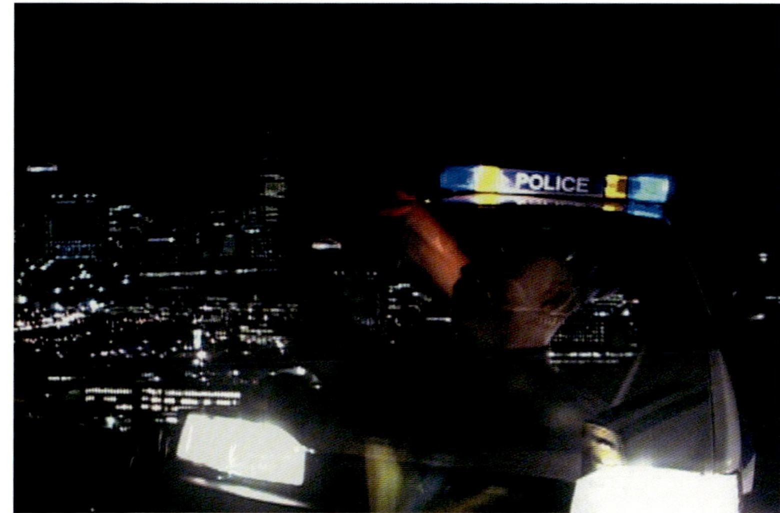
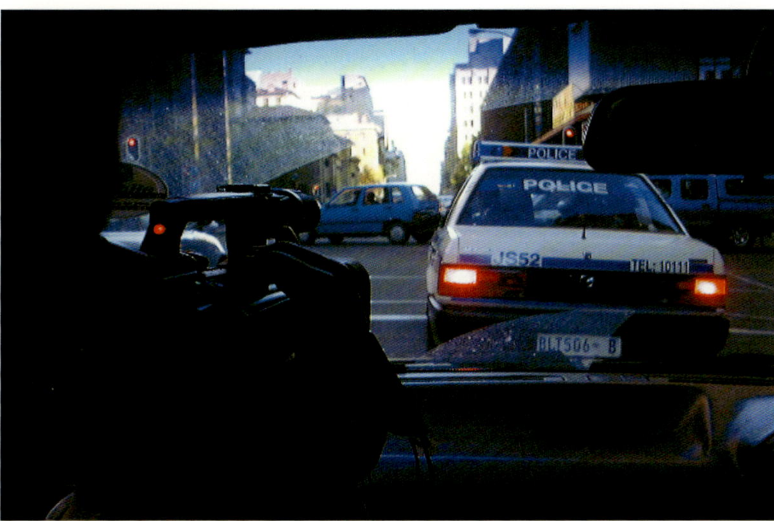
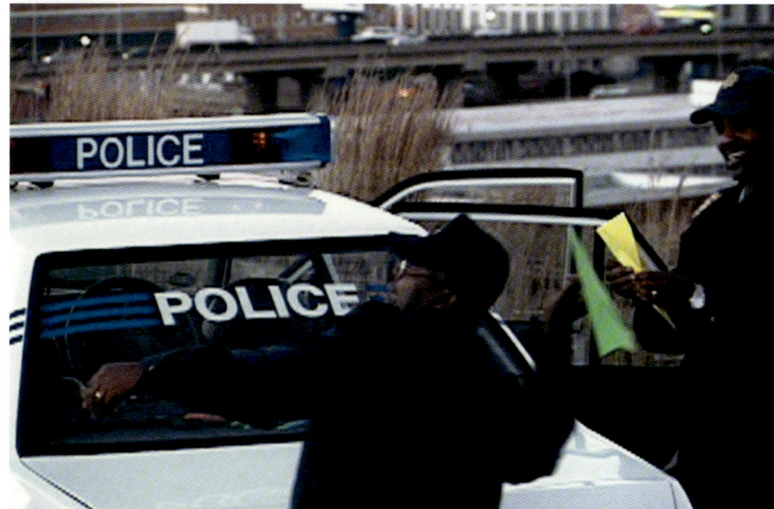

Mama & Ritos Viciosos
Mama & Vicious Rituals

Made in collaboration with US Federal Immigration and Customs K-9 Officers, these videos reveal the daily work of the officers and their dogs, trained to find drugs and illegal immigrants at the San Diego/Tijuana US/Mexican border.

Bringing together a man's two best friends—his dog and his mother—in *Mama* Dias & Riedweg paint an acerbic picture of an unstoppable south/north immigration at the world's most crossed border. Definitions of power and authority given by officers point to possible analogies between military power and motherhood. *Mama* investigates how private psychologies affect and constitute public space and vice versa. *Vicious Rituals* also depicts a scene that defies comprehension, in which a group of illegal immigrants from the south insist on jumping over the fence built to separate the US from Mexico, and are inevitably caught by police.

- Public art project and video installation
  Commissioned for InSite 2000
  Twin video installations with 2 wall panels with
  40 backlit photographs
  Loops, 15:55/2:04
  Dimensions variable

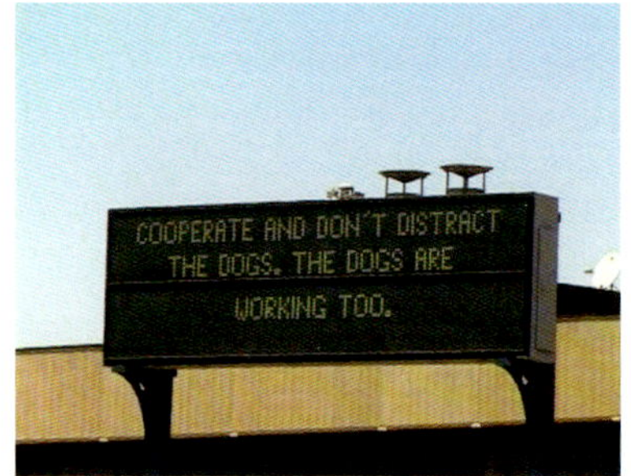

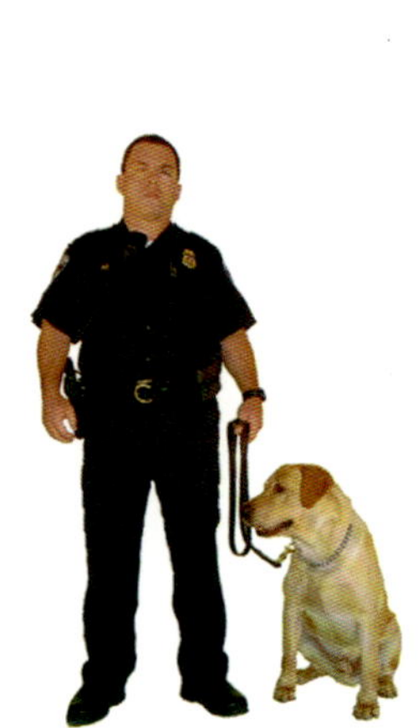

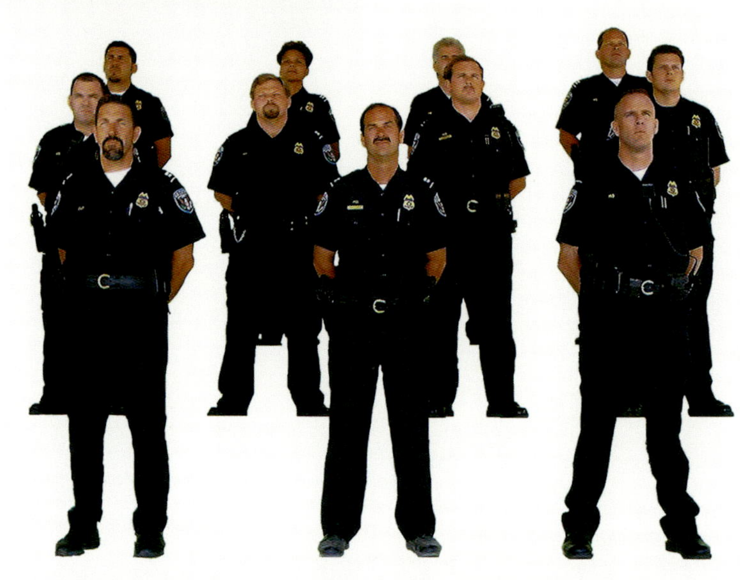

Meu nome na tua boca
My Name on Your Lips

Maria, Pedro, John, Karin, Roland, Cristina … Names are remembered and smoothly recited by lips projected onto bed sheets that are hung as if from a mundane washing line. At the turn of the millennium, Dias & Riedweg individually asked diverse people to close their eyes and try to remember and name, using only first names, everybody they had slept with until the moment of the recording.

Only the speakers' lips were recorded in close-up, which revealed the delicate effort of remembrance and forgetfulness when magnified. Small private confessions about intimate memories were thus transformed into something repetitive and anonymously collective in the public sphere.

- Public art project and video installation
  Loops, 44:44/33:10
  Dimensions variable

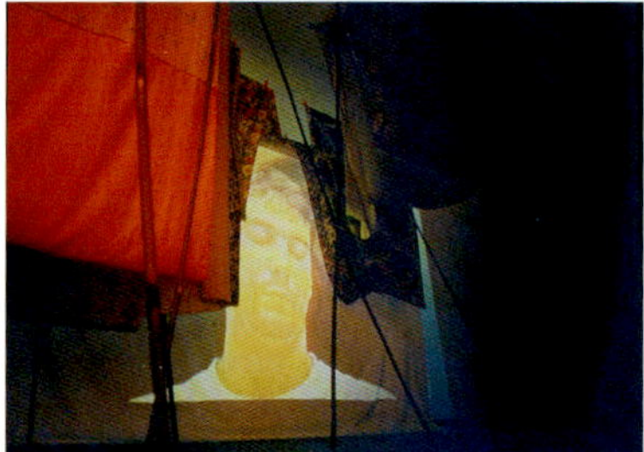

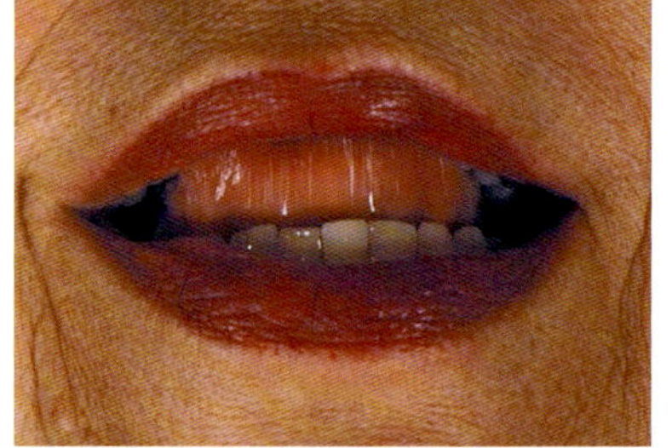

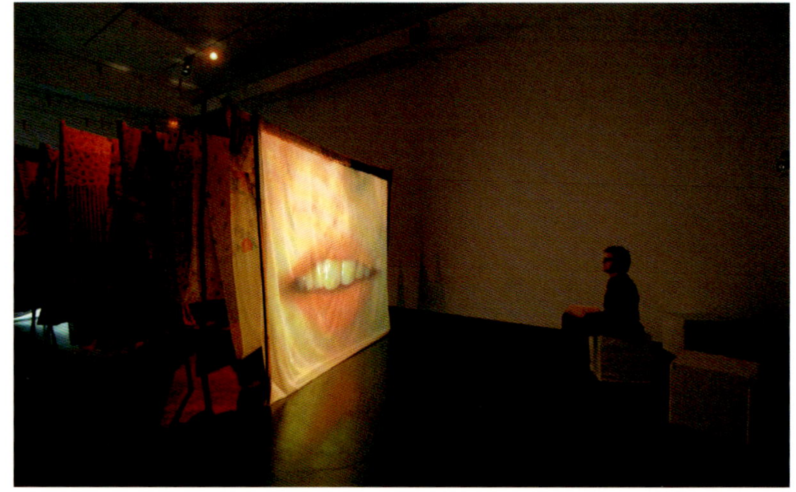

Tutti Veneziani
All Venetians

36 Venetians from different neighbor-hoods and social classes were filmed at the time of day when they changed clothes. Whether at home or at work, the video captured the passage from private to public in all its intimacy and fragility as a kind of automatized ritual of modern life when the inner and outer worlds meet.

Every gesture in Venice takes on a theatrical quality. The city itself is like a stage. Images of the city are so often printed and mediated that when we see the original it is linked to mediated, mythical images. Venice stages Venice daily. Inhabitants of the city are actors in the drama. Throughout the centuries, the myth of the sinking city has created the perfect stage for the drama of our civilization. Air and water meet on uncertain ground.

- Public art project and video installation
  Commissioned by Harald Szeemann for the
  48th Venice Biennale
  Loops, 68:14/07:17
  Dimensions variable

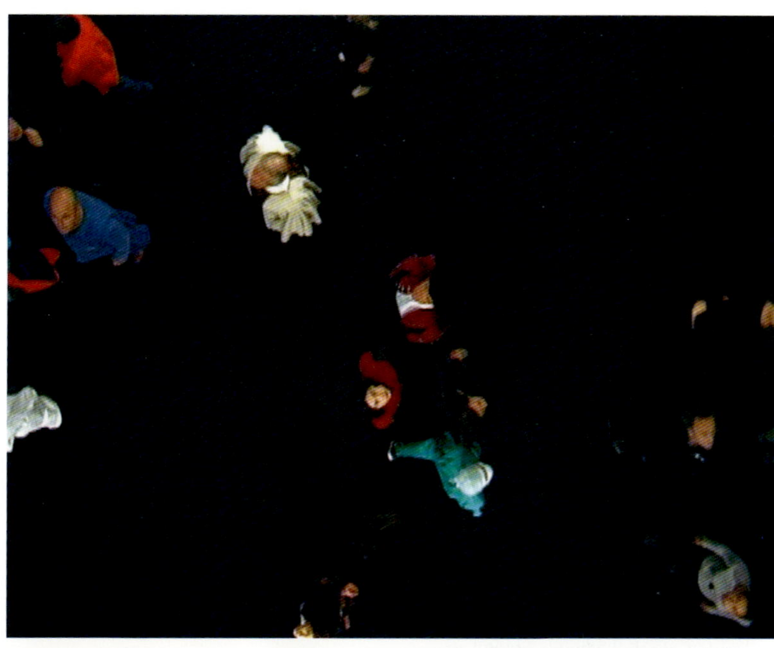

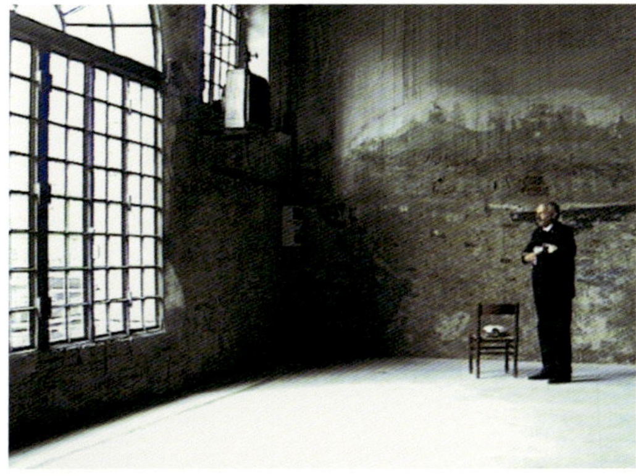

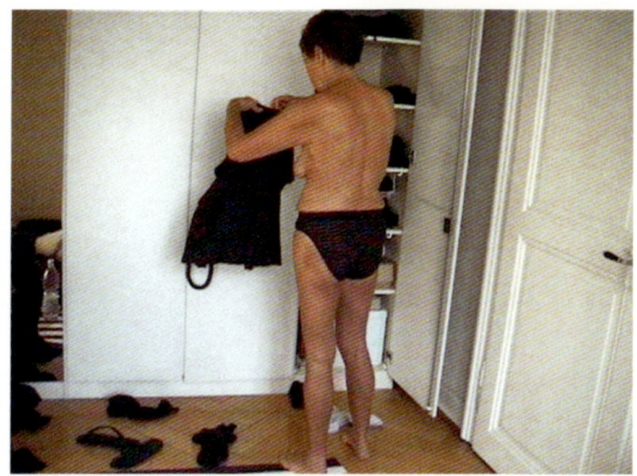

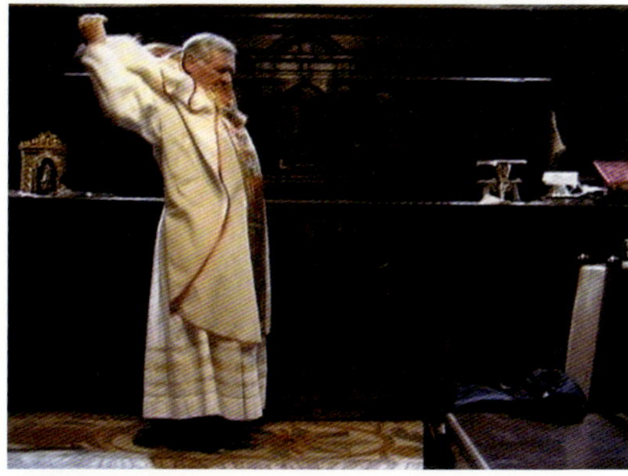

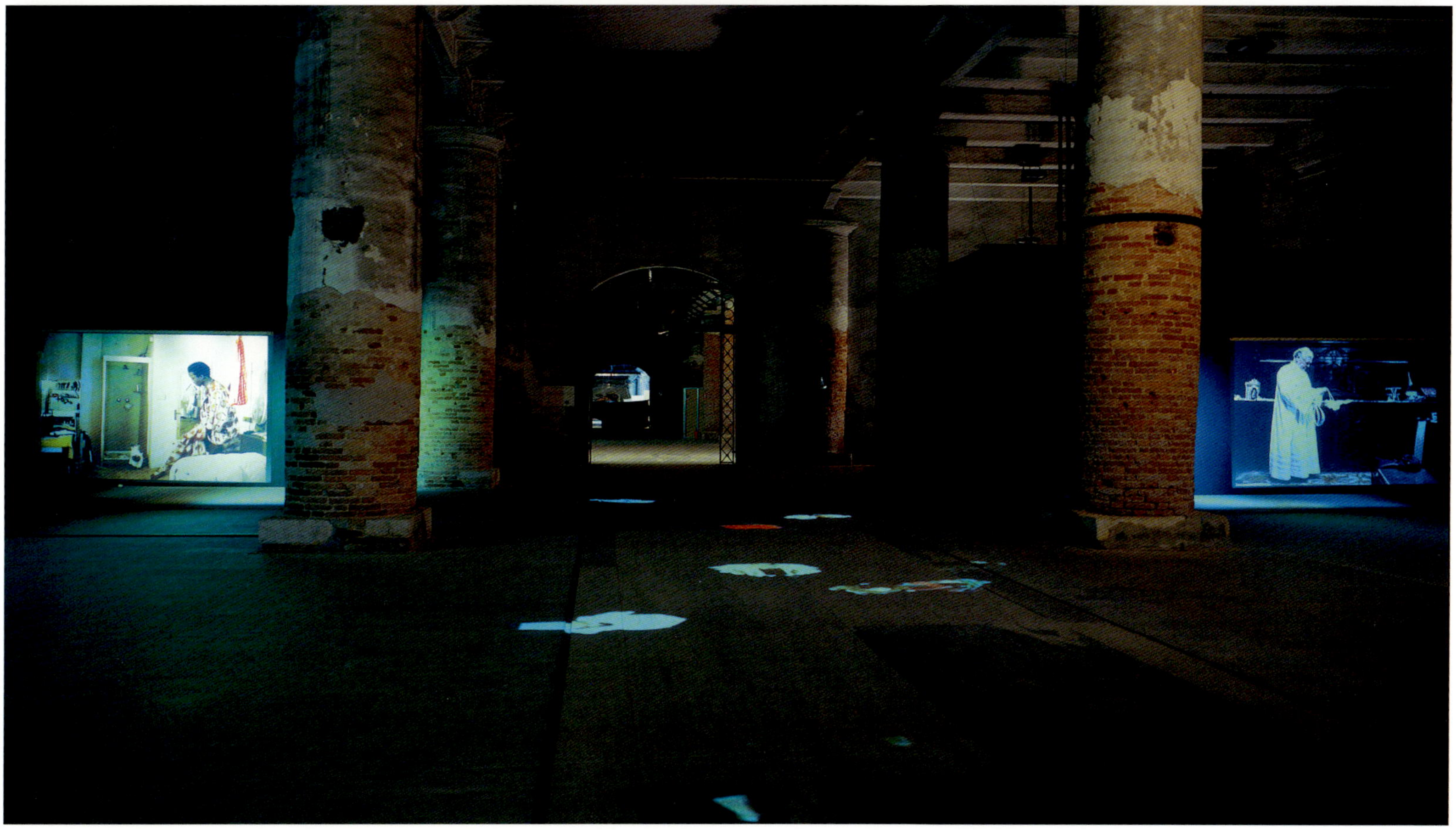

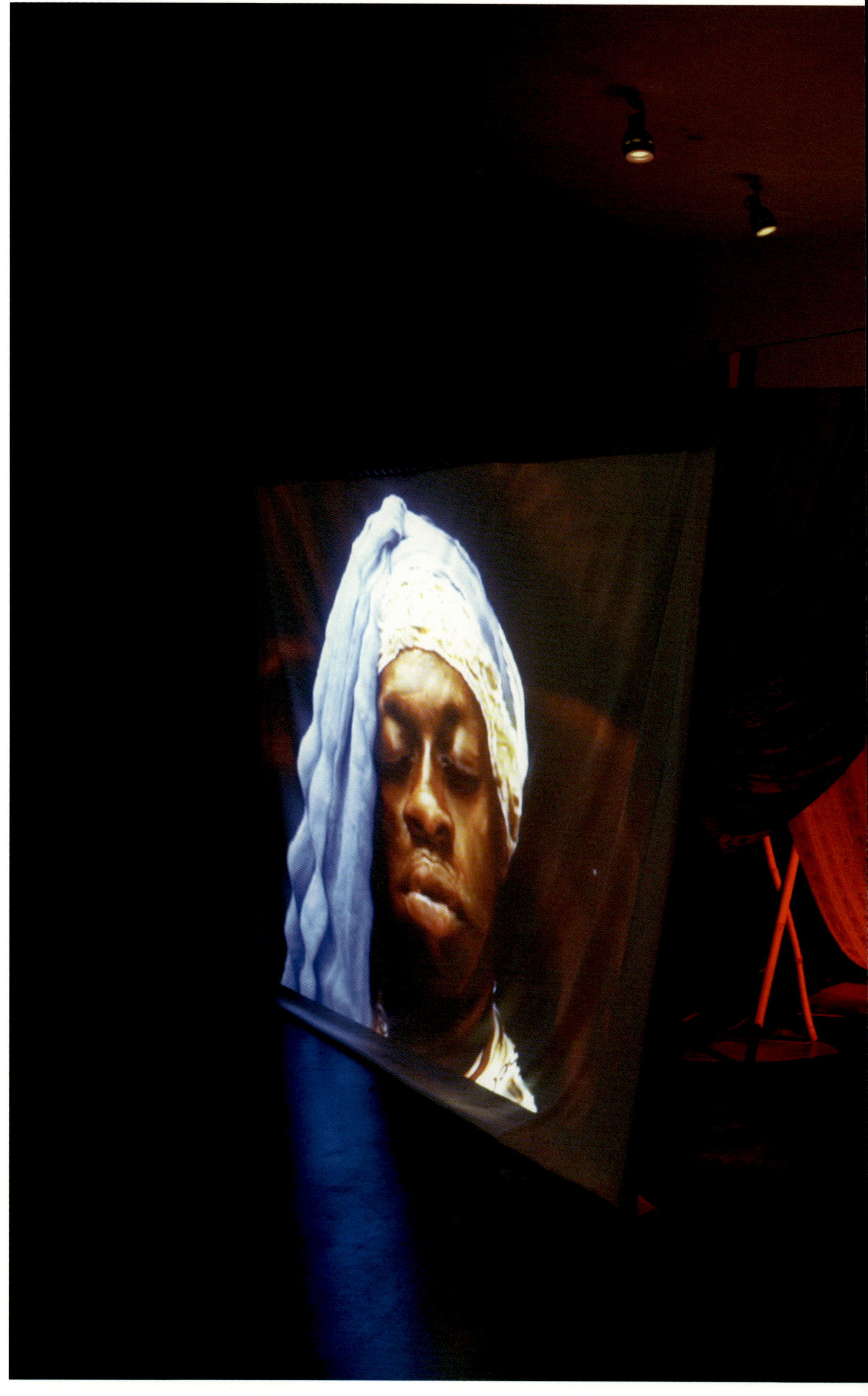

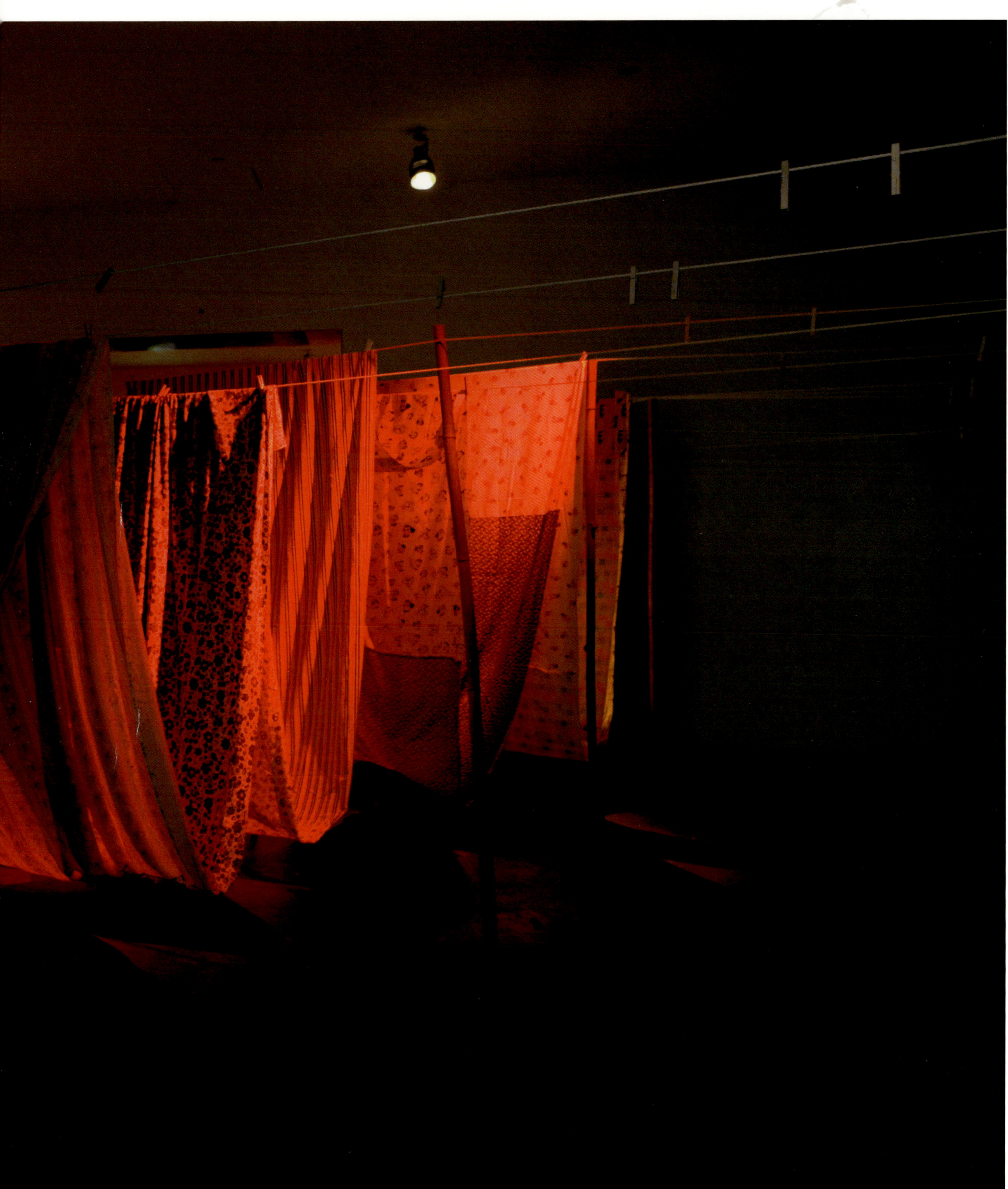

This Is Not Egypt

A script of 11 short stories told in a simultaneous three-channel video installation recreates a sensual and fragmented, but potentially critical and provocative portrait of what the artists could (not) perceive and translate from their sojourn on a Pro Helvetia residency project in Cairo and Alexandria.

The chosen titles of the short stories—*Freedom*, *Beauty*, *Desire*, *Reciprocal Curiosity*, *Pleasure*, *Resignation*, *Instructions*, and *Tourist*—reveal a mixture of fascination and disappointment that culminates in the negative expression that entitled the piece.

- Video installation
  Loop, 31:14
  Dimensions variable

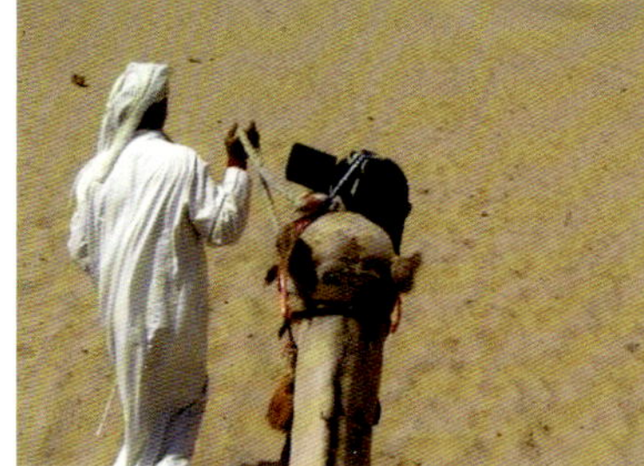
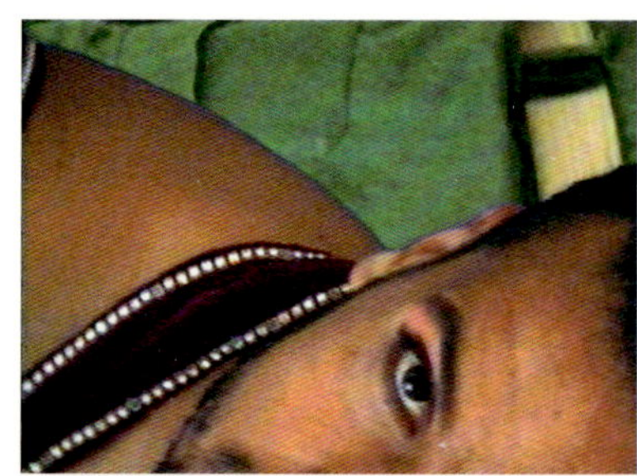
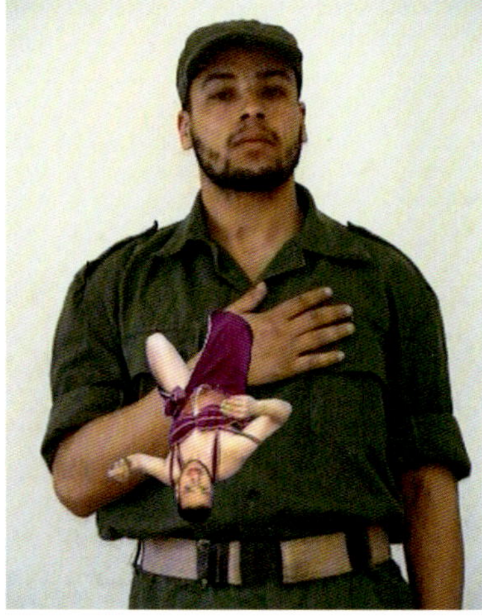
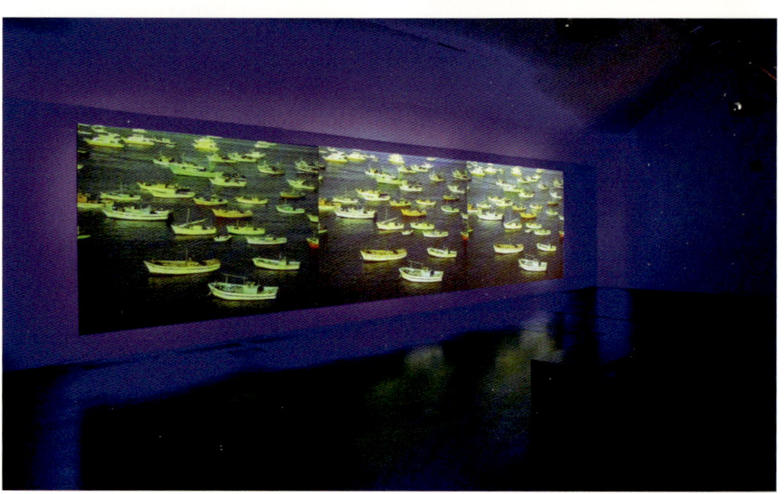

Os Raimundos, os Severinos e os Franciscos
The Raimundos, the Severinos and the Franciscos

This video brings together narratives from 30 janitors of residential buildings of the city of São Paulo, about their routine of working and living in these towers. The doormen, all migrants from northeast Brazil, all have one of three names typical names of this region: Raimundo, Severino, or Francisco. The piece builds up a panel of stories of immigration and integration of men who have been inscribed in the history of civil construction in Brazil, and in almost all Brazilian metropolises.

The final scene is a small choreography in which they all exist inside an approximate replica of their own living spaces, built by themselves with the artists, using their own belongings. One after another, each doorman enters this space as if he were alone, after having worked in the lobby until the end of the day. The space soon becomes overcrowded, thus demonstrating the lack of generosity and democracy in contemporary civil architecture in Brazil.

About 90% of all janitors and servants working in residential buildings in São Paulo and Rio are immigrants from northeast Brazil. Mostly they are men who came to work in the construction of the buildings, and ended up staying to work and live as janitors, housekeepers, and servants in the same towers. Their massive presence in Brazilian cities exposes the discrepancies of the country's economic reality today, in which borders are more clearly defined between social classes than in geographical terms.

- Public art project and multimedia installation
  Commissioned by Paulo Herkenhoff for the 24th São Paulo Biennale
  Loop, 52:00; final scene, 04:09
  Dimensions variable

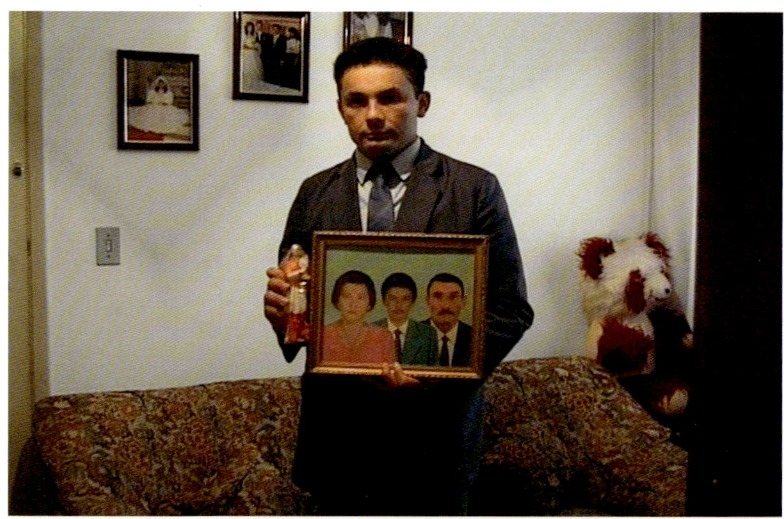
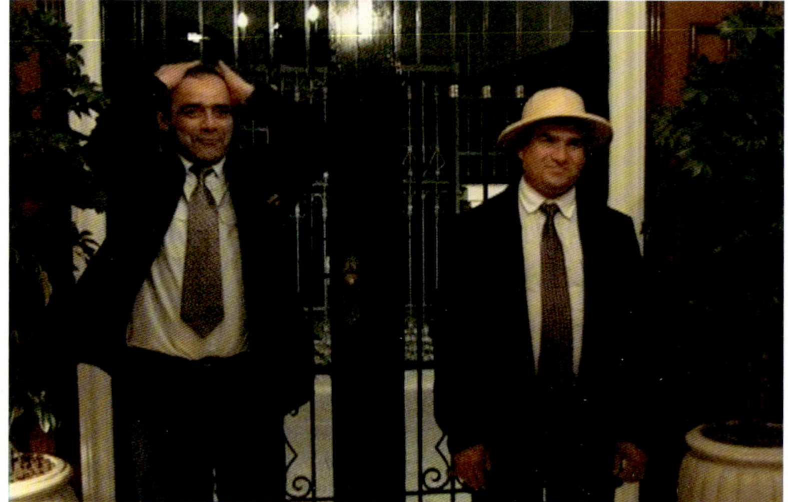

Inside & Outside the Tube

In collaboration with a group of refugees claiming political asylum in Switzerland, the artists developed a series of audio workshops that aimed to associate the senses of smell, touch, hearing, and sight to the fields of individual memory and imagination, and thus create conversations and biographical reflections between a group of people staying at the Reception Center for Refugees in Adliswil. These conversations were recorded on sound CDs and later placed inside metal pipes normally used for heating, but turned into sound sculptural bodies installed in a public space.

Refugees arrive in Europe daily from diverse countries with socio-economic and/or political problems. They have to be received and kept in these refugee centers while their cases are legally examined and decided by the authorities. Although the refusal rates are high, the numbers of refugees keeps increasing, making this issue one of the most difficult and challenging in Europe today. The waiting time for an asylum request is long, complex, and painful.

- Public art project and sound installation with metal pipes
  Sound loop, 04:09
  Dimensions variable

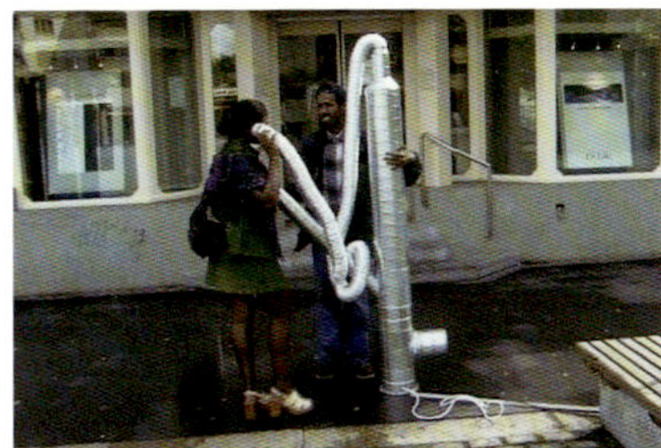
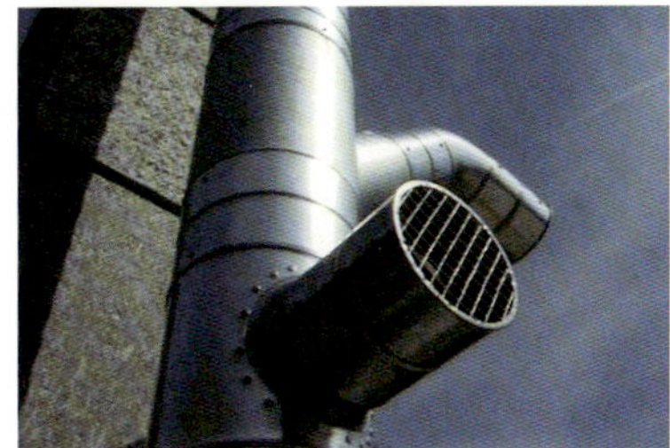
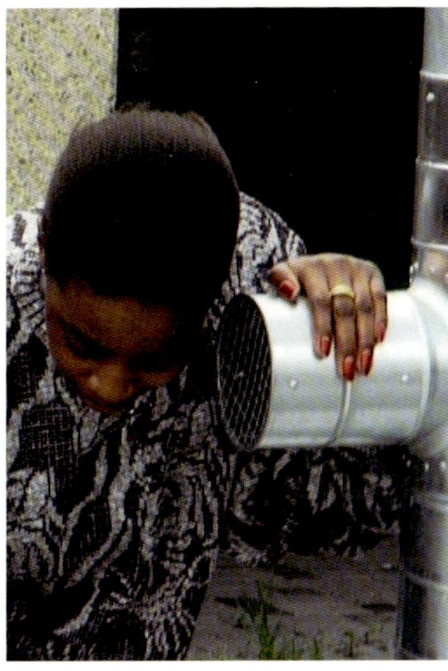

Question Marks

Question Marks was a communication and art project between two groups of prisoners who did not know each other: a group of ten adult prisoners (all of them serving long-term sentences) at Atlanta's Federal Penitentiary, and a group of 30 teenagers who at the time were in a detention center for youngsters at the Fulton County Child Treatment Center. Daily workshops at both sites started a communication process between these groups over a three-month period, through the regular exchange of videos made by the men about their own issues of living in confinement. This exchange was then edited by the artists and extended to a series of interventions in public space in order to carry these reflections from the prison out to society.

The artistic program entitled *Conversations at the Castle*, conceived, curated, and produced by Mary Jane Jacob and Homi Bhabha as a critical counterpoint to the Olympic Games in Atlanta in 1996, became one of the most radical and important exhibitions of the decade in the United States. The penal institutions chosen by Dias & Riedweg were situated in the immediate environs of the Olympic stadium. One of the artists' actions was to fix car license plates containing questions formulated by prisoners and painted in their own handwriting on cars parked in the city. In the US, official license plates are produced by prisoners during their sentences.

- Public art project and video installation
  Loop, 62:00
  Dimensions variable

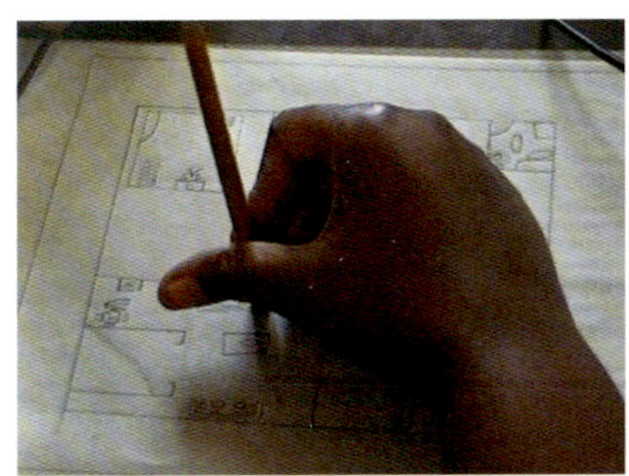
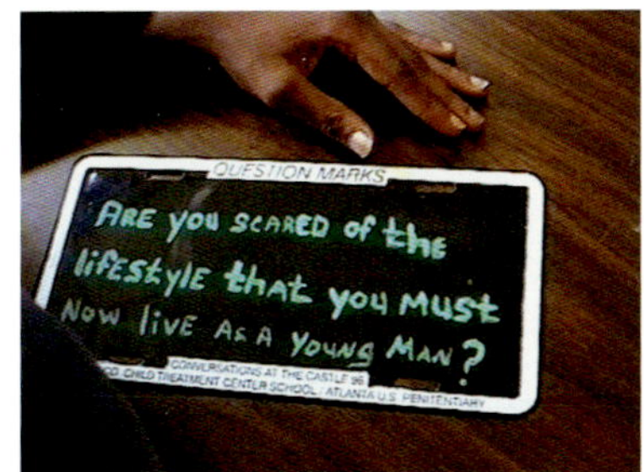

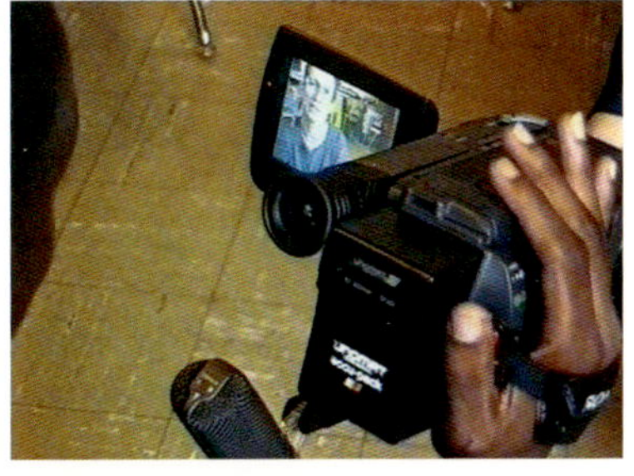

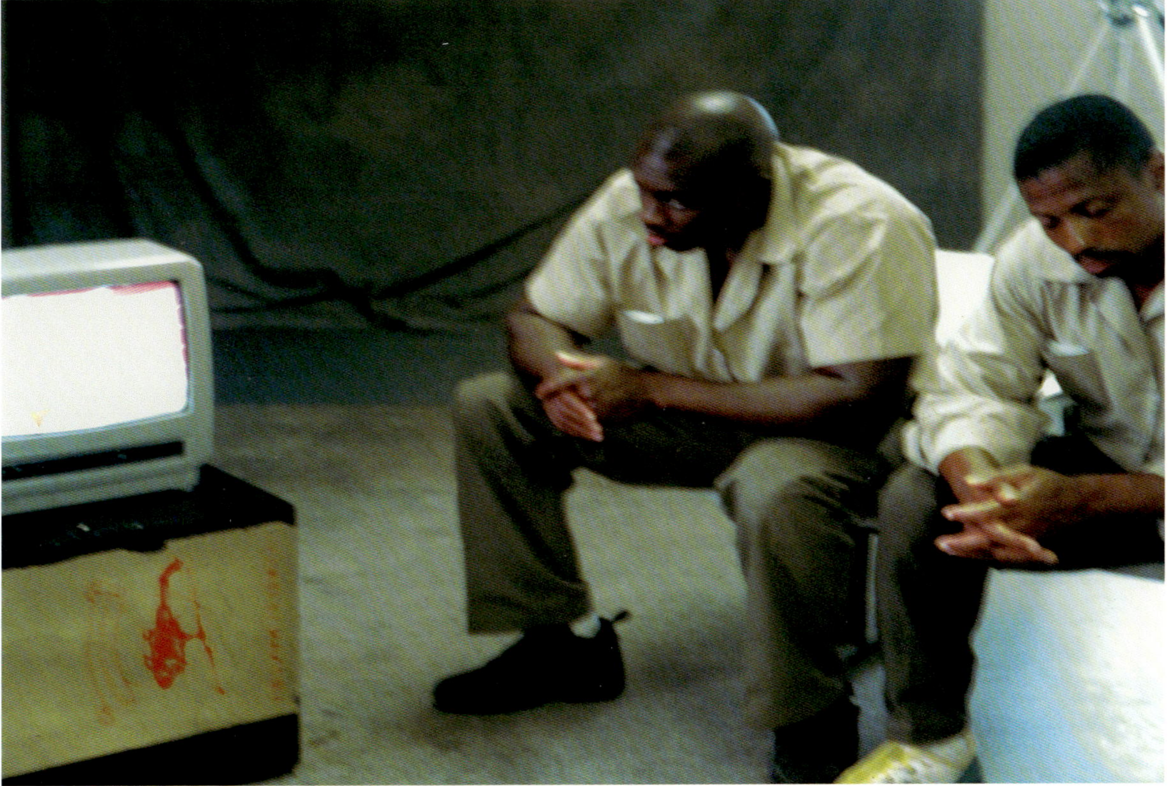

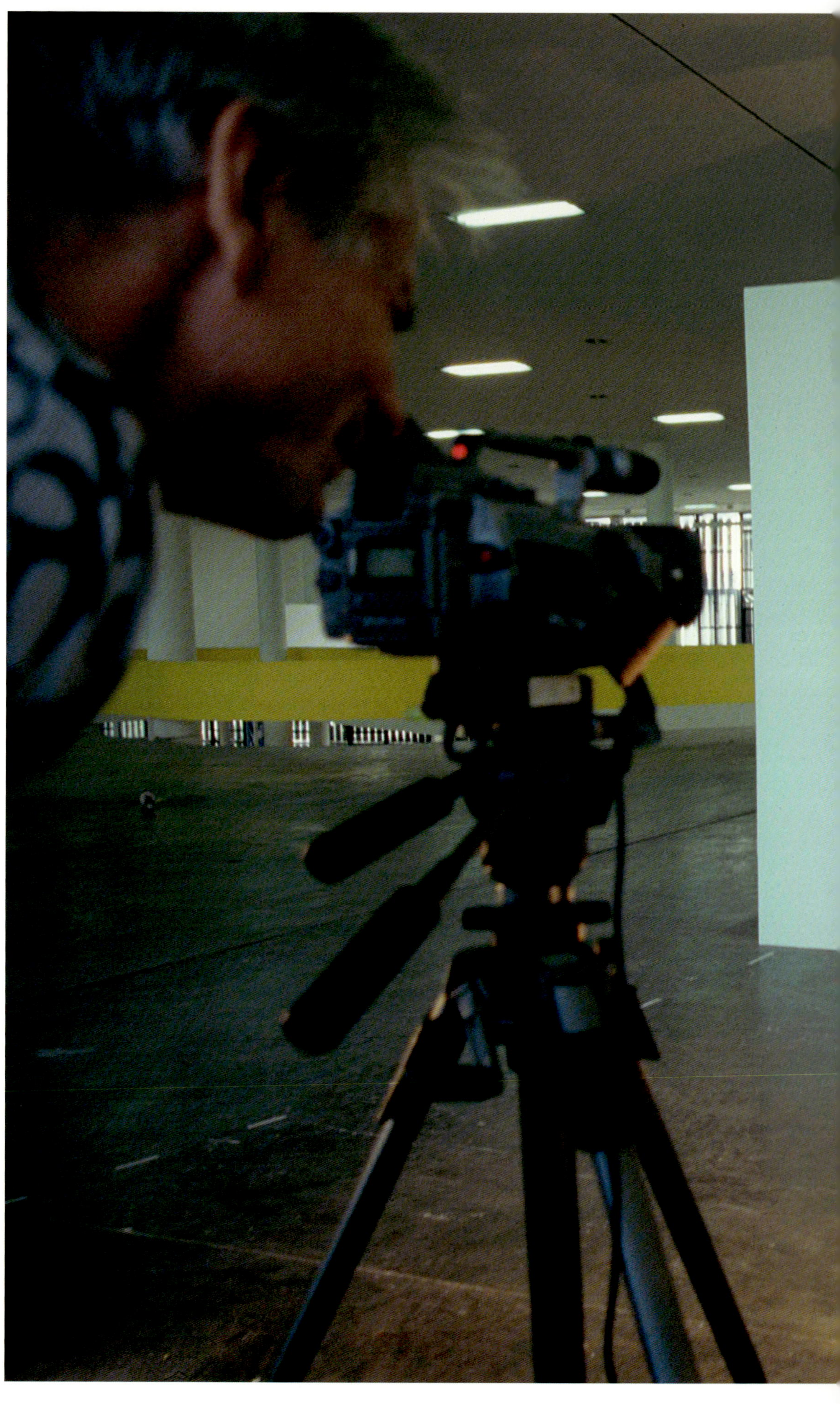

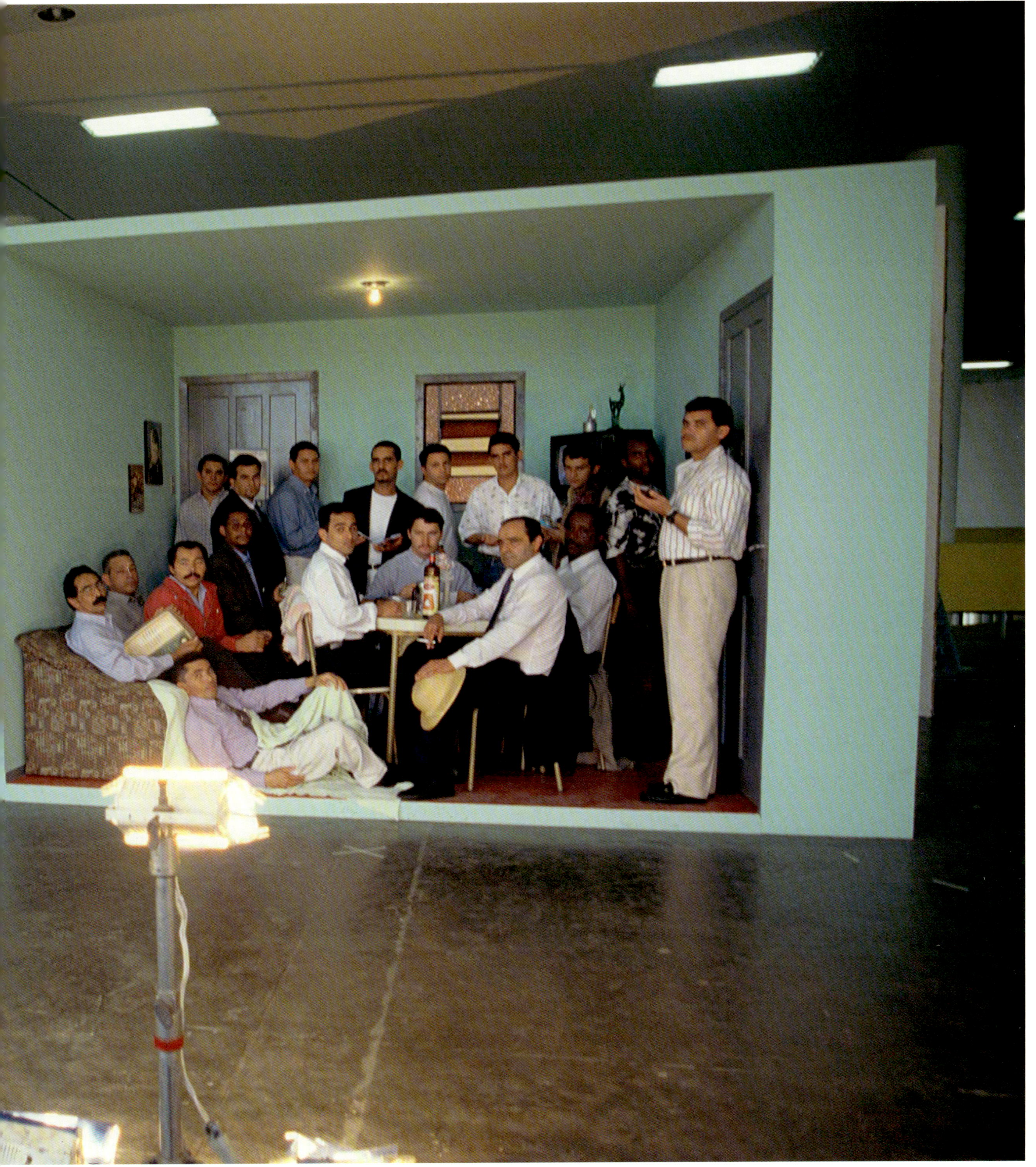

Innendienst
Inner Services

In collaboration with immigrant children recently arrived in Switzerland and just starting the public school system, the artists proposed a series of actions in their school classes, and later directly in the exhibition space at the Shedhalle in Zurich. Through exercises with smells, images, and objects associated with memories of the sites of their former homelands, and contemporary descriptions of the city of Zurich, the youngsters and the audience were invited to reflect on the acquisition (and loss) of language in the process of immigration. *Inner Services* is an attempt to record the delicate flux between inner and outer worlds in order for an individual to name things and find their own path from perception to expression.

Since the beginning of the 1990s, a high percentage of foreign children immigrate to Switzerland when their parents receive a residency permit to live in the country after having worked in low-grade jobs for almost a decade. The public school system is, therefore confronted with this new reality, and has created a so-called initiation classes, made up of these children, to teach them the official language and help them integrate into the country.

- Public art project and video installation
  Loop, 68:14
  Dimensions variable

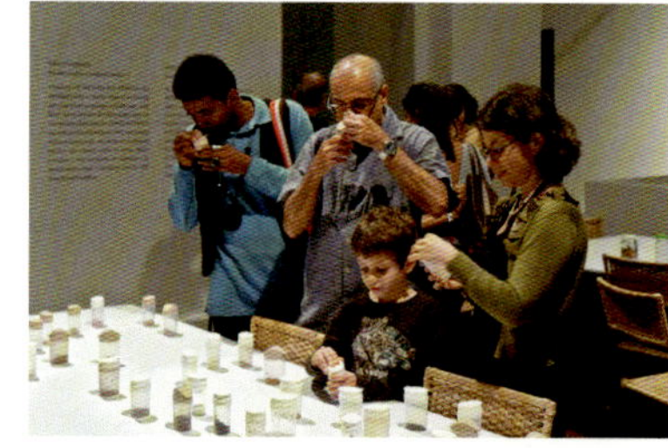

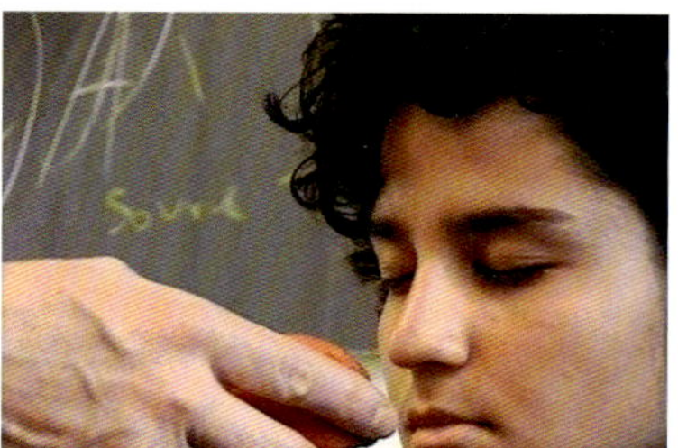

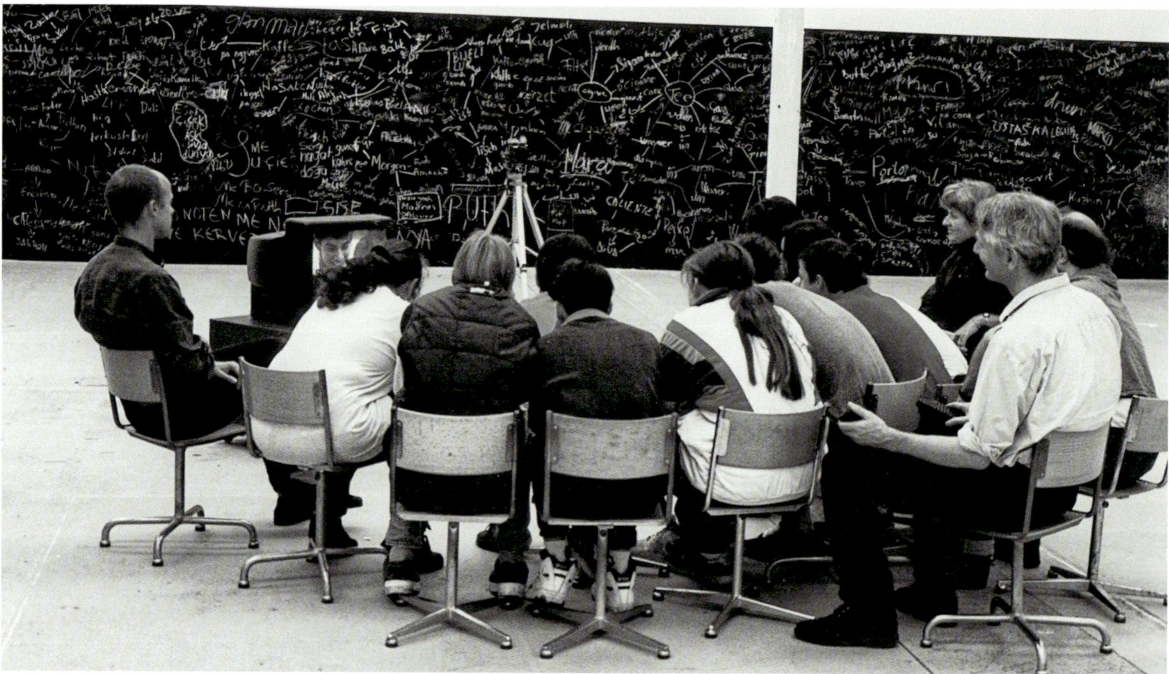

Devotionalia

Throughout 1994 Dias & Riedweg realized a mobile workshop with children and adolescents living on the streets of Rio de Janeiro. The artists taught the youngsters to make wax casts of their own hands and feet, in the tradition of amulets and ex-votos, symbolic objects that carry a wish or a need. A video of the process, along with the 1,286 casts were presented in a large-scale installation, a sort of collective ex-voto, displaced from religious territory into the museum, and thus directed at society.

In the period of the work's execution, Rio witnessed frequent and serious attempts against the lives of children and adolescents living on the streets, among them the mass murder around the city's cathedral, Candelária, and in the community of Vigário Geral. Such urban violence is directly linked to drug dealing and to the mistaken response of a corrupt police force. Although various social movements and NGOs emerged, public care and educational policies have only just started, and when the *Devotionalia* project ended in 2004, more than half of its 600 participants had lost their lives under violent circumstances. Catherine David commissioned a video documenting the ten-year process, and the original installation was donated by the artists to the National Museum of Fine Arts of Rio, where it remains as a document of the existence of these children.

- Public art project and video installation
  Video installation with 1,286 wax casts and 2,500 plaster molds
  Loop, 46:34
  Dimensions variable

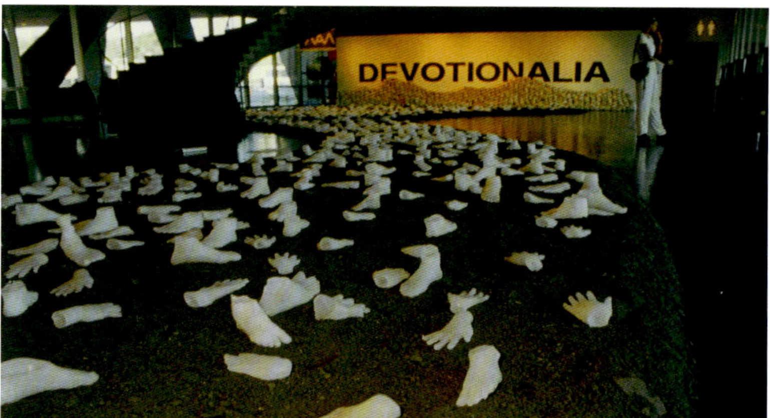

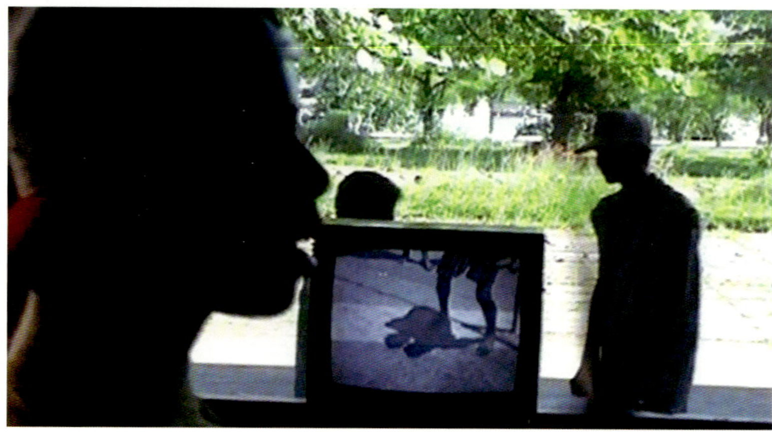

Index of Stills

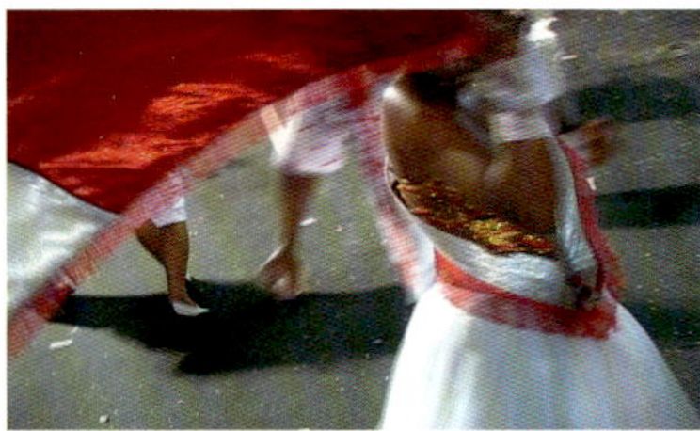

Câmera Foliã/Sambing Camera
2004

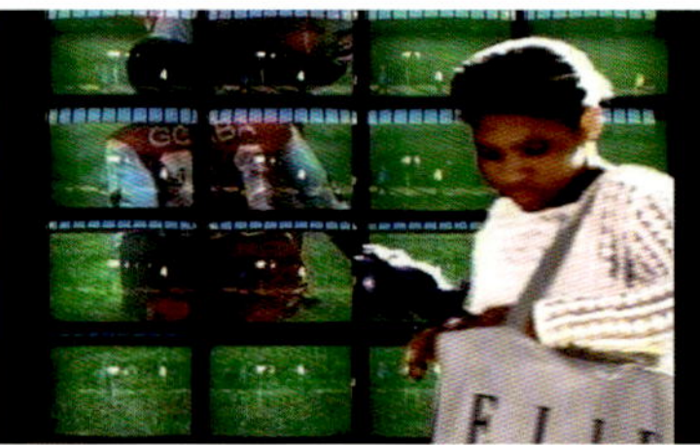

Video Wall
2001

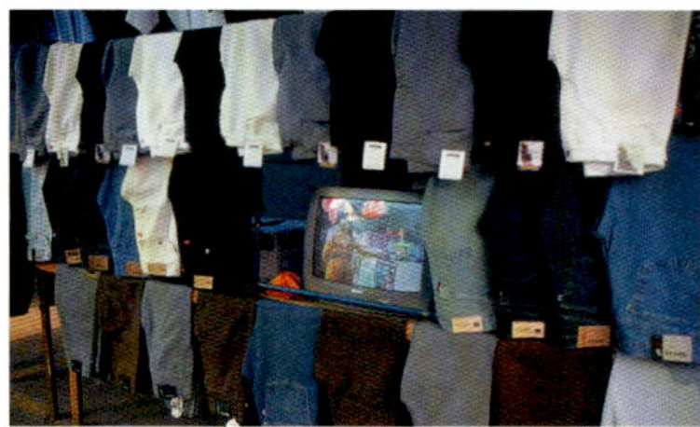

Mera Vista Point/Mere View Point
2002

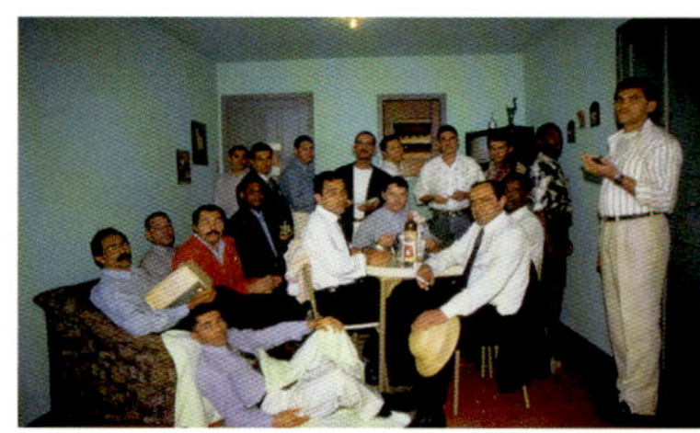

*Os Raimundos, os Severinos e
os Franciscos/The Raimundos,
the Severinos and the Franciscos*
1998

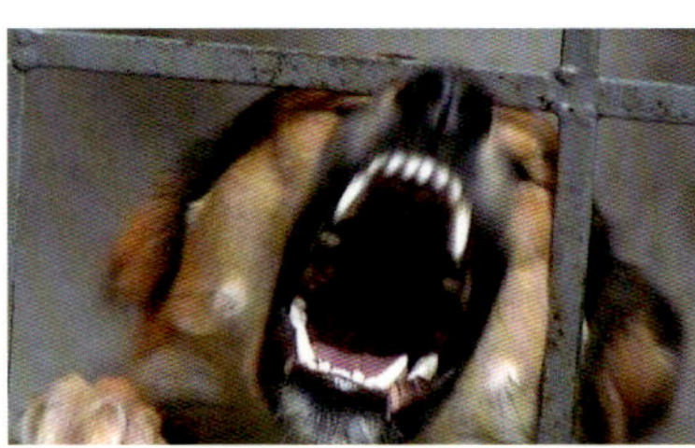

Dogs and Politicians
1999

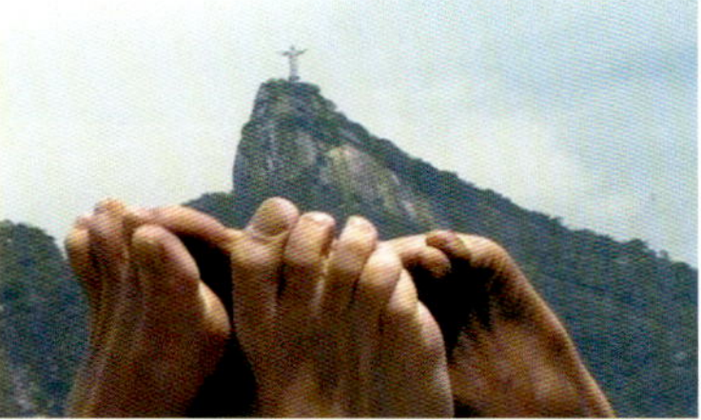

*Porque eu poderia perder/
Because I Might Lose*
2001

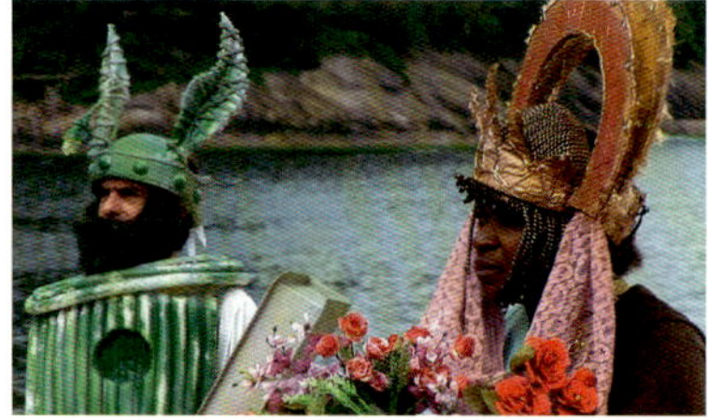

Corpo Santo/Holy Body
2012

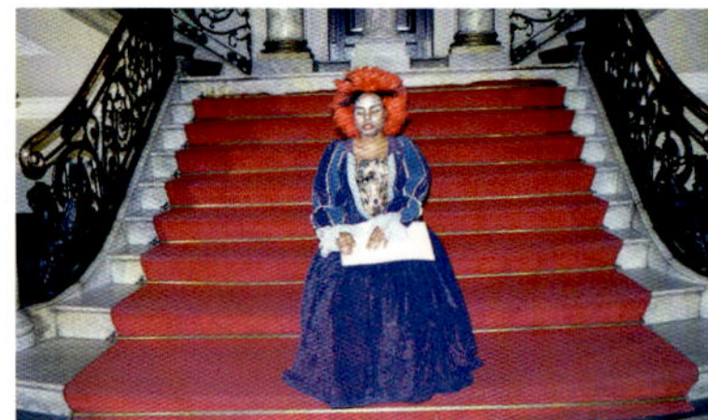

*Belo é tudo aquilo que também não
foi visto/Beautiful Is also that which Is
Unseen*
2002

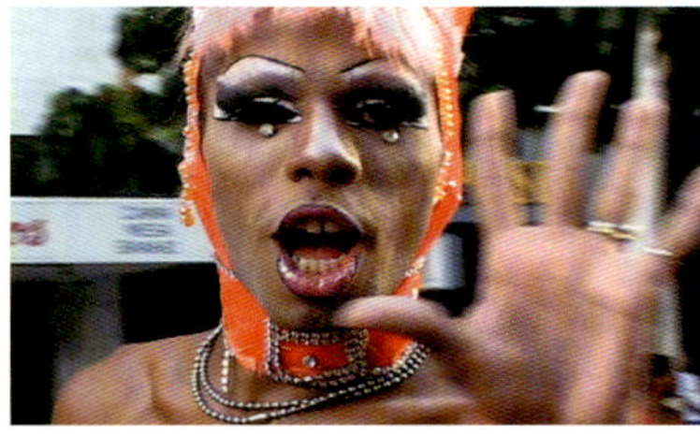

Deus é boca/God's Lips
2002

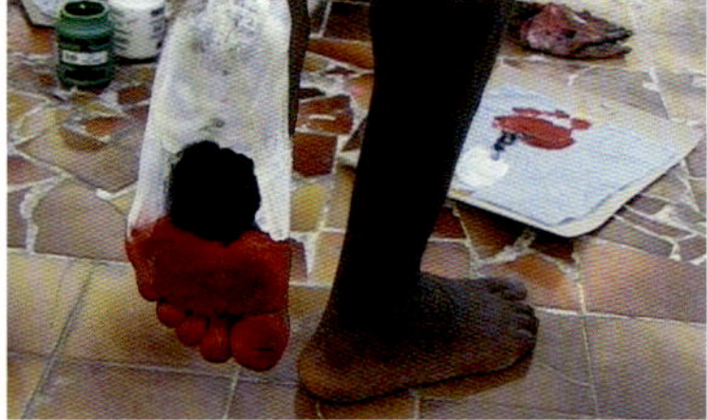

Devotionalia
1994

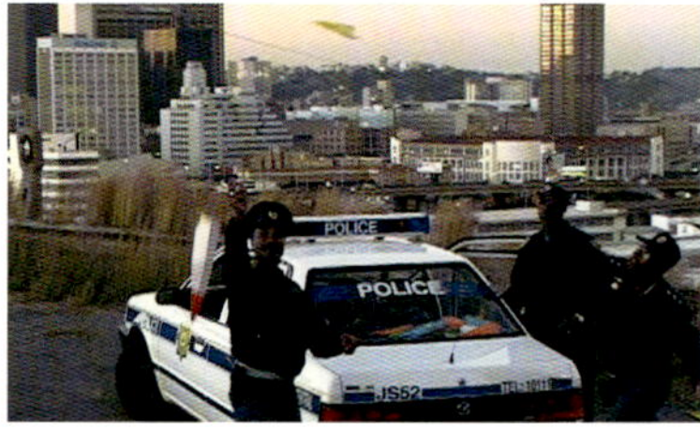

Night Shift
2001

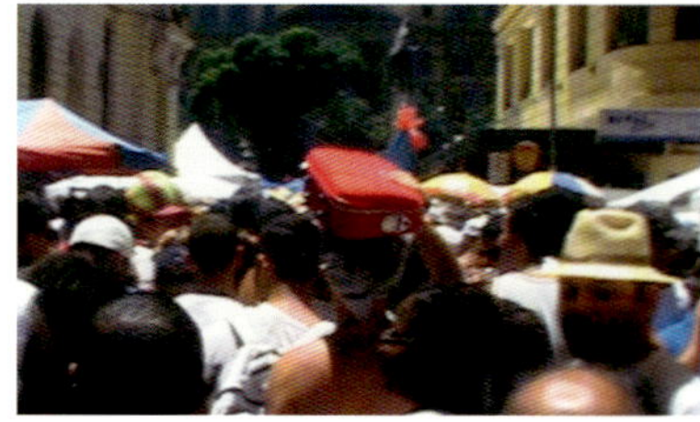

Malas para Marcel/Suitcases for Marcel
1998

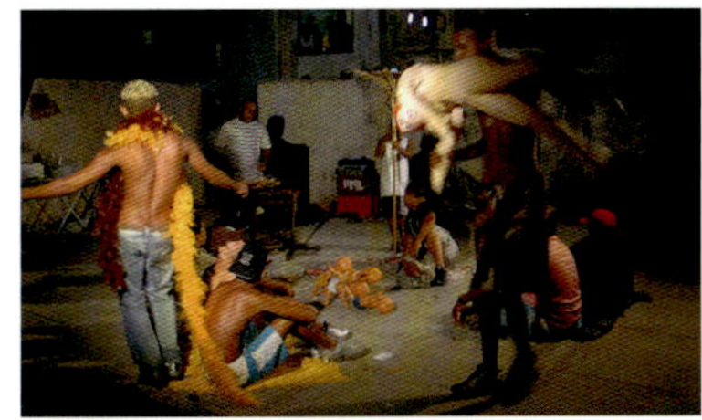

Funk Staden
2007

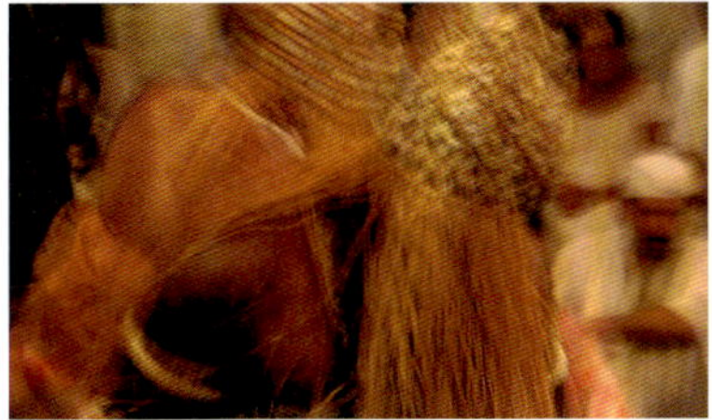

Não sou eu quem me navega/
Not Me Who Navigates Myself
2006

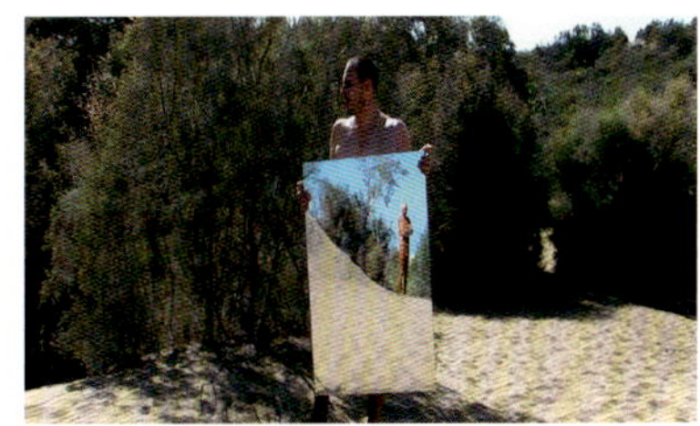

Paradiso Cansado/Exhausted Paradise
2009

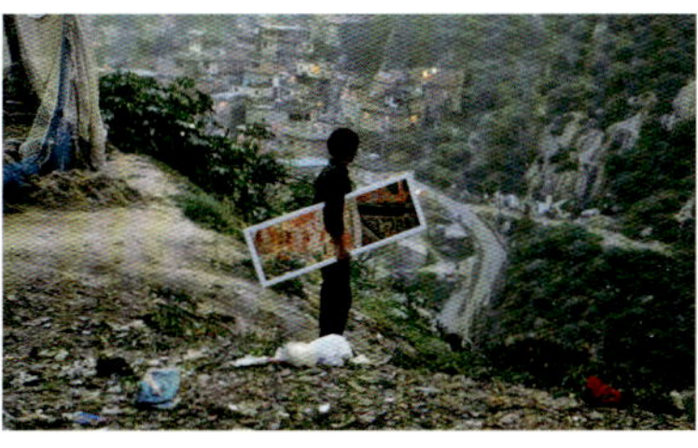

O Espelho e a Tarde/
The Mirror and the Dusk
2011

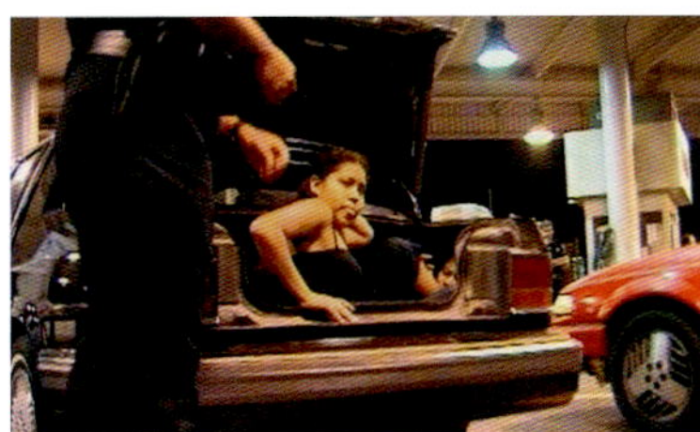

Mama & Ritos Viciosos/
Mama & Vicious Rituals
2000

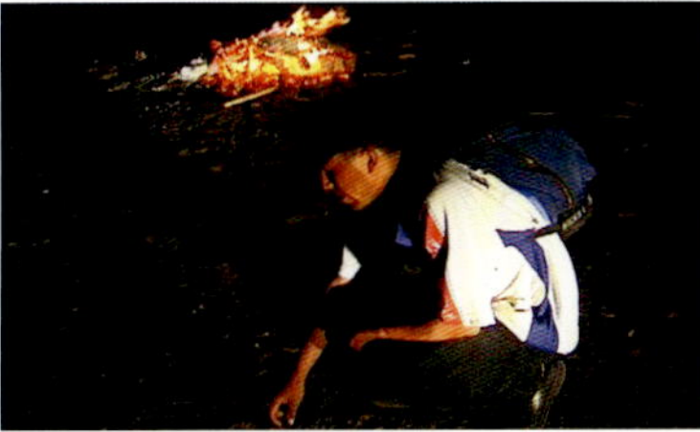

Mama & Ritos Viciosos/
Mama & Vicious Rituals
2000

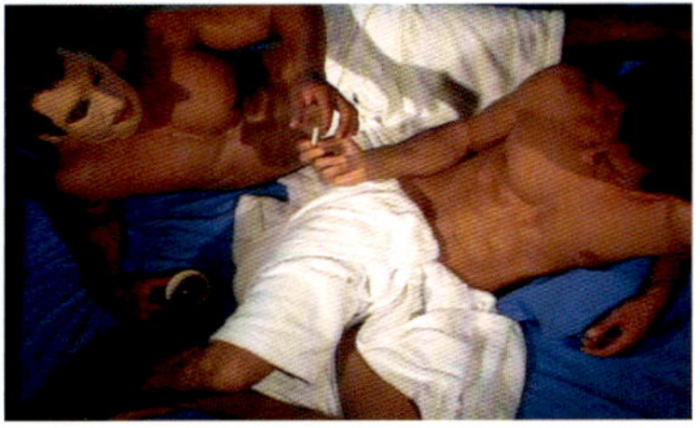

Voracidad Maxima/Maximal Voracity
2003

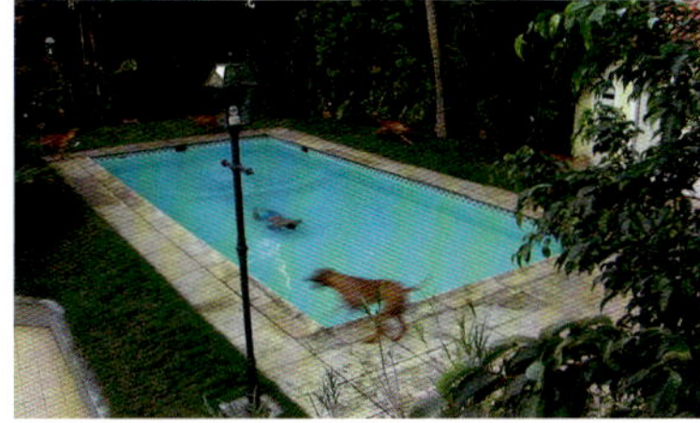

A Casa/The House
2007

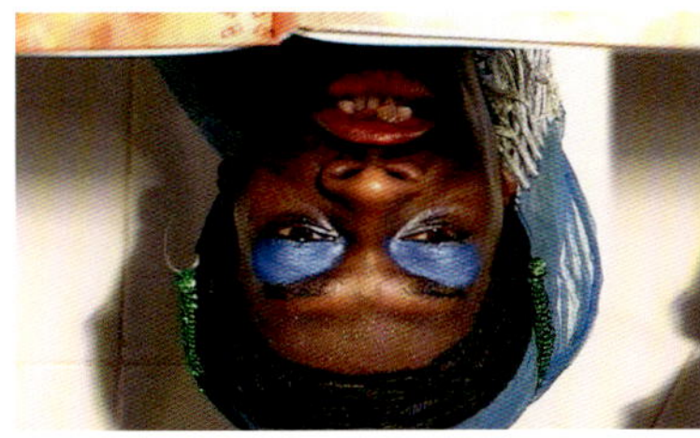

Do Universo do Baile/
Of the Universe of the Ball
2008

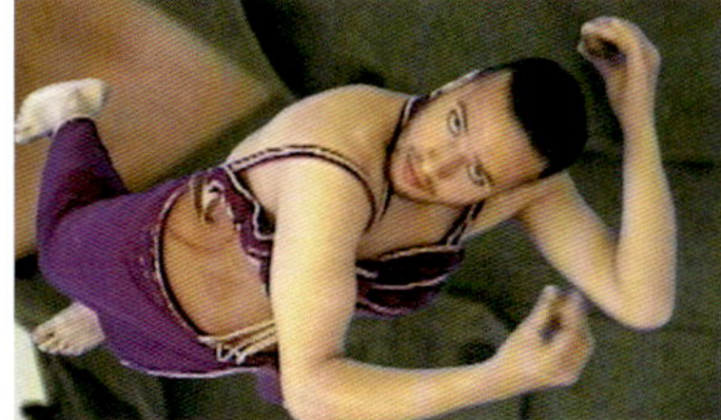

This Is Not Egypt
1999

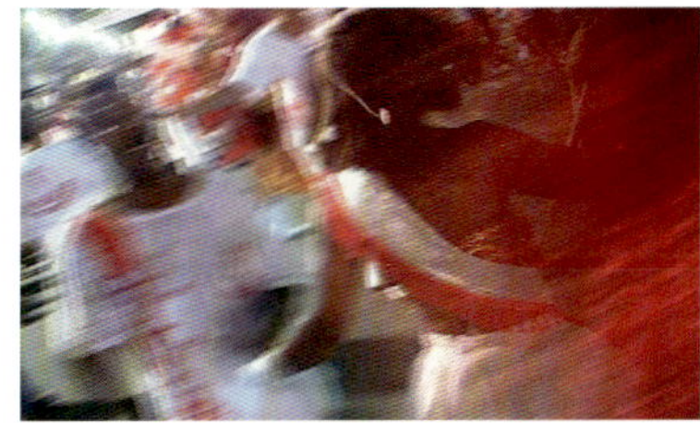

Câmera Foliã/Sambing Camera
2004

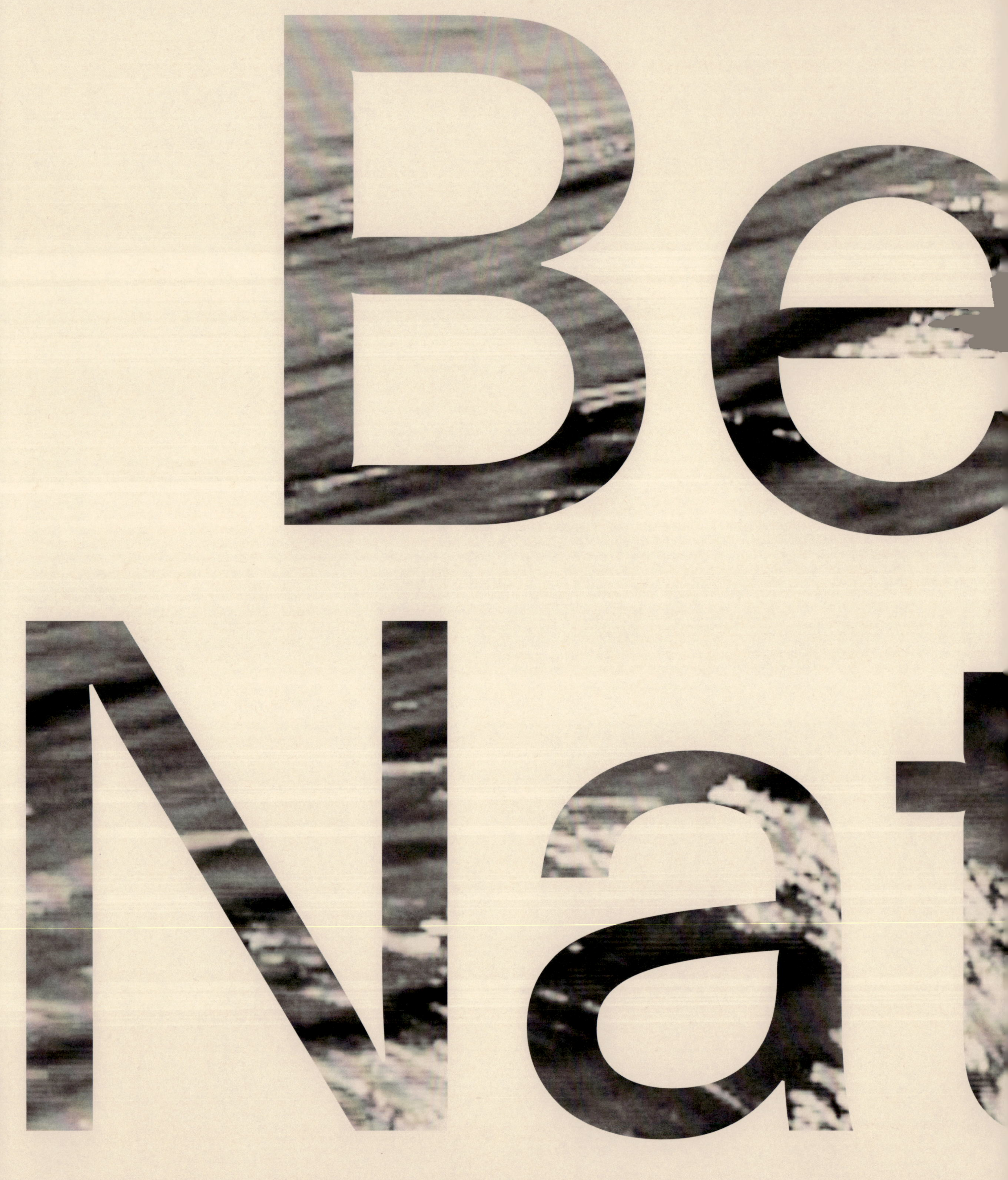

Be
Nat

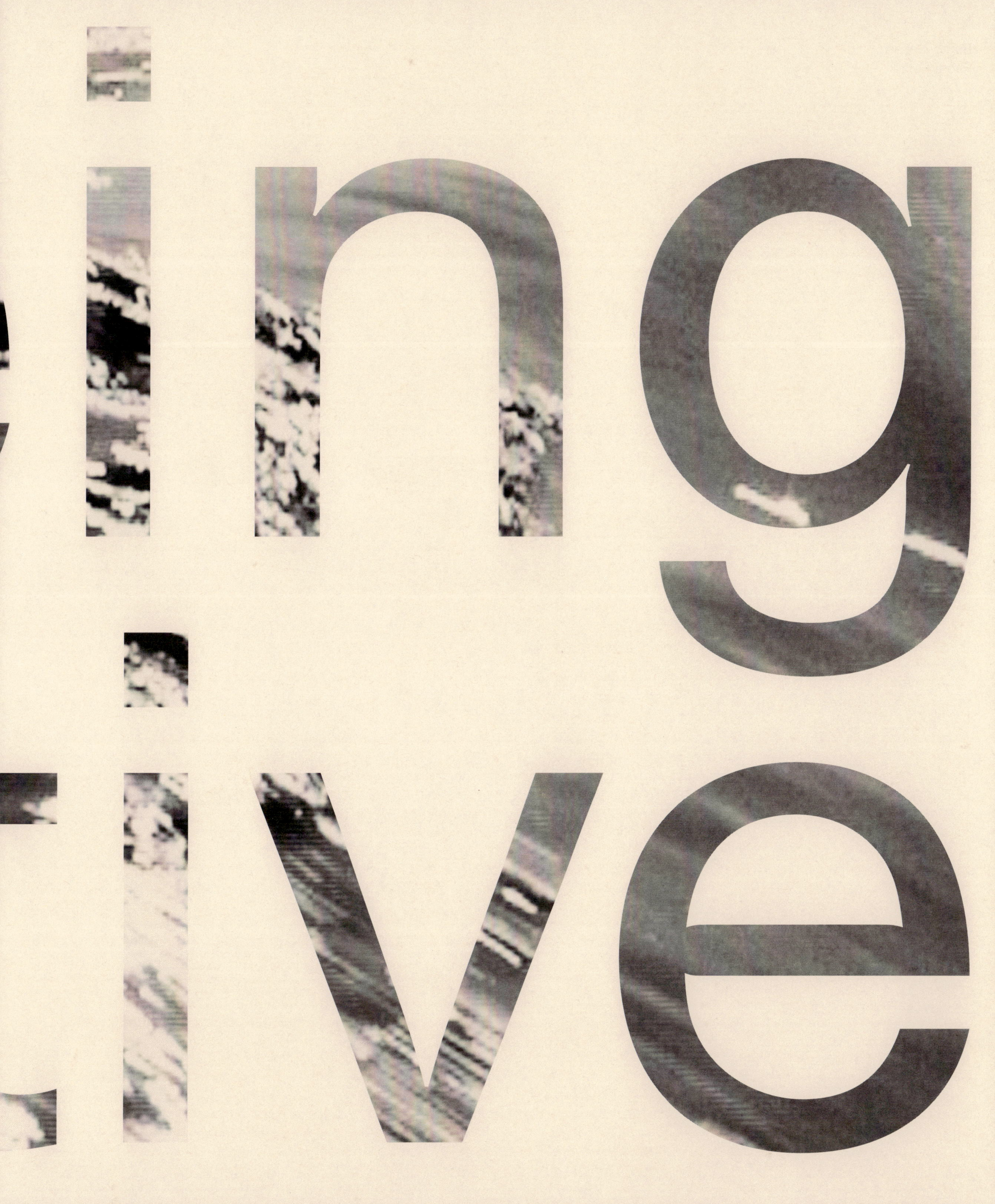

Dias & Riedweg sind Geschichtenerzähler. Aber vielleicht ist dieser Begriff nicht präzise genug, weil zu eng. Dias & Riedweg sind nämlich auch Geschichtenfinder. Nicht Erfinder, sondern Finder. Sie finden ihre Geschichten überall, vor allem aber in ihren Gegenübern. In der direkten Begegnung mit den beiden gibt es keinen Moment der Fremdheit. Sie stellen unmittelbar Vertrautheit her, indem sie Geschichten erzählen: ihre eigenen, von aktuellen Projekten, Reisen und Ideen, aber auch zu ihrem Leben, ihrer Herkunft und zu ihrer Beziehung. Die Künstler erzählen freimütig, wie sie sich kennengelernt haben, woran sie gerade arbeiten, wen sie treffen, wie sie leben. In diesem selbstverständlichen Bericht aus ihrem Alltag, ihrem Haus in Rio de Janeiro, ihrem Freundeskreis, ihrer Familie fehlt es nicht an Zufällen, an Missgeschicken, an Wut und Freude. Ihre Erzählungen verschaffen eine direkte Nähe. Das Gegenüber ist involviert in ihren Alltag und eingeladen teilzuhaben.

Storytelling ist eine Methode, mit der explizites, aber vor allem implizites Wissen in Form einer Metapher oder einer Erzählung weitergegeben und durch Zuhören aufgenommen wird, im Fall von Dias & Riedwegs Videos und Fotografien auch durch Schauen. Das Publikum wird in die erzählte Geschichte eingebunden und kann so den Gehalt der Erzählung leichter verstehen. Das vermittelte Wissen wird dadurch stärker verinnerlicht, denn Geschichten sind essentielle Erfahrungen: Sie bestimmen, wie wir uns verhalten, uns fühlen und wie wir Sinn aus neuen Erfahrungen konstruieren. Geschichten organisieren die Informationen über unsere Gegenwart, sie formen die Perspektive, mit der wir unser Leben, unsere Vergangenheit und unsere Zukunft betrachten. Geschichten sind für unser Zusammenleben und Wohlbefinden zentral. Aber woher kommen sie, wer erzählt sie und wie werden sie erzählt?

Diese Fragen greifen Dias & Riedweg in ihren Videos direkt auf. Frühe Arbeiten gehen noch vermehrt von dokumentarischen Recherchen aus (*Mama & Ritos Viciosos*, 2000, *Meu nome na tua boca*, 2000) oder geben den involvierten Menschen präzise Metaphern vor. In den sich über mehrere Monate hinziehenden Workshops mit erwachsenen und jugendlichen Gefangenen für *Question Marks* (1996) richteten die Delinquenten ihre Fragen, festgehalten auf Autonummernschildern, an die Öffentlichkeit (nicht das einzige Setting für Storytelling, das nach Abschluss des künstlerischen Projekts von den Behörden weitergeführt wurde); in *Tutti Veneziani* (1999) berichten Menschen von ihrem Tod, als läge dieser bereits hinter ihnen. Ein schönes Bild für die versinkende, ewig moderne Stadt Venedig. Aber auch ein klarer Rahmen, was erzählt werden soll und worüber gesprochen wird. In jüngeren Projekten bringen die beiden Künstler die Menschen dazu, in noch viel freierer Form ihre Geschichten zu erzählen. Dabei sind es keine Heldentaten, über die berichtet wird. Oftmals werden Verluste (*Juksa*, 2006) oder die Konstruktion von Identität (*Os Raimundos, os Severinos e os Franciscos*, 1998, *Paradiso Cansado*, 2009) thematisiert. Schwierige Aspekte wie Migration, Sexualität, Armut oder Heimat werden dabei nicht ausgespart, sondern explizit ins Zentrum der Aufmerksamkeit gerückt. Weiter gelingt es Dias & Riedweg, mit präzisen Metaphern für Globalisierung, Handel oder Mobilität ebenso vergnügliche wie beeindruckende Bilder zu schaffen (*Malas para Marcel*, 2006, *Caminhão de Mudança*, 2009).

In Seminaren zur Interviewtechnik, ob im Journalismus oder in den Sozialwissenschaften, wird gelehrt, dass ohne Preisgabe des Selbst, wenigstens ansatzweise, auch das Gegenüber nichts preisgeben wird. Dies gilt natürlich im selben Mass für das Storytelling: Wie wird jemand dazu gebracht, ihre oder seine Geschichte zu erzählen? Der Moment des Erzählens ist intim. Die Aufmerksamkeit gehört ganz der Erzählerin, dem Erzähler. Durch Geschichten wird Vertrauen hergestellt, sie werden daher oft getauscht: Dein Erlebnis gegen meine Erfahrung, deine Geschichte gegen meine Schilderung. Das ist nicht kompetitiv zu verstehen, sondern Voraussetzung dafür, dass sich die Zungen lösen und die Münder lockern. Dias & Riedweg scheinen diesen Lehrsatz vom Geben und Nehmen verinnerlicht zu haben. Wobei der Begriff „preisgeben" impliziert, dass es sich um etwas eher Unangenehmes handelt; aber dies trifft im Fall von Dias & Riedweg sicher nicht zu. Für sie ist es eher eine Teilhabe als eine Preisgabe. Nicht beobachtend teilnehmen wie in der Ethnologie, sondern involviert sein mit Haut und Haar, wie es ihrer Kunst ganz eigen ist. Sie sind Teil der Geschichten, die sie in ebenso komplexe wie atmosphärische Videoinstallationen transformieren. Sie kennen die Settings nicht nur, sie leben in und mit ihnen. Erst diese Nähe erlaubt es ihnen, in *Funk Staden* (2007) mit einheimischen Jugendlichen eine Parodie auf europäische Vorurteile aus dem 16. Jahrhundert bezüglich der kannibalischen, sexuell hemmungslosen Wilden Südamerikas zu inszenieren. Für uns, das westliche Publikum, ist die Szenerie exotisch. Wir fühlen uns durch die Rhythmen der Musik und Körper verführt und von den Puppen und Fleischbrocken unangenehm berührt. Für die Künstler hingegen ist die Situation nicht befremdend, sie sind Teil der thematisierten Kultur. Nur deshalb können sie ihre Akteurinnen und Akteure so ausserordentlich glaubwürdig zum Spiel mit Vorurteilen und Klischees motivieren. Die aussergewöhnliche Authentizität in Dias & Riedwegs Werk entsteht gerade durch ihr Heimisch-Sein in den präsentierten Geschichten.

Das heisst nicht, dass Dias & Riedweg in der Favela leben, aber es bedeutet, dass ihr Umgang mit den Menschen in den Favelas sehr vertraut ist. So sehr, dass sich diese Menschen bereitwillig auf ihre Projekte einlassen. Dies gilt nicht nur für partizipative Projekte wie *Devotionalia* (1994), *Sugar Seekers* (2004) oder *Deus é boca* (2002), bei denen im Prinzip jede und jeder mitmachen kann. Es gilt mindestens ebenso für inhaltlich heiklere Arbeiten, bei denen die beteiligten Menschen entweder persönliche und intime Aspekte einbringen oder sich mit Vorurteilen ihrer Person, Herkunft, Rasse gegenüber auseinandersetzen. Die Künstler sind dabei dermassen involviert, dass die Projekte keinen klaren Anfang und auch kein klares Ende zu haben scheinen. Zwischen Kunst und Leben, Arbeit und privat wird nicht unterschieden. Beispielsweise sind die Menschen von *A cidade fora dela* (2011), der allerersten Arbeit der Serie *Pequenas Histórias de Modéstia e Dúvida (seit 2011)*, so sehr Teil von Dias & Riedwegs Alltag, dass sich die Zwillinge Vitor und Vitoria nach Abschluss der Dreharbeiten nicht von den beiden Künstlern trennen mögen. Mauricio Dias entschliesst sich daraufhin zur Adoption der beiden Kinder.

Ein Haus in Rio, thematisiert in den beiden Werken *A Casa* (2007) und *O Jardim* (2008), ist Wohnort von Mauricio Dias und den beiden Kindern. Hier arbeiten Dias & Riedweg zusammen mit ihren Assistentinnen und Assistenten, hier gehen Gäste ein und aus, jederzeit herzlich willkommen. Hier werden die Geschichten, die eigenen und die mitgebrachten, verdichtet und zu packenden Videoinstallationen gefügt. Dieses Haus mit den vielen Zimmern, den historischen Details und dem grossen Garten bietet den idealen Ausgangspunkt für künstlerische Recherchen. Es ist aber auch ein Ort für die vielen mit Dias & Riedweg verbundenen Menschen. Konsequenterweise lassen sie uns, das Publikum, daran teilhaben, führen uns in *A Casa* und in *O Jardim* durch dieses Haus und diesen Garten. Wir begegnen dabei Walter Riedweg und Mauricio Dias: Sie blicken uns vervielfältigt an, multipliziert laufen sie um den Pool und tanzen durch die Räume. Nie ist dabei ganz klar, was Spiel, was Alltag ist, was für ein Paar sie da gerade sind – aber die kleinen Videos, präsentiert auf Screens, montiert in einen hübsch gezeichneten Grundriss von Haus und Garten, wirken ausserordentlich privat. Diese Intimität ist verführerisch, schon ziehen wir gedanklich ein, übernehmen vielleicht einen Teil der anstehenden Gartenarbeit oder engagieren uns anderweitig in Haus und Atelier. Wir wollen dazugehören und identifizieren uns dabei übermässig mit dem Gegenüber, dem Fremden.

„Going Native" bezeichnet die Überidentifikation der Anthropologin, des Ethnologen mit dem Gegenstand ihrer, seiner Untersuchung. Heimisch werden, sich als Eingeborene, Eingeborener fühlen und dabei die kritische, für die Reflexion nötige Distanz verlieren, ist in den Sozialwissenschaften ein Fehlverhalten, weil es den wissenschaftlichen Kriterien komplett zuwiderläuft: dem Grundsatz nämlich, dass jede und jeder unter denselben Umständen zu denselben Ergebnissen kommen kann. *Going Native* impliziert im Tempus des Verbs „to go" als „going", in dieser Unmittelbarkeit des Jetzt, dass eine Bewegung der Annäherung stattfindet. Die Feldforscherin, der Feldforscher ist ursprünglich nicht *native*, eingeboren, heimisch, sondern wird es im Laufe ihrer, seiner Studien und teilnehmenden Beobachtungen. Was aber, wenn die im *Going Native* überwundene Distanz gar nie vorhanden war? Oft wurde im Zusammenhang mit Dias & Riedwegs Werk über das Andere, die Reflexion des Selbst im Gegenüber geschrieben. Dies entspricht der Perspektive von uns, dem Publikum. Für die Künstler selbst trifft diese Distanz zum Anderen nicht zu; die beiden sind Teil des Gegenüber, sie werden nicht erst eingeboren oder einheimisch, sie sind es bereits. Dias & Riedweg sind die Anderen, auch wenn sie nicht in einer Favela wohnen oder als Stricher arbeiten. *Being Native* ist die Haltung, die überhaupt erst das Erzählen der Geschichten ermöglicht.

Wir begegnen den Künstlern beispielsweise ganz unmittelbar auf den blau bezogenen Betten in *Voracidad Maxima* (2003) und zwar erneut verdoppelt. Diesmal ist die Verdoppelung von Walter Riedweg und Mauricio Dias aber kein technischer Kniff, sondern die Künstler leihen ihre Gesichter in Form von Masken männlichen Prostituierten, die aus ihrem Leben erzählen. Dazu liegen die Stricher halbnackt, in weisse Frotteemäntel gehüllt und maskiert mit Walters respektive Mauricios Gesicht entspannt auf einem blau bezogenen Bett und unterhalten sich mit demjenigen Künstler, dessen Gesicht sie sich geliehen haben. Dias & Riedweg zeichnen dabei nicht nur für die Inszenierung verantwortlich, sie sind Teil der Szene und im Bild ebenfalls halbnackt zu sehen. *Being Native*: Die Künstler lassen gar nicht erst eine Distanz zu den Prostituierten aufkommen, wodurch jeglicher Voyeurismus unmöglich ist. Die Neugier, mit der wir als Betrachterin, Betrachter in der Ausstellung nun Platz nehmen auf einem blau bezogenen Bett zwischen den Videoprojektionen, ist wohlwollend und anteilnehmend.

In der umfangreichen Arbeit *Corpo Santo* (2012) entwickeln Dias & Riedweg ausgehend von Zeichnungen psychisch angeschlagener Menschen fantastische Kostüme, die wiederum Patientinnen und Patienten einer psychiatrischen Klinik anziehen für die Videoaufnahmen der beiden Künstler. Im gut einstündigen Video berichten diese fantastischen Figuren auf so anrührende

Weise mit Musik, Tanz, Erzählungen und einem Ausflug ans Meer von ihren Gefühlen und ihrem Leben, dass jegliche Distanz beim Publikum verloren geht. Die Begegnung mit den Insassinnen und Insassen der Psychiatrie geschieht so unmittelbar, dass kein Raum für Sentimentalitäten wie Mitleid, Abscheu oder Furcht bleibt. Selbst die Differenzierung in „Wir" und „die Anderen" ist nicht mehr möglich, weil *Corpo Santo* dafür viel zu poetisch und viel zu anziehend ist.

Diese fehlende Distanz generiert die ausserordentliche Authentizität in Dias & Riedwegs Werk. Erstaunlicherweise gelingt es den beiden Künstlern trotz ihrer enormen Involviertheit, kritisch zu bleiben und eine vielschichtige Sicht zu entwickeln. Vielleicht ist die unglaubliche Nähe zu den Akteurinnen und Akteuren auch gerade Voraussetzung für die Entwicklung der komplexen Erzählstränge – so als ob die Künstler über Menschen und ihre Schicksale berichteten, die sie bereits seit langem, wenn nicht schon immer kennen. In dieser familiären Atmosphäre kommen wir als Publikum über die Kunstwerke ungeahnt nah an das Andere, die Anderen heran. Die charakteristische Unmittelbarkeit der Künstler lässt uns dabei selbst die Distanz verlieren und zum Anderen, zur Anderen werden. *Going Native* eben.

Dias & Riedwegs Arbeiten sind oft in Südamerika, ja in Rio selbst realisiert worden – aber nicht ausschliesslich. Denn sie sind keine südamerikanischen Künstler, sie sind vielmehr überall auf der Welt eingeboren. Für der Serie *Pequenas Histórias de Modéstia e Dúvida* entwickeln sie zu den vier Kapiteln aus Südamerika zwei weitere aus Europa. Sie nehmen uns mit in ihre Stadt, aber auch in die Schweiz. Das Land, in dem zumindest der eine der beiden Künstler ein Einheimischer ist – wenn auch ein vor langer Zeit schon Ausgewanderter. Dias & Riedweg führen uns nachts auf einen hell beleuchteten Fussballplatz (*Peladas Noturnas*, 2011), in einen Vergnügungspark (*Sábado à noite no Parquinho*, 2011), durch das sich vom Zentrum zu seinen Rändern hin verändernde Rio (*O Espelho e a Tarde*, 2011). Der Spaziergang dieser letzten *kleinen Geschichte von Bescheidenheit und Zweifel* zeigt die Metropole fragmentiert und vermittelt das Lebensgefühl in dieser Stadt gerade deshalb so eindrücklich. Die Handlung ist einfach, wenn nicht gar simpel, doch die Metapher ist komplex: Ein junger Mann schreitet mit einem Spiegel unter dem Arm vom Stadtzentrum aus in seine Favela hinauf. Der Spiegel reflektiert die umliegende Stadt, die bunten Gassen. Es sind also sowieso immer schon zwei Bilder im Bild zu erkennen. Dias & Riedweg steigern die Komposition, indem sie dieses Bild mit zwei weiteren Projektionen überlagern. Das projizierte Rechteck ist kein Mono-Channel, sondern eine Dreifach-Projektion. Die farbigen Sprengsel, die Bilder im Bild zu erkennen ist anspruchsvoll, verwirrend und gleichzeitig sehr sinnlich. Sein Weg führt den jungen Mann mit dem Spiegel von der hektischen Innenstadt durch die verwinkelten Gassen über steile Stufen in die Favela oben am Hang mit Sicht auf Rio. Dabei sind die städtebaulichen Bemühungen erkennbar, mit denen die raueren Aussenbezirke dank neuer Treppen erschlossen und gezähmt werden sollen. Eine in ihrer Farbigkeit vielleicht tatsächlich südamerikanische Arbeit, die die Vertrautheit der Künstler mit der Stadt Rio klar belegt. Wären da nicht die beiden neusten Kapitel der Serie *Pequenas Histórias de Modéstia e Dúvida*, die anlässlich der Ausstellung im Kunstmuseum Luzern realisiert wurden. Die kleinen Geschichten von Vreni & Fritz und Esther & Heinz erzählen in *Zwei aus Vier* (2014) vom Zusammenleben, vom Leben in der Schweiz, vom Mittelstand, vom Land und von der Stadt. Erneut ist sofort spürbar, wie vertraut die beiden Künstler mit ihren Akteurinnen und Akteuren sein müssen, um diese Nähe in den Videos einfangen zu können. Wobei „einfangen" ein zu jägerischer Jargon ist, vielmehr schaffen die beiden den Raum, in dem ihre Gegenüber so offen ihre Geschichten erzählen mögen. Weil Dias & Riedweg hier heimisch sind: Hier auf dem Land ist Walter Riedweg aufgewachsen und rieb sich an den dörflichen Strukturen, an der Kleinteiligkeit des ländlichen Lebens, bis er auszog, um Musik, Pantomime und Kunst zu studieren. Hier in dieser Stadt (Basel) begegnete ihm in den 1980er Jahren Mauricio Dias im damals legendären VIA (Video Audio Atelier Basel). Beide aufgebrochen, anderswo heimisch zu werden. Nach Jahren in Basel wechseln sie den Kontinent, bewahren jedoch die Freundschaften und familiären Beziehungen.

Dieses Ausziehen in die Welt hinaus, aber auch dieses Heimischwerden im Überall, in sich und dem Gegenüber zeichnet Dias & Riedwegs künstlerische Arbeit aus. Sie überschreiten viele Grenzen, auch ihre eigenen, werden distanzlos und lassen sich mit ausgesprochener Sensitivität für politische Themen, für Migrantinnen, Migranten, Flüchtlinge, Arbeitslose, für Fragen zur Identität, Sexualität, Reichtum, Bildung oder Urbanismus, auf alles ein. In ihrem Werk berichten sie davon, wie viel wir gewinnen können an Intensität, wenn wir die Distanz zum Anderen, zu den Anderen aufgeben. *Being Native* meint immer, wir sind involviert, wir sind zuhause, einheimisch, heimisch, mit den Sitten und Gebräuchen vertraut, eingeboren. Was, wenn wir *Being Native* global, umfassend und weit verstünden, über die Kontinente hinweg, wie dies Dias & Riedweg tun? Denn wir sind alle Eingeborene, da oder dort.

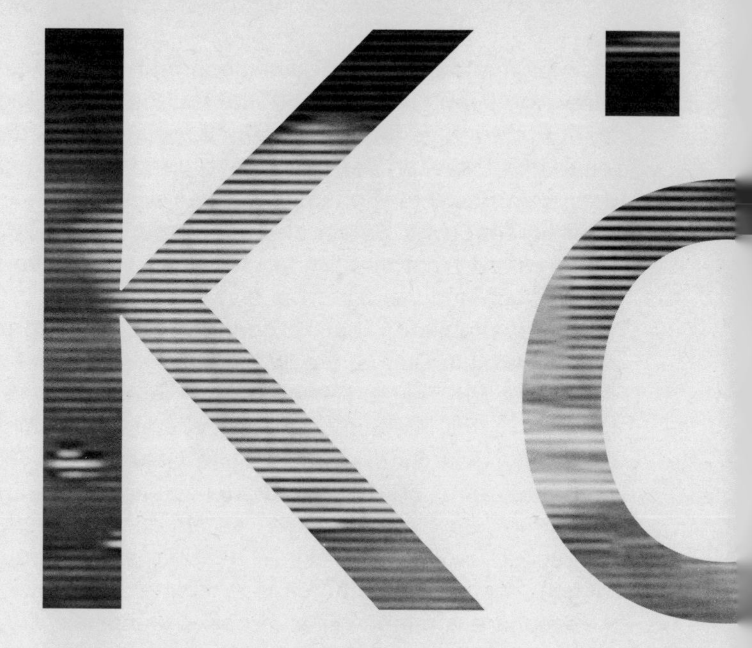

örper

an

örper

„Alles auf der Welt begann mit einem Ja. Ein Molekül sagte zu
einem anderen Molekül ja, und das Leben wurde geboren."
– Clarice Lispector, *Die Sternstunde*[1]

In seinem Buch *Die Erschaffung der Welt oder Die Globalisierung*
trägt Jean Luc-Nancy die unterschiedlichen Bedeutungen der
Worte *globalisation* und *mondialisation* (Welt-Erschaffung) vor.[2]
Im Französischen können beide Begriffe verwendet werden,
Nancy nuanciert diese jedoch, indem er ihre möglichen Bedeutungen differenzierend voneinander abhebt. *Globalisation* wird
als abstraktes, summarisches Phänomen verstanden, aus dem
sich eine lineare Entwicklung ableiten lässt. *Mondialisation* ist
konkreter; es impliziert Bewegung, Aufsplitterung und Verände-
rung. Die Sprache spielt hier eine Rolle bei der Definition von
Welterscheinungen und der „Verkörperung" der verschiedenen
Bedeutungen, die sie haben können. Die Sprache erfasst
lediglich Bruchstücke der Wirklichkeit. Sie neigt dazu, Reales
in Definitionen zu verpacken, die durch das Lexikon oder die
Enzyklopädie zur Norm erstarren. Die Aufgabe der Philosophie
ist es, den normativen Charakter der Sprache zu hinterfragen,
Wörter neu zu definieren und neue Bedeutungen zu entwickeln.
Maurice Merleau-Ponty gehörte zu einer Generation von
Philosophinnen und Philosophen, die in der Mitte eines Jahrhunderts lebten, in dem Gewalt und Konflikte durch die beiden
Weltkriege ein noch nie da gewesenes Ausmass erreichten.
Er zählte jedenfalls zu denen, die die Grenzen der Philosophie
kennen. Merleau-Ponty dachte, dass man sich in Zukunft auf
der Suche nach Sinn und Bedeutung am ehesten der Kunst
zuwenden müsste.[3]

Dias & Riedweg könnte man als Philosophen unserer Zeit
verstehen, als Philosophen, die in einer vom Phänomen der
Globalisierung beherrschten Welt lieber mit Bildern arbeiten als
mit Worten. Wo ist dieses Duo im Problemfeld „globalisation/
mondialisation" anzusiedeln?

Bevor wir versuchen, diese Frage in den Griff zu bekom-
men, möchte ich nochmals auf Nancy zurückkommen, da
seine Gedanken in diesem speziellen Fall hilfreich sein könn-
ten. Lassen Sie mich Nancys Einleitung zur französischen
Originalausgabe seines Werks zitieren:

„Die Erschaffung der Welt *oder* Die Globalisierung":
Die Konjunktion muss gleichzeitig und abwechselnd in
ihrer disjunktiven, substitutiven und konjunktiven Wertigkeit
verstanden werden.
Gemäss der ersten: die Erschaffung der Welt oder die
Globalisierung, es gilt zu wählen, die eine bedeutet den
Ausschluss der anderen.
Gemäss der zweiten: die Erschaffung der Welt, mit
anderen Worten die Globalisierung, diese muss als jene
verstanden werden.

Gemäss der dritten: die Erschaffung der Welt oder die Globalisierung führen uns, beide gleichermassen, zu ein und demselben Resultat (das noch zu bestimmen ist). Die Verknüpfung dieser drei Wertigkeiten läuft darauf hinaus, eine einzige Frage zu variieren: Kann das, was man „Globalisierung" nennt, eine Welt ins Leben rufen, oder deren Gegenteil?

Und da es weder darum geht, die Zukunft zu prophezeien noch sie zu beherrschen: wie sollen wir uns geben (uns öffnen), um vor uns zu schauen, dorthin wo nichts sichtbar ist, unser Blick von diesen beiden Begriffen geleitet, deren Sinn sich uns entzieht – die „Schöpfung" (die bisher dem theologischen Mysterium vorbehalten war), die „Globalisierung" [*mondialisation*] (die bisher den ökonomischen und technischen Tatsachen vorbehalten war und die im Französischen auch als *globalisation* bezeichnet wird)?[4]

Nancy betrachtet den Prozess der Mondialisierung als identisch mit jenem der Schöpfung, als Prozess, in dessen Verlauf die Welt erschaffen wird. Er ist weltbildend in dem Sinn, dass die Welt nicht mehr etwas Gegebenes ist, sondern weiterverarbeitet oder neu zusammengesetzt werden muss. Diese Zukunft kennen wir während ihrer Entstehung noch nicht. Sie kann der Globalisierung entgegenwirken, die gewöhnlich mit der Dominanz von Wirtschaft und Technik einhergeht. Nancy fragt sich jedoch: Was ist „Schöpfung"? Deren Bedeutung entzieht sich uns, es fehlt die klare Richtschnur, alles was wir tun können, ist, uns zu öffnen, „um vor uns zu schauen".

Dias & Riedweg sind Künstler aus Brasilien, oder besser: Künstler, die in Brasilien leben und arbeiten, genauer gesagt: in Rio de Janeiro. Mauricio Dias ist Brasilianer, Walter Riedweg Schweizer. Der eine ist gelernter Druckgrafiker, der andere hat eine Theater- und Musikausbildung absolviert. Ihre Zusammenarbeit als Duo hat ihre Kunst grundlegend verändert, da sie zu einem gemeinsamen Unterfangen wurde. Doch wie wir sehen werden, macht gerade die Kombination der beiden Standpunkte, dem des Druckgrafikers, dem des darstellenden Künstlers, das Spezifische des Duos aus. Der Druckgrafiker will einen materiellen Abdruck der Welt[5] erreichen, der darstellende Künstler spielt in der Welt vorkommende Tropen und Situationen durch. Beide sind körperlich mit einem Kunst-Machen verbunden, das mit Weltgestaltung zu tun hat.

2006 wurde ich anlässlich einer Ausstellung Brasilianischer Skulpturen ins Henry Moore Institute in Leeds eingeladen.[6] Als Herausgeberin von *Parachute* hatte ich damals gerade ein Heft über São Paulo publiziert.[7] Die damit einhergehenden Recherchen hatten mich dazu gebracht, das „Körper an Körper"-Konzept zu entwickeln, das meinem Vortrag den Titel gab. Ich kannte Dias & Riedweg und ihr Werk damals schon seit einigen Jahren, und es stand für mich ausser Zweifel, dass sie ebenfalls in diese besondere Sparte der brasilianischen Kunst gehörten, die man als Körper-an-Körper-Erkundung beschreiben kann. Besonders die Kunst von Lygia Clark, Lygia Pape und Helio Oiticica hatte mich dazu gebracht, dieses Konzept zu entwickeln, aber auch Tungas Arbeit und jene von Cildo Meireles hingen meiner Ansicht nach mit diesem Tropus zusammen. Dias & Riedweg haben andere Wege und Mittel entwickelt, aber im Kern folgt ihre Arbeit einer bestimmten Tradition oder Weltanschauung, in der sich alles um den aktiven Prozess der Weltgestaltung dreht. Parallel dazu liegt diesem Prozess eine fortwährende Erkundung der Frage nach dem Anderen zugrunde.

Brasilien lebt weiterhin als „Neue Welt". Nachdem es über Jahrhunderte zur Heimat zahlloser Immigranten aus anderen Kontinenten wurde, bekanntlich vorwiegend aus Afrika und Europa, wird es heute aufgrund seiner boomenden Wirtschaft und seines demografischen Wachstums zu einem zunehmend neuralgischen Punkt unseres Planeten. Seine vielen Ballungsräume, einschliesslich São Paulo und Rio, mit ihren vielfältig gemischten Rassen und Ethnien, sind Laboratorien des heutigen Lebens auf der Erde. Die aktuelle Situation zwingt uns, „vor uns zu schauen", in einer unvergleichlichen Mutmassung, die sich aus der Vermischung vieler Welten und Kulturen ergibt, und dies in einer Weltregion, die sich inmitten einer unglaublich starken Naturumgebung befindet. Einer Natur, die mit einer brodelnden Urbanisierung konfrontiert ist, die ihrerseits die Entwicklung von Städten zu bewältigen hat, die so gross sind wie andernorts ganze Länder. São Paulo zählt mittlerweile fast 12 Millionen Einwohner und Rio 7 Millionen.

Rio, die Heimat der meisten hier erwähnten Künstlerinnen und Künstler, auch die von Dias & Riedweg, wird vom atlantischen Ozean begrenzt. Der Atlantik erinnert hier ständig daran, dass es ein „Anderes" da draussen gibt, das immerfort an die Tür klopft. Ein sehr grosses und atemberaubendes Anderes.

Das Leben ist eine Herausforderung für diese Künstlerinnen und Künstler, die in ihrer Kunst versuchen, Lebensbedingungen zu erarbeiten. Dias & Riedweg haben sich von Anfang an mit diesen Fragen auseinandergesetzt, im Sinn einer an andere gerichteten gemeinsamen Aussage. Sie sprechen das Thema Gemeinsamkeit ständig an, was den einen mit dem anderen verbindet, wie das Gemeinsame funktioniert, und zwar im zeitgenössischen Kontext.

Das Zeitgenössische bezeichnet die Gegenwart, es umfasst all
die vielen Themen und Lebensweisen, die unsere Epoche aus-
machen, alles, was die Zeiten, die wir durchleben, zum Ereignis
macht. Doch anders als Historiker und Politiker akzeptieren
sie die Tatsache, dass das Zeitgenössische schwer fassbar ist,
nicht feststeht. Was zeitgenössisch ist, muss fast jeden Tag
neu bestimmt werden. Das hängt eng mit dem demokratischen
Prozess zusammen. Die Ausübung der Demokratie muss Pro-
zesse in Gang setzen, die den Geist und neue Möglichkeiten
öffnen und Veränderungen begünstigen. Wobei diese Veränderungen sowohl auf kollektiven als auch auf individuellen
Beiträgen beruhen.

Betrachten wir einige der Arbeiten, die seit den 1990er
Jahren entstanden sind. 1994 haben Dias & Riedweg ein Projekt
namens *Devotionalia* gestartet. Sie arbeiteten in Lapa in Rio
de Janeiro (einem blühenden Viertel voller Musik und Bars, in
der sich eine Jugendkultur zusammenfand), zogen mit einer
mobilen Werkstatt herum und kommunizierten mit Kindern und
Teenagern. Sie fragten diese, ob sie einen Abguss ihrer Hand
oder eines Fusses machen wollten. Diese wurden zu Votivgaben,
die später als Installation in einem Museum ausgestellt wurden.
In Kirchen werden solche Votivgaben in der Regel hinterlegt,
um einen Wunsch oder eine Sehnsucht zum Ausdruck zu bringen. In diesem Fall bildete die schiere Anhäufung der Abgüsse
lebendiger junger Körper einen mächtigen Chor von Stimmen,
welche die Verwirklichung unausgesprochener Träume erflehten.

Die älteste Arbeit in der Ausstellung im Kunstmuseum
Luzern, *Os Raimundos, os Severinos e os Franciscos* (1998),
verfolgt ebenfalls dieses Interesse am Vermischen von Privatem
und Öffentlichem, Individuellem und Kollektivem, und an der Entwicklung einer sich daraus ergebenden künstlerischen Aussage,
die aufzeigen könnte, wie Gemeinsamkeit funktioniert. Das Werk
ist eine „Untersuchung" à la Dias & Riedweg, die sich mit in
São Paulo arbeitenden Portiers befasst, und entstand anlässlich
der 24. Biennale in São Paulo.

Viele dieser Portiers stammten aus dem Norden Brasiliens.
Sie wurden gebeten, vor der Videokamera über ihre Arbeit zu
sprechen. Ausgewählt wurden sie aufgrund der Tatsache, dass
sie einen dieser Vornamen trugen: Raimundo, Severino oder
Francisco. Hinter der Gemeinsamkeit des Namens tritt die
Einzigartigkeit jedes einzelnen der Gefilmten umso deutlicher
hervor. Sie erzählen von Immigration, Wanderschaft, Arbeits-
bedingungen, Beziehungen und vermitteln uns ein Bild der
Verflechtung ihres persönlichen Lebens mit der schnelllebigen,
hektischen Stadt. Darüber hinaus wurden die Portiers eingeladen, kollektiv in einer fiktiven Endszene eines Theaterstückes

mitzuspielen, für welches sie das Bühnenbild gemeinsam bauten
und für das sie Möbel und private Objekte mitbrachten. Dieses
Bühnenbild war zusammen mit dem dokumentierenden Video
an der Biennale ausgestellt, so dass sich die Geschichten der
einzelnen Protagonisten mit der fiktiven, dargestellten Szene ver-
mischten. Auch hier wird die Frage nach dem Anderen gestellt,
und das persönliche Schicksal ist mit kollektiven Interaktionen
und Ermächtigungen vermischt.

Voracidad Maxima, entstanden 2003 in Barcelona, ist ein
für den Werdegang von Dias & Riedweg wichtiges Werk. Hier
stellen sie sich nicht nur den Mitgliedern einer Gemeinschaft,
sondern fassen einander buchstäblich selbst ins Auge. Die
Gesichter im dabei entstandenen Video sind stark geschminkt.
Für diese Arbeit wurden in Barcelona männliche Prostituierte
gesucht, elf von ihnen waren schliesslich an der Entstehung
von *Voracidad Maxima* beteiligt. Sie wurden gebeten, über ihre
Arbeit zu sprechen, über ihre persönliche Geschichte, über ihre
Kunden und ihre Sexualität, während sie sich in Bademänteln
auf einem Bett räkelten, das Gesicht hinter Masken verborgen,
die Mauricio und Walter ähnelten. Der Raum war mit Spiegeln
ausgestattet, um gleichzeitig Vorder- und Rückansichten zu
ermöglichen. Dank der Überspitzung brechtscher Leitsätze in
Kombination mit dem Drehen eines Videos und dem damit verbundenen Installationsapparat gibt dieses intime Theaterstück
den Anliegen und Lebensbedingungen einer Gemeinschaft
Raum, die in unserer Gesellschaft bis heute marginalisiert wird.
Die Verwendung von Masken mit den Gesichtszügen der Künstler
erzeugt einen besonderen Blickwinkel hinsichtlich der Frage der
Repräsentation. Durch die Ausweitung der bekannten Diskurse
zum Thema der männlichen Prostitution auf mit Sexualität
verquickte wirtschaftliche Fragen dekonstruieren Dias & Riedweg
die Möglichkeit der Existenz eines einzigen übermächtigen
Narrativs, welches das vor den Augen der Betrachter erörterte
Phänomen beherrscht. Ausserdem verweist die Verwendung
von Masken auf die stellvertretende Präsenz der Künstler im
Werk, eine Präsenz, die normalerweise nicht vorhanden (sichtbar) ist. Dieses Werk handelt von Macht, genauer von den
machtgetränkten Beziehungen zwischen Prostituierten und
Freiern. Schliesslich zerlegt es die Mechanismen, die in dieser
Sexualökonomie meistens wirksam sind. Und es ermöglicht,
dass andere Worte, andere Bilder auftauchen. Es installiert eine
Gegenmacht, indem es sich mit einer Situation auseinandersetzt,
die als extrem „zehrend" betrachtet werden kann, weil sie an
der Selbstachtung und Autonomie der Betroffenen nagt.

Die Strategie, die eigene Rolle zu spielen und sich gleichzeitig davon zu distanzieren, ist auch in weiteren Arbeiten von

Dias & Riedweg anzutreffen. So wird sie beispielsweise in *Corpo Santo* (2012) unter einem anderem Blickwinkel betrachtet. Hier arbeitete das Duo mit Insassen einer psychiatrischen Klinik (The Psychiatric Institute of the Federal University Hospital of Rio de Janeiro), wobei die Patientinnen und Patienten frei Theaterszenen kreierten und Kostüme trugen, die von Gemälden und Zeichnungen aus der Prinzhorn-Sammlung inspiriert waren (der Sammlung des Psychiaters, Kunsthistorikers und Sammlers Hans Prinzhorn in Heidelberg). Die während dieser „Aufarbeitungs"-Sitzungen entstandenen Videos werden jeweils zusammen mit diesen Kostümen gezeigt.

Die Spiegelung kann als eine der wichtigsten und augenfälligsten Strategien vieler Werke von Dias & Riedweg bezeichnet werden. Die Spiegelung und die Metapher, wie sie in der frühen Arbeit *Devotionalia* zum Einsatz kamen. Die Metapher ist eine andere Form der Spiegelung, nämlich eine begriffliche. Sie besteht in der nochmaligen Verdoppelung der Bedeutung zwecks Erweiterung des Bewusstseins einer Situation, eines Gefühls oder einer Sinneserfahrung. Auch die Geschichte könnte man im Bereich der Spiegelung ansiedeln. Diese Frage hat das Duo bei seinen Untersuchungen ebenfalls beschäftigt. Das Werk, das sie an der documenta 2007 vorstellten, *Funk Staden*, handelt von der Entstehung jenes Meta-Narrativs, auf dem Geschichte traditionell beruht. Die Installation besteht aus drei Spiegeln, kombiniert mit drei grossformatigen Videoprojektionen. Hans Staden war ein deutscher Soldat und Abenteurer, der im 16. Jahrhundert von den Tupinambá an jener Küste gefangen genommen wurde, welche heute zu Brasilien gehört. Später wurde er freigelassen und schrieb ein Buch über seine Erlebnisse, *Warhafftig Historia und Beschreibung eyner Landschafft der wilden, nacketen, grimmigen Menschenfresser Leuthen, in der Newen welt America gelegen* (1557). Claude Lévi-Strauss hat sich sehr für dieses Werk interessiert, da es zu den frühesten Berichten eines Europäers über die Begegnung mit dem Anderen gehört. In *Funk Staden* stehen Bilder von Tänzen und Ritualen heutiger Funk-Fans aus Rio, den *funkeiros*, die im heutigen Brasilien eine echte Subkultur darstellen, Bildern gegenüber, die kannibalistische Szenen und Eingeborenenrituale aus dem 16. Jahrhundert zeigen. Doch zu diesen Körpern kommen noch jene des Publikums hinzu, die sich selbst in den Spiegeln rundum reflektiert sehen. So wird durch Vergangenheit und Gegenwart, Nahes und weit Entferntes eine gebrochene, phantasmatische Vision der Geschichte erzeugt, die den Mythos einer einzig möglichen kanonischen Sicht der Geschichte, ja, sogar jeglicher Erzählung, ins Wanken bringt. Die unheimliche Kameraführung in *Funk Staden* trägt zur Destabilisierung des Körpergefühls bei, indem

sie Rituale vergangener Zeiten und heute mögliche Rituale mimt. Es gilt jedoch festzuhalten, dass jede Inszenierung, die Dias & Riedweg unternehmen, mit dem Begriff des Rituals per se in Widerspruch steht. Ein Ritual muss sich wiederholen und man greift darauf zurück, um Traumata, Ängste und so weiter auszutreiben. Dieses Werk lässt sich jedoch nicht ohne weiteres einer solchen Kategorie zuordnen. Durch seinen dekonstruktiven Ansatz geht es weiter als die brechtschen Regeln zur Verfremdung der in einem Stück behandelten Inhalte für das Publikum. Vom Ritual wird lediglich die Idee der kollektiven Versammlung beibehalten sowie das Ansprechen einer Frage, die für eine spezifische Gemeinschaft von Belang sein kann. Auf dieser Spezifizierung muss beharrt werden, denn wie sich in jeder beliebigen Situation zeigt, ist es dieser spezifische Kontext, der angesprochen wird, zusammen mit den „Akteurinnen/Akteuren" aus diesem Kontext, seinen wichtigsten Vertretern. Die Schauspieler und Schauspielerinnen sind hier „reale" Menschen, die ihr tägliches Leben spielen. Sie spielen keine Rollen, die vorgeschrieben wären und aus ihnen etwas anderes machen würden, als sie bereits sind. Im Rahmen einer Gemeinschaft wird immer jedes Individuum und seine individuelle Befindlichkeit angesprochen. Das könnte eine Definition der Demokratie sein in einer Welt, der viele Illusionen abhanden gekommen sind, etwa jene des Kapitalismus, des Kommunismus und der nationalen Identität.

Dias & Riedweg greifen die Frage nach dem Anderen durchgehend in vielfältigen Weisen und Kontexten auf. Halten wir fest, dass der psychoanalytische Prozess des „Aufarbeitens" dabei an die Stelle des geheimnisumwitterten Begriffs des Rituals tritt.

In einer Arbeit wie *Paradiso Cansado* (2009) inszeniert das Duo eine Performance am Strand von Gran Canaria. Zwei Männer gehen am Strand entlang, ohne ein Wort zu wechseln, der eine weiss gekleidet, der andere schwarz. Ihre Begegnung ist eine von der Kamera aufgezeichnete „Unmöglichkeit", ein flüchtiger Moment des Auf-der-Welt-Seins, der die existenzielle Kluft offenbart, die jedes Wesen in sich trägt. Man denkt unweigerlich an Maurice Blanchots „uneingestehbare Gemeinschaft", die Vorstellung einer Gemeinschaft, die in einem stetigen, nie abgeschlossenen Prozess begriffen ist. An einem Punkt in dieser Strandszene taucht absurderweise ein Spiegel auf. Die innerhalb ihres Werks laufend wiederkehrende Trope des Spiegels erscheint hier erneut, diesmal im intimen Rahmen von nur zwei sich gegenüberstehenden Personen. In dem Moment, wo die zwei aufeinandertreffen, gibt das Video den anderen im Spiegel zu erkennen und es wird einem klar, dass beide Männer von demselben Schauspieler gespielt werden. Die zwei sich jagenden Männer sind also tatsächlich nur einer. Der Andere ist das Spiegelbild des Ich, behauptete Jacques Lacan. Das Sein ist mit einem dauerhaften Verlust verknüpft, ein Verlust, der mit einer ewigen Suche nach Leben und Liebe einhergeht. Diese Arbeit ähnelt sehr stark einer anderen, *A Casa* (2007), einer Videoinstallation, in der die Künstler selbst auftreten. Es handelt sich um ein Selbstporträt, das mit dem Zusammenleben und Zusammenarbeiten zu tun hat sowie mit der Visualisierung dieser Beziehung im Kontext, in dem sich eine künstlerische Praxis herauskristallisiert (in diesem Fall ist es das eigene Zuhause der Künstler in Rio).

Die Art des Filmens und der Präsentation der fünf resultierenden Videos lässt die Ungewissheiten und Diskrepanzen der Realität noch stärker hervortreten, insbesondere jene, die mit jedem Versuch, eine Identität oder Beziehungen zu definieren, verbunden sind.

Der Spiegel kommt auch in einer neueren Arbeit, *Pequenas Histórias de Modéstia e Dúvida*, zum Einsatz. Das in Rio begonnene und sich weiter entwickelnde Werk besteht bis heute aus sieben Teilen: *A cidade fora dela*, *Sábado à noite no parquinho*, *O Espelho e a Tarde, Peladas Noturnas* (alle 2011), *O ceú e o dia, Caminho sem volta* (beide 2013) und das bisher noch nicht gezeigte *Zwei aus Vier* (2014), welches in der Retrospektive-Ausstellung in Luzern ausgestellt wird. Die Serie hat ursprünglich Bilder von in Rio beobachteten Phänomenen, Interaktionen mit Einwohnerinnen und Einwohnern und verschiedenen Gemeinschaften innerhalb der Stadt versammelt. Die ersten Teile der *Pequenas Histórias* zeigen das Brasilien von heute, ein Brasilien voller gesellschaftlicher und wirtschaftlicher Phänomene, die in diesem Fall eine noch nie da gewesene Entwicklung nehmen, wie etwa die rhizomartigen Favelas. Auch die später in Bahia, Uruguay und der Schweiz entstandenen Teile des Werks kommentieren alle städtebaulichen und architektonischen Erscheinungen durch die Augen der Künstler und jene der Stadtbewohner. Die fortlaufende Serie ist in beidem, in Form und Inhalt, eine kontinuierliche Recherche und Ausarbeitung zum Motiv der Bescheidenheit und des Zweifels als übergeordnete Tugenden der menschlichen Subjektivität in Zeiten eines harschen Kapitalismus geworden.

Diese Mikro-Geschichten, die durch die verschiedenen Videos in ihrer ganzen Vielfalt wiedergegeben werden, präsentieren eine Stadt, die niemals in ihrer Ganzheit erfasst werden kann, in der jedoch das Hervortreten individueller Eigenarten noch viel packender ist als der grandiose Blick auf Rios berühmten Strand, wo die Serie begann. Für die Ausstellung im Kunstmuseum Luzern haben Dias & Riedweg die *kleinen*

Geschichten um zwei Schweizer Kapitel erweitert. Die Arbeit *Zwei aus Vier* porträtiert zwei Paare, Vreni und Fritz sowie Esther und Heinz. Darin nehmen andere Protagonisten eine andere Umgebung unter die Lupe. Der Kontext ist ein komplett anderer als in Brasilien. Der Ansatz von Dias & Riedweg bleibt jedoch derselbe: Multiperspektivisch nehmen sie das Andere in den Blick und liefern eine von persönlichen Überlegungen begleitete Schilderung realer Lebensbedingungen. Ein ebenfalls „global denkender", aus einem anderen Ballungsgebiet stammender mexikanischer Kunstkritiker und Kurator, Cuauhtémoc Medina, meint mit Recht: „Brasilien ist kein brasilianisches Problem: es ist entscheidend für die Beschreibung der Welt." [8] Die Einstellung zur Welt, die Dias & Riedweg pflegen, ist geprägt von einer wachen Aufmerksamkeit für Brasiliens derzeitige „Performance" (mittels eines eindrucksvollen Instrumentariums an performativen Strategien); in diesem Sinn öffnet ihr Werk Türen zum Verständnis des Zeitgenössischen, des heutigen Zustands der Welt.

1
Clarice Lispector, *A hora da estrela*
(1977), zit. nach der deutschen
Übersetzung von Curt Meyer-Clason,
Suhrkamp, Frankfurt am Main 1985,
S. 11.

2
Jean-Luc Nancy, *La création du monde
ou la mondialisation*, Editions Galilée,
Paris 2002. Deutsch: *Die Erschaffung
der Welt oder Die Globalisierung*,
aus dem Französischen von Anette
Hoffmann, Diaphanes, Zürich/Berlin
2003.

3
Merelau-Ponty schreibt: „meine These:
diese Dekadenz der Philosophie ist
unwesentlich; es ist die einer gewissen
Art des Philosophierens (nach Sub-
stanz, Subjekt-Objekt, Kausalität). Die
Philosophie wird Unterstützung finden
in der Poesie, Kunst usw., in einer
engeren Beziehung zu ihnen wird sie zu
neuem Leben erwachen und ihre eigene
metaphysische Vergangenheit – die nicht
vergangen ist – neu interpretieren." Im
Original: „ma thèse: cette décadence de
la philosophie est inessentielle; est celle
d'une certaine manière de philosopher
(selon substance, sujet-objet, causalité).
La philosophie trouvera aide dans
poésie, art, etc., dans un rapport beau-
coup plus étroit avec elles, elle renaîtra
et réinterprétera ainsi son propre passé
de métaphysique – qui n'est pas passé."
(Maurice Merleau-Ponty, *Notes de cours*,
1959–60, Gallimard, Paris 1996, S. 39.)
Vgl. auch: Merleau-Ponty, *Das Sichtbare
und das Unsichtbare*, Wilhelm Fink
Verlag, München 1986.

4
Nancy, op cit. (Anm. 2), S. 9.

5
Vgl. Georges Didi-Huberman, *La
Ressemblance par contact*, Minuit,
Paris 2008. *L'empreinte*, Éditions
du Centre Georges Pompidou, 1997.
(Deutsche Ausgabe: *Ähnlichkeit und
Berührung*, DuMont, Köln 1999.)

6
*Espaço Aberto/Espaço Fechado:
Sites for sculpture in modern Brazil*,
Henry Moore Institute, Leeds,
5. Februar–14. April 2006.

7
Parachute 106, *São Paulo*, 10.11.12.
2004. Siehe auch Glória Ferreira,
„Encounters with the Other: An interview
with Mauricio Dias and Walter Riedweg",
in *Parachute* 111, *Démocratie_Democracy*,
07.08.09. 2003.

8
„The Tropics exists: Cuauhtémoc Medina
interviews Dias & Riedweg", in *Dias &
Riedweg, Até que a rua nos spare (Until
the street do us part)*, Rio de Janeiro:
NAU; Imago Escritório de Arte, 2012,
S. 167 (Zitat aus dem Engl. übers.).

eim-
kehr-
mittel

Das Bauen als Wohnen, d.h. auf der Erde sein, bleibt (...)
für die alltägliche Erfahrung des Menschen das im vorhinein,
wie die Sprache so schön sagt, „Gewohnte".
– Martin Heidegger, „Bauen Wohnen Denken"[1]

Im Frühsommer 2012 machten meine Begleiterin und ich, auf
unserer Reise quer durch Europa von einer Biennale zur nächsten,
einen Umweg durch den deutschen Schwarzwald, um zu einem
der berühmtesten Häuser der abendländischen Philosophie zu
pilgern – Heideggers Hütte im winzigen Dorf Todtnauberg, rund
30 Kilometer südlich der Universitätsstadt Freiburg im Breisgau.
Es war ein ausgesprochen trüber Regentag, und wir hatten
sowohl versäumt, unsere Route von Freiburg nach Todtnauberg
richtig zu planen, als auch unser Auto vollzutanken; wir fuhren
stundenlang in der nassen, sanften Hügellandschaft herum,
fragten auch mehrmals nach dem Weg (ältere Leute, von denen
wir dachten, sie müssten „den Martin" noch gekannt haben, was
tatsächlich der Fall war), aber am Ende gelang es uns trotzdem
nicht, das berühmteste Haus der abendländischen Philosophie
aufzuspüren und sicher zu identifizieren – dieses Objekt einer
besonderen Form der architektonischen Verehrung. Für einen
Teilzeit-Heideggerianer, der in seinen kunsttheoretischen Schriften reichlich Gebrauch von den diversen philosophischen Werk-
zeugen gemacht hat, die in diesem schwer auffindbaren, rätsel-
haften Schlupfwinkel geschmiedet wurden (der übrigens nach
wie vor im Besitz der Familie Heidegger und nicht öffentlich zu-
gänglich ist, geschweige denn betreten werden darf), war dies
natürlich eine grosse Enttäuschung – eine Frustration, die wir
dadurch zu beseitigen beschlossen, dass wir die wesentlich
einfacher zu findende Villa aufsuchten, in der Martin und Elfride
Heidegger den grössten Teil ihres Lebens in Süddeutschland
zubrachten. Im Gegensatz zu besagter Hütte, in welcher der
mürrische Meisterdenker die Grundgedanken seiner bekanntesten Schriften ausbrütete, taugt das ganz und gar banale zwei-
stöckige Gebäude an einer kurvenreichen Strasse im grünen
Vorstadtgürtel Freiburgs nicht als architektur-philosophisches
Reiseziel. Selbst Heidegger, der ja ein bekennender Philosoph
der Wohnstätte, des Ortes und der Wohnlichkeit war – ein Punkt,
auf den wir in Kürze zurückkommen werden –, befand dieses
Domizil der philosophischen Reflexion nicht wirklich würdig; vielleicht war es zu eng mit dem ganz unphilosophischen Geschäft
seiner Freiburger Universitätskarriere verknüpft – deren Tiefpunkt
bekanntlich Heideggers Zugehörigkeit zur NSDAP während seiner
Zeit als Rektor darstellt. So wirkte der profane Alltagswohnsitz
um ein Vielfaches realer – nicht nur in philosophischer Hinsicht –
als die sorgfältig gehegte und zurechtgelegte Fantasievorstellung
der unauffindbaren Hütte: lieber die echte Heimstatt der Existenz-
philosophie des 20. Jahrhunderts samt ihren zahllosen Gespens-
tern, Phantomen und Geistern als die romantische Bauernlegende,
durch welche die Grübeleien des Meisters über Identität und
Differenz eine so verhängnisvolle Prägung erhielten.

Doch warum dieser lange, verschlungene Pfad, um auf das Werk von zwei Künstlern – Mauricio Dias und Walter Riedweg – zu sprechen zu kommen, deren Interessen von jenen des mürrischen Magiers von Todtnauberg unfassbar weit entfernt zu sein scheinen und deren Tätigkeit so eng an eine Stadt – Rio de Janeiro – gebunden ist, die in mancher Hinsicht das genaue Gegenteil der ländlichen, puritanischen und radikal antimodernen Gedankenwelt von *Sein und Zeit* verkörpert? Die Arbeit von Dias & Riedweg (letzterer, das sollte festgehalten werden, wurde gar nicht so weit weg von der gebeutelten Heimat des Existenzialismus geboren) verfügt über eine dichte Textur, einen geradezu kaleidoskopischen Wirbel von Memen, Motiven, Themen und Tropen; doch unter diesen vielfältigen thematischen Strängen sticht der klar heideggersche Komplex von „Bauen, Wohnen, Denken" deutlich genug hervor, um ein gezieltes genaueres Hinsehen zu rechtfertigen und Einblick zu nehmen in die – gebaute und ungebaute – Welt der beiden Künstler.

*

Ich sollte vielleicht noch einmal auf meine erste Begegnung mit Mauricio Dias und Walter Riedweg zurückkommen – der wenig später mein schrittweises Vertrautwerden mit ihrer Arbeit folgte (für die Argumentation in diesem Essay ist es nicht unerheblich, dass ich die beiden zuerst als Menschen kennenlernte und erst danach als Künstler). Diese erste Begegnung fand 2004 in Rio de Janeiro statt, in ihrem Haus in Santa Teresa. Es war sofort klar, dass dieses Haus, das den beiden bis heute als Atelier dient, etwas Einmaliges ist – in einem Stadtteil, der seinerseits mit keinem anderen Carioca-Viertel zu vergleichen ist. Ich war daher nicht wirklich überrascht, als ich fünf Jahre später entdeckte, dass das Zuhause von Dias & Riedweg mit dem liebevollen Namen Villa Laurinda – benannt nach Laurinda Santos Lobo, einer führenden Dame der Gesellschaft Santa Teresas, die sich für die Rechte der Frauen einsetzte und eine entscheidende Rolle für die Entstehung der Bohème im Rio des frühen 20. Jahrhunderts spielte – tatsächlich Gegenstand eines Video-Diptychons mit den Titeln *A Casa* (2007) und *O Jardim* (2008) geworden war. *A Casa* besteht aus fünf Videos, gezeigt auf Bildschirmen, die in ein schematisches Wandbild integriert sind; zu sehen ist eine Vielzahl digitaler Mauricios und Walters, die ihren Beschäftigungen nachgehen – manche sind deutlich weniger alltäglich als andere und vieles ist unverkennbar komisch; das Ganze spielt vor dem wunderschön gepflegten Hintergrund der Wohn- und Arbeitsumgebung der Künstler. Tatsächlich ist es bezeichnend, dass die am unverhohlensten autobiografische

Arbeit, wohl ihr bisher umfassendstes Selbstporträt, innerhalb eines Werks, das sich so grundlegend und programmatisch mit „Anderen" und der quälenden Frage des Andersseins beschäftigt, die Form einer *architektonischen* Fantasie annimmt, die um das *Zuhause* der Künstler kreist – das sprichwörtliche Labyrinth, in dem *architektonische* Kategorien wie „ich" und „der Andere" tatsächlich zusammenbrechen und sich auflösen.[2] Es ist dieser Prozess der Verdoppelung und Verdunkelung, der das Zuhause ungemütlich werden lässt oder genauer: *unheimlich*, indem er das architektonische Pendant des solidesten vorstellbaren Ichgefühls zum möglichen Schauplatz der wahnhaften Auflösung desselben Ichs macht. Wie Anthony Vidler in seiner Studie *unHEIMlich. Über das Unbehagen in der modernen Architektur* in Bezug auf den „bei weitem beliebteste(n) Aspekt des Unheimlichen im 19. Jahrhundert [...], das Spukhaus" bemerkt: „Das Haus war ein besonders bevorzugter Ort für unheimliche Störungen: seine offensichtliche Häuslichkeit, seine Funktion als Hort für Familiengeschichten und -erinnerungen, seine Rolle als letzter und intimster Schutz privater Behaglichkeit liessen den Gegensatz zum Schrecken in Form eines Eindringens fremder Geister besonders scharf hervortreten."[3] In gewissem Sinn – und äusserst passend für eine künstlerische Praxis, die immer wieder den Begriff oder den Akt der „Besetzung durch fremde Geister" sucht – sind die fremden Geister in *A Casa* und *O Jardim* die Künstler Dias & Riedweg selbst (auf jeden Fall sind sie dazu passend gekleidet): fremde Invasoren ihrer eigenen Ichs, Eindringlinge in ihrem eigenen Zuhause.[4]

*

Dias & Riedweg legen in ihrer Arbeit kein besonderes Augenmerk auf die Architektur als solche – aber sie interessieren sich, denke ich, für die materiellen und immateriellen Lebensbedingungen: für Bauen, Wohnen, Wohnstätten. In diesem Sinn sind sie ein zutiefst *globales* Künstlerduo: Künstler, die so weit gereist und in der Welt zu Hause sind, so mobil und kosmopolitisch, das heisst so (von Berufs wegen) ohne Wurzeln und nomadisch, dass der Traum von einer Zuflucht (einem „Zuhause") häufig als zentrales gedankliches Anliegen in ihrer Arbeit auftaucht – eine Beobachtung, die offensichtlich auch damit zusammenhängt, dass das Wohnungswesen in ihrer Heimatstadt Rio de Janeiro ein brisantes politisches Thema ist. Man denke an die wuchernden Favelas mit ihren berüchtigten, manchmal euphemistisch als „informelle" Architektur bezeichneten Wohnformen (etwa jene, die 2002 den Rahmen für das Kunstprojekt *Mera Vista Point* bildeten), und an die prekären Umstände, in denen

Millionen von Einwohnern Tag für Tag leben müssen. Die nackte Gewalt der Globalisierung als erbarmungsloser zentrifugaler Prozess der Entterritorialisierung und Verlagerung, des Reisens, Transferierens und Handelns, der Migrationsbewegungen und der unablässigen Zirkulation kann mit Sicherheit als Anlass dafür betrachtet werden, dass sich ihre Arbeit gerne mit Fragen der Zugehörigkeit und alternativen Formen des Verwurzeltseins und der Identifikation durch Trennung und Verlagerung befasst. Diese Fragen stehen ganz klar im Zentrum einiger ihrer berühmtesten Werke, aber auch einiger weniger bekannter Arbeiten: Dazu gehören *Os Raimundos, os Severinos e os Franciscos* (1998), ein aufwändig inszeniertes Gruppenbild mit 30 Türstehern und Portiers aus dem Nordosten Brasiliens, dem ärmsten Teil des Landes, der zugleich ein wichtiges Kraftfeld in der Geschichte der brasilianischen Binnenmigration darstellt. Zur Zeit der Dreharbeiten lebten und arbeiteten sie alle in São Paulo. Aber auch *David & Gustav* (2005), ein Doppelporträt von zwei Protagonisten der Londoner Kunstszene der Swinging Sixties (David Medalla und Gustav Metzger), das „den Kontrast zwischen zwei Perspektiven unterstreicht, die unsere Identitätsbildung entscheidend beeinflussen können, wenn wir fernab der Heimat leben – die des Kosmopoliten oder des Exilanten"[5]; ferner *Juksa* (2006), ein Video, das drei verschiedene Momente im Leben dreier Menschen auf einer kleinen Insel vor der Küste Norwegens dokumentiert, deren Existenz sich im Lauf der Zeit grundlegend verändert hat durch die Globalisierung der Fischfangindustrie, der einstmals einzigen verlässlichen Existenzgrundlage dieser Insel; dann *Paradiso Cansado* (2009), das durch die Augen eines Exilkubaners gesehene Porträt einer anderen Insel (sie gehört zu den Kanarischen Inseln, die vor allem für ihren Sextourismus bekannt sind – eine nur allzu bekannte, deprimierende Nebenwirkung unserer globalisierten Wirtschaft, die sich in den Migrationsmustern niederschlägt).[6] Auf die eine oder andere Weise befassen sich alle diese Arbeiten – am nachdrücklichsten vielleicht *Os Raimundos, os Severinos e os Franciscos* – mit der Frage der Heimat, des sich häuslich Einrichtens, der Zuflucht vor dem Sturm des Weltgeschehens. Sie beschwören die vergebliche Sehnsucht nach Stabilität in einer Welt, die vom Prinzip der Mobilität (im engeren Sinn) regiert wird. Tatsächlich ist es nicht ganz bedeutungslos, dass eines der bekanntesten öffentlichen Kunstwerke der beiden ein nicht abgeschlossenes Projekt ist, zu dem ein in Bewegung befindlicher Lastwagen gehört, dieses profanste und kraftstrotzendste aller Symbole des globalen Mobilitätswahns – aus dem wirren Knäuel der Sehnsüchte, Zwänge und Erfordernisse, stets unterwegs zu sein. Auf einer elementaren konzeptuellen Ebene funktioniert diese Arbeit als

performative Reflexion über die Ursprünge und Bedeutungen des Begriffs „bewegtes Bild" an sich. Es ist aufschlussreich, sich hier daran zu erinnern, dass einer der Kurzfilme der Gebrüder Lumière, den man gewöhnlich mit der Geburt des Kinos in Verbindung bringt, der 50-Sekunden-Film *Arrival of a Train at La Ciotat Station* von 1896 ist. Die Künstler haben sich über dieses spezifische Werk in den virologischen Begriffen der zeitgenössischen Bildkultur geäussert. Die Tatsache bleibt jedoch bestehen, dass der rollende Lastwagen als eine Art Heimkehrmittel unser Erleben des Werks auf die räumlichen Begriffe von Architektur, Mobilität, Unterkunft und Umzug zurückbringt.

Dieselbe Symbolik bildet auch den Unterton eines weiteren Videoinstallationsprojekts *in progress*, nämlich *Malas para Marcel* (Koffer für Marcel, 2006): einer zwölfteiligen Erzählung in bewegten Bildern, in der wir die surreale Odyssee eines Koffers durch Rio de Janeiro mitverfolgen. Das Werk verbindet kunstgeschichtliche Anspielungen – das Objekt der Verehrung ist Marcel Duchamps *boîte-en-valise* als eine Art Talisman – mit einer umfassenderen Reflexion der Wechselfälle der Kultur des bewegten Bildes und ihrer Verstrickung in die rasenden Produktions- und Konsumzyklen der Weltwirtschaft. In mancher Hinsicht liegt jedoch der Schlüssel zu einem tieferen Verständnis des Verhältnisses zwischen der Kunst und dem täglichen Leben der Künstler in einem dreizehnten Video, das gewöhnlich auf eine nahe Wand projiziert wird und in dem Dias & Riedweg selbst zu sehen sind, wie sie an einem Flughafen, bezeichnenderweise in einer Stadt, in die sie als Gäste und ausstellende Künstler eingeladen wurden, zwölf Koffer aufsammeln. In dieser nachgestellten pseudodokumentarischen Episode sieht man, wie die Künstler, auf der Reise vom Flughafen zum Museum und wieder zurück, ihre Kunstwerke und ihr persönliches Gepäck schleppen – die typischen modernen Nomaden, für die ein Koffer buchstäblich zum „Zuhause fern von Zuhause" wird, wie auch die läppische Redensart „aus dem Koffer leben" besagt. Hier muss ich hervorheben, dass ich das Glück hatte, dieses Werk im Herbst 2011 in einer von mir kuratierten Ausstellung im Museum van Hedendaagse Kunst Antwerpen (M HKA) zu zeigen – als Höhepunkt eines Dialogs mit den Künstlern, der bereits im Sommer 2004 in ihrem Haus in Santa Teresa seinen Anfang genommen hatte. Der Titel der Ausstellung lautete *A Rua* (Die Strasse) und nahm sowohl das Einzigartige des Strassenlebens in den Carioca-Vierteln als auch die Besonderheiten von Rios Stadtgefüge als Ausgangspunkt für eine vertiefte Betrachtung der Beziehung zwischen einer künstlerischen Praxis und ihrem Ort oder Schauplatz; auf vielerlei Weise betrachtete *A Rua* die Strasse als ursprüngliche Heimat der Carioca-Kunst.[7] Wenn man den zwölfteiligen Zyklus, den *Malas*

para Marcel darstellt, als Tribut an die Strassen von Rio de
Janeiro, die natürliche Arbeitsstätte der Künstler, verstehen kann,
so lässt sich das dreizehnte Kapitel mit ortsspezifischem Epilog
zum selben Werk als leicht melancholisches Nachsinnen über die
zur Normalität gewordene Befindlichkeit des heutigen Künstlers
lesen: seine stete Heimatlosigkeit und sein Heimweh – die buchstäblich schmerzhafte Sehnsucht nach der Heimstätte von einst –
als unumgängliche Elemente des unsteten Künstlerlebens.

*

In den Strassen von Rio zu Hause zu sein – wie Dias & Riedweg
und die wechselnden Protagonisten ihrer vielen Videoarbeiten –
führt uns zurück zu Heideggers Hütte in Todtnauberg, zu seinem
Haus in Freiburg und zur zentralen Erkenntnis in seinem Text
„Bauen Wohnen Denken", nämlich, dass das „Wohnen" im Titel,
die Kunst, sich zu Hause zu fühlen, letztlich sehr wenig zu tun
hat mit dem „Bauen" im selben Titel, mit Architektur. In den in
diesem Essay erwähnten Arbeiten von Dias & Riedweg ist das
Wohnen, das sich häuslich Einrichten in häufig ungemütlichen
Räumen, der klar hervorstechende Topos, und nicht das *Bauen*;
eher das Haus als die Hütte ist, laut Heidegger, „der Grundzug
des Seins, demgemäss die Sterblichen sind." [...] „Der Bezug
des Menschen zu Orten und durch Orte zu Räumen beruht im
Wohnen. Das Verhältnis von Mensch und Raum ist nichts anderes als das wesentlich gedachte Wohnen."[8] Dieses Verhältnis
steht, wie ich hier deutlich machen möchte, in den Werken von
Dias & Riedweg regelmässig an erster Stelle und bestimmt teil-
weise das viel emphatischere Verhältnis zwischen dem Ich und
dem Anderen – Identität und Differenz –, in welches es manchmal auch direkt übersetzt wird. Heideggers Essay endet mit einer
Reflexion über den modernen Zustand der Unbehaustheit, die
besonders gut hierher zu passen scheint, nicht zuletzt wegen
ihrer Bedeutung in einem soziokulturellen Kontext (jenem von
Rio de Janeiro), in dem Obdachlosigkeit zugleich eine akut durch-
lebte Tragödie und ein philosophisches Rätsel darstellt: „Die
eigentliche Not des Wohnens beruht darin, dass die Sterblichen
das Wesen des Wohnens immer erst wieder suchen, dass sie
das Wohnen erst lernen müssen. Wie, wenn die Heimatlosigkeit
des Menschen darin bestünde, dass der Mensch die *eigentliche*
Wohnungsnot noch gar nicht *als die* Not bedenkt?"[9] Das Werk
von Dias & Riedweg lehrt uns das eine oder andere über diese
Notlage; indem es dabei verweilt, lehrt es uns, richtig zu ver-
weilen – zugleich unbehaust in uns selbst und zu Hause in
anderen zu sein, andernorts.[10]

1
Martin Heidegger, „Bauen Wohnen
Denken", in Heidegger, *Gesamtausgabe,
I. Abteilung: Veröffentlichte Schriften
1910–1976*, Bd. 7 (Vorträge und Aufsätze),
Vittorio Klostermann, Frankfurt am Main
2000, S. 149.

2
Hier scheint eine kurze Rückbesinnung
auf Heideggers Hütte angebracht –
immerhin war sie der Entstehungsort
der philosophischen Abhandlung, die
Heidegger selbst als seine bedeutend-
ste neben *Sein und Zeit* betrachtete,
nämlich die Schrift mit dem prägnanten
Titel *Identität und Differenz*, die er im
September 1957 in Todtnauberg zu Papier
brachte. In diesem Text stellt Heidegger
fest: „Sein Denken wird demnach
nur dann sachlich, wenn wir es in der
Differenz mit dem Seienden denken und
dieses in der Differenz mit dem Sein.
So kommt die Differenz eigens in den
Blick." Martin Heidegger, *Identität und
Differenz*, Neske, Pfullingen 1957, S. 53.
In gewissem Sinn kennzeichnet dieser
Essay (eigentlich eine Verbindung zwei-
er Vorlesungen, einer „über" Identität
und einer „über" Differenz – die eine
bezeichnenderweise in Freiburg gehalten,
die andere in Todtnauberg) den schwer
fassbaren Ursprung des kontinentaleu-
ropäischen Denkens der Differenz und
des Andersseins, das sich so nachhaltig
und folgenschwer auf die intellektuelle
und kulturelle Landschaft der Nachkriegs-
zeit auswirken sollte.

3
Anthony Vidler, *unHEIMlich. Über das
Unbehagen in der modernen Architektur*,
aus dem Englischen übers. v. Norma
Kessler, Edition Nautilus, Hamburg 2002,
S. 37.

4
Hier lohnt sich der Verweis auf eine
Installation aus dem Jahr 1968 von Lygia
Clark, der Matriarchin der sinnlichen
Konzeptkunst Brasiliens: Ihr Titel lautete
A casa e o corpo („Das Zuhause ist
der Körper") – eine Formel, die unser
aktuelles Thema, nämlich Häuslichkeit
und Gemütlichkeit, programmatisch mit
einem anderen Schlüsselelement der
Kunst von Dias & Riedweg verbindet,
nämlich der Politik des Körpers (man
denke etwa an so breit diskutierte
Schlüsselwerke wie *Corpo Santo*,
Funk Staden und *Voracidad Maxima*).

Dias & Riedweg haben mehrfach auf
dieses spezifische Werk von Clark Bezug
genommen.

5
Dias & Riedweg, *… and it becomes
something else*, New York: Americas/
Society, 2009. David Medalla kam 1942
in Manila, der Hauptstadt der Philip-
pinen, zur Welt und zog in den frühen
1960er Jahren nach London; Gustav
Metzger wurde 1926 in Deutschland
als Kind polnischer Juden geboren
und gelangte 1939 als Flüchtlingskind
nach London.

6
Das Bild des exilierten Protagonisten,
der einen Spiegel durch die karge,
windgepeitschte Dünenlandschaft der
Insel trägt, erinnert unweigerlich an das
Spiel der Spiegelungen in *A Casa*; das
aufgeladene Bild taucht auf direktere
Weise in einer Videoarbeit aus dem Jahr
2011 erneut auf, *O espelho e a tarde*;
dort ist ein Einwohner von Rio de Janeiro
zu sehen, der einen Spiegel durch die
Strassen, Plätze und Gassen der vor
Menschen wimmelnden tropischen
Metropole trägt, so dass insbesondere
die rasante Urbanisierung einer von
Rios berüchtigten alten Favelas in den
Blick rückt. Hier ist nicht der Ort für
eine vertiefte Untersuchung der Verwendung von Spiegeln und Spiegelungen
im Bildvokabular von Dias & Riedweg;
vorerst mag der Hinweis genügen, dass
der Spiegel ein archetypisches Symbol
für die Dialektik, Dynamik und Mechanik
der Reflexion ist, die für ihre Praxis und
ihr Werk insgesamt so entscheidend
sind.

7
Eine der Hauptquellen der literarischen
Inspiration zu diesem Ausstellungs-
projekt war eine Träumerei *des* Carioca-
Literaten des frühen 20. Jahrhunderts
schlechthin, Joao do Rio, dessen Text,
A alma encantadora das ruas (Die
bezaubernde Seele der Strassen) wurde
im Ausstellungskatalog abgedruckt.
Der Geist von João do Rio taucht als
richtungsweisendes Licht wieder auf
in der Einzelausstellung von Dias &
Riedweg im Herbst 2013 im Centro de
Artes Helio Oiticica in Rio de Janeiro
mit dem treffenden Titel *Até que a
rua nos separe* (Bis die Strasse uns
scheidet).

8
Martin Heidegger, op. cit. (Anm. 1),
S. 163 und 160.

9
Ebenda, S. 163.

10
Same Time Else Where war der Titel
einer Ausstellung von Dias & Riedweg
im Kunstnernes Hus in Oslo 2008.
In ihrem einführenden Katalogessay
verweist die Kuratorin Maaretta Jaukkuri
auf die Frage der *cohabitation* als eines
der wichtigsten Anliegen der Künstler.
Im vorliegenden Essay habe ich versucht,
diese Frage auf jene der *habitation*
einzugrenzen.

Biography

Mauricio de Mello Dias, born in Rio de Janeiro, October 27,
1964. Studied at Universidade Federal do Rio de Janeiro;
Schule für Gestaltung Basel, Switzerland; and at The
Printmaking Workshop, New York City.

Walter Stephan Riedweg, born in Luzern, Switzerland, December
26, 1955. Studied at Musik-Akademie Luzern, and Scuola di
Teatro Dimitri, Verscio, Switzerland; and at workshops at
The Performance Studies Departement, New York University.

Over more than 20 years of an intense and fruitful collaboration,
Dias & Riedweg have created a unique body of work that
investigates how the individual psyche influences and forms
public space, and vice versa. In their collaborative art projects
they act as translators between different worlds, and create
space and expression in a wide variety of encounters with
people, using their respective individual experiences in visual
arts and performance.

2014
Kleine Geschichten von Bescheidenheit und Zweifel,
Kunstmuseum Luzern, Switzerland

2013
Amparo y Desamparo, Fotograma 13, Montevideo,
Uruguay
Possible Archives, Kunsthal Nikolaj Copenhagen,
Denmark
Until the Street Do Us Part, Centro de Artes Hélio
Oiticica, Rio de Janeiro, Brazil

2012
Corpo Santo, Museum der Prinzhorn Sammlung,
Heidelberg, Germany
Strangely Possible, Museum of Modern Art of Bahia,
Salvador, Brazil
The Mirror and the Dusk, ARCO, Madrid, Spain; PINTA,
London, UK
Peñas de Pena, CajaSol, Sevilla, Spain

2011
Peñas de Pena, CajaSol, Jerez de la Frontera, Spain

2010
Cold Stories, FIAC Art Fair, Bendana-Pinel Art
Contemporain, Paris, France
Parties of Sorrow, Sicardi Gallery, Houston, USA
Che–Project Room, PINTA, London, UK; Galeria
Filomena Soares, Lisbon, Portugal

2009/2010
Periphery of your Eyes, MUAC–Museum of
Contemporary Art, Mexico City, Mexico

2009
Possible Paradises, Instituto Tomie Ohtake, São Paulo,
Brazil
*Senses Without Directions and Other Directions of
Sense*, Galeria Filomena Soares, Lisbon, Portugal
… and It Becomes Something Else, Americas Society,
New York, USA
Moving Truck and Recent Works, Argos, Kunstenfestival
des Arts, Brussels, Belgium
Each Thing its Place, Other Place Another Thing,
Galerie Bendana-Pinel, Paris, France

2008
Else Where Same Time, Kunsthalle, Oslo, Norway
Funk Staden, Brazilian Embassy, Buenos Aires,
Argentina
Of the Universe of the Ball, ARCO, Madrid, Spain
Funk Staden, Vleeshal Middelburg, Netherlands

2007
Funk Staden/Voracidade Máxima, documenta 12,
Kassel, Germany

Promenade, Frieze, London, UK
Gravities, Museu da República, Rio de Janeiro, Brazil

2006
Juksa, Lofoten International Art Festival, Norway

2005
The Unfinishing World, Espace Le Plateau, Festival
d'Automne à Paris, France
Cabra criada, Galeria Vermelho, São Paulo, Brazil
Sambing Camera, Villa Arson, Nice, France

2004
Possibly Speaking about the Same, Kiasma Museum
of Contemporay Art, Helsinki, Finland

2003
MACBA – Museu d'Art Contemporani de Barcelona,
Spain

2002
The Other Begins Where Our Senses Meet the World,
Centro Cultural Banco do Brasil, Rio de Janeiro,
Brazil

2000
Dias & Riedweg, Kunsthalle Palazzo, Liestal, Switzerland

1997
Devotionalia, National Parliament, Brasilia, Brazil
Dias & Riedweg, Stroom, The Hague, Netherlands
Dias & Riedweg, O.T. Galerie/Kornschütte, Lucerne,
Switzerland

1996
Kaskadenkondensator, Basel, Switzerland
Dias & Riedweg, Musée d'art moderne et
contemporain, Geneva, Switzerland
Dias & Riedweg, Museu de Arte Moderna do Rio
de Janeiro, Brazil

Group Exhibitions

2014
Cruzamentos, Contemporary Art in Brazil – Wexner
Center for the Arts, Columbus, USA

2013/2014
Brasiliana–Installations from 1960 to the Present,
Kunsthalle Schirn, Frankfurt, Germany
Futebol, Brasília, Salvador, Rio de Janeiro, Fortaleza,
Santa Cruz de la Sierra, Montevideo, Buenos Aires,
La Paz, São Paulo, Belo Horizonte, Lima, Cordoba,
Bogota, Caracas, Santiago de Chile, Quito

2013
Arte e Crime, Galeria Vermelho, São Paulo, Brazil
Art Rio, Galeria Vermelho, Galeria Filomena Soares,
Rio de Janeiro, Brazil

Sistema/Ecos, Praça Victor Civitas, São Paulo, Brazil
Opening Exhibition, MAR, Museu de Arte do Rio de
Janeiro, Brazil; Pinta, London, UK

2012
1st Biennale de Montevideo, Uruguay
Nikolaj Kunsthal, Arts Festival Copenhagen, Denmark
From the Margin to the Edge, Somerset House,
London, UK
Paris Photo, Galeria Filomena Soares, Paris, France
The Subject Object, Grassi Museum für Völkerkunde
zu Leipzig, Germany
Une Tension en Chewing-Gum, Bâtiment d'Art
Contemporain, Geneva, Switzerland
The Spiral and the Square, Sorlandets Kunstmuseum,
Kristiansand, Norway; Kunstmuseum Trondheim,
Norway
Pinta, Bendana-Pinel Arts Contemporain, London,
UK
ARCO, Galeria Filomena Soares, Madrid, Spain
VIP Art Fair, Galeria Filomena Soares, Internet

2011
The Spiral and the Square, Bonniers Konsthall
Stockholm, Sweden
A Rua, Muhka, Antwerp, Belgium
Meu Meio, Sesc Interlagos, São Paulo, Brazil
Werkbeitrag, Kunstkredit, Basel, Switzerland
Videocriação, Centro de Artes Hélio Oiticica,
Rio de Janeiro, Brazil
Art Rio, Galerie Bendana-Pinel Art Contemporain,
Galeria Filomena Soares, Galeria Vermelho,
Rio de Janeiro, Brazil
SP Arte, Galeria Filomena Soares, São Paulo, Brazil
Ordem e Progresso, Museu de Arte Moderna de
São Paulo, Brazil

2010
Novas Aquisições, Museu de Arte Moderna do Rio
de Janeiro, Brazil
MACO, Galeria Vermelho, Sicardi Gallery, Mexico City,
Mexico
The Traveling Show, La Coleccion Jumex, Mexico City,
Mexico
Brussels Art Fair, Galeria Filomena Soares, Brussels,
Belgium
Armory Show, Galeria Filomena Soares, New York,
USA
Jogos de Guerra, Memorial da América Latina,
São Paulo, Brazil
Centro Cultural da Caixa Econômica Federal, Rio de
Janeiro, Brazil

2009
2ª Bienal de Canarias, Tenerife Espacio de las Artes
(TEA), Tenerife, Spain
En Todas Partes, Centro Galego de Arte Contemporáneo,
Santiago de Compostella, Spain
Medium Religion, ZKM, Karlsruhe, Germany
Tragicomedia, Museo de Cadiz e Centro Andaluz
de Arte Contemporáneo, Seville, Spain

2008
Tropen, Martin Gropius Bau, Berlin, Germany
Seja Marginal, Seja Herói, Galerie Vallois, Galerie
    Serousi, Paris, France
Lugares Comunes, Centro José Guerrero, Granada,
    Spain
Islands + Ghettos, Heidelberger Kunstverein,
    Heidelberg, Germany
Peripherical Look and Collective Body, Museion,
    Bolzano, Italy
Vertrautes Terrain, ZKM, Karlsruhe, Germany
Loop, Galeria Filomena Soares, Barcelona, Spain
Acervo, Galeria Vermelho, São Paulo, Brazil
Trópicos, Centro Cultural Banco do Brasil, Rio de
    Janeiro, Brazil
ARCO, Galeria Filomena Soares, Galeria Vermelho,
    Madrid, Spain
Mimetismes, Extra City, Antuérpia/Antwerp, Belgium

2007
Miami Basel Art Fair, Galeria Vermelho, Miami, USA
Paris Photo 2007, Galeria Filomena Soares, Musée
    du Louvre, Paris, France
Trópicos, Centro Cultural Banco do Brasil, Brasília,
    Brazil
SPA das Artes, Recife, Brazil
Por um Fio, Paço das Artes, São Paulo and Campinas
    (SP), Brazil
documenta 12, Kassel, Germany
Biennale de Valencia, Spain
ARCO, Galeria Filomena Soares, Madrid, Spain

2006
Miami Basel Art Fair, Galeria Vermelho, Miami, USA
Paris Photo 2006, Galeria Filomena Soares, Musée
    du Louvre, Paris, France
Mørke Nu Festival, Bodø, Norway
Kunstkredit Basel Werkjahr, Switzerland
6th Gwanju Biennial, Gwanju, South Korea
6th Lofoten International Arts Festival, Svolvaer,
    Norway
Luft Holen, Unikum, Klagenfurt, Austria
Artes Mundi Awards, Cardiff, UK
Satellite of Love, Witte de With, Rotterdam,
    Netherlands

2005
Jogo da Memória, Museu de Arte Moderna do Rio
    de Janeiro, Brazil
Populism, Stedelijk Museum, Amsterdam, Netherlands
Museum of Fine Arts, Oslo, Norway
Kunstverein, Frankfurt, Germany
Centre of Contemporary Arts, Vilnius, Lithuania
Citizens, PM Gallery, London, 2005; City Gallery
    Leicester, UK

2004
4th Liverpool International Biennial, FACT & Tate
    Liverpool, UK
5th Shanghai Biennale, China
Body & Nostalgia, MOMA Tokyo, MOMA Kyoto, Japan

2003
8a Bienal de Havana, Cuba
4a Bienal do Mercosul, Porto Alegre, Brazil

2002
Arte Cidade, São Paulo, Brazil
25a Bienal de São Paulo, Brazil

2001
Johannesburg Art Gallery, Johannesburg, South Africa
L'État des choses, Kunst-Werke Berlin, Berlin,
    Germany
Rede de Tensão, 50 Anos da Bienal de São Paulo,
    Brazil

2000
InSite 2000, San Diego & Tijuana, USA/Mexico
Centre d'Art Contemporain, Geneva, Switzerland

1999
Arguments, Ataturk Centre, Istanbul Biennial Foundation,
    Turkey
49th Biennale di Venezia, Italy

1998
24a Bienal de São Paulo, Brazil

1996
Conversations at the Castle, Atlanta, USA

1995
Shedhalle, Zurich, Switzerland

Screenings

2014
Beat Bieri, Ruedi Leuthold, *Stern Stunde*, Zurich,
    Switzerland

2009
Moving Truck and Recent Works - documentation
    of solo exhibition at Argos Centre for Art
    and Media
Dias & Riedweg. Documenta Vídeo Brasil, São Paulo,
    Brazil

2007
Os Trópicos - visões a partir do centro do globo,
    CCBB Brasília

2002
Marco del Fiol, Fabiana Werneck, *MAU WAL –
    Translated Encounters*, *Authors Collection*,
    52 minutes, Videobrasil, São Paulo, Brazil

1997
Jochen Bechler, Thomas Schunke, *Conversations
    in Atlanta*, documentary, 52 minutes, Geneva
    and Berlin

Awards and Grants

2011
Kunstkredit Basel, Werkbeitrag, Basel, Switzerland

2010
First Prize, Madrid Foto, Madrid, Spain

2007
Jury Prize, Videobrasil, São Paulo, Brazil

2006
Kunstkredit Basel, Werkbeitrag, Basel, Switzerland
Acquisition, Artes Mundi International Awards,
    Cardiff, UK

2004
Kunstkredit Basel, Atelier Ankauf, Basel, Switzerland

2002
The J. S. Guggenheim Foundation Fellowship,
    New York, USA
Authors Collection, Videobrasil, São Paulo, Brazil

2001
Grant Pro Helvetia Foundation, Residency project
    in South Africa

2000
Vitae Foundation Grant, São Paulo, Brazil

1999
Basel Cultural Acknowledgment Prize, Switzerland
Grant Pro Helvetia Foundation, Residency project
    in Egypt

1998
Grant of the City of Basel, Switzerland

1997
Collection Cahier d'Artiste Pro Helvetia, Switzerland

Selected Works in Public Collections

MAR – Museu de Arte do Rio, Rio de Janeiro, Brazil
Pinacoteca de São Paulo, Brazil
Musée National d'art Moderne Centre Georges
    Pompidou, Paris, France
MOCA – Museum of Contemporary Art,
    Los Angeles, USA
MACBA – Museu d'Art Contemporani de Barcelona,
    Spain
Kiasma Museum of Contemporary Art, Helsinki,
    Finland
National Museum of Wales, Cardiff, UK
Frac Ile-de-France, Paris, France
Colección Bergé, Madrid

MUAC – Museo Universitario de Arte Contemporaneo, Mexico City, Mexico
Museu Nacional de Belas Artes do Rio de Janeiro, Brazil
Museu de Arte Moderna de São Paulo, Coleção Pedro Barbosa, São Paulo, Brazil
Museu de Arte Moderna do Rio de Janeiro, Coleção Gilberto Chateaubriand, Rio de Janeiro, Brazil
Centro Cultural Belém, Coleção Joe Berardo, Lisbon
Kunstkredit Basel, Basel, Switzerland
Kunststiftung Heute, Bern
Videothek Baselland, Switzerland

Selected Works in Private Collections

Coleção Maria Lúcia Veríssimo, São Paulo, Brazil
Coleção Cris Bicalho e Ricardo Brito Pereira, São Paulo, Brazil
Sammlung Hanspeter Zemp, Rio de Janeiro, Brazil
Credit Suisse Collection, Zurich, Switzerland
Colección Anibal Josami & Marlise Ilhesca, Buenos Aires, Argentina
Coleção Gilberto Chateaubriand, Rio de Janeiro, Brazil
Coleção José Olympio, São Paulo, Brazil
Coleção Pedro Barbosa, São Paulo, Brazil
Coleção Phillipe e Roger Wright, São Paulo, Brazil
Colección Sagrário Perez Souto, San José, Costa Rica
Collection Anna Sukoloff, New York, USA
Colección Irene Goro, Buenos Aires, Argentina
Collection Jane and Leonard Kormann, Philadelphia, USA
Collection Lucille Rooney, San Diego, USA
Coleção Miguel Rios, Lisbon, Portugal
Collection Joël Girard, Paris, France
Collection Marsha and Darell Anderson, USA
Coleção José Marton, São Paulo, Brazil
Coleção Luisa Strina, São Paulo, Brazil
Collection Guillaume et Juan Bendana-Pinel, Paris, France
Coleção Eliana Finkelstein, São Paulo, Brazil

Selected Bibliography

2013
Rafael Cardoso, Martina Weinhart, Max Hollein, *Brasiliana - Installations from 1960 to the Present*, catalogue, Verlag der Buchhandlung Walther König (Schirn Kunsthalle Frankfurt)
Alfons Hug, *Zeitgenössiche Künstler aus Brasilien*, Goethe-Institute, Akademie der Künste, München, Berlin, Deutschland
Martina Weinhart, Max Hollein, *Brasiliana - Installations from 1960 to the Present*, exh. cat., Schirn Kunsthalle Frankfurt/Verlag der Buchhandlung Walther König, Frankfurt/Cologne
Ingrid von Beyme, Thomas Röske, *ungesehen und unerhört - Künstler reagieren auf die Sammlung Prinzhorn*, Sammlung Prinzhorn, Wunderhorn, Heidelberg

Alfons Hug, Paz Guevara, *Futebol - o jogo só acaba quando termina*, Goethe-Institute, Rio de Janeiro

2012–2013
Alfons Hug, Paz Guevara, Patricia Bentancur, *1a Bienal de Montevideo - En Gran Sur*, exh. cat., Montevideo
Revista s/n Brasil, *Estradas*, vol. 18

2012
Paulo Herkenhoff, Catherine David, Cuauhtémoc Medina, Gabriela Rangel, *Até que a Rua nos Separe/Until the Street Do Us Part*, Imago, Rio de Janeiro
Solange Farkas, Stella Carrozzo, *Estranhamente Possível/Strangely Possible*, exh. cat., Museu de Arte Moderna da Bahia, Salvador
Javier Codesal, Robin Held, *Peñas de Pena*, Flamenco Series Intervalo, Cajasol, Seville
Anna-Sophie Springer, *The Subjective Object*, Museum für Völkerkunde zu Leipzig/k-verlag, Berlin
"Entretien avec Xavier Franceschi," *Le Plateau, 10 ans*, Fonds régional d'art contemporain, Ile de France, Paris

2011
Beatriz Pimenta Veloso, *Dias & Riedweg – Alteridade e experiência estética na arte contemporânea brasileira*, Apicuri, Rio de Janeiro
Glória Ferreira, *Entrefalas*, Zouk, Porto Alegre
Eduardo de Jesus, *Arte e novas espacialidades – Relações contemporâneas*, Oi Futuro, Rio de Janeiro
Gabriela Rangel, *Puntos ciegos/Blind Spots – SITAC VIII*, Patronato de Arte Contemporáneo A. C., Mexico City
Dieter Roelstraete, *A rua. Rio de Janeiro & The Spirit of the Street*, M HKA, Antwerp

2010
Felipe Chaimovich, *Ecológica*, exh. cat., MAM–SP, São Paulo
Dias & Riedweg, "Interterritorialidade e atemporalidade da imagem em movimento," *Tempo e psicanálise – Cadernos de psicanálise*, SPCRJ, Rio de Janeiro
Novas aquisições 2007–2010, exh. cat., MAM–RJ, Rio de Janeiro

2009
Paulo Herkenhoff, *Arte & Ensaios*, no. 18, UFRJ, Rio de Janeiro
Rosa Olivares et al., *100 Video artistas/100 video artists*, Exit Publicaciones, Madrid
Silencio – 2ª Bienal de Canarias, exh. cat., Tenerife, Spain
Gabriela Rangel, Paulo Herkenhoff, John Hanhardt, Beatriz Jaguaribe, *… and It Becomes Something Else*, exh. cat., Americas Society, New York
Aguinaldo Farias, *Paraísos possíveis*, exh. cat., Instituto Tomie Ohtake, São Paulo
Holland Cotter, " … and It Becomes Something Else," Art in Review, *New York Times*, July 9
Carol Boubés, "Dias & Riedweg – Fiac 2009," *Art Presse*, July-August, Paris

Luciano Figueiredo, "Câmera folia," Katia Maciel, *Transcinemas*, Contra Capa, Rio de Janeiro
Taiyana Pimentel, "Dias & Riedweg," *Tragicomedia*, exh. cat., Cajasol y Centro Andaluz de Arte Contemporâneo, Seville
Paolo Bianchi, "Trance in den Tropen," *Kunstforum International*, vol. 195, Berlin
Boris Groys, Peter Weibel, *Medium Religion*, Walther König/ZKM Center for Art and Media, Cologne/Karlsruhe
Gregor Jansen, Thomas Thiel, *Vertrautes Terrain*, Kehrer/ZKM, Heidelberg/Karlsruhe

2008
David Barro, Paolo Reis, *Parangolé – Fragmentos desde los 90: Brasil*, Dardo, Valladolid
Maaretta Jaukkuri, Daniel Hora, *Same Time Else Where*, exh. cat., Kunsternes Hus, Oslo
Roland Groenenboom, *Funk Staden*, exh. cat., Vleeshal Middelburg, Netherlands
Marianne Le Métayer, Benjamin Seroussi, *Seja Marginal, Seja Herói - 13 artistes brésiliens* - Sculpture Contemporaine, exh. cat., Galerie Vallois, Paris

2007
Consuelo Lins, Daniel Hora, "Dias & Riedweg – *Funk Staden*," *Revista Cultura e Pensamento*, Ministério da Cultura do Brazilian Ministry of Culture
Suely Rolnik, "Funk Staden," *Documenta 12*, exh. cat., Kassel
Susanne Jaegger, "Maximum Voracity," *Documenta 12*, exh. cat., Kassel
Peter Fischer, Christoph Lichtin, Susanne Neubauer, *Top of Central Switzerland*, exh. cat., Museum of Art Lucerne, Lucerne

2006
Maaretta Jaukkuri, "The Story Killers," *Artes Mundi International Awards*, exh. cat., Cardiff
Nathalie Delbard, "Dias & Riedweg – Le Monde Inachevé, Le Plateau," *Parachute*, no. 122, Montreal

2005
Valérie da Costa, "Transfiguration de l'espace social," *Revue Mouvement*, no. 36/37
Guy Brett, "The Unfinished World," *Le Monde Inachevé*, exh. cat., Le Plateau/Festival d'Automne
Lars Bang Larsen, Cristina Ricupero, Nicolaus Schafhausen, *Populism*, exh. cat., Lukas & Sternberg, New York and Berlin
Alberto Ligaluppi et al., *Grupo Recolectivo – No estábamos hechos para los mismos caminos … *, Goethe–Institut, Córdoba

2004
Luciano Figueiredo, "Câmera foliã," *Carnaval*, exh. cat., Centro Cultural Banco do Brasil, Rio de Janeiro, Brazil
Suely Rolnik, "Alterité à Ciel Ouvert," *Revue Multitudes*, vol. 15, Paris

2003-2004
Catherine David, Dias & Riedweg, Suely Rolnik, Dias
    & Riedweg – *Possiblemente hablemos de lo mismo/
    Possibly Speaking About the Same* (Actar & Macba,
    Barcelona, Espanha/Spain)

2003
Gloria Ferreira, "Entretién avec Dias & Riedweg,"
    Parachute Art Contemporain, vol. 111,
    Montreal/Paris
*Concinitas – Revista de Arte da Universidade Estadual
    do Rio de Janeiro*
Ignácio Averos, "Dias & Riedweg: Mera Vista Point,"
    Quaderns, Barcelona
Dias & Riedweg, "Devotionalia," *8ª Bienal de Havana*,
    exh. cat., Havana
Alfons Hug, "The Chimborazzo Delirium," *4a Bienal
    Mercosul*, exh. cat., Porto Alegre, Brazil
Jorge Mestre, Ivan Bercedo, *Quaderns d'arquitecura i
    urbanisme, Collegi d'arquitectes de Catalunya*

2002
Catherine David, *O outro começa onde nossos sentidos
    encontram o mundo – Dias & Riedweg/The Other
    Begins Where our Senses Meet the World – Dias &
    Riedweg*, exh. cat., Centro Cultural Banco do Brasil,
    Rio de Janeiro
Dias & Riedweg, "*Alles andere interessiert mich*," in
    "*Dürfen die das? Kunst als sozialer Raum*,"
    Ed. Stella Rollig e Eva Sturm, Vienna

2001
Catherine David, Klaus Biesenbach, *L'Etat des Choses*,
    exh. cat., Kunst-Werke, Berlin

2000
Dias & Riedweg, "Der Anderer beginnt da, wo unsere
    Sinne der Welt begegnen," *Total Global*,
    Christoph-Merian/Museum Für Gegenwartskunst
    Basel, Basel
Dias & Riedweg, "2000: Viu?" *Veredas*, Centro Cultural
    Banco do Brasil, Rio de Janeiro
Paolo Colombo, Viktor Durschei, *Arguments*,
    Istanbul Biennial Foundation-Pro Helvetia, Istanbul/
    Geneva
Paulo Reis, *Brasilidades*, Centro Cultural Light, exh.
    cat., Rio de Janeiro
Harald Szeemann, "Dias & Riedweg – Tutti Veneziani,"
    48ª Biennale di Venezia, exh. cat., Rizzoli, Milan

1998
Homi Bhabha, "Os Raimundos, os Severinos e os
    Franciscos por Dias & Riedweg," in 24ª Bienal
    de São Paulo, catálogo/catalogue, Brazil

1998-1999
Paolo Bianchi (ed.), "Maurício Dias & Walter Riedweg:
    Querschnitte Durch die Realität," *Lebenskunstwerke
    (LKW) – Kunstforum International*, vol. 142/143,
    Berlin

1997
Mary Jane Jacob, Homi Bhabha, Michael Brenson,
    et al., *Conversations at The Castle–Changing
    Audiences and Contemporary Art*, MIT Press,
    Cambridge, Massachusetts/London
Sebastian López, Maureen Sherlock, Martina Wohlthat,
    et al., *Mauricio Dias & Walter Riedweg*, Collection
    Cahier d'Artistes, Pro Helvetia/Lars Müller, Zurich

1996-1997
Mary Jane Jacob, Lygia Pape, Anabela Paiva,
    Annemarie Monteil, Catherine Queloz, Lily van
    Ginneken, *Devotionalia*, special supplements, *Jornal
    do Brasil* (Rio de Janeiro, Brazil), *Journal de Genève*
    (Geneva, Switzerland), *WOZ Wochen Zeitung*
    (Zurich, Switzerland), *Stadskrant* (The Hague,
    Netherlands), *Correio Braziliense* (Brazil)

1996
Maureen Sherlock, "Unruly Publics," *New Art Examiner*,
    Chicago

Selected Web Pages

Galeria Vermelho
http://www.galeriavermelho.com.br
(last accessed March 2014)

Galeria Filomena Soares
http://www.gfilomenasoares.com
(last accessed March 2014)

Galerie Sicardi
http://www.sicardi.com
(last accessed March 2014)

Videobrasil
http://www2.sescsp.org.br/sesc/videobrasil/
site/dossier028/apresenta_en.asp
(last accessed March 2014)

Mau Wal – youtube
http://www.youtube.com/user/mauwalvideos
(last accessed March 2014)

Imprint

This book was published on the occasion of
the exhibition *Mauricio Dias & Walter Riedweg.
Kleine Geschichten von Bescheidenheit und Zweifel*
at Kunstmuseum Luzern, March 8–June 22, 2014.

Exhibition

Exhibition Curator/Director
Fanni Fetzer

Curatorial Assistant
Lena Friedli

With the collaboration of
Nicole Asprion (Administration), Doris Bucher (Events
and Sponsoring), Anita Hoess (Restoration), Dominik
Müller (Research Assistant), Jürg Peter (Head of
Administration), Heinz Stahlhut (Collections Curator)

Technical Team
Tobias Oehmichen (Head of Installation), Daniel Amhof,
Christian Aregger, Samuli Blatter, Tatjana Erpen,
Michael Greppi, Raphael Muntwyler, Benedikt Notter,
Irene Suppiger, Steven Tod, Anita Zumbühl

Art Education Team
Brigit Kämpfen-Klapproth (Head of Art Education), Petra
Breitschmid, Sandra Genhart, Lorenz Hegi, Susanne
Kudorfer, Irene Lussi-Fries, Kevin Oehler, Kathrin Schär,
Monika Twerenbold, Amanda Unger

Kunstmuseum Luzern
Europaplatz 1
6002 Luzern
Switzerland
www.kunstmuseumluzern.ch

Acknowledgments

Dias & Riedweg would like to thank:
Galeria Vermelho, São Paulo; Galeria Filomena Soares,
Lisbon, and Sicardi Galery, Houston; the Authors, Fanni
Fetzer, Chantal Pontbriand, and Dieter Roelstraete;
Lionel Bovier, Renata Catambas, Lukas Haller, Nicolas
Eigenheer, and Vera Kaspar at JRP|Ringier; Fanni Fetzer,
Lena Friedli, Tobias Oehmichen, Steven Tod, and the
entire team at Kunstmuseum Luzern; as well as Esther
Meier and Heinz Szadrowsky, Marina Knell and Heiner
Kohlhaas, VIA and I-Art, in Basel; Lisa Fuchs, Fritz and
Vreni Riedweg-Roos in Lucerne; Agnes Brügger and
Bernhard Schmid in Zürich; Cleiton dos Santos, Jorge
Soledar, Juliana Franklin in Rio de Janeiro, and Joël
Girard in São Paulo.

Publication

Editor
Fanni Fetzer

Editorial Coordination
Renata Catambas, Lena Friedli

Texts
Fanni Fetzer, Chantal Pontbriand, Dieter Roelstraete,
Mauricio Dias & Walter Riedweg (chronology)

Editing and Proofreading
Fanni Fetzer, Lena Friedli, Clare Manchester (EN),
Karin Prätorius (DE)

Translations
Shaun Whiteside (Fanni Fetzer DE/EN),
Suzanne Schmidt (Chantal Pontbriand EN/DE;
Dieter Roelstraete EN/DE)

Design
Nicolas Eigenheer, Vera Kaspar

Typeface
Unica Haas

Cover
O Espelho e a Tarde/The Mirror and the Dusk, 2011

Photo Credits
Stefano Schröter (Installation shots Kunstmuseum
Luzern)

Color separation & Print
Musumeci S.P.A., Quart (Aosta)

This publication has received generous support from

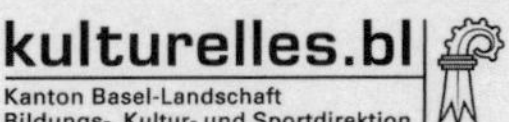

LANDIS & GYR STIFTUNG
Siemens Building Technologies

STANLEY THOMAS
JOHNSON FOUNDATION

prohelvetia

kulturelles.bl
Kanton Basel-Landschaft
Bildungs-, Kultur- und Sportdirektion

All rights reserved. No part of this publication may be
reproduced, stored in a retrieval system, or transmitted,
in any form, or by any means, electronic, mechanical,
or otherwise without prior permission in writing from
the publisher.

© 2014, the authors, the artists; and JRP|Ringier
Kunstverlag AG

Printed in Europe

Published by

JRP|Ringier
Limmatstrasse 270
CH–8005 Zurich
T +41 (0) 43 311 27 50
F +41 (0) 43 311 27 51
E info@jrp-ringier.com
www.jrp-ringier.com

ISBN: 978-3-03764-358-7

JRP|Ringier publications are available internationally at
selected bookstores and from the following distribution
partners:

Switzerland
AVA Verlagsauslieferung AG, Centralweg 16,
CH-8910 Affoltern a.A.,
verlagsservice@ava.ch, www.ava.ch

Germany and Austria
Vice Versa Distribution GmbH,
Immanuelkirchstrasse 12, D–10405 Berlin,
info@vice-versa- distribution.com,
www.vice-versa-distribution.com

France
Les presses du réel, 35 rue Colson, F-21000 Dijon,
info@lespressesdureel.com, www.lespressesdureel.com

UK and other European countries
Cornerhouse Publications, 70 Oxford Street,
UK-Manchester M1 5NH,
publications@cornerhouse.org,
www.cornerhouse.org/books

USA, Canada, Asia, and Australia
ARTBOOK|D.A.P., 155 Sixth Avenue, 2nd Floor,
USA-New York, NY 10013,
orders@dapinc.com, www.artbook.com

For a list of our partner bookshops or for any
general questions, please contact JRP|Ringier directly
at info@jrp-ringier.com, or visit our homepage
www.jrp-ringier.com for further information about
our program.